COMPARATIVE PERSPECTIVES
THEORIES AND METHODS

COMPARATIVE PERSPECTIVES

THEORIES AND METHODS

Edited and with Introduction by

AMITAI ETZIONI
Columbia University

FREDRIC L. DUBOW
University of California, Berkeley

LITTLE, BROWN AND COMPANY   Boston

LIBRARY OF CONGRESS CATALOG CARD NO. 69-16923

FIRST PRINTING

Printed simultaneously in Canada by
Little, Brown & Company (Canada) Limited

PRINTED IN THE UNITED STATES OF AMERICA

PREFACE

> All capitals have their problems. To understand Washington's you
> have to look at somebody else's. Washington's problems are intoler-
> able unless you consider Moscow's or Peking's or somebody else's.
> Everything is relative: the slums of New York or Newark or Los
> Angeles are unbearable unless you look at the slums of Mexico City,
> which, in turn, are better than the slums of Rio de Janeiro.[1]

Comparisons play a central role in our daily lives, in logic, and in substantive theories. "*Dr. Strangelove* is a better movie than *Fail-Safe*," " 'a' is
larger than 'b'," and "the suicide rate of Norway is lower than that of
Sweden" are all examples from the larger universe of comparative statements. In this collection, we attempt to provide key discussions of the
analytical and methodological assumptions upon which such comparative
statements rest. Hopefully, he who masters the contents of the works collected here will be better able to understand the comparative approach
and will work to expand and enrich it. We are not interested in any particular kind of comparisons, but in the art of comparing in general.

In the past ten years, there has been an unprecedented growth in comparative studies within the social sciences. What was previously the realm
of anthropologists and a small but influential group of other social scientists has become a major enterprise in all of social science. While we
draw illustrative material chiefly from the fields of sociology, political
science, and anthropology, we expect that most of the points elaborated
here would hold for other social sciences, including psychology, economics, and history.

The large number of comparative studies that have appeared in recent
years has forced us to omit many potential selections which would have
merited inclusion in a larger volume. Those interested in comparisons of

[1] James Reston, *New York Times*, July 23, 1967.

vii

a specific kind or area will find material in other volumes published in this series or in a recent bibliography by Robert Marsh.[2]

As we note in some detail in the introduction, the comparative perspective is more than a scientific technique — it provides a basic intellectual outlook that helps one overcome natural inclinations to view the world through egocentric or ethnocentric lenses. When this liberating perspective is pushed too far, it opens the door to bottomless relativism, but, as we shall see, the comparative perspective has a tendency to curb this danger itself.

The readings are divided into six groups. Chapter II provides general discussions of the nature of the comparative perspective or "method." Radcliffe-Brown states the case for the comparative approach. Sjoberg specifies the bases of comparison and the alternative directions among which comparative work must choose. Bloch explores two specific strategies of comparative research.

The third chapter deals with the extent to which we are all alike or substantially different, a question closely related to another issue: the extent to which our social life can be undone and redone, restructured in formats which are significantly different from those we now know. Benedict represents the position which prevailed a generation ago in social sciences, stressing that man is highly variable. Brown presents empirical evidence which casts doubts on the validity of the Benedict position. Wolf, speaking for the contemporary generation, updates the view of man as a "mix" of universal features and features particular to a specific period and culture.

The fourth chapter is designed for more advanced students seeking to familiarize themselves with specialized developments in the field of comparative studies. Eggan's report deals chiefly with qualitative developments; Rokkan concentrates on quantitative ones.

Chapter V assumes that it is useful to view society as a set of Chinese nesting boxes, with smaller units encompassed by larger ones. The problems involved in comparing various kinds of units are discussed, and various levels of comparison are illustrated. Elder's work illustrates comparative studies of families in various nations. Goode, in comparing a family attribute, takes into account both class membership and societal membership. Etzioni compares societies in terms of attributes of their control systems and the consequences of the use of control for the societal orientations of their members. Young and Moreno deal with the 48 states. The question is: are they 48 societies, such that each state should be treated as an autonomous unit? Hopkins and Wallerstein close the section with general comments about the level on which comparisons ought to proceed.

[2] Robert Marsh, "Comparative Sociology, 1950-1963," *Current Sociology*, 19 (1966).

While the preceding chapter deals with differences in the social world, the sixth chapter, like the fourth one, focuses on differences in the modes of studying it. There are half a dozen ways to compare, and the merits and demerits of each approach, with examples, are explored here. Mill's treatment is on the level of logic, while all the other articles in this section deal with inferences from data. Folsom proceeds by listing descriptive items about two family systems — a "primitive" one and ours in the United States — to gain insight through extreme contrast. Notice that few intrasocietal differences (e.g., among classes) or societal attributes per se are specified. Levy compares two societies close to each other, explaining differences within one societal attribute (economic development) in terms of several others. While Levy's work is qualitative, McElrath approaches the same question by a highly quantified method and is typically much more concerned with precision of measurement than with conceptual clarification. Janowitz and Segal illustrate the power of combining an explicit theory (Levy) with careful evaluation of data (McElrath) in conducting comparative analysis (for another example see the selection by Goode).

Most comparisons are static: they compare two or more units in the same time period (or as if they co-exist) without studying their changes. Bendix's comparison has historical roots; for he compares, in effect, processes rater than structures, which were compared in most of the preceding selections. His work is basically qualitative, and to this Schwartz and Miller add a quantitative analysis which is also *dynamic* (e.g., processual).

All of the issues mentioned so far are conceptual or theoretical in that they deal with the question of how we can best think comparatively. The last chapter deals with methods of verification. Once we have evolved a viewpoint, proposition, or theory about comparative relations, how can we find out if our notions are valid ones, that is, if they fit the empirical world?

Almond and Verba used questionnaire data for one of the most well-known and highly regarded comparative studies. They explore the difficulties they encountered and the solutions they employed. Scheuch extends their analysis by studying the ways in which quantitative data in general — not only survey data — are used in comparative studies.

The remaining two selections deal with specific issues; and as well as their importance in their own right, they illustrate the problems encountered in conducting a specific piece of research. Any notion that one prints a questionnaire, sends it to a sample of persons in a few societies, and compares the data which come in is dispelled after viewing the complexities raised by linguistic and cultural differences among societies. Phillips explores the actual problem of translation. Campbell raises the same basic issue: the establishment of equivalent items in two or more

societies in terms of questions to be asked and cultural items in general.
The introduction, Chapter I, addresses itself to three issues which underlie the readings: the *intellectual* insights into the nature of man provided by comparative study; the *theoretical* issues raised by various
attempts to conceptualize the data which are being compared; and the
methodological issues involved in the effort to verify comparative statements. It is an essay on comparative analysis rather than a detailed com-
mentary on the selections included in this volume. We hope that, by
providing a perspective on some key issues in comparative analysis, it
also offers a perspective within which the readings may be viewed.

The reader may feel by now that we are about to embark on a complicated dull drill; actually, while to fully understand comparative study is
a fairly intricate enterprise, it is also one of the most exciting ones in the
social sciences. The issue at hand, we must remind each other, is really
what man is like and how, and to what extent he can be changed.

Amitai Etzioni, *New York*
Fredric L. DuBow, *Dar es Salaam*

TABLE OF CONTENTS

COMPARATIVE PERSPECTIVES

THEORIES AND METHODS

I

Introduction

AMITAI ETZIONI AND
FREDRIC L. DUBOW

While a fascination with remote and exotic social phenomena has often
been a stimulus for comparative research, at least as powerful a motivation has been the search to better understand ourselves through the recognition of differences and similarities across a wide range of societies. The
deeper roots of this quest lie in a desire not merely to understand our
immediate social, cultural, and personal selves, but to comprehend our
underlying human nature. We seek answers to questions such as "Who
are we?" "Why are we the way we are?" and "What else could we be?"
These questions can be answered to some extent by personal and societal
introspection and self-study. But this approach makes it difficult to determine whether an attribute, for instance, aggressiveness, is shared by all
men (and is hence probably, although not necessarily, unchangeable),
shared only by members of our society and similar societies, or is an

1

idiosyncratic quality. Here, comparisons help; actually, such questions may be unanswerable without some systematic comparative study or reflection.

Unfortunately, the intellectual assistance and vigor provided by the comparative approach are not without cost; it is a rather intricate business. What to compare to what and how to do it are the subjects of the selections in this volume.

THE INTELLECTUAL DIMENSION: THE NATURE OF MAN

Comparisons of our society with others are, at least potentially, liberating exercises. If we approach the data with an open mind, we quickly discover that habits and beliefs which we consider fundamental may be viewed by others as marginal, and vice versa. Institutions we consider natural turn out to be only our particular way of doing things, and we may see other routes by which our problems have been approached. For instance, we handle drug addiction through police, courts, and jails; Britain does it mainly through health authorities and doctors.

Among the first attitudes challenged by comparative studies are those of cultural superiority. We soon see that many nations and societies consider themselves superior, frequently assessing themselves by utilizing different sets of criteria than those we use. For example, we think it desirable to be efficient while others may pride themselves on their sophistication. And people who are often considered inferior by many criteria — preliterate tribes, for example — are found upon examination to live by esthetic, moral, or community values that we are striving to regain. Thus, the study of other cultures and societies provides a powerful corrective for a common tendency toward ethnocentrism and unexamined, uncritical evaluations.

When it comes to determining what can be done about aspects of our society we would like to change, comparisons can be further enlightening. For instance, the U.S. might learn much that could be worthwhile about family allowances, legalized abortion, and toleration of adult homosexuals from observations of other societies, especially Holland and Scandinavia. On the other hand, other societies absorb from us such diverse notions as modern musicals (e.g., *West Side Story*) and methods of mass production in science and technology (research and development corporations).

While comparative analysis is liberating, it also "relativizes." Its first impact is often to call into question not only specific commitments, but also the concept of absolute commitment. Since almost any form of behavior can be found somewhere, why should one adhere to a particular pattern unless it is enjoyable or expedient? For example, we see in a world-wide sociological panorama some families which are polygamous while others are matrilineal, and we may then ask why we should lead monogamous lives in patrilineal families. Arriving at answers to such questions involves, in part, learning to separate normative commitments from notions of superiority and assumptions of universality. Indeed, there is no reason to assume that others must live up to our values, much less that all should live by one set of standards. Yet this realization does not invalidate our values, our commitments; their strength does not depend on their superiority or universality, but on their moral validity — for us. The comparative perspective can help us to clarify and revise our commitments, but we ought not allow it to undermine their normative potency, any more than we ought to stop contributing to cancer research because we find out that some of our neighbors do not.

Relativism is also being curbed on the basis of developments in comparative research itself. In several key anthropological works written before 1945, there was a strong emphasis on cultural variability — the many faces of the family of man — which nourished relativism. After World War II, there developed an increased emphasis on the limits of these variations and a rising recognition of the universal facets of the human and social condition. Some realization of the limits of human variability had always existed, but the bounds were considered to be extremely broad; within these limits, human nature was believed capable of a high degree of adaptation (see Benedict, pp. 42-52).* More recently, there has been a growing recognition — especially in anthropology and, to a lesser extent, in sociology — of a fundamental human nature which seems to reappear, with considerable regularity and specificity, in a universe of societies (see Wolf, pp. 69-71).

A striking example of the universality of certain aspects of human development has been found in a series of cross-cultural and interclass studies of the moral development of children as first described by Piaget.[1] In all the familial and cultural settings studied, children between the ages of six and twelve were found to undergo a basically similar change in their attitudes toward rules of moral constraint. Starting with a passive orientation toward rules as the "given" products of higher authority, children between the ages of ten and twelve came to regard moral norms as changeable products of cooperative effort.[2] Similarly, recent interpretations of societal institutions as varied as slavery, popular protest movements, and mental hospitals have noted the degree to which individuals act to maintain a degree of rationality, dignity, and autonomy under even the most imposing social constraints.[3] The number of studies which deal with the universality of human characteristics is small, but, for reasons one of the editors has spelled out elsewhere,[4] a much richer

* References in parentheses are to selections included in this volume.

set of findings would result from a search of the social science literature
with this question in mind.

We take the position that there are basic human needs, such as those
for recognition and affection, which are not determined by cultural or
social conditions.* While members of a society can adapt to roles which
provide little and infrequent gratification of these needs, and can even
reach a point where they state a preference for such roles, we suggest that
roles which are less rewarding will: (1) entail significantly higher socialization costs, i.e., it will take longer and cost more to educate people
to accept these roles; (2) require significantly more social control, i.e.,
more sanctioning agents and resources, to sustain conformity; and (3)
produce pressure on the part of the role-incumbents to alter their roles
in a more gratifying direction.

Similar statements to those just made about adaptations to roles may
be made with regard to total social structures and cultural patterns. The
"alienation school" holds that modern industrial society with its bureaucratic institutions and materialistic culture is much less responsive to
human needs than were primitive communities. Others assert that
pluralistic polities and their affluent economies are the most responsive
social structures man has ever known, while totalitarian regimes are the
most frustrating ones. These holistic comparative propositions can be
subjected, at least in principle, to empirical testing. The attitudes of a
national sample of the citizens of a society may be studied in ways similar
to those in which the satisfaction of workers has been examined.[5] The
task would not be an easy one because society and culture are more complex than a factory and their component parts are less interrelated. However, these difficulties do not seem insurmountable.[6]

If we are correct in suggesting that some societies, cultures, and
polities are, *in toto*, less responsive than others to human needs, then
comparative research leads to a new concept, that of a *deviant society*.
As long as we assume that human beings are highly malleable, there is
little reason not to expect that most members of a given society will be
socialized effectively and will internalize societal prescriptions.[7] The only
deviancy which could occur would be the result of ineffectual, incomplete,
or conflicting socialization. While social conditions might be responsible
for such malsocialization, those members of the society who do not
adjust are the deviants. However, once we recognize the possibility of a
universal human nature, we gain a critical vantage point which allows us
to advance the hypothesis (open to empirical testing) that a particular
societal structure is unresponsive or less responsive than some other

* One new to this field ought to be alerted to the fact that while many anthropologists and psychiatrists use the concept of basic human needs, many sociologists and psychologists reject it as vague and unempirical.

specified structures to universal human needs. Deviants in such a society are likely to include those who carry the societal seeds of a more responsive set of social arrangements — they are more than merely the malsocialized or malcontent.

The historical context must be taken into account in making such comparisons. At each point in time, members of a society are socialized to some structure and culture. If a new societal structure is introduced, as may happen after a revolution, we do not expect to be able to evaluate the responsiveness of the new structure immediately. Transition may have its own costs.[8] But if, after a period of exposure to a new structure, especially after a new generation has been born and socialized, the social and psychic costs of the "new world" are still significantly higher than those of the "old world" and the pressures to change are in the direction of the old structures, we must hold — until it is proven otherwise — that the new structures are inherently less responsive. For example, if it is correct that most of the regimes which have made austerity a central theme — the Soviet Union in its first years, the *kibbutzim*, Catholic orders — have experienced a continual pressure towards a less austere life, then it may be assumed — until proven otherwise — that the desire for comfort and material goods are part of basic human nature. How can we otherwise explain its presence in such different social, cultural, and historical contexts?

The value of comparative research stands out when we apply the points just made to a well-known study which did not, initially, employ a comparative base. American children have been shown to prefer democratic to authoritarian leadership; they find it more satisfying.[9] But something which is often overlooked in the references to this study is the fact that these children came from middle class homes, especially homes of professionals, where a "democratic" family structure is reported to prevail. Thus, these children may have simply preferred the form of authority to which they were accustomed. (One child from a home in which the father was an army officer preferred authoritarian leadership.) If this study were repeated with lower class children and with children of other cultures where family and political structures are more authoritarian, we would expect to find that the children would initially prefer the modes of authority to which they were accustomed. A confirmation of the proposition that democratic leadership is more responsive to basic human needs would come from evidence that long range exposure to the two forms of leadership resulted in a preference for the democratic form *regardless of the child's previous milieu.**

---

* A note on research techniques is needed here. Techniques differ in the depth to which they explore the personality. Since external conformity is likely to arise

So far, we have proceeded by comparing the degrees of unresponsiveness that various roles or societies reveal in terms of the extent to which they fail to satisfy basic human needs. Another basis for such comparisons can be the needs of social units, such as organizations or total societies. A comparative study of organizations within one culture — Western culture — has shown that organizations tend to specialize in the means of control they use to guide their participants. Some organizations rely more heavily on force (e.g., prisons), others on utilitarian rewards (e.g., factories), and still others on normative means, particularly the manipulation of symbols (e.g., churches). (See Etzioni, pp. 137-161.) Organizations differ in the societal needs they serve. Some are mainly concerned with maintaining law and order; others, with production; and still others with socialization, resocialization, and cultural activities. The means of societal control employed and the societal functions served are closely associated. Force is used more by organizations which specialize in maintaining order, utilitarian means by productive organizations, and normative means by organizations which deal with socialization. Each organization uses other means to some degree. Police carry out citizen education programs, factories have pep talks, and churches organize raffles. But these activities are marginal; at most, they are secondary tasks and means of control. The reasons for the correlation between the main societal function served and the primary means of control used need not concern us here. What we seek to describe is an example in which comparative analysis provides new insights into the relations between societal needs and societal control.

We have seen that on the individual level, endless variation in human needs is not found to exist. The same seems to hold on the social level. While there are no definitive studies, there is sufficient evidence to suggest that societies which vary tremendously in their social structures, cultures, economies, and polities have rather similar organizational patterns when the organizations deal with the same basic societal needs. Thus the average prison in Sweden, Japan, the U.S.S.R., Ghana, and Peru uses more force than the average factory in the same country, and the average factory relies more on monetary rewards or sanctions than most schools. Moreover, the relationship holds for more subtle gradations; e.g., the control of professionals seems to be more normative and less monetary than that of manual workers in all of these societies. (The former may be paid more, but money is used less for control purposes.)

---

from the pressure of the social environment, we need a test which seeks to assess the presence and degree of latent or hidden rejection. The proponents of questionnaire survey research would agree that their methods are ill-suited to such a comparative study; depth interviewing and projection tests are more likely to be fruitful.

The differences which do exist among societies are in *relative* emphases and *relative* "distances," but not in rank orders. Thus, the Swedish prison system is less coercive than the American one, but it is still mainly coercive, more coercive than the productive organizations of either country. The reason for this relationship may lie in the similarities of the underlying human nature: most people of all cultures may find being locked up a condition they will not accept voluntarily for the long run. And to gain the kind of cooperation required for effective work in most areas seems to necessitate rewarding people, not forcing them. Forced labor camps and slavery are notoriously inefficient.

By unveiling the universal features of man and separating them from his variable attributes, the comparative perspective further helps to define the limits of guided change. For example, efforts of reform to do away with coercion in prisons or to replace the economic basis of commitment in factories with rewards of differential prestige soon face the counter-pressures of these universal features, and do not usually endure.

We stand here on the forefront of social science, for many of the observations just made require considerable additional research. They are presented here as examples of the potential of the comparative perspective rather than as firm conclusions.

THE THEORETICAL DIMENSION: CONCEPTUALIZATION OF THE UNITS OF COMPARISON

Investigators have given highly divergent answers to the question of the range of the phenomenon to be explored in comparative studies. Neil Smelser's position is that the comparative method "is employed in the scientific analysis of historical data, [where] the number of cases . . . is too small to permit statistical manipulation. This method is most evidently required in the comparative analysis of national units . . . and other subnational social units."[10] Johan Galtung has suggested a much more inclusive definition of comparative research as "a design whereby the same process of data-collection and data-analysis is carried out within a number of spatial units."[11] This encompasses a comparative study of individuals as well as of social units of any size. Must one choose between these and many other views of the scope of comparative research? And what are the consequences of choosing one definition over another? It could be argued that these differences are a matter of semantics rather than a substantive issue or an empirical question; then all that would be required of any social scientist is that he be consistent in applying the term. However, when the concept of comparison is extended to cover a wide array of instances, the danger arises that its meaning may become diluted to the point where the concept loses much of its power. If any statement about two states of being is comparative (e.g., Jane is taller than Jim), or comparison is implied in one statement (e.g., Jane is tall) in conjunction with an implicit frame of reference of all beings (or all Jane-like beings), then there is nothing left which is not at least implicitly comparative. But there is very little that we can say specifically about the comparative enterprise. What we gain in scope we lose in depth.

Early comparative studies dealt primarily with comparisons of whole societies, especially primitive ones (see Sjoberg, pp. 25-38). This usage is similar to that suggested by Smelser. More recently, social scientists have tended to dimensionalize the differences among societies rather than treating them holistically.[12] Rather than compare Britain with Ghana, or a modern with a developing nation, they pay more attention to differences in gross national product, population data, or other specific characteristics of the societies. The dimensions on which societies are compared are scored in terms of measures derived from aggregates of member units, such as firms or families. In addition, units other than societies — for instance, ethnic groups within one or more societies — have been compared in the same manner. Thus, the contemporary tendency of comparative studies seems to move toward Galtung's formulation.

If the trend toward diluting the concept continues to a point at which all possible comparisons are considered to be part of "comparative research," it will lose any discriminating power, since every table, correlation, or measurement is, in some sense, a comparison. It is hence fruitful to designate a subfield of intellectual effort which has attributes and problems of its own. Therefore, we suggest that it is useful to *distinguish comparative analysis from comparative description*. Almost any description may indeed be comparative, at least implicitly, but not every frame of analysis is. And the problems involved in building analytic frameworks for comparison are distinctive from those encountered by other theory-builders.

All analysis entails the breaking up and abstraction of data in terms of units which, in themselves, are not encountered but are the concepts and tools of the analyst. These concepts serve comparative analysis only when they focus attention on *similarities* and *differences* of at least two entities.

Once the analytic basis of comparison is thus defined, several more specific approaches arise. Some scholars prefer to compare units with each other directly (for example, comparing two American families in terms of a given variable). Others use two levels of units (comparing American families of two classes). Still others add a consideration of the *relation* of the "lower" level units (the families) to the "higher" level, more encompassing ones (classes) and make the relation a third basis of comparison. This may then be extended to units at additional levels (for instance, families in two classes in two societies), and so on (perhaps to regions or cultures). Examples of all these levels of comparison are found in Chapter V.

A different approach is to work with a general model or theory and to compare each unit under study to the model, which itself undergoes modification on the basis of the analysis of data from a variety of social and cultural settings. For instance, we may have a conception of bureaucracy, and then ask to what extent the civil service of a specific country, city, or agency approximates the concept.

There is considerable opposition to *both* of these forms of comparative analysis. Anthropologists argue that to understand the meaning of a cultural item one must immerse himself in the particular culture involved. Anthropologist Paul Bohannan, in his warning against the study of African legal systems through the imposed analytic grid of the alien researcher, states:

> It would be possible, once one had elicited all the rules which one could find in all the cases, to arrange them into some order and set them forth as the procedural law of Tiv courts. . . . The error would be that the arrangement is not part of the Tiv way of looking at it, and hence would be false.[13]

Similarly, historians have argued that we must involve ourselves in the *zeitgeist* both of a period *and* of a particular society; and Gestalt psychologists and phenomenologists demand immersion in the particular personal or cultural context. It is even maintained that a researcher can attain a high degree of understanding of at most only one culture, period, or society, and that any use of analytic concepts (other than those of the observed actors) separates the researcher from his subject and thus distorts the meaning and richness of what he observes.

In its extreme version, this position rules out not only comparative analysis but all analysis, at least in the form of a generalizing science. In the more moderate version (see Bloch, pp. 39-41), critics stress the dangers of a glib use of ethnocentric assumptions and generalizing concepts and favor comparative research among relatively similar rather than highly divergent societies. The British anthropologist Evans-Pritchard argued in favor of what he called "intensive comparative investigation" which restricted inquiry "to limited topics or to societies of a certain type."[14] Those who do not subscribe to the extreme version of this viewpoint may still see much merit in the moderate one, for it seems that for many purposes comparisons of less divergent societies will be more useful than comparisons of highly divergent ones. In the latter case there are likely to be too many uncontrolled yet relevant variables; but in societies having similar cultures, histories, or levels of economic development, a number of factors may be considered "controlled" and disregarded for the purpose of explaining differences among these societies.

Comparisons of large numbers of societies, however similar to each other, may well require collaboration among experts who have specialized on each society and who can pool their knowledge and serve as checks on each other's perceptions.[15] And while comparative studies of meaning (cultural systems in particular) may require a high degree of involvement in a culture, it is possible for a researcher to learn through comparing economic, demographic, communications, and other forms of "hard" data from numerous societies (see Scheuch, pp. 365-386). Thus, large scale comparative research seems possible. While one researcher may be able to cover only one or a few similar societies, the cumulative work of several researchers may allow, at a later stage, the development of an abstract and generalizing theory.

Even among those who favor analytic theory, there are some who would limit themselves to a "middle range" approach, comparing units and stating analytic differences and similarities without attempting to relate these to an overall theory. There is prudence in this position, but, as we see it, the analytic effort is incomplete unless the bases of comparison are variables of a general theory. There are endless dimensions along which units may be compared. Unless some systematic criteria for choosing one set of dimensions over another and for formulating propositions which relate the dimensions to each other are employed, we may drown in a sea of hundreds of relatively trivial specific comparisons. True, we must avoid premature closure; the dimensions we choose may not be the most productive ones and will therefore need revision. But we hold that without systematic attention to such generalized frameworks, comparative analysis foregoes much of its potential.

The fact that comparative analysis needs anchoring in a general theory is a statement about methodological needs, not about proper order; comparative research may precede theory-building. The selections in Chapter VI illustrate various approaches which are being applied: Mill starts from pure logic (pp. 205-213); Folsom draws inductive inferences from heavily descriptive material (pp. 213-224); and Levy (pp. 225-267) and Janowitz and Segal (pp. 289-311) attain a rare balance between derivative theory and induction from data. The collective enterprise of comparative analysis makes use of all kinds of theorizing and methodology and it may well be futile to ask which is *the* superior approach. At most, we venture to say that there seems to be an abundance of highly deductive and richly descriptive work, but a dearth of the kind of endeavor exemplified by Levy and Janowitz and Segal.

When it comes to the analysis of comparative data, there are basically two ways to relate variables to each other, to build explanations and theories: (1) *genetically,* by explaining later indications in terms of earlier events (common to historical and clinical studies); and (2) *contextually,* by explaining events in terms of synchronical (or co-existent) variables. Studies of structures — be they of buildings, symphonies, or societies — serve as cases in point. If we see an arch and ask who built it and why, we are asking genetic questions. If we ask why it does not collapse, or what the tensions are between the parts, we seek a contextual explanation. As this example suggests, we can, of course, seek both kinds of explanations and endeavor to relate the two: we may find that the arch is relatively tension free and ask where the builder obtained the design.

Comparative Analysis as a Rule Deals with Contextual Explanations. It deals with units which are *assumed* to be (1) independent of each other rather than causally related, and (2) occurring at the same point in time. This contextual focus is maintained when the units which are compared are not in the same period by disregarding the time differences or explicitly assuming them to be irrelevant. For instance, when primitive societies are compared to modern ones, differences in the historical stages within each group of societies are frequently not taken into account. Similarly, mutual effects among the units compared are usually ignored, deliberately disregarded, or, rarely, controlled: comparisons of Japan and China rarely study Japan's effects on China. Finally, information about various periods of the same unit is treated in comparative analysis as if it were information about two different units, as in comparisons of colonial and post-colonial periods of the same society.

A major debate running through the development of comparative studies has concerned the extent to which these assumptions of independence and atemporality can be made without doing violence to the resulting explanation. In an early form, the debate involved the degree to which the diffusion of cultural traits from one cultural group to another invalidated cross-cultural comparative analyses. If the presence of a cultural item in one society could be explained in terms of its diffusion from another society, then, it was argued, an analysis in which the two societies are compared as independent units would be misleading. Two instances in which this problem is encountered are the comparative studies of parliaments and political parties in Western nations and former colonies and in occupational evaluations among secondary school students in various countries.[16] To observe that countries X and Y have democratic institutions while A and B do not, and to explain the difference in terms of the countries' societal structures (or levels of GNP, education, and so forth), may ignore the fact that X and Y are former colonies of Britain, while A and B were colonies of Spain. This is to suggest not that the societal attributes of these countries will have no effect on their predispositions toward democratic institutions, but rather that their historical *and* present linkages to their colonial powers cannot be disregarded. In the case of occupational evaluations, it has been argued that the great similarity in response among secondary school students in many countries when they are asked to rank occupations suggests a relationship between the requirements of systems of social stratification and evaluations of occupational status; for instance, all countries need doctors more than farmers and, hence, the former are ranked higher in all countries. Yet an alternative possibility exists. The "culture" of secondary school education may embody certain values which are spread throughout the world by expatriate teachers and foreign-educated elites, as well as by the mass media, but these values may not reflect the actual relationships between occupations and the needs of non-Western societies.[17]

Recent studies of diffusion have developed techniques for evaluating its significance *and* have drawn on contextual factors in explaining diffusion itself.[18] That is, while units — and even total societies — can rarely be viewed as unaffected by other units which act in the same situation and period, this fact does not invalidate comparative analysis; just because what X does is affected by what Y does, we are not prevented from treating them as analytically autonomous units. First, the effects of diffusion (from Y to X) can be separated from those of intra-unit factors. Second, when an item (for instance, the American Constitution) has been "diffused" from one unit and accepted by another (a Latin republic) and acquires a function in the second unit, this function is affected not only by the nature of the substance of the item which is "diffused" but also by the structure of the receiving unit. Third, the process of diffusion itself is affected by the respective structures. Hence, the comparative study of the units is both logically possible and of interest.

Similarly, theories of social change which depict recurring "stages" of development (e.g., economic take-off) have been criticized for not taking into account the significance of the fact that some societies develop before others. Comparative studies of nations such as Great Britain, Russia, and Turkey must be sensitive to the ways in which the paths of development in Russia and Turkey are somewhat dependent on the prior British experience. "Latecomers" to development are influenced by "what has worked or failed" elsewhere and by the awareness of their own "backwardness."[19] A comparison of the early forms of industrialization in each of these three countries would have to take into account the extent to which Turkey or Russia had borrowed from Britain and other more developed countries. But again, these historical (genetic) linkages do not render comparative analysis impossible; they merely warn us against unduly simple, naive comparisons.

Finally, as we have already suggested, genetic and contextual explanations may be combined. A study of a context at one point in time, including its internal points of tension, and an application of these explanatory factors over time lead to a genetic analysis of contextual transformation. This combination of the two perspectives, which make contextual analysis dynamic or genetic analysis comparative, is a very demanding but not impossible task.[20]

THE UNITS OF ANALYSIS

It seems rather self-evident that the units of analysis must be chosen according to what is relevant for the question under study and, more generally, the line of inquiry which the analyst seeks to develop. Units of comparative analysis could be persons (comparative psychology), firms (comparative micro-economics), political institutions (comparative politics), total societies, or cultures. It seems useful to state explicitly what units are to be focused upon and, rather than argue that it is proper to compare societies and not to compare cultures, refer to different kinds of comparative analyses — of societies, of cultures, of law, and so forth (cf. Hopkins and Wallerstein, pp. 183-204). Confusion can arise not so much because the wrong kinds of units are compared, but rather because units which are not of one and the same kind, for instance, a society and a culture, are compared as if they were. The same thing may happen when assumptions about the implications of the concept are treated as verified propositions; for example, a country like Nigeria is referred to as a "society" or "nation" and is therefore assumed to constitute one macroscopic action unit.

Comparative analysis often proceeds by focusing on two or more levels of units, as when a comparison is made between families in different societies. Here, the comparison is not of families or of societies but of families-in-societies, because the supra-units (the societies) affect the member units (the families) and/or the relations among them (e.g., intermarriage). (For such an approach, see Goode, pp. 116-137.) Such interlevel effects, it must be stressed, cannot be assumed; their existence, quality, and magnitude are all propositions that must be tested. A single study may, on the basis of earlier work or anticipated future studies, take such suppositions for granted, but the discipline, the accumulation of collective knowledge, cannot accept them unless empirical evidence is available.

While it is quite proper to conduct a comparative analysis on one level (e.g., to compare five societies) as well as on several levels (e.g., families in five societies), two traps ought to be avoided: (1) the supraunit should not only be named but also *specified* in the sense that its relevant attributes should be clearly indicated; and (2) the units accounting for the variations in the factors under study cannot simply be assumed to be internal to any specific society.

Regarding the first point, the names of countries may be understood as short-hand references for a set of scores on different variables; comparative analysis entails the specification of which of the many scores (or combinations of such scores) account for internation differences found on some other level. Thus, it is not enough to refer to differences between the family structures in France and the U.S.A. for the reader to be able to realize which of the many attributes of the two countries are the relevant ones to account for the differences in the family structures. Without such specifications, we may have comparative descriptions or data but not analysis, because one variable (family structure) is not related to any other.

Second, it seems troublesome to assume that nation-states constitute the ultimate units of comparative analysis, although they are the units most frequently used. Often it is assumed that the national boundaries are coterminous with a national society which is the most powerful context for intrasocietal relations and serves best to explain differences between member-units (e.g., families) and the same units in different societies. As we see it, one cannot assume, a priori, that the nation-state is coterminous with a society and, hence, with the most powerful contextuating unit. In many "weak" nation states, a tribe or a region may be relatively more self-contained. Thus, in a comparison of nineteenth century developments between Japan and China, it would be important for most purposes to conceive of China as not one but many societies having relatively independent relations with external forces.[21] External elites may prove to be crucial contextuating factors which would be ignored if the nation-state were assumed to be the primary nexus of explanation. For example, to explain the changing relations among tribes in Ghana and the Ivory Coast, it may be necessary to take into account differences in their respective relations with Britain and France. The case of interunit relations is similar: the rise of the Central American common market may be more understandable in terms of an analysis of the internal dynamics of the United States than of either the nations involved or Central America per se. (For another example illustrating the same point, see Young and Moreno, pp. 161-183.)

THE METHODOLOGICAL DIMENSION: CROSS-CULTURAL VERIFICATION

The problems raised in the application of research techniques to comparative analysis are complex and deserve much additional study. We can here point only to one general issue which affects all comparative research to one degree or another. We need instruments which will allow us to study different cultures without the results of measurements being affected by the culture in which the instruments are designed and tested. The same problem exists in comparative studies within one society when members of different sub-cultures and sub-communities, for instance, whites and Negroes, are compared. The problem is accentuated when cross-societal-cultural comparisons are attempted, especially on a large scale or between highly divergent cultures. For instance, it was originally assumed that significant variations measured by IQ tests among groups and societies were indicative of inherent differences. However, more sophisticated methods of testing have demonstrated that the tested differences between groups were largely not innate, but the results of tests which were socio-culturally bound. For instance, lower-class Negro children scored lower than white middle-class children on tests slanted toward the white middle-class. The tests have been improved to some extent and are now less culture-bound,[22] but it is not clear to what extent they have been, or even if they can be, rendered culturally neutral.

The same basic issue appears in working with survey techniques, in efforts to construct (or translate) questionnaires for cross-cultural studies. Here, too, the aim is to devise instruments which have equivalent meanings in both cultures in order to ascertain that the variation found is due to real differences rather than to those inherent in the research tools. One can show logically that the question of equivalence cannot be completely solved. However, accommodations can be made to eliminate many "translation" pitfalls (see Phillips, pp. 387-406; and Campbell, pp. 407-410).

As in most areas of science, the student approaching this field with a romantic notion of finding great precision, high objectivity, and the accumulation of verified truth will find these attributes to some extent, but will also find an exciting struggle to gain a foot-hold on slippery slopes, a considerable measure of conflict and even intellectual turmoil, and, occasionally, a genuine insight. Thus, as he gains an understanding of the difficulties of verifying comparative statements, he may also gain insight into the ways in which the social sciences progress.

References

1. Jean Piaget, *The Moral Judgment of the Child* (New York: Free Press, 1948).
2. For a review of cross-cultural applications of Paiget's ideas see L. Kohlberg, "Moral Development and Identification," in National Society for the Study of Education, 62nd Yearbook, *Child Psychology* (Chicago: University of Chicago Press, 1963).
3. Kenneth M. Stampp, *The Peculiar Institution: Slavery in the Ante-Bellum*

South (New York: Vintage Books, 1956); George Rude, *The Crowd in History, 1730-1848* (New York: John Wiley & Sons, Inc., 1964); Erving Goffman, *Asylums: Essays on the Social Situation of Mental Patients and Other Inmates* (Garden City, New York: Doubleday & Company, Inc., 1961).

4. Amitai Etzioni, *The Active Society: A Theory of Societal and Political Processes* (New York: Free Press, 1968), Chapter 21.

5. Robert Blauner, *Alienation and Freedom* (Chicago: University of Chicago Press, 1964).

6. See, for example, Gabriel Almond and Sidney Verba, *The Civic Culture* (Princeton: Princeton University Press, 1963); and Norman M. Bradburn and David Caplowitz, *Reports on Happiness* (Chicago: Aldine, 1965).

7. Cf. Dennis Wrong, "The Oversocialized Concept of Man," *American Sociological Review,* 26 (1961), pp. 183-92.

8. For a suggestive discussion of the costs of revolution see Barringon Moore, *The Social Origins of Dictatorship and Democracy* (Boston: Beacon Press, 1966), pp. 407-10.

9. Kurt Lewin, Ronald Lippitt, and Ralph K. White, "Patterns of Aggressive Behavior in Experimentally Created 'Social Climates'," *Journal of Social Psychology,* 10 (1939), pp. 271-99. For a review of some comparative data see Sidney Verba, *Small Groups and Political Behavior* (Princeton: Princeton University Press, 1961).

10. Neil Smelser, "Notes on the Methodology of Comparative Analysis of Economic Activity," *Social Science Information,* 6 (1967), p. 16.

11. Johan Galtung, "Some Aspects of Comparative Research," *Polls,* 2 (1967), p. 1.

12. Jack Sawyer, "Dimensions of Nations: Size, Wealth and Politics," *American Journal of Sociology,* 73 (1967), pp. 145-72.

13. Paul Bohannan, *Justice and Judgment Among the Tiv* (New York: Oxford University Press, 1957), p. 69.

14. E. E. Evans-Pritchard, *The Comparative Method in Social Anthropology* (London: Athlone Press, 1963), pp. 19, 22.

15. Robert Ward and Dankwart Kustow (eds.), *Political Modernization in Japan and Turkey* (Princeton: Princeton University Press, 1964), suggest a direction for future collaborations.

16. Peter N. Rossi and Alex Inkeles, "National Comparisons of Occupational Prestige," *American Journal of Sociology,* 61 (1956), pp. 329-39.

17. R. M. Thomas, "Reinterpreting a Structural Position on Occupational Prestige," *American Journal of Sociology,* 67 (1962), pp. 660-65.

18. Elihu Katz et al., "Traditions of Research on Diffusion of Innovations," *American Sociological Review,* 28 (1963), pp. 237-52.

19. Alexander Gerschenkron, *Economic Backwardness in Historical Perspective* (New York: Frederick A. Praeger, 1965); and Reinhard Bendix, *Nation-Building and Citizenship* (New York: John Wiley & Sons, 1964).

20. For an attempt to compare four structural developments genetically, using short periods of time and a processual model, see Amitai Etzioni, *Political Unification* (New York: Holt, Rinehart & Winston, 1965).

21. Wolfram Eberhard, "Concerns of Historical Sociology," *Sociologus,* 14 (1964), pp. 3-17.

22. Torsten Husen (ed.), *The International Study of Achievement in Mathematics* (New York: Wiley & Sons, 1967).

II

General Statements

1   A. R. RADCLIFFE-BROWN

A Case for the Comparative Method

What is meant when one speaks of "the comparative method" in anthropology is the method used by such a writer as Frazer in his *Golden
Bough*. But comparisons of particular features of social life can be made
for either of two very different purposes, which correspond to the distinction now commonly made in England between ethnology and social
anthropology. The existence of similar institutions, customs or beliefs
in two or more societies may in certain instances be taken by the
ethnologist as pointing to some historical connection. What is aimed at
is some sort of reconstruction of the history of a society or people or
region. In comparative sociology or social anthropology the purpose of

Reprinted from *The Journal of the Royal Anthropological Institute*, 1951,
15-22. By permission of the Council of the Royal Anthropological Institute
of Great Britain and Ireland. The original title was "The Comparative Method
in Social Anthropology."

17

comparison is different, the aim being to explore the varieties of forms of social life as a basis for the theoretical study of human social phenomena. Franz Boas, writing in 1888 and 1896, pointed out that in anthropology there are two tasks to be undertaken. One kind of task is to "reconstruct" the history of particular regions or peoples, and this he spoke of as being "the first task." The second task he describes as follows:

. . .

A comparison of the social life of different peoples proves that the foundations of their cultural development are remarkably uniform. It follows from this that there are laws to which this development is subject. Their discovery is the second, perhaps the more important aim of our science. . . . In the pursuit of these studies we find that the same custom, the same idea, occurs among peoples for whom we cannot establish any historical connection, so that a common historical origin cannot be assumed and it becomes necessary to decide whether there are laws that result in the same, or at least similar, phenomena independently of historical causes. Thus develops the second important task of ethnology, the investigation of the laws governing social life.

The frequent occurrence of similar phenomena in cultural areas that have no historical contact suggests that important results may be obtained from their study, for it shows that the human mind develops everywhere according to the same laws.

. . .

Thus, the comparative method in social anthropology is the method of those who have been called "arm-chair anthropologists" since they work in libraries. Their first task is to look for what used to be called "parallels," similar social features appearing in different societies, in the present or in the past. At Cambridge sixty years ago Frazer represented arm-chair anthropology using the comparative method, while Haddon urged the need of "intensive" studies of particular societies by systematic field studies of competent observers.

Without systematic comparative studies anthropology will become only historiography and ethnography. Sociological theory must be based on, and continually tested by, systematic comparison.

The only really satisfactory way of explaining a method is by means of illustration. Let us therefore consider how the method can be applied in a particular instance. We may take our start with a particular feature of some tribes in the interior of New South Wales. In these tribes there is a division of the population into two parts, which are named after the eaglehawk and the crow (Kilpara and Makwara). There is a rule by which a man should only take a wife from the division other than his own, and that the children will belong to the same division as their mother. The system is described in technical terms as one of totemically represented exogamous matrilineal moieties.

One way of explaining why a particular society has the features that it does have is by its history. As we have no authentic history of these or other Australian tribes the historical anthropologists are reduced to offering us imaginary histories. Thus the Rev. John Mathew would explain these divisions and their names by supposing that two different peoples, one called Eaglehawks and the other Crows, met in this part of Australia and fought with each other. Ultimately they decided to make peace and agreed that in future Eaglehawk men would only marry Crow women and *vice versa*.

Let us begin looking for parallels. There is a very close parallel to be found amongst the Haida of north-west America, who also have a division into two exogamous matrilineal moieties which are named after the eagle and the raven, two species which correspond very closely indeed to the eaglehawk and crow of Australia. The Haida have a legend that in the beginning only the eagle possessed fresh water which he kept in a basket. The raven discovered this and succeeded in stealing the water from the eagle. But as he flew with the basket over Queen Charlotte Island the water was spilled from the heavy basket and formed the lakes and rivers from which all birds can now drink; and salmon made their way into the streams and now furnish food for men.

In some parts of Australia there are similar legends about the eaglehawk and the crow. One is to the effect that in the beginning only the eaglehawk possessed a supply of fresh water, which he kept under a large stone. The crow, spying on him, saw him lift the stone and take a drink, then replace the stone. The crow proceeded to lift the stone, and after he had taken a drink of fresh water scratched the lice from his head into the water and did not replace the stone. The result was that the water escaped and formed the rivers of eastern Australia in which the lice became the Murray cod that were an important item of food for the aborigines just as salmon are in north-west America. If we accept the criteria formulated by the diffusionists, such as Graebner, we have here what they would say is evidence of a historical connection between Australia and the Pacific coast of North America.

Once we begin looking for parallels to the eaglehawk-crow division of Australia we find many instances of exogamous moieties, in some instances, matrilineal, in others patrilineal, in the rest of Australia, and frequently the divisions are named after or represented by birds. In Victoria we find black cockatoo and white cockatoo, in Western Australia white cockatoo and crow. In New Ireland there is a similar system in which the moieties are associated with the sea-eagle and the fish-hawk. At this point we may feel inclined to ask why these social divisions should be identified by reference to two species of birds.

In Eastern Australia the division of the population into two sexes is represented by what is called sex totemism. In tribes of New South Wales the men have for their "brother" the bat, and the women have for their "sister" the night owl in some tribes and the owlet nightjar in others. In the northern part of New South Wales the totems are the bat for men and the tree-creeper for women. (It must be remembered that the Australian aborigines classify the bat as a "bird.") So we find another dichotomy of society in which the divisions are represented by birds.

Throughout most of Australia there is a very important social division into two alternating generation divisions or endogamous moieties. One division consists of all the persons of a single generation together with those of the generation of their grandparents and the generation of their grandchildren, while the other division includes all those of the generation of their parents and the generation of their children. These divisions are rarely given names but in some tribes may be referred to by terms, one of which a man applies to his own division and its members while the other is applied to the other division. But in one part of Western Australia these endogamous moieties are named after the kingfisher and the bee-eater, while in another part they are named after a little red bird and a little black bird.

Our question "Why all these birds?" is thus widened in its scope. It is not only the exogamous moieties, but also dual divisions of other kinds that are identified by connection with a pair of birds. It is, however, not always a question of birds. In Australia the moieties may be associated with other pairs of animals, with two species of kangaroo in one part, with two species of bee in another. In California one moiety is associated with the coyote and the other with the wild cat.

. . .

A comparative study . . . reveals to us the fact that the Australian ideas about the eaglehawk and the crow are only a particular instance of a widespread phenomenon. First, these tales interpret the resemblances and differences of animal species in terms of social relationships of friendship and antagonism as they are known in the social life of human beings. Secondly, natural species are placed in pairs of opposites. They can only be so regarded if there is some respect in which they resemble each other. Thus eaglehawk and crow resemble each other in being the two prominent meat-eating birds. When I first investigated the sex totems of New South Wales I supposed, quite wrongly, that what was the basic resemblance of the bat and the night owl or nightjar was that they both fly about at night. But the tree-creeper does not fly at night and is the totem of the women in the northern part of New South Wales. As I was sitting in the region of the Macleay River with a native a tree-creeper made its appearance, and I asked him to tell me about it. "That is the bird that taught women how to climb trees," he told me. After some conversation I asked, "What resemblance is there between the bat and the tree-creeper?" and with an expression on his face that showed surprise that I should ask such a question he replied, "But of course they both live in holes in trees." I realised that the night owl and the nightjar also live in trees. The fact that certain animals eat meat constitutes a sort of social similarity, as of eaglehawk and crow or dingo and wild cat. Similarly the habit of living in holes in trees.

We can now answer the question "Why eaglehawk and crow?" by saying that these are selected as representing a certain kind of relationship which we may call one of "opposition."

The Australian idea of what is here called "opposition" is a particular application of that association by contrariety that is a universal feature of human thinking, so that we think by pairs of contraries, upwards and downwards, strong and weak, black and white. But the Australian conception of "opposition" combines the idea of a pair of contraries with that of a pair of opponents. In the tales about eaglehawk and crow the two birds are opponents in the sense of being antagonists. They are also contraries by reason of their difference of character, Eaglehawk the hunter, Crow the thief. Black cockatoo and white cockatoo which represent the moieties in Western Victoria are another example of contrariety, the birds being essentially similar except for the contrast of colour. In America the moieties are referred to by other pairs of contraries, Heaven and Earth, war and peace, up-stream and down-stream, red and white. After a lengthy comparative study I think I am fully justified in stating a general law, that wherever, in Australia, Melanesia or America, there exists a social structure of exogamous moieties, the moieties are thought of as being in a relation of what is here called "opposition."

Obviously the next step in a comparative study is to attempt to discover what are the various forms that the opposition between the moieties of a dual division takes in actual social life. In the literature there are occasional references to a certain hostility between the two divisions described as existing or reported to have existed in the past. All the available evidence is that there is no real hostility in the proper sense of the term but only a conventional attitude which finds expression in some customary mode of behaviour. Certainly in Australia, although in some instances where there is a dispute it is possible to observe the members of the two patrilineal moieties forming separate "sides," real hostility, of the kind that may lead to violent action is not between the moieties but between local groups, and two local groups of the same patrilineal moiety seem to be just as frequently in conflict as two groups belonging to different moieties. Indeed, since a common source of actual conflict is the taking by one man of a woman married to or betrothed to another the two antagonists or groups of antagonists in such instances will both belong to the same patrilineal moiety.

The expression of opposition between the moieties may take various forms. One is the institution to which anthropologists have given the not very satisfactory name of "the joking relationship." Members of opposite divisions are permitted or expected to indulge in teasing each other, in verbal abuse or in exchange of insults. Kroeber (*Handbook of Indians of California*) writes that amongst the Cupeño "a sort of good natured opposition is recognized between the moieties, whose members frequently taunt each other with being unsteady and slow-witted, respectively." Strong (*Aboriginal Society in Southern California*) reports the same thing.

> A good-natured antagonism between the moieties exhibits itself in joking between persons of the one and the other. The coyote people taunt the wild cat people with being slow-witted and lazy like their animal representative and the wild cat people retaliate by accusing their opponents with being unsteady. There are indications that this teasing of one moiety by another entered into their serious ceremonies. There were songs of a satirical kind that could be sung by one moiety against the other. However, the opposition between the moieties seems to have been much less strong than between certain pairs of clans, sometimes belonging to the same moiety, which were traditionally "enemies." These clans, on certain occasions would sing "enemy songs" against each other.

This institution, for which it is to be hoped that some one will find a better name than "joking relationship," is found in a variety of forms in a number of different societies, and calls for systematic comparative study. It has for its function to maintain a continuous relationship between two persons, or two groups, of apparent but factitious hostility or antagonism. I have offered a suggestion towards a comparative study of this institution in a paper published in the journal *Africa*.

Another significant custom in which is expressed the relation of opposition between the two moieties is that by which, in some tribes of Australia and in some of North America the moieties provide the "sides" in games such as football. Competitive games provide a social occasion on which two persons or two groups of persons are opponents. Two continuing groups in a social structure can be maintained in a relation in which they are regularly opponents. An example is provided by the two universities of Oxford and Cambridge.

There are other customs in which the opposition of moieties is expressed. For example, in the Omaha tribe of North America the camp circle was divided into two semi-circles, and when a boy of the one half crossed into the other he took companions with him and there was a fight with the boys of the other moiety. We need not and can not here examine these various customs.

. . .

Viewed in relation to social structure the meaning or symbolic reference of these customs ought to be obvious. The solidarity of a group requires that the loss of one of its members shall be recognized as an injury to the group. Some expression of this is therefore called for. The taking of a woman in marriage is represented as in some sense an act of hostility against her kin. This is what is meant by the saying of the Gusii of East Africa "Those whom we marry are those whom we fight."

It is in the light of this that we must interpret the custom of marriage by exchange. The group or kin of a woman lose her when she marries; they are compensated for their loss if they receive another who will become the wife of one of them. In Australian tribes, with a few exceptions, the custom is that when a man takes a wife he should give a sister to replace her. In the Yaralde tribe of South Australia, which did not have a system of moieties, when a man married a woman of another local clan, his own clan was expected to provide a wife for some member of the clan from which the bride came. Otherwise the marriage was regarded as irregular, improper, or we might almost say illegal. It has been reported from the tribes of the eastern part of Victoria (Gippsland) that the only proper form of marriage was by exchange. The system of exogamous moieties provides a system of generalisation of marriage by exchange, since every marriage is one incident in the continual process by which the men of one moiety get their wives from the other.

A comparative study shows that in many primitive societies the relation established between two groups of kin by a marriage between a man of one group and a woman of the other is one which is expressed by customs of avoidance and by the joking relationships. In many societies a man is required to avoid any close social contact with the mother of his wife, frequently also with her father, and with other persons of that generation amongst his wife's kin. With this custom there is frequently associated the custom called the "joking relationship" by which a man is permitted or even required to use insulting behaviour to some of his wife's kin of his own generation. I have elsewhere suggested that these customs can be understood as being the conventional means by which a relationship of a peculiar kind, which can be described as a compound of friendship or solidarity with hostility or opposition is established and maintained.

In a complete study there are other features of the dual organization that would need to be taken into consideration. There are instances in which there are regular exchanges of goods or services between the two moieties. In that competitive exchange of food and valuables known as "potlatch" in North America, the moieties may be significant. Amongst the Tlingit, for example, it is members of one moiety who potlatch against members of the other moiety. The two moieties provide the "sides" for what is a sort of competitive game in which men "fight with property."

Our comparative study enables us to see the eaglehawk–crow division of the Darling River tribes as one particular example of a widespread type of the application of a certain structural principle. The relation between the two divisions, which has here been spoken of by the term "opposition" is one which separates and also unites, and which therefore gives us a rather special kind of social integration which deserves systematic study. But the term "opposition" which I have been obliged to use because I cannot find a better, is not wholly appropriate, for it stresses too much what is only one side of the relationship, that of separation and difference. The more correct description would be to say that the kind of structure with which we are concerned is one of the union of opposites.

.   .   .

We began with a particular feature of a particular region in Australia, the existence of exogamous moieties named after the eaglehawk and the crow. By making comparisons amongst other societies, some of them not Australian, we are enabled to see that this is not something particular or peculiar to one region, but is one instance of certain widespread general tendencies in human societies. We thus substitute for a particular problem of the kind that çalls for a historical explanation, certain general problems. There is, for example, the problem of totemism as a social phenomenon in which there is a special association of a social group with a natural species. Another, and perhaps more important, problem that has been raised, is that of the nature and functioning of social relationships and social structures based on what has been called "opposition." This is a much more general problem than that of totemism for it is the problem of how opposition can be used as a mode of social integration. The comparative method is therefore one by which we pass from the particular to the general, from the general to the more general, with the end in view that we may in this way arrive at the universal, at characteristics which can be found in different forms in all human societies.

The Comparative Method
in the Social Sciences

INTRODUCTION

American social scientists, with the possible exception of the anthropologists, have typically been ethnocentric in their writings and research. Most of their studies are simply unique to a particular institutional complex, possessing little generality beyond a single socio-cultural system. Nevertheless, social scientists nowadays are evincing increased interest in comparative studies. They are coming to realize that many of their generalizations may be found wanting when tested in the laboratory of world cultures. For the solution of many significant problems cross-cultural comparison seems essential — the relationships among the variables involved must be examined under diverse cultural conditions.

An attempt is made herein to survey the principal obstacles to a comparative science of society. Three problems seem to be of primary concern. First, the question, "What is going to be compared?" immediately introduces a number of issues. Then there are impediments to cross-cultural comparison stemming from difficulties both in the sampling process and in attempts to standardize researchers' observations. This paper further demonstrates how these problems are interrelated and suggests procedures which might help to resolve some of these difficulties. Most of the examples for this discussion have been drawn from anthropology and sociology, although the principles enunciated are applicable to other social sciences as well.

Several kinds of comparison are possible. Comparison can be made within a single socio-cultural system of "units" from a given time period or of units from different time periods. Neither approach is given special attention in this paper. Instead, emphasis is placed upon the comparative study of different socio-cultural systems (or segments thereof) without spatial or temporal restrictions. Unfortunately some of what

Gideon Sjoberg, "The Comparative Method in the Social Sciences," *Philosophy of Science*, 22: 106-117. Copyright © 1955, The Williams & Wilkins Co., Baltimore, Md. 21202, U.S.A. Reprinted by permission of the author and publisher.

comes under the rubric of "comparative" social sciences is hardly comparative at all. This is to a considerable extent true of the field which is referred to as "area research"; here studies are often conducted in non-Western cultural settings, but little effort is made to relate the findings to those obtained from other areas. Those social scientists who seem to regard area studies as the only possible kind of "comparative" research neglect some of the fundamental issues pertaining to comparative social science.

THE BASES OF COMPARISON

As Clyde Kluckhohn (3) has observed, ". . . genuine comparison is possible only if nonculture-bound units have been isolated." Certain "invariant points of reference" or "universal categories"[1] are required which are not merely reflections of the cultural values of a particular social system. Comparable and relatively stable units must be consciously perceived if comparative study is to progress. Only through the use of invariant points of reference is it possible to test adequately various hypotheses in a cross-cultural setting.[2] None of the social sciences seems to have attained the level of sophistication developed, for example, in the field of linguistics, where more satisfactory universal categories (i.e., phonemes and morphemes) exist. It has often been remarked that more adequate theoretical formulations are sorely needed in the social sciences. Here the problem is the development of a theory of a special type: one which would make possible cross-cultural comparison.

One fundamental assumption must be made by all those who seek to establish invariant points of reference. This is that limits are imposed upon human behavior, whether by biological, geographical, or sociocultural factors. And as a result only a limited number of stable patterns can arise. Social scientists who reject this premise also will not accept the fact that a science of society is an objective possibility.

[1] In this study problems of terminology arise which are on occasion resolved in a rather arbitrary fashion. The terms, "invariant point of reference" and "universal category," are herein used synonymously. However, as becomes apparent from the discussion below, something may be "universal" simply to a special universe — e.g., that of industrialized social systems — but not necessarily to all socio-cultural systems (although the achievement of the latter appears to be a most desirable goal). Also, it seems obvious that reference points which are invariant within one frame of reference may be variable in another.

The employment of the adjective, "invariant," is not intended to invest universal categories with absolutism. Thus "probability" might be allowed for in the construction of some of these. In fact, von Neumann (13) seems to have done just this with his concept of the minimax in his *Theory of Games*.

[2] Studies of single socio-cultural systems, if they are to have any real significance, also should utilize general categories. For the "unique" takes on meaning only insofar as it can be related to the "general."

Although much of social science inquiry has been relatively uncon-
cerned with the construction of universal categories, some progress has
nevertheless been made in this direction, especially in the fields of
sociology and anthropology. One of the earliest efforts was Wissler's
"universal pattern," (15) a crude empirical catalogue of culture traits
which supposedly occur in all social orders. This formulation has proved
to be inadequate. Murdock (8), following in much the same tradition,
although starting from somewhat different assumptions, has sought to
isolate certain "common denominators" of culture which may serve as
guides not only to research but to cross-cultural comparison as well. This,
too, is a systematic listing of rather "empirical" categories,[3] although it
represents a definite advance over that presented by Wissler.

In contradistinction to the aforementioned scholars are those who
have sought to establish "abstract" categories for use in cross-cultural
analysis. For example, Malinowski (5) claims to have isolated seven universal institutions which he believes are functionally necessary to meet
the biological requirements of human beings. In a somewhat similar vein,
Aberle *et al.* (1) have pointed up certain basic patterns which they contend are functional prerequisites to the survival not only of individuals
but, more particularly, of social systems. Two other abstract theories will
be discussed in somewhat greater detail. Florence Kluckhohn has set
forth five invariant points of reference around which she believes all
cultural systems revolve. Through these, cross-cultural comparison of a
certain kind is held to be possible. She writes (4):

> The five common human problems which are tentatively singled
> out as those of key importance can be stated quite directly in the
> form of questions: (1) What are the innate predispositions of men?
> (2) What is the relation of man to nature? (3) What is the signifi-
> cant time dimension? or What is the direction in time of the action
> process? (4) What type of personality is to be most valued? (5)
> What is the dominant modality of the relationship of man to
> other men? The problems as stated are constant; they arise inevitably
> out of the human situation. The phraseology of them is variable but
> variable only within limits.
>
> The limits of the variability, suggested here as at least a testable
> conceptualization of it, are three-point ranges for each of the main
> orientation dimensions.

Perhaps the most extensive approach on the abstract level to be offered
by an anthropologist or sociologist in recent years is that of Talcott

[3] The use of the term, "empirical," is not meant to imply that no abstraction
is involved here. It is simply intended to convey the idea that this kind of
category (or concept) is more "closely associated" with empirical reality than is
an abstract category.

Parsons and his colleagues (10), who have constructed a system around what they term the pattern variable schema, the core of a rather complex theory.

> . . . a *pattern variable* is a dichotomy, one side of which must be chosen by an actor before the meaning of a situation is determinate for him, and thus before he can act with respect to that situation. We maintain that there are only five *basic* pattern variables (i.e., pattern variables deriving directly from the frame of reference of the theory of action) and that, in the sense that they are *all* of the pattern variables which so derive, they constitute a system. Let us list them . . .
>
> 1. Affectivity — Affective neutrality.
> 2. Self-orientation — Collectivity-orientation.
> 3. Universalism — Particularism.
> 4. Ascription — Achievement.
> 5. Specificity — Diffuseness.[4]

Without embarking upon a detailed analysis of this schema (this would lead us far afield), suffice it to say that Parsons *et al.* have contended that these pattern variables enter into consideration upon the personality, societal, and cultural levels, although they are inherently patterns of cultural value orientation — culture being a more generalized concept than society or personality. Inasmuch as these basic "dilemmas" occur in all cultural situations, and inasmuch as they are logically exhaustive, they should, Parsons argues, facilitate cross-cultural comparisons. More specifically Parsons seems most interested in testing hypotheses which concern the relation of values and social structure, the former being viewed as the "independent" variable.

The preceding discussion serves as an introduction to some pertinent observations. The first is that a number of systems of universal categories have been suggested as possible solutions to the general problem of cross-

---

[4] Parsons unfortunately has developed a somewhat "private" vocabulary. The following brief discussion, therefore, suggests the meanings given these terms. Each is considered here from a cultural point of view. Affectivity is the normative pattern which grants an actor permission in a given situation to take advantage of an opportunity for immediate gratification without regard to evaluative considerations; affective neutrality is the converse of this. Self-orientation is that pattern which permits an actor to pursue his private interests without regard to the interests of other actors; collectivity-orientation is the converse of this. Universalism obliges an actor to be oriented toward objects (e.g., persons) in the light of general standards rather than in the objects' possession of certain properties related to those of the actor; particularism is the converse of this. Ascription is the pattern which prescribes that an actor should, in his selection of differential treatment for social objects, give priority to attributes they possess over their performances; achievement is the converse of this. Specificity is that pattern which prescribes that an actor should confine his concern with an object to a specific sphere; diffuseness is the converse of this.

cultural analysis. Only some of the more significant have been mentioned. Some social scientists become sceptical when confronted by a variety of categories. But different theories may well require different invariant reference points. Put in other terms, an economic or technological determinist who attempts to correlate various aspects of social organization with his most generalized independent variable may necessarily have to select a different set of categories from the social scientist who takes as his focus of study the interrelationships between a society's value system (viewed as the independent variable) and its social structure. So, too, a psychologist starting from different assumptions and faced with different problems would employ still other categories. And it appears that even those who take the same independent variable as their point of departure may be justified in developing different invariant points of reference, depending upon their assumptions and whether the problems to be considered are of a special nature (e.g., if they are treating some limited sub-universes). This practice does not appear to be out of line with that in the physical sciences, which also must resort to various theoretical systems to explain different phenomena. Although the ideal is the development of a unified theory, this is far from reaching fruition not only in the physical but especially in the social sciences. The latter must be wary of relying too heavily upon a single theory and a single set of reference points. The fact that different theories (and the different hypotheses which stem from these theories) may require different universal categories has direct bearing upon the nature of comparative research, a fact which is indicated below.

It should be stressed that the isolation of invariant points of reference is not an end in itself. Nor should these be used simply to classify various social phenomena. Rather they should permit the testing of hypotheses in a cross-cultural setting. Before Max Weber could "demonstrate" relationships between the religious system and the economic system, it was necessary that he isolate certain "trans-cultural" reference points which would facilitate comparisons among European, Chinese, Indian, and other societies (9). Furthermore, only when invariant points of reference have been isolated is prediction possible. Because of their intrinsic importance, much more attention needs to be given them by the researcher.

Now, various problems arise in the selection of universal categories. First, should the social scientist choose concrete (empiric) or abstract categories? Although no sharp division exists between these two types of concepts and the choice to be made is to a degree a function of the particular research project, certain general issues appear. Many social scientists have sought to employ categories which are relatively concrete in nature. Their studies possess the very definite advantage that their generalizations have empirical meaning and content. On the other hand, we find numerous instances in contemporary social science where this procedure has led to some startling contradictions. The use of the concept, "divorce," as a category for examining family or societal solidarity in various cultures seems to be a case in point. Miner in his recent study of the city of Timbuctoo took as his working hypothesis the assumption that all urban centers exhibit a degree of secularization and/or disorganization (6). His choice of divorce as a criterion of disorganization was in accordance with the practice of students of European and American urban life. But for a cross-cultural study such as Miner's the choice was a rather unfortunate one. The result is that Miner has implied that the sacred writings of the Koran, which justify divorce in Moslem society, are not sacred at all. Actually, divorce in one society may be an institutionalized and a highly orderly and acceptable procedure, whereas in another it may represent a form of societal disorganization. As an invariant point of reference for this kind of research it displays inherent limitations. Other social scientists who have used the concept of divorce in cross-cultural studies as a reference point for familial disorganization have been faced with similar contradictions. This is just one example of the social scientist's capture by culture-bound concepts; still others could be enumerated. In fact, it may develop that most of the categories currently employed in socio-cultural inquiry are quite inadequate for comparative analysis. It should never be assumed that reference points which hold for one cultural setting are applicable to all others.

In an effort to resolve the contradictions which seem to be inherent in highly empiricized concepts, social scientists such as Florence Kluckhohn and Parsons have been searching for more abstract categories. This is in line with the trend in all services toward utilization of abstract concepts to circumvent problems arising on the "common-sense" level of inquiry. The disadvantages of abstract conceptualization, however, seem apparent enough. Some of the concepts employed by Parsons, e.g., universalism and particularism, and the universal categories offered by Florence Kluckhohn are so general that they are subject to numerous interpretations on the part of the investigator. They require empirical indicators — or better yet certain specified "operational" procedures — which will relate them to empirical reality. Otherwise these invariant reference points will be part of a "neat" theory the empirical relevance of which is negligible. The charge of "over-abstraction" has been leveled against many social scientists — not only verbal theorists but also logico-mathematical "model builders" like the econometricians — who often lose sight of the empirical relevance of their models. Certainly if any theory is to be of value in comparative research the universal categories employed must be established in a manner which will permit their use in the testing of specific hypotheses. Although it is apparent that for some time to come much of cross-cultural research will be dependent upon rather loose and somewhat impressionistic conceptualization, social scientists must strive for a more rigorous approach.

A number of writers have stressed the need for a compromise between the strictly empirical and the rationalistic conceptual schemes. Nowhere is this requirement more strongly felt than in efforts to establish invariant points of reference for cross-cultural research. The use of abstract or concrete categories can not be an either/or proposition. Actually the co-existence of these two approaches serves as a check upon the abuses to which each is susceptible. The process of constructing an adequate set of invariant reference points must, then, be one of continual trial and error and, fundamentally, one of self-criticism. For it appears that most of the systems currently employed in the social sciences will serve merely to "clear away the underbrush" for future scholars; not only are present-day categories unsatisfactory for predictive purposes but they are inadequate for most descriptive purposes as well.

Still other problems present themselves. Invariant points of reference, if they are to be meaningful, should be integrated into a logically consistent system.[5] Few of the early comparative social scientists such as Spencer and Sumner were particularly concerned with this question. Their premises were not clearly stated nor did they attempt to relate their "categories" logically one to the other. In recent years attempts to improve this situation have occurred in the verbal as well as in the logico-mathematical traditions. Among verbal theorists Parsons has been a pioneer in that he has stressed the need for logical consistency. However, it is doubtful that he (or anyone else) has developed a satisfactorily consistent verbal theory. For example, Parsons' pattern variable schema does not appear to be homologous; by his own admission its categories do not appear to be derivable from a single principle, but rather from three (11, p. 66). Yet, through his effort the attention of social scientists has been directed to the need for more rigorous analysis in cross-cultural research.

Possibly the logico-mathematical tradition will give the greatest impetus to the formulation of a more rigorous set of universal categories. Although as presently constituted many logico-mathematical deductive models seem to have little empirical import, this does not appear to be an inherent limitation of the approach. Some effort is currently being made, especially through the use of "qualitative" mathematical models, to adjust these systems so that they will conform more closely to empirical reality. The classic work of von Neumann and Morgenstern (13) is an example of a mathematically derived model which has definite implica-

---

[5] Also, whenever categories are developed for a "limited universe," e.g., a kinship system or a class system, they should in turn be related to a still broader frame of reference.

tions for cross-cultural research of a special type. The concepts developed
— the minimax, coalitions, and randomized strategy — seem applicable
to the study of conflict and competition under a variety of cultural conditions. Even when this mathematical model is translated into verbal
form it offers some major advances in insight and rigor over previous
formulations in the field of social conflict (12). The proliferation of the
logico-mathematical approach within the social sciences would do much
to further cross-cultural research.

SAMPLING AND THE STANDARDIZATION
OF OBSERVATIONS

Let us turn our attention for a moment from the question of universal
categories or invariant points of reference to problems of a more technical
nature. First, just how are we to proceed in selecting "cases" for the
comparative study of diverse socio-cultural systems or sub-systems? Here
we might profitably take Murdock's recent work (7) as a starting point
for this discussion. His comparative analysis of kinship systems is one of
the studies which has drawn upon the data amassed by the Human Relations Area Files (at New Haven, Conn.) on numerous literate and nonliterate societies. Murdock's contribution is significant here for his use of
sampling and probability statistics in comparative research (we shall not
be concerned with his conclusions). Although this procedure can serve
as a profitable implement to social science research, certain difficulties
arise when probability statistics are applied on a cross-cultural basis.
Murdock's sampling design with respect to world societies invites some
serious criticisms. Just what is the universe from which his sample has
been selected? The fact that he has included within his sample some
historically "extinct" societies means that his universe embraces all
societies which have ever existed. But we lack sufficient knowledge about
this universe. It consists of societies for which we have adequate data,
others upon which our knowledge is limited, and finally those about
which we really know nothing. There is no way of determining how societies for which we lack information are related to those upon which we
have information. Under these circumstances it is most difficult to consider his sample as "random"; some major "biases" may in fact be
present. And if a random sample is not employed, extreme caution must
be exercised in interpreting (if not actually in applying) inductive statistical techniques — e.g., the chi-square test which Murdock utilizes to
generalize from his "sample" to the universe. Too often social scientists
employ statistical procedures without examining the assumptions upon
which their analyses necessarily rest.

Not only is it difficult to determine the nature of a universe, but problems are encountered in establishing the boundaries of societal or cultural

systems. Many of these are interrelated historically. Are they to be treated as one, or separately? For example, should the Chinese in Malaya be classed as a separate socio-cultural system or as part of the Chinese social order? To a degree this is a function of the particular research problem. Yet historical interrelationships among socio-cultural systems serve to complicate the drawing of a sample by introducing the question of the "independence" of sampling units. The situation is made all the more confused by the absence of convenient standards for delineating the sub-systems of a social order. Some formalized procedures are certainly required if sampling is to be utilized in cross-cultural research.

Sampling units must also be comparable. If such units as household or community are employed, these can be subject to different cultural interpretations. A "household" in one socio-cultural system may be quite different from a "household" in another. Here, too, we are confronted with the need for "trans-cultural" or "nonvaluational" categories. Still another source of confusion — one of a logical nature — appears often in the literature. It seems fashionable nowadays to take the "community" as a unit for comparison. But can we really compare the Tikopia of Oceania (a nonliterate "community" which is co-terminous with the "society") with Yankee City or Chicago? In many instances this kind of comparison can lead to some questionable conclusions. Whereas the Tikopia constitute a functionally self-sufficient system, American communities such as Chicago are only partial systems. A primitive community logically needs to be compared not with an urban or rural community but with the total society of which the latter are integral parts. Yet comparison between sub-systems and total systems is common practice in the social sciences.

The application of statistical techniques in the face of the aforementioned problems might be rationalized by the investigator in certain types of cross-cultural studies. However, due consideration must be given to the limitations of using random sampling and probability statistics in most cross-cultural research. In fact, as is indicated below, even social scientists who make comparisons within a single socio-cultural system are plagued by similar handicaps, although this is not often recognized.

Not only do pitfalls appear in the sampling process but considerable difficulty is encountered in standardizing the observations of researchers working in diverse cultural settings. Social scientists must strive toward the attainment of some degree of standardization: otherwise each field worker will record impressions which can not be validated by others. To be sure, rigorous research designs, sampling procedures, sociograms, and questionnaires have all contributed toward making social science research more than an individual venture. Possibly the greatest advances have been in the field of microscopic research — i.e., the study of small

groups — where the situational factors seem somewhat more easily controlled. Nevertheless, some crucial aspects of the problem of standardizing observations, especially in cross-cultural research, remain relatively
untouched. There is particular need for standardizing and objectifying the
procedures by which imputations are made concerning the "subjective"
aspects of human experience, data which are not directly observable.
Just how to standardize the imputation of meanings to human action
is a pressing issue in all the socio-cultural sciences. When a person enters
a place of "worship," just what "meaning" is to be attached to his action? One can observe and record the act easily enough, but imputing
meanings to it is another matter. At times it can prove quite trying for
social scientists to reach a consensus concerning the meaning of certain
acts in their own socio-cultural system, to say nothing of other cultural
settings. Yet some standardization within this sphere nevertheless seems
possible of attainment.

Another troublesome area, interrelated with that just mentioned, concerns standardizing the imputations of observers about the mechanics
of large-scale, complex social systems — e.g., a governmental bureaucracy. Although considerable effort has been given to refining questionnaires and similar research tools, these have proved to be of very limited
value for analyzing the functioning of complex social structures. There is
clearly a need for standardizing the observations of participant observers
in this kind of setting. Furthermore, efforts to standardize researchers'
imputations from published records concerning the functioning of large-
scale social systems (e.g., through the use of content analysis) are still
far from satisfactory. Too many inconsistent interpretations concerning
the nature of large-scale social systems have been put forth. Even a partial solution to these problems would do much to enhance cross-cultural
research.

POSSIBLE DIRECTIONS

At this point it seems appropriate to seek out the relationships among
those facets of cross-cultural research discussed above — namely, invariant
points of reference and the more strictly methodological problems of
research as sampling and the standardization of observations — and
through this means to uncover possible solutions to some of the aforementioned difficulties. In order better to perceive their functional interrelationships some slight digression seems necessary. In comparative
research it appears that in the selection of cases (whether these be total
systems or sub-systems) for testing hypotheses, social scientists must
accept the fact that a crude statistical approach, or more often than not
some kind of qualitative analysis, is required. This is probably all that can
ever be achieved on a cross-cultural basis (especially on the macroscopic

level) for some time to come. Among other factors, data simply are lacking on too many societies; therefore, reliance must be placed in most instances upon some kind of "judgmental" sample. This principle should be followed: utilize quantitative and other rigorous procedures where these are required and can legitimately be employed (especially within case studies, e.g., that of a single community), but recognize that certain kinds of problems can not be treated in a rigorous statistical fashion, especially through the use of probability statistics, at the present time. Unless the social scientist is willing to accept this obvious limitation, the whole of comparative study (which appears to form the basis of social science) must be conceded to have no future.

Even the granted limitations imposed upon research in comparative social science, the situation is not without hope. One approach might be pursued to advantage — i.e., the giving of increased emphasis to deviant or unique cases. Such a step may point up some hypotheses which should be rejected — or perhaps define more precisely the conditions under which the original hypotheses are valid — or even demonstrate the need for a broader hypothesis to cover the deviant cases. It is through deviant case studies that reference points can best be perceived or those already in use sharpened and clarified. Some social scientists seem to hold to the view that intensive knowledge of our own culture is required before we are justified in attempting analyses of other socio-cultural systems. But this brings us to a major impasse: the general and stable elements in our own culture can best be understood when the latter is compared with divergent cases.

The physical sciences took centuries to formulate and refine their invariant points of reference, and it seems unlikely that the social sciences will uncover any convenient short-cuts to this goal. Therefore, instead of merely searching for confirmatory evidence, as some social scientists prefer, it seems necessary purposively to gather contradictory evidence, then, in light of this, rework and reformulate the so-called invariant points of reference as well as the hypotheses being tested: A number of social scientists implicitly recognize the value of this procedure. However, there is need for more explicit recognition of its *essentiality* in cross-cultural research. This procedure, incidentally, is in conformance with the ideas of such philosophers of science as Popper and Wisdom (14), who argue that one can only disprove, never really prove, scientific hypotheses, and that the scientific method therefore basically embodies a negative approach.

Not only do carefully-designed case studies, especially deviant ones, sharpen invariant points of reference, but certain other facts should be noted. To the extent that invariant reference points or categories have been isolated for a particular research problem, a case study (whether

of a society or community or other social group) takes on added significance. Not only can we perceive its general aspects but we can appre-
ciate more fully the significance of its unique features.

The essential role of case studies for comparisons within a single socio-
cultural system is also often overlooked. It is common practice nowadays
to use the community as a setting within which to test various hypotheses
concerning the functioning of the class structure, ecological system,
kinship organization, etc. And it is a relatively simple matter to apply
random sampling within this "primary" universe, if this is desirable.
However, the community is still only a case study with respect to other
communities in the total social order, to say nothing of in the world.
It is considerably more difficult to draw a random sample of communities
and to study a number of these even within a single socio-cultural system. Thus, social scientists usually take a case study of community life
and generalize freely from it to other communities. But they give all too
little attention to the question: Is the community representative both
spatially and *temporally* of other communities within the socio-cultural
system? Generalization from one or only a few cases is often necessary,
but this is valid only if certain invariant reference points have been
isolated. Put in more concrete terms, research projects in such communities as Yankee City and Middletown are significant for an understanding
of other communities in the United States to the extent that their findings have been related to certain general and comparable categories.

Some other relationships between research and invariant points of reference merit attention. Social scientists should recognize that different
theoretical systems may require different invariant reference points and
that descriptive data for various case studies need therefore to be collected
with this in mind. The practice of limiting observations to a single set of
categories (as well as to a single hypothesis) can be far from satisfactory.
If the need for a broader perspective were more explicitly recognized by
researchers interested in comparative analysis, their case studies of societies, communities, kinship systems, etc. would be greatly enhanced. We
can not be certain which set of reference points will prove to be most
adequate: those which we now use are just too approximate. Why, then,
gamble on collecting data simply in terms of a single set of categories?
If more than one is consciously employed, more of our existing reference
points can be sharpened or perhaps discarded, or the need for new ones
clearly seen. Also, some comparative work must necessarily be done by
non-field workers — the sheer impossibility of one individual ever conducting research in more than just a few cultures during a life-time seems
obvious enough. There must be specialists to correlate these findings from
various socio-cultural settings.

Finally, a few remarks about standardizing observations. This, too, is strikingly interrelated with invariant points of reference. For to the degree that relatively stable reference points have been isolated, standardization of observation becomes a more objective possibility. Observation necessarily takes place, whether implicitly or explicitly, in terms of some particular theoretical structure. If a researcher is dealing with universal and comparable categories, he is more likely to observe the same kind of social phenomena as do other researchers. This is especially true for studies of large-scale social systems. It seems to this writer that one of the principal reasons for the research difficulties encountered in the last-named area is that no really satisfactory invariant reference points have been isolated. Techniques alone can not resolve these issues.

This is not to imply that all that is required is the construction of conceptual categories. Measurement and operational procedures also have a place. Scales and indices are currently being developed and applied with the expectation that these will somehow standardize observations. And to a degree they may succeed. Unfortunately, however, these devices are often utilized without attention to general and comparable categories. The following question must be kept in mind: "What is going to be measured?" Sociologists are attempting to construct indexes and scales which will aid in depicting, for example, the American class structure or urban ecological patterns. But they are plagued by numerous discrepancies, one reason being that so much attention is given the "unique" rather than to universal reference points.

It is also the writer's contention that social scientists should employ less "stereotyped" methods in attempting to standardize observations. One such deviant approach is suggested by Firey and Belknap (2). They argue that society itself has refined techniques for imputing meanings to social action; one of these is the "jury system" with its judges, witnesses, advocates, etc. Social scientists, they believe, might well utilize some of the principles embodied in this approach as an aid to standardizing the imputation of meaning to social action. This is just one example of how a deviant technique might be employed to advantage, particularly if it is used in relation to sets of universal categories.

SUMMARY

It should be emphasized that most social science research evinces no real effort to generalize beyond single socio-cultural systems, the United States in particular. There is a marked tendency to lose sight of the basic function of science — i.e., to generalize. Although the social sciences may never achieve the "predictability" of the natural sciences, a deeper understanding of society than is now apparent seems possible through the comparative method.

Given the intrinsic importance of comparative study, cognizance should be taken of the problems encountered in cross-cultural research. This paper has sought to isolate three of the most significant. Perhaps the major emphasis should be given to developing more satisfactory invariant reference points or universal categories. *In order to test the relationships among variables in various socio-cultural settings, certain comparable and relatively stable categories must be employed.* Some of these invariant points of reference, of course, might be applicable only to limited universes. Also, attention has been called herein to two pressing methodological problems, sampling and the standardization of observations. But even these, as has been shown, are interrelated with invariant reference points; the social scientist should keep this in mind when he seeks to resolve problems in cross-cultural research.

References

1. Aberle, D. F. *et al.*, "The Functional Prerequisites of a Society," *Ethics*, LX, 1950, pp. 100-11.
2. Firey, Walter and Ivan Belknap, "The Problem of Standardizing Observations in Sociology," *Proceedings of the Southwestern Sociological Society*, I, 1951, pp. 60-67. (mimeo.)
3. Kluckhohn, Clyde, "Universal Categories of Culture," in A. L. Kroeber, *Anthropology Today*, University of Chicago Press, 1953, pp. 507-23.
4. Kluckhohn, Florence, "Dominant and Substitute Profiles of Cultural Orientations: Their Significance for the Analysis of Social Stratification," *Social Forces*, XXVIII, pp. 376-93.
5. Malinowski, B., *A Scientific Theory of Culture*, University of North Carolina Press, 1944.
6. Miner, Horace, *The Primitive City of Timbuctoo*, Princeton University Press, 1953.
7. Murdock, George P., *Social Structure*, Macmillan Co., 1949.
8. Murdock, George P. *et al.*, *Outline of Cultural Materials*, 3rd rev. ed., Human Relations Area Files, Inc., 1950.
9. Parsons, Talcott, *The Structure of Social Action*, The Free Press, 1949.
10. Parsons, Talcott and Edward A. Shils (eds.), *Toward a General Theory of Action*, Harvard University Press, 1951.
11. Parsons, Talcott *et al.*, *Working Papers in the Theory of Action*, The Free Press, 1953.
12. Sjoberg, Gideon, "Strategy and Social Power: Some Preliminary Formulations," *Southwestern Social Science Quarterly*, XXXIII, 1953, pp. 297-308.
13. von Neumann, John and Oskar Morgenstern, *Theory of Games and Economic Behavior*, 2nd ed., Princeton University Press, 1947.
14. Wisdom, John O., *Foundations of Inference in Natural Science*, Methuen & Co., 1952.
15. Wissler, Clark, *Man and Culture*, Thomas Y. Crowell, 1923.

3   MARC BLOCH

Two Strategies of Comparison

The term "comparative history," now in current use, has had the fate of almost all common words: shifts in meaning. We will leave aside certain usages of the term which are definitely wrong; but, even apart from such errors, an ambiguity remains. In the social sciences the term "comparative method" is generally used in such a way as to include two very different intellectual procedures. Only linguists have made a sustained effort to keep these two meanings carefully apart. Now it is our turn, as historians, to make a precise distinction.

In the first place, what does it mean if a historian "compares"? Without any doubt it means this: he selects two or more phenomena which appear at first sight to be analogous and which occur in one or more social milieus. He finds out how these phenomena resemble or differ from one another, traces their evolution, and, as far as possible, explains the similarities and differences. In order to have historical comparison, two conditions must be fulfilled: a certain similarity or analogy between observed phenomena — that is obvious — and a certain dissimilarity between the environments in which they occur. If I study the landholding system of the Limousin region, for instance, I will constantly compare fragments of evidence drawn from the records of this or that *seigneurie*. This is comparison in the common sense of the word, but, nevertheless, I do not think that I engage here in what is, technically speaking, comparative history; for the various objects of my study are all derived from parts of the same society, a society which in its totality forms one large unit. It has become common practice to reserve the term "comparative history" almost exclusively for the confrontation of phenomena which have occurred on different sides of the boundary of a state or nation. Political and national contrasts are indeed the most striking and immediately evident of all social contrasts. But, as we shall see, this restricted conception of the comparative method is a rather gross simplification. Let us

Reprinted with permission from *Enterprise and Secular Change*, by Frederic C. Lane and Jelle C. Riemersma (eds.) (Homewood, Ill.: Richard D. Irwin, Inc., 1953). The original title was "Toward a Comparative History of European Societies."

therefore use here the notion of a "difference of environment" — a notion which is more flexible and more precise.

All forms of the comparative method have in common the procedure of comparison defined above. Depending on the field of inquiry, there are two altogether different ways in which the method can be applied, different both in principle and in results.

First case: the units of comparison are societies far removed from one another in time or space. Analogous phenomena observed in these societies cannot be explained, therefore, by mutual influences or by a common origin. Such a comparison is exemplified by the confrontation of the Greek and Roman civilizations of ancient times with presently existing primitive societies. This application of the comparative method has become common since the days of Father Lafitau, S.J. (1724), who invited his readers to "compare the customs and manners of American savages" with those of "the earliest times." Within the relatively advanced civilization of the early Roman Empire one ritual stood out like a strange and cruel discrepancy. Very near Rome was a little temple of Diana on the beautiful shores of Lake Nemi. Anyone could become a priest of this temple, but only after fulfilling one specific and inescapable requirement: he had to kill the priest whose place he intended to take. "If we can show that a barbarous custom, like that of the priesthood of Nemi, has existed elsewhere; if we can detect the motives which led to its institution; if we can prove that these motives have operated widely, perhaps universally, in human society, producing in varied circumstances a variety of institutions specifically different but generally alike; if we can show, lastly, that these very motives, with some of their derivative institutions, were actually at work in classical antiquity; then we may fairly infer that at a remoter age the same motives gave birth to the priesthood of Nemi."[1] Here we have the starting point of the immense inquiry of *The Golden Bough*, a most famous and illustrative example of a study based upon evidence from all parts of the world. Such an application of the comparative method has rendered various and important services. It has done so especially for the study of Mediterranean antiquity. Humanistic education had accustomed us to regard Hellas and Rome as much too similar to ourselves. The ethnographers and their comparisons, by a sort of mental shock, restored the sense of a contrast between ourselves and the ancients. Thereby we regained that peculiar sense of the exotic which is a prerequisite for a sound understanding of the past. Other benefits of the comparative method in the grand manner are of a more general nature. Gaps in documentation may be overcome by hypotheses based on analogies, comparisons may suggest research in new directions

[1] James G. Frazer, *The Golden Bough: A Study in Magic and Religion*, Vol. I (3rd ed., London: Macmillan & Co., Ltd., 1911), p. 10.

and, in particular, may explain many "survivals" which hitherto had remained strange and unintelligible. By "survivals" I mean customs which are retained and crystallized in a milieu entirely different from (and later than) the psychological environment in which the customs originated. Such phenomena would appear bizarre and inexplicable, were it not for the existence of similar traits in other cultures which allow precise reconstruction of that vanished social environment; the ritual murder of Nemi is a case in point. This comparative method on the grand scale can be summarized as essentially a procedure of interpolation of lines of development. The basic postulate of this method, as well as the conclusion to which it constantly returns, is the fundamental unity of the human spirit or, if you wish, the monotony and astonishing poverty of human intellectual resources during the course of history. This poverty is most evident in the ages when, in a first crude attempt, primitive humanity elaborated a philosophy of life (Frazer).

There exists another application of the comparative procedure: that in which the units of comparison are societies that are geographical neighbors and historical contemporaries, constantly influenced by one another. During the historical development of such societies, they are subject to the same over-all causes, just because they are so close together in time and space. Moreover, they have, in part at least, a common origin. This second form of the comparative method corresponds, within the historical discipline, to the approach of comparative linguistics (dealing with one related group of languages, for instance the Indo-Germanic). The comparative method in the grand manner, on the other hand, would correspond approximately to general linguistics, which deals with all human languages. From the scientific point of view the method with the more restricted outlook appears to be the most promising; this holds for history as well as for linguistics. The latter method may arrive at more precise and less hypothetical conclusions, because its classifications can be more rigorous and critical. . . .

III

Variety and Universals

4   RUTH BENEDICT

The Diversity of Cultures

A chief of the Digger Indians, as the Californians call them, talked to me a great deal about the ways of his people in the old days. He was a Christian and a leader among his people in the planting of peaches and apricots on irrigated land, but when he talked of the shamans who had transformed themselves into bears before his eyes in the bear dance, his hands trembled and his voice broke with excitement. It was an incomparable thing, the power his people had had in the old days. He liked best to talk of the desert foods they had eaten. He brought each uprooted plant lovingly and with an unfailing sense of its importance. In those days his people had eaten "the health of the desert," he said, and knew nothing of the insides of tin cans and the things for sale at butcher shops. It was such innovations that had degraded them in these latter days.

From *Patterns of Culture* by Ruth Benedict. (Boston: Houghton Mifflin Company). Reprinted by permission of the publisher.

One day, without transition, Ramon broke in upon his descriptions of grinding mesquite and preparing acorn soup. "In the beginning," he said, "God gave to every people a cup, a cup of clay, and from this cup they drank their life." I do not know whether the figure occurred in some traditional ritual of his people that I never found, or whether it was his own imagery. It is hard to imagine that he had heard it from the whites he had known at Banning; they were not given to discussing the ethos of different peoples. At any rate, in the mind of this humble Indian the figure of speech was clear and full of meaning. "They all dipped in the water," he continued, "but their cups were different. Our cup is broken now. It has passed away."

Our cup is broken. Those things that had given significance to the life of his people, the domestic rituals of eating; the obligations of the economic system, the succession of ceremonials in the villages, possession in the bear dance, their standards of right and wrong — these were gone, and with them the shape and meaning of their life. The old man was still vigorous and a leader in relationships with the whites. He did not mean that there was any question of the extinction of his people. But he had in mind the loss of something that had value equal to that of life itself, the whole fabric of his people's standards and beliefs. There were other cups of living left, and they held perhaps the same water, but the loss was irreparable. It was no matter of tinkering with an addition here, lopping off something there. The modelling had been fundamental, it was somehow all of a piece. It had been their own.

Ramon had had personal experience of the matter of which he spoke. He straddled two cultures whose values and ways of thought were incommensurable. It is a hard fate. In Western civilization our experiences have been different. We are bred to one cosmopolitan culture, and our social sciences, our psychology, and our theology persistently ignore the truth expressed in Ramon's figure.

The course of life and the pressure of environment, not to speak of the fertility of human imagination, provide an incredible number of possible leads, all of which, it appears, may serve a society to live by. There are the schemes of ownership, with the social hierarchy that may be associated with possessions; there are material things and their elaborate technology; there are all the facets of sex life, parenthood and post-parenthood; there are the guilds or cults which may give structure to the society; there is economic exchange; there are the gods and supernatural sanctions. Each one of these and many more may be followed out with a cultural and ceremonial elaboration which monopolizes the cultural energy and leaves small surplus for the building of other traits. Aspects of life that seem to us most important have been passed over with small regard by peoples whose culture, oriented in another direction, has been far from poor. Or the same trait may be so greatly elaborated that we reckon it as fantastic.

It is in cultural life as it is in speech; selection is the prime necessity. The numbers of sounds that can be produced by our vocal cords and our oral and nasal cavities are practically unlimited. The three or four dozen of the English language are a selection which coincides not even with those of such closely related dialects as German and French. The total that are used in different languages of the world no one has even dared to estimate. But each language must make its selection and abide by it on pain of not being intelligible at all. A language that used even a few hundreds of the possible — and actually recorded — phonetic elements could not be used for communication. On the other hand a great deal of our misunderstanding of languages unrelated to our own has arisen from our attempts to refer alien phonetic systems back to ours as a point of reference. We recognize only one *k*. If other people have five *k* sounds placed in different positions in the throat and mouth, distinctions of vocabulary and of syntax that depend on these differences are impossible to us until we master them. We have a *d* and an *n*. They may have an intermediate sound which, if we fail to identify it, we write now *d* and now *n*, introducing distinctions which do not exist. The elementary prerequisite of linguistic analysis is a consciousness of these incredibly numerous available sounds from which each language makes its own selections.

In culture too we must imagine a great arc on which are ranged the possible interests provided either by the human age-cycle or by the environment or by man's various activities. A culture that capitalized even a considerable proportion of these would be as unintelligible as a language that used all the clicks, all the glottal stops, all the labials, dentals, sibilants, and gutturals from voiceless to voiced and from oral to nasal. Its identity as a culture depends upon the selection of some segments of this arc. Every human society everywhere has made such selection in its cultural institutions. Each from the point of view of another ignores fundamentals and exploits irrelevancies. One culture hardly recognizes monetary values; another has made them fundamental in every field of behaviour. In one society technology is unbelievingly slighted even in those aspects of life which seem necessary to ensure survival; in another, equally simple, technological achievements are complex and fitted with admirable nicety to the situation. One builds an enormous cultural superstructure upon adolescence, one upon death, one upon after-life.

The case of adolescence is particularly interesting, because it is in the limelight in our own civilization and because we have plentiful information from other cultures. In our own civilization a whole library of psychological studies has emphasized the inevitable unrest of the period of puberty. It is in our tradition a physiological state as definitely characterized by domestic explosions and rebellion as typhoid is marked by fever. There is no question of the facts. They are common in America. The question is rather of their inevitability.

The most casual survey of the ways in which different societies have handled adolescence makes one fact inescapable: even in those cultures which have made most of the trait, the age upon, which they focus their attention varies over a great range of years. At the outset, therefore, it is clear that the so-called puberty institutions are a misnomer if we continue to think of biological puberty. The puberty they recognize is social, and the ceremonies are a recognition in some fashion or other of the child's new status of adulthood. This investiture with new occupations and obligations is in consequence as various and as culturally conditioned as the occupations and obligations themselves. If the sole honourable duty of manhood is conceived to be deeds of war, the investiture of the warrior is later and of a different sort from that in a society where adulthood gives chiefly the privilege of dancing in a representation of masked gods. In order to understand puberty institutions, we do not most need analyses of the necessary nature of *rites de passage*; we need rather to know what is identified in different cultures with the beginning of adulthood and their methods of admitting to the new status. Not biological puberty, but what adulthood means in that culture conditions the puberty ceremony.

Adulthood in central North America means warfare. Honour in it is the great goal of all men. The constantly recurring theme of the youth's coming-of-age, as also of preparation for the warpath at any age, is a magic ritual for success in war. They torture not one another, but themselves: they cut strips of skin from their arms and legs, they strike off their fingers, they drag heavy weights pinned to their chest or leg muscles. Their reward is enhanced prowess in deeds of warfare.

In Australia, on the other hand, adulthood means participation in an exclusively male cult whose fundamental trait is the exclusion of women. Any woman is put to death if she so much as hears the sound of the bull-roarer at the ceremonies, and she must never know of the rites. Puberty ceremonies are elaborate and symbolic repudiations of the bonds with the female sex; the men are symbolically made self-sufficient and the wholly responsible element of the community. To attain this end they use drastic sexual rites and bestow supernatural guaranties.

The clear physiological facts of adolescence, therefore, are first socially interpreted even where they are stressed. But a survey of puberty institutions makes clear a further fact: puberty is physiologically a different matter in the life-cycle of the male and the female. If cultural emphasis followed the physiological emphasis, girls' ceremonies would be more marked than boys'; but it is not so. The ceremonies emphasize a social fact: the adult prerogatives of men are more far-reaching in every culture than women's, and consequently, as in the above instances, it is more common for societies to take note of this period in boys than in girls.

Girls' and boys' puberty, however, may be socially celebrated in the same tribe in identical ways. Where, as in the interior of British Columbia, adolescent rites are a magical training for all occupations, girls are included on the same terms as boys. Boys roll stones down mountains and beat them to the bottom to be swift of foot, or throw gambling-sticks to be lucky in gambling; girls carry water from distant springs, or drop stones down inside their dresses that their children may be born as easily as the pebble drops to the ground.

In such a tribe as the Nandi of the lake region of East Africa, also, girls and boys share an even-handed puberty rite, though, because of the man's dominant rôle in the culture, his boyhood training period is more stressed than the woman's. Here adolescent rites are an ordeal inflicted by those already admitted to adult status upon those they are now forced to admit. They require of them the most complete stoicism in the face of ingenious tortures associated with circumcision. The rites for the two sexes are separate, but they follow the same pattern. In both the novices wear for the ceremony the clothing of their sweethearts. During the operation their faces are watched for any twinge of pain, and the reward of bravery is given with great rejoicing by the lover, who runs forward to receive back some of his adornments. For both the girl and the boy the rites mark their *entrée* into a new sex status: the boy is now a warrior and may take a sweetheart, the girl is marriageable. The adolescent tests are for both a pre-marital ordeal in which the palm is awarded by their lovers.

Puberty rites may also be built upon the facts of girls' puberty and admit of no extension to boys. One of the most naïve of these is the institution of the fatting-house for girls in central Africa. In the region where feminine beauty is all but identified with obesity, the girl at puberty is segregated, sometimes for years, fed with sweet and fatty foods, allowed no activity, and her body rubbed assiduously with oils. She is taught during this time her future duties, and her seclusion ends with a parade of her corpulence that is followed by her marriage to her proud bridegroom. It is not regarded as necessary for the man to achieve pulchritude before marriage in a similar fashion.

The usual ideas around which girls' puberty institutions are centered, and which are not readily extended to boys', are those concerned with menstruation. The uncleanness of the menstruating woman is a very widespread idea, and in a few regions first menstruation has been made the focus of all the associated attitudes. Puberty rites in these cases are of a thoroughly different character from any of which we have spoken.

Among the Carrier Indians of British Columbia, the fear and horror of a girl's puberty was at its height. Her three or four years of seclusion was called "the burying alive," and she lived all that time alone in the wilderness, in a hut of branches far from all beaten trails. She was a threat to any person who might so much as catch a glimpse of her, and her mere footstep defiled a path or a river. She was covered with a great headdress of tanned skin that shrouded her face and breasts and fell to the ground behind. Her arms and legs were loaded with sinew bands to protect her from the evil spirit with which she was filled. She was herself in danger and she was a source of danger to everybody else.

Girls' puberty ceremonies built upon ideas associated with the menses are readily convertible into what is, from the point of view of the individual concerned, exactly opposite behaviour. There are always two possible aspects to the sacred: it may be a source of peril or it may be a source of blessing. In some tribes the first menses of girls are a potent supernatural blessing. Among the Apaches I have seen the priests themselves pass on their knees before the row of solemn little girls to receive from them the blessing of their touch. All the babies and the old people come also of necessity to have illness removed from them. The adolescent girls are not segregated as sources of danger, but court is paid to them as direct sources of supernatural blessing. Since the ideas that underlie puberty rites for girls, both among the Carrier and among the Apache, are founded on beliefs concerning menstruation, they are not extended to boys, and boys' puberty is marked instead, and lightly, with simple tests and proofs of manhood.

The adolescent behaviour, therefore, even of girls was not dictated by some physiological characteristic of the period itself, but rather by marital or magic requirements socially connected with it. These beliefs made adolescence in one tribe serenely religious and beneficent, and in another so dangerously unclean that the child had to cry out in warning that others might avoid her in the woods. The adolescence of girls may equally, as we have seen, be a theme which a culture does not institutionalize. Even where, as in most of Australia, boys' adolescence is given elaborate treatment, it may be that the rites are an induction into the status of manhood and male participation in tribal matters, and female adolescence passes without any kind of formal recognition.

These facts, however, still leave the fundamental question unanswered. Do not all cultures have to cope with the natural turbulence of this period, even though it may not be given institutional expression? Dr. Mead has studied this question in Samoa. There the girl's life passes through well-marked periods. Her first years out of babyhood are passed in small neighbourhood gangs of age mates from which the little boys are strictly excluded. The corner of the village to which she belongs is all-important, and the little boys are traditional enemies. She has one duty, that of baby-tending, but she takes the baby with her rather than stays home to mind it, and her play is not seriously hampered. A couple of years before puberty, when she grows strong enough to have more difficult tasks required of her and old enough to learn more skilled techniques, the little girls' play group in which she grew up ceases to exist. She assumes woman's dress and must contribute to the work of the household. It is an uninteresting period of life to her and quite without turmoil. Puberty brings no change at all.

A few years after she has come of age, she will begin the pleasant years of casual and irresponsible love affairs that she will prolong as far as possible into the period when marriage is already considered fitting. Puberty itself is marked by no social recognition, no change of attitude or of expectancy. Her pre-adolescent shyness is supposed to remain unchanged for a couple of years. The girl's life in Samoa is blocked out by other considerations than those of physiological sex maturity, and puberty falls in a particularly unstressed and peaceful period during which no adolescent conflicts manifest themselves. Adolescence, therefore, may not only be culturally passed over without ceremonial; it may also be without importance in the emotional life of the child and in the attitude of the village toward her.

Warfare is another social theme that may or may not be used in any culture. Where war is made much of, it may be with contrasting objectives, with contrasting organization in relation to the state, and with contrasting sanctions. War may be, as it was among the Aztecs, a way of getting captives for the religious sacrifices. Since the Spaniards fought to kill, according to Aztec standards they broke the rules of the game. The Aztecs fell back in dismay and Cortez walked as victor into the capital.

There are even quainter notions, from our standpoint, associated with warfare in different parts of the world. For our purposes it is sufficient to notice those regions where organized resort to mutual slaughter never occurs between social groups. Only our familiarity with war makes it intelligible that a state of warfare should be alternate with a state of peace in one tribe's dealings with another. The idea is quite common over the world, of course. But on the one hand it is impossible for certain peoples to conceive the possibility of a state of peace, which in their notion would be equivalent to admitting enemy tribes to the category of human beings, which by definition they are not even though the excluded tribe may be of their own race and culture.

On the other hand, it may be just as impossible for a people to conceive of the possibility of a state of war. Rasmussen tells of the blankness with which the Eskimo met his exposition of our custom. Eskimos very well understand the act of killing a man. If he is in your way, you cast up your estimate of your own strength, and if you are ready to take it upon yourself, you kill him. If you are strong, there is no social retribution. But the idea of an Eskimo village going out against another Eskimo village in battle array or a tribe against a tribe, or even of another village being fair game in ambush warfare, is alien to them. All killing comes under one head, and is not separated, as ours is, into categories, the one meritorious, the other a capital offence.

I myself tried to talk of warfare to the Mission Indian of California, but it was impossible. Their misunderstanding of warfare was abysmal. They did not have the basis in their own culture upon which the idea could exist, and their attempts to reason it out reduced the great wars to which we are able to dedicate ourselves with moral fervour to the level of alley brawls. They did not happen to have a cultural pattern that distinguished between them.

War is, we have been forced to admit even in the face of its huge place in our own civilization, an asocial trait. In the chaos following the World War all the wartime arguments that expounded its fostering of courage, of altruism, of spiritual values, give out a false and offensive ring. War in our own civilization is as good an illustration as one can take of the destructive lengths to which the development of a culturally selected trait may go. If we justify war, it is because all peoples always justify the traits of which they find themselves possessed, not because war will bear an objective examination of its merits.

Warfare is not an isolated case. From every part of the world and from all levels of cultural complexity it is possible to illustrate the overweening and finally often the asocial elaboration of a cultural trait. Those cases are clearest where, as in dietary or mating regulations, for example, traditional usage runs counter to biological drives. Social organization, in anthropology, has a quite specialized meaning owing to the unanimity of all human societies in stressing relationship groups within which marriage is forbidden. No known people regard all women as possible mates. This is not in an effort, as is so often supposed, to prevent inbreeding in our sense, for over great parts of the world it is an own cousin, often the daughter of one's mother's brother, who is the predestined spouse. The relatives to whom the prohibition refers differ utterly among different peoples, but all human societies are alike in placing a restriction. No human idea has received more constant and complex elaboration in culture than this of incest. The incest groups are often the most important functioning units of the tribe, and the duties of every individual in relation to any other are defined by their relative positions in these groups. These groups function as units in religious ceremonials and in cycles of economic exchange, and it is impossible to exaggerate the importance of the rôle they have played in social history.

Some areas handle the incest tabu with moderation. In spite of the restrictions there may be a considerable number of women available for a man to marry. In others the group that is tabu has been extended by a social fiction to include vast numbers of individuals who have no traceable ancestors in common, and choice of a mate is in consequence excessively limited. This social fiction receives unequivocal expression in the terms of relationship which are used. Instead of distinguishing lineal from collateral kin as we do in the distinction between father and uncle, brother and cousin, one term means literally "man of my father's group (relationship, locality, etc.) of his generation," not distinguishing between direct and collateral lines, but making other distinctions that are foreign to us. Certain tribes of eastern Australia use an extreme form of this so-called classificatory kinship system. Those whom they call brothers and sisters are all those of their generation with whom they recognize any relationship. There is no cousin category or anything that corresponds to it; all relatives of one's own generation are one's brothers and sisters.

This manner of reckoning relationship is not uncommon in the world, but Australia has in addition an unparalleled horror of sister marriage and an unparalleled development of exogamous restrictions. So the Kurnai, with their extreme classificatory relationship system, feel the Australian horror of sex relationship with all their "sisters," that is, women of their own generation who are in any way related to them. Besides this, the Kurnai have strict locality rules in the choice of a mate. Sometimes two localities, out of the fifteen or sixteen of which the tribe is composed, must exchange women, and can have no mates in any other group. Sometimes there is a group of two or three localities that may exchange with two or three others. Still further, as in all Australia, the old men are a privileged group, and their prerogatives extend to marrying the young and attractive girls. The consequence of these rules is, of course, that in all the local group which must by absolute prescription furnish a young man with his wife, there is no girl who is not touched by one of these tabus. Either she is one of those who through relationship with his mother is his "sister," or she is already bargained for by an old man, or for some lesser reason she is forbidden to him.

That does not bring the Kurnai to reformulate their exogamous rules. They insist upon them with every show of violence. Therefore, the only way they are usually able to marry is by flying violently in the face of the regulations. They elope. As soon as the village knows that an elopement has occurred, it sets out in pursuit, and if the couple are caught the two are killed. It does not matter that possibly all of the pursuers were married by elopement in the same fashion. Moral indignation runs high. There is, however, an island traditionally recognized as a safe haven, and if the couple can reach it and remain away till the birth of a child, they are received again with blows, it is true, but they may defend themselves.

After they have run the gauntlet and been given their drubbing, they take up the status of married people in the tribe.

The Kurnai meet their cultural dilemma typically enough. They have extended and complicated a particular aspect of behaviour until it is a social liability. They must either modify it, or get by with a subterfuge. And they use the subterfuge. They avoid extinction, and they maintain their ethics without acknowledged revision. This manner of dealing with the *mores* has lost nothing in the progress of civilization. The older generation of our own civilization similarly maintained monogamy and supported prostitution, and the panegyrics of monogamy were never so fervent as in the great days of the red-light districts. Societies have always justified favourite traditional forms. When these traits get out of hand and some form of supplementary behaviour is called in, lip service is given as readily to the traditional form as if the supplementary behaviour did not exist.

Such a bird's-eye survey of human cultural forms makes clear several common misconceptions. In the first place, the institutions that human cultures build up upon the hints presented by the environment or by man's physical necessities do not keep as close to the original impulse as we easily imagine. These hints are, in reality, mere rough sketches, a list of bare facts. They are pin-point potentialities, and the elaboration that takes place around them is dictated by many alien considerations. Warfare is not the expression of the instinct of pugnacity. Man's pugnacity is so small a hint in the human equipment that it may not be given any expression in inter-tribal relations. When it is institutionalized, the form it takes follows other grooves of thought than those implied in the original impulse. Pugnacity is no more than the touch to the ball of custom, a touch also that may be withheld.

Such a view of cultural processes calls for a recasting of many of our current arguments upholding our traditional institutions. These arguments are usually based on the impossibility of man's functioning without these particular traditional forms. Even very special traits come in for this kind of validation, such as the particular form of economic drive that arises under our particular system of property ownership. This is a remarkably special motivation and there are evidences that even in our generation it is being strongly modified. At any rate, we do not have to confuse the issue by discussing it as if it were a matter of biological survival values. Self-support is a motive our civilization has capitalized. If our economic structure changes so that this motive is no longer so potent a drive as it was in the era of the great frontier and expanding industrialism, there are many other motives that would be appropriate to a changed economic organization. Every culture, every era, exploits some few out of a great number of possibilities. Changes may be very disquieting, and involve great losses, but this is due to the difficulty of change itself, not to the fact that our age and country has hit upon the one possible motivation under which human life can be conducted. Change, we must remember, with all its difficulties, is inescapable. Our fears over even very minor shifts in custom are usually quite beside the point. Civilizations might change far more radically than any human authority has ever had the will or the imagination to change them, and still be completely workable. The minor changes that occasion so much denunciation today, such as the increase of divorce, the growing secularization in our cities, the prevalence of the petting party, and many more, could be taken up quite readily into a slightly different pattern of culture. Becoming traditional, they would be given the same richness of content, the same importance and value, that the older patterns had in other generations.

The truth of the matter is rather that the possible human institutions and motives are legion, on every plane of cultural simplicity or complexity, and that wisdom consists in a greatly increased tolerance toward their divergencies. No man can thoroughly participate in any culture unless he has been brought up and has lived according to its forms, but he can grant to other cultures the same significance to their participants which he recognizes in his own.

5   JULIA S. BROWN

A Comparative Study of Deviations from Sexual Mores

In every society certain patterns of sexual behavior are accepted as proper and approved ways of expressing sexual urges, while alternative forms of behavior are rejected. Members who act in accordance with the mores are rewarded by social approval, but individuals who deviate from the mores receive social censure or other more specific punishments.

From *American Sociological Review*, vol. 17, no. 2 (April 1952), pp. 135-146. Reprinted by permission of the author and the American Sociological Association.

In general, anthropologists interested in the mores have emphasized the conformity of behavior of members of simple societies and have been chiefly concerned with the manner in which the approved patterns are maintained and transmitted to later generations. The present study, however, stresses deviations from the mores and the means which societies employ to discourage and punish such nonconformity. In order to determine which forms of behavior are most generally forbidden, quantitative techniques are utilized to measure the frequency with which specific types of behavior are considered deviant by a sample of primitive societies, and to estimate the severity with which these forms of sexual behavior are punished. Specifically, the following problems are considered:

(1) The relative frequency with which specific types of sexual behavior are considered to be deviant by a number of societies, where frequency is defined as the percentage of the societies which tabu the behavior. For example, is adultery punished by more societies than is premarital indulgence?

(2) The relative severity with which various deviant sexual practices are punished. For example, is incest punished more severely than adultery by most societies?

(3) The degree of correspondence between frequency and severity of punishment. Are those forms of sexual behavior (e.g., incest or rape) which are tabued by most societies also the forms most severely punished?

(4) The degree of correspondence between the punishments accorded various deviant sexual practices by the same society. Do societies which punish one offense severely (e.g., adultery) also tend to punish other offenses severely (e.g., premarital indulgence)?

(5) The nature of the sanctions which support the mores. Under what circumstances do individuals punish offenders, and under what circumstances is punishment alleged to derive from supernatural sources?

COLLECTION AND SCOPE OF DATA

The major portion of the data for this study was collected in 1942 from materials catalogued by the Human Relations Area File, Inc., although additional information was subsequently secured from other sources.

A preliminary examination of the data resulted in the discarding of those societies whose sexual mores were insufficiently documented. The remaining 110 societies which form the sample for the present analysis are listed below according to their geographical distribution.

Africa (20 societies)
Ashanti, Azande, Bena, Chewa, Chagga, Fez, Jukun, Kababish, Lamba, Lango, Masai, Mbundu, Nama, Rif, Siwans, Tanala, Thonga, Tiv, Venda, Wolof

North America (23 societies)

Cahita, Comanche, Copper Eskimo, Creek, Crow, Hopi, Kickapoo, Kutchin, Kwakiutl, Maricopa, Menomini, Naskapi, Natchez, Omaha, Ponca, Sanpoil, Surprise Valley Paiute, Taos, Tarahumara, Teton-Dakota, Tubatulabal, Yurok, Zuni

South America (24 societies)

Abipone, Alacaluf, Apinaye, Araucanians, Aymara, Barama River Caribs, Canella, Cayapa, Chapakura, Choroti, Colorado, Cuna, Guaikuru, Jivaro, Macusi, Matako, Ona, Taulipang, Tehuelche, Toba, Tupinamba, Wapisiana, Witoto, Yahgan

Eurasia (17 societies)

Ainu, Baiga, Chukchee, Gond, Kazak, Khasi, Kurd, Lepcha, Mongols, Osset, Rwala, Samoyed, Sema Naga, Toda, Vedda, Yakut, Yukaghir

Oceania (26 societies)

Alorese, Andamanese, Arunta, Balinese, Buka (Kurtatchi), Dieri, Dobuans, Dusun, Easter Islanders, Ifugao, Kamilaroi, Kiwai Papuans, Kwoma, Lesu, Mala, Maori, Marquesans, Miriam, Murngin, Orokaiva, Pukapukans, Tasmanians, Tikopia, Tongans, Trobrianders, Yungar

Subsequent to the selection of the sample, a listing was made of every type of sexual behavior considered deviant by any of the 110 societies. After miscellaneous minor tabus were eliminated from the list due to the paucity of data, the following behavior items remained.

1. Incest
2. Premarital relations
3. Illegitimate impregnation of an unmarried girl
4. Seduction of another man's fiancee
5. Sexual relations with own betrothed
6. Adultery
7. Seduction of prenubile girl
8. Homosexuality
9. Rape
10. Bestiality
11. Masturbation
12. Abduction of married woman
13. Sexual relations during menstruation
14. Sexual relations during pregnancy
15. Sexual relations during postpartum period
16. Sexual relations during lactation period
17. Sexual relations during mourning period
18. Sexual relations during war period
19. Sexual relations during periods devoted to specific food-getting activities

The data for each society were next checked to determine which of the above types of behavior were permitted, which were tabued, and whether differential punishments were accorded men and women, children and adults, single and married individuals.[1]

The unit of this sample is the society, here defined simply as a group of individuals living together who recognize themselves as a separate group, and who have been so recognized by ethnologists. Historical anthropologists may challenge the value of predictions and generalizations derived from this analysis on the basis that the units are not independent because of the historical connections of some of the societies included. However, the present investigator assumes that selectivity enters into the process of cultural change, with the elements of any given culture tending to consistency. Once this functionalist viewpoint is adopted, cultural contact can no longer be considered the decisive element in determining the absence or presence of traits, and individual societies may justifiably be treated as discrete units despite their historical contacts.

METHOD

Two measures were devised to determine the relative strengths of the tabus applied to the various sexual aberrations. The first was the percentage of societies which forbade a specific form of behavior. The second was designed to serve as a numerical index of the relative severity with which different infringements of the mores were punished. Since only rarely have ethnologists reported the manner in which members of particular cultural groups rate their punishments, a rating scale was devised in order that the severity of a number of punishments might be estimated by judges conversant with anthropological phenomena. A list was compiled of the actual punishments mentioned in the literature as customary for specific types of deviant sexual behavior. Seventeen judges then rated the itemized punishments as mild, moderate, severe or very severe. These

---

[1] The tabus noted for exhibitionism, for violations of the levirate or sororate, for promiscuity, elopement, cross-class and cross-generation alliances were eliminated due to lack of data. Desertion was originally included in the list of tabued types of behavior, but was later removed because of the multiplicity of factors involved in determining the treatment of the deserting spouse. Frequently desertion was not considered an offense but merely the initial step in the breakup of a marriage. Many societies permitted desertion for stipulated reasons such as adultery or sterility, and others freely permitted desertion provided the brideprice was restored.

Notation was also made of instances of relaxation of the tabus. Sixteen societies of the sample reported instances of relaxation in the form of general ceremonial license, and three societies reported instances of highly immoral acts permitted under special circumstances to particular individuals. Thus, the Thonga or Lamba father may commit incest with his daughter before embarking on an elephant hunt, in order to achieve great courage. A study of folktales might better demonstrate the secret envy with which persons who break tabus are regarded by others of their societies.

56   JULIA S. BROWN

ratings were given values of 1, 2, 3, and 4, respectively. The means of the
values assigned by the judges to each of the punishments are presented
in Table 1. These values were then used in order to estimate the severity
of the punishments inflicted for each of the sexual deviations noted in the
sample of societies. Thus it was possible to compare punishments for
different deviations within a given society, and to compare punishments
for the same deviation from society to society.

TABLE 1. PUNISHMENTS RATED FOR SEVERITY ON A FOUR-
POINT SCALE BY SEVENTEEN JUDGES, AND THE
CORRESPONDING MEAN SEVERITY VALUES OBTAINED
FROM THE RATINGS

Mean Severity Value Obtained	Punishments Rated for Severity
1.0	Small fine
1.2	Fistfight
1.4	Quarreling within family
1.5	Parental reproof
1.8	Beating by member of family
2.1	Duel
2.2	Public ridicule and disgrace
2.2	Enforced marriage
2.2	Illness
2.2	Bad Luck
2.3	Danger to near kin
2.4	Ceremonial penance
2.4	Lowered brideprice
2.4	Knifing
2.5	Temporary exile
2.5	Humiliation at wedding
2.5	Heavy fine
2.5	Enslavement of relative
2.5	Divorce, and return of brideprice
2.5	Public flogging
2.6	Difficulty in acquiring a husband
2.6	Failure at hunting or fishing
2.6	Desertion of spouse
2.7	Puniness of offspring, injury to child
2.9	Divorce with disgrace, no remarriage permitted
2.9	Facial mutilation
2.9	Multiple mutilation
2.9	Madness
3.0	Spearing of legs
3.1	Repudiation of bride by groom
3.1	Sorcery to injure or kill
3.3	Loss of virility
3.4	Public raping
3.4	Enslavement
3.4	Destruction of major property
3.5	Barrenness
3.6	Permanent exile
3.7	Life imprisonment
3.7	Torture, resulting possibly in death
3.7	Enforced suicide
3.9	Death

RESULTS

The results obtained from tabulating the percentages of societies punishing various types of sexual behavior are presented in Table 2. From an examination of these percentages it may be seen that incest, abduction and rape are the behavioral items most frequently tabued by the societies of the present sample. Conversely, premarital affairs and intercourse with one's own betrothed are the sexual acts least frequently forbidden.

TABLE 2. THE NUMBER OF SOCIETIES FOR WHICH DATA WERE AVAILABLE CONCERNING SPECIFIC TYPES OF SEXUAL BEHAVIOR, AND THE PERCENTAGES OF THESE SOCIETIES WHICH PUNISHED THESE SPECIFIC TYPES OF BEHAVIOR

No. of Societies[a]	Percentage Punishing	Type of Behavior and Person Punished
54	100	Incest[b]
82	100	Abduction of married woman
84	99	Rape of married woman
55	95	Rape of unmarried woman
43	95	Sexual relations during postpartum period
15	93	Bestiality by adult
73	92	Sexual relations during menstruation
88	89	Adultery (paramour punished)
93	87	Adultery (wife punished)
22	86	Sexual relations during lactation period
57	86	Infidelity of fiancee
52	85	Seduction of another man's fiancee
74	85	Illegitimate impregnation (woman punished)
62	84	Illegitimate impregnation (man punished)
30	77	Seduction of prenubile girl (man punished)
44	68	Male homosexuality
49	67	Sexual relations during pregnancy
16	44	Masturbation
97	44	Premarital relations (woman punished)
93	41	Premarital relations (man punished)
12	33	Female homosexuality
67	10	Sexual relations with own betrothed

[a]The figures in this column represent the number of societies for which data were available concerning the permitting or forbidding of each specific type of sexual behavior. Thus, information concerning incest could be secured for 54 of the sample societies, information concerning abduction of a married woman could be secured for 82 of the societies, etc.

[b]Although ethnographers for only 54 of the societies of the sample stated specifically that incest was punished, it might be assumed that the entire 110 societies actually tabu incest. Some of these societies reported that incest was simply unknown, and therefore penalties could not be stated for non-existent crimes.

One difficulty in the way of determining the penalties for incest is the fact that anthropologists have only rarely defined the term "incest," using it to refer both to affairs within the nuclear family and to affairs within larger kin groups. Where information exists, parent-child incest and sibling incest are held in greater horror than is incest with classificatory relatives. It is logical to assume this is generally the case even when differential punishments are not mentioned. For this study, only data referring to incest within the nuclear family are utilized.

Adultery falls between these two groups of acts, being tabued far more frequently than premarital indulgence, but less frequently than incest, abduction or rape. When the differences in percentages of societies punishing the following pairs of items were subjected to statistical test, they proved to be significant at approximately the 1 per cent level of confidence: (a) premarital indulgence and adultery; (b) intercourse with one's own betrothed and adultery; (c) adultery and rape; (d) adultery and abduction of a married woman; (e) adultery and incest.[2]

The positions on the scale of strength-of-tabu occupied by some of the remaining items are dubious, since differences in percentages of these items and adjacent items are not statistically reliable. Thus, on the basis of this measure, it cannot be concluded that punishment of a man is less frequent for the illegitimate impregnation of a single girl than for adultery, since the difference in percentages is not statistically significant. On the other hand, the finding that illegitimate impregnation of an unmarried girl is more frequently punished than a premarital affair not resulting in pregnancy proved to be highly significant ($CR = 5.4$).

The above findings drawn from the data of Table 2 are further supported by the results obtained from the use of the scale of severity of punishment. Table 3 presents for each specified type of deviant behavior the mean scale value of the punishments inflicted by the societies of the sample. This mean value was determined for each type of behavior by applying the severity ratings of Table 1 to each punishment, and then averaging the obtained values. On the assumption that severity of punishment reflects the seriousness of an offense, it may be tentatively concluded from Table 3 that incest, abduction and rape are the most serious offenses. Adultery is less serious than these acts, but more serious than the illegitimate impregnation of an unmarried girl, and this in turn is a more serious offense than premarital indulgence. These conclusions are supported by statistical tests which yield highly significant differences between the mean scale values of the punishments for the following pairs of deviations: (a) abduction of a married woman and adultery by a man; (b) rape and adultery by a man; (c) adultery and premarital indulgence by a man; (d) adultery and premarital indulgence by a woman.[3]

[2] The test of significance employed was the ratio of the difference between two percentages to the standard error of that difference. See Joy P. Guilford, *Psychometric Methods*, New York and London: McGraw-Hill Publications in Psychology, 1936, p. 60. The critical ratios found were all 2.5 and over.

[3] The customary *t*-ratio was employed here to test the significance of the differences. This is the ratio of the difference of the means to the standard error of the difference of the means. See Allen L. Edwards, *Statistical Analysis for Students in Psychology and Education*, New York: Rinehart, 1946, pp. 182 ff. The *t*'s secured varied from 4.7 to 8.75, and were all significant at the 1 per cent level of confidence or better.

TABLE 3. THE NUMBER OF SOCIETIES FOR WHICH DATA
WERE AVAILABLE CONCERNING SPECIFIC TYPES OF
SEXUAL BEHAVIOR, AND THE AVERAGE SCALE VALUES
OF PUNISHMENTS INFLICTED FOR THESE TYPES OF
SEXUAL BEHAVIOR BY THE SOCIETIES OF THE SAMPLE

Number of Societies[a]	Average Scale Value of Punishments[b]	Type of Behavior and Person Punished
25	3.7	Abduction of married woman
50	3.3	Incest
32	3.3	Rape of married woman
8	3.0	Bestiality by adult
23	2.4	Rape of unmarried woman
89	2.3	Adultery (wife punished)
80	2.3	Adultery (paramour punished)
16	2.2	Sexual relations during lactation period
31	1.9	Sexual relations during menstruation
12	1.9	Sexual relations during postpartum period
16	1.9	Seduction of prenubile girl (man punished)
38	1.8	Illegitimate impregnation (man punished)
53	1.8	Illegitimate impregnation (woman punished)
18	1.7	Seduction of another man's fiancee
15	1.5	Infidelity of fiancee
29	1.3	Male homosexuality
28	1.2	Sexual relations during pregnancy
88	0.9	Premarital relations (woman punished)
11	0.8	Female homosexuality
86	0.8	Premarital relations (man punished)
16	0.7	Masturbation
66	0.1	Sexual relations with own betrothed

[a]The figures of this column do not coincide with those of the first column of Table 2, since anthropologists often report that an act is tabued, but fail to cite the customary penalties.

[b]In computing these averages, a punishment scale value of zero was entered for each society which permitted a specific type of behavior.

In order to determine the degree of correspondence between frequency and severity of punishment, a product-moment correlation coefficient was computed between the percentages of societies punishing the stipulated forms of sexual behavior and the average scale values of the punishments for those types of behavior.[4] From the extremely high correlation obtained ($r = .87$, $df = 20$), it may be concluded that the more frequently a given type of sexual behavior was tabued by the sample societies, the more severe the punishment, and vice versa. This high degree of correspondence between the positions of the behavior items on the scales constructed by the two measures of strength-of-tabu suggests that the relative positions of the items on the scale are reasonably stable.

Correlations were also computed between the punishments for various pairs of offenses, using the scale values of Table 1, to determine whether societies that punish one offense severely tend also to punish other offenses

[4] See Edwards, *op. cit.*, p. 91, formula #23.

60   JULIA S. BROWN

severely. High positive correlations were found between the punishments for the following pairs of deviations: (a) premarital indulgence by a man, and adultery with another man's wife; (b) premarital indulgence and adultery by a woman; (c) premarital indulgence by a man and rape of an unmarried girl; (d) premarital indulgence by a man and premarital indulgence by a woman; (e) adultery by a man and adultery by a woman; (f) adultery and rape by a man.[5] The fact that these correlations exist is of interest since it tends to support the view that there may be generalized attitudes of permissiveness or punitiveness towards sexual activity. Murdock has recently expressed doubt that such generalized sexual tabus exist save for a very few individual societies.[6] However, these correlations seem to indicate a tendency on the part of societies to be generally lenient or severe despite the fact of great variability within any given society. Such a conclusion is in agreement with the hypothesis that there is a strain towards consistency within the mores.

The above data have demonstrated a gradation in the strength of various sexual tabus. It may now be asked why incest and abduction are tabued more strongly than is adultery, and why the tabus on adultery are generally more stringent than those on premarital indulgence.

One possible explanation for the variability in the strength of the tabus is the presence or absence of the element of aggression or assault. This is supported by data from the present study since acts which imply aggression are punished both more frequently and severely than are similar acts without obvious aggressive content. Thus a man is usually punished more severely for raping an unmarried girl than for seducing her. (The difference in punishments is highly significant: $t = 4.3$, $df = 20$). Likewise a man is punished more severely for raping or abducting a married woman than for having an illicit affair with her. However, aggression is insufficient of itself to explain why the punishment for raping a married woman is greater than the punishment for raping an unmarried girl.

[5] The r's and degrees of freedom for each of the pairs were as follows:

Pair	r	df
(a)	.36	62
(b)	.21	70
(c)	.59	19
(d)	.66	77
(e)	.83	66
(f)	.77	26

All these coefficients with the exception of that for Pair (b) were significant beyond the 1 per cent level of confidence. The r for Pair (b) was significant between the 5 and 10 per cent levels only.

[6] George P. Murdock, *Social Structure*, New York: The Macmillan Company, 1949, pp. 263-4.

A second factor that may aid in accounting for the gradation in strength of tabus is the marriage status of the person or persons involved. Thus, sexual acts by or with married individuals are generally more seriously regarded than are similar acts by unmarried individuals. Adultery is punished more than premarital indulgence, both for men and for women, and the rape of a married woman is more severely tabued than the rape of an unmarried girl. Likewise, affairs involving betrothed individuals are more serious for most of the societies than are affairs involving individuals not promised in marriage.

Still a third variable is the sex of the individual concerned. This factor, however, did not appear to be especially important. There seems little difference in the extent to which men and women are punished for premarital indulgence or for adultery. Thus, punishments of an unfaithful fiancee and of her extra-betrothal partner are nearly identical (see Table 3). Nonetheless, it should be mentioned that the persons who punish a man for a given act usually stand in a different relationship to him than do the persons who customarily punish a woman for a similar transgression. A man is punished not so much by his own family or mate as by the family of the woman partner to his act, since it is the woman's relatives who suffer through injury to the woman's potential or actual marital status. The woman's marital status, not the man's, appears to be the prime consideration.

A fourth factor determining strength of tabus, which may be even more significant than the others, might be labelled the factor of social involvement. Other things equal, it appears that societies punish more frequently and severely those acts which injure larger numbers of individuals. Conversely, the fewer the individuals adversely affected, the less strong the tabu.

Table 4 represents an attempt to determine the influence of this factor of social involvement. Here sexual acts have been grouped into three categories. Category 1 includes those acts which appear from the documented data to be interpreted by the various societies as concerning only the individuals performing the act, or members of their immediate families. Thus, violating pregnancy or lactation tabus is considered by most societies as injurious only to the parents or the child, or to both. Most societies conceive the breaking of tabus against premarital intercourse as injuring only the boy, the girl, and their families. The girl's family may be deprived of a maximum bride-price for the girl, and the boy's family suffers demands for retribution made by the girl's family. Similarly it may be argued for the other items in this category that only members of the immediate families of the offenders are affected by the acts.

Category 2 includes types of behavior believed by the societies studied to injure individuals other than the deviators or their blood kin. Thus, in

62 JULIA S. BROWN

TABLE 4. SEVERITY OF PUNISHMENT FOR SPECIFIC TYPES
OF SEXUAL BEHAVIOR AS A FUNCTION OF THE FACTOR
OF SOCIAL INVOLVEMENT

Type of Behavior and Person Punished	Number of Societies	Average Scale Value of Punishment
Category 1: Acts interpreted by the sample societies as affecting only the participants or members of their immediate families.		
Incest	35	3.2
Bestiality by adult	5	2.4
Rape of unmarried woman	23	2.4
Sexual relations during lactation period	16	2.2
Sexual relations during menstruation	30	1.9
Sexual relations during postpartum period	12	1.9
Seduction of prenubile girl (man punished)	14	1.6
Illegitimate impregnation (man punished)	34	1.7
Illegitimate impregnation (woman punished)	49	1.7
Male homosexuality	27	1.2
Sexual relations during pregnancy	28	1.2
Premarital relations (woman punished)	86	0.9
Female homosexuality	10	0.6
Premarital relations (man punished)	86	0.8
Masturbation	16	0.7
Sexual relations with own betrothed	66	0.1
Total	537	Ave. 1.2
Category 2: Acts interpreted by the sample societies as affecting members of families other than the immediate families of the participants.		
Abduction of married woman	24	3.7
Rape of married woman	30	3.2
Adultery (wife punished)	88	2.3
Adultery (paramour punished)	78	2.3
Seduction of another man's fiancee	18	1.7
Infidelity of fiancee	15	1.5
Sexual relations during mourning period	10	2.6
Total	263	Ave. 2.5
Category 3: Acts interpreted by the sample societies as affecting the whole clan, tribe, community.		
Abduction of married woman	1	3.9
Incest	15	3.6
Rape of married woman	2	3.9
Bestiality by adult	3	3.9
Adultery (wife punished)	1	2.5
Adultery (paramour punished)	2	3.2
Sexual relations during menstruation	1	2.2
Seduction of prenubile girl	2	3.9
Illegitimate impregnation (man punished)	4	2.7
Illegitimate impregnation (woman punished)	4	2.4
Male homosexuality	2	3.1
Premarital relations (woman punished)	2	1.8
Female homosexuality	1	2.5
Sexual relations during war period	16	3.9
Total	56	Ave. 3.4

adultery, not only are the wife and her family involved, but also the paramour and his family, and the husband and his family. Violations of mourning tabus affect members of the dead husband's family as well as the widow and lover. Likewise, the other types of behavior in the second category affect families besides those of the offenders.

Category 3 includes acts interpreted by the societies concerned as bringing injury to the whole group, such as a clan, tribe or village, through crop failures, divine displeasure, plagues and disasters. Thus, 15 societies reported that incest harmed the society as a whole, two societies claimed male homosexuality affected the entire community, and three societies believed bestiality did likewise.

Three conclusions may be drawn from Table 4. First, it seems relatively uncommon for sexual acts to be interpreted as harming the whole society, since the total number of cases in Category 3 is small when compared to the totals in the other two categories. Second, it appears that punishment becomes more severe as more individuals are affected, since the average punishment for all acts in Category 3 (3.4) exceeds the average for acts in Category 2 (2.5), which in turn exceeds the average for acts in Category 1 (1.2). Third, it may be noted that identical acts are punished more severely by societies which interpret them as injurious to the whole community than by societies which do not so interpret them. Thus, those societies which express the belief that incest hurts the whole society average a more severe punishment for that deviation (scale value = 3.6) than do societies which do not specify such a belief (scale value = 3.2). The average punishment of men for homosexuality in societies conceiving the act as harming the community is 3.1 in contrast to an average of 1.2 for societies not believing this to be true. The comparison may be continued for other items.

Certain comments need be made concerning Table 4. Within Category 1, the values for incest, bestiality and rape are the ones most at variance with the values of the other items in the group. Although only 15 of the 50 societies for which information on incest was available reported specifically that incest was an offense against the community, fuller information might evince the fact that others of these 50 societies held to a similar belief. Those incest cases would then be shifted to Category 3, and the homogeneity of Category 1 would be increased. In like manner, with better information it might be found that many cases of bestiality classified in Category 1 properly belong in Category 3. Supporting this possibility is the evidence that members of certain societies occasionally interfere and punish those guilty of incest or bestiality, if the families of the offenders fail to exact the customary penalties. This fact implies that these non-relatives consider themselves affected by the offenses.

Finally, the punishment for rape is exceptionally high for items in Category 1 for two reasons. First, as mentioned earlier, the punishment for

rape must compound the punishments for assault and for a sexual deviation. Second, in the case of rape, although members of two families (the
man's and the woman's) are involved, the act still involves an innocent
party. Possibly, on the basis of such reasoning, the act should be classed
in Category 2. If these changes were instituted, the extreme cases would
be shifted, the variability within categories cut down, and the differences
between the averages of the categories would be increased.

Despite the variability within categories, the differences in average
punishments for the three categories tend to justify the view that social
involvement is *one* of the several factors to be considered in explaining
the graduated penalties accorded by the sample societies to various forms
of sexual behavior. Moreover, the gradation of punishment on the basis
of social involvement is reasonable when one remembers that many primitive societies possess no institutions to judge or to punish. In such societies, individuals and their kin protect their rights and avenge their
injuries, while persons not directly harmed refrain from interference.
Affairs in which members of a family injure other members of the same
family will tend to be adjusted within the family structure. In such cases,
punishment of the guilty is tempered by considerations of sentiment, of
the value of the offender to the family group, and by the need for ingroup
self-preservation. Such considerations do not operate to the same extent
outside the immediate family group, and punishment will therefore be
greater where members of other family groups perform the injury. Nevertheless, it appears that a family will not exact as extreme a penalty from
these outsiders if its own members were also at fault. Thus, a father will
not tend to punish a man more severely for having an affair with his
daughter, than he will punish his daughter, if she were equally responsible
for the transgression.

A final problem for consideration is the nature of the sanctions supporting the tabus. Where specific behavior is proscribed, the tabus may be
sustained (a) by human agents; (b) by natural or supernatural sanctions;
or (c) by both human agents and supernatural sanctions conjointly. Table
5 presents data concerning the punitive agents for specific types of sexual
behavior in the sample societies. It may be seen from this table that the
role assigned to supernatural agents is of unequal importance for different
types of behavior and on occasion it appears negligible. Some sociologists
might hold that the types of behavior not sustained by supernatural sanctions should not be termed mores, since they define mores as religiously
sanctioned patterns of behavior and tabus as religiously prohibited patterns of behavior. This viewpoint, though justifiable, appears not to be
fruitful. Sumner has pointed out that the mores are mass phenomena
which have evolved gradually. First, the individual reacts to a problem in

7 William G. Sumner and Albert G. Keller, *The Science of Society*, New
Haven: Yale University Press, 1927, Vol. 1, pp. 32-4.

a random fashion. As the individual hits on a bit of adjustive behavior, it is incorporated into a habit system. Other individuals may imitate his behavior, or may independently chance upon the same behavior, until gradually more and more individuals are responding consistently in a similar fashion. In this way folkways are created. As they become settled and carry the conviction of rightness, they evolve into mores, which are eventually reinforced by the sanction of ghost-fear. Here finally are the fully formed mores. However, when one observes cultural phenomena, it is almost impossible to indicate the precise points on the continuum of behavior at which random acts become habits, at which similar individual acts become collectively folkways, and at which the folkways are transformed into mores. It is obvious that patterns which might be considered mores are not all equally well crystallized, and that not all are equally backed by religion. This inequality in the degree of religious sanctioning is shown by Table 5.

Not only are supernatural sanctions of varying importance for different mores, but they are less important than are social sanctions. Thus, from Table 5 it appears that in 73.6 per cent of the cases the punitive agents are human alone; in 12.6 per cent of the cases punishment is relegated to supernatural agents alone; and in another 13.8 per cent both human and supernatural sanctions are combined. Supernatural sanctions are present, then, in only 26 per cent of the cases as against the 87 per cent in which social sanctions operate.[8]

A third conclusion to be derived from the table is that some deviations occur without retribution by human agents, save for the general tone of public opinion. Punishment is left almost entirely to supernatural agents for violations of such tabus as those built about the reproductive functions — the lactation tabu, the post-partum tabu, tabus operating during pregnancy, and, to a lesser degree, tabus during the menstrual period.

Another possible conclusion, though this is not clearcut, is that supernatural tabus usually reinforce social tabus for those offenses considered to be serious. Where the two types of sanction are employed, the punishments are likely to be very severe. For instance, incest and adultery are the most frequently doubly sanctioned types of deviations, and they are

[8] It might be mentioned that the individuals who ordinarily administer the punishments are those persons most directly injured by the deviation. A woman's family punishes her for premarital lapses, and a husband punishes his wife for infidelity. The girl's family punishes the man responsible for seducing her if such seductions are disapproved, and the outraged spouse punishes his wife's paramour. The dead man's relatives punish his widow for infringements of the mourning tabu, and a fiancee or the fiancee's family punish the unfaithful fiancee and her seducer. Occasionally, members of the community outside the immediate families will punish incest and bestiality cases, especially if the family of the offender(s) fail to carry out the customary penalties.

TABLE 5. AGENTS OF PUNISHMENT FOR SEXUAL DEVIATIONS

Number of Societies Punishing Specified Act[a]	Type of Behavior and Person Punished	Human Only	Super- natural Only[b]	Both Human and Super- natural
			Punitive Agents	
25	Abduction of married woman	23	0	2
50	Incest	23	6	21
31	Rape of unmarried woman	27	0	4
7	Bestiality by adult	4	0	3
20	Rape of unmarried woman	18	0	2
77	Adultery (wife punished)	70	0	7
70	Adultery (paramour punished)	60	1	9
13	Sexual relations during lactation period	0	13	0
25	Sexual relations during menstruation	3	20	2
10	Sexual relations during postpartum period	0	10	0
9	Seduction of prenubile girl (man punished)	5	1	3
28	Illegitimate impregnation (man punished)	23	0	5
41	Illegitimate impregnation (woman punished)	37	0	4
10	Seduction of another man's fiancee	9	1	0
7	Infidelity of fiancee	6	1	0
15	Male homosexuality	12	1	2
12	Sexual relations during pregnancy	0	11	1
34	Premarital relations (woman punished)	31	1	2
3	Female homosexuality	2	0	1
31	Premarital relations (man punished)	26	0	5
7	Masturbation	6	1	0
6	Sexual relations with own betrothed	6	0	0
531	Cases of tabued behavior Totals	391	67	73

[a]The figures in this column represent the number of societies of the sample which tabued a specific act and which also cited the punitive agents. These figures, there- fore, do not necessarily coincide with those of the first column of Table 3 since the latter included some societies which permitted the type of behavior, or which failed to cite the punitive agents.

[b]The writer originally intended to distinguish between natural punishments and those deriving from supernatural or supersocial agents. It was quickly found that either primitive peoples do not distinguish clearly between such categories, or that anthropologists have failed to report their distinctions.

both heavily punished. On the other hand, it must be admitted that for the 25 societies for which the punishment for abduction has been docu- mented, there are only two instances of a dual punishment.

Table 6 demonstrates in more detail the role of supernatural (or natural) agents. In Group A are listed those tabus whose violation is sel- dom punished by other members of the societies. Fear of the inevitably unpleasant consequences imposed by nature or by supernatural agents serves as a deterrent to would-be offenders. These tabus seek mainly to restrict marital relations. It may be that the punishment for their infringe- ment is left to supernatural agents for the simple reason that violations are difficult to detect. A second reason for the absence of social sanctions may be that the injured and the injurer belong to the same family group, and

A *Comparative Study of Deviations from Sexual Mores* 67

TABLE 6. THE ROLE OF SUPERNATURAL AGENTS IN
PUNISHING SPECIFIC TYPES OF SEXUAL BEHAVIOR

Type of Behavior and Person Punished	Number of Societies Citing Punishment	Percentage of Societies Citing Supernatural Agents
Group A: Types of tabued behavior for which supernatural sanctions are predominant.[a]		
Sexual relations during war period	16	100%
Sexual relations during crises	8	100
Sexual relations when engaged in certain occupations	11	100
Sexual relations when engaged in food-getting activities	23	100
Sexual relations during lactation period	13	100
Sexual relations during postpartum period	10	100
Sexual relations during pregnancy	12	100
Sexual relations during menstruation	25	92
Group B: Types of tabued behavior for which supernatural sanctions are moderately important.[b]		
Incest	50	54
Sexual relations during mourning period	10	50
Seduction of prenubile girl	9	44
Bestiality	7	43
Female homosexuality	3	33
Group C: Types of tabued behavior for which supernatural sanctions are relatively unimportant.[c]		
Male homosexuality	15	20
Illegitimate impregnation (man punished)	28	18
Premarital relations (man punished)	31	16
Adultery (paramour punished)	70	14
Infidelity of fiancee	7	14
Masturbation	7	14
Rape of married woman	31	13
Group D: Types of tabued behavior for which supernatural sanctions are least important.		
Rape of unmarried woman	20	10
Seduction of another man's fiancee	10	10
Illegitimate impregnation (woman punished)	41	10
Adultery (wife punished)	77	9
Premarital relations (woman punished)	34	9
Abduction of married woman	25	8
Sexual relations with own betrothed	6	0

[a]Only rarely did members of the societies actively punish violators of the tabus in Group A. The Lamba exiled a woman who had intercourse during menstruation. The Kamilaroi and Ashanti killed both parties to intercourse during menstruation, but the source material did not specifically state supernatural agents to be involved in any way. The Masai flogged a man and killed his cattle if his child was stillborn, for this was presumed to be the result of intercourse during pregnancy.

[b]In almost every instance in Group B, supernatural sanctions are reinforced by active punishments by other members of the society.

[c]All violations in Groups C and D are punished by human agents. The supernatural punishments which exist appear to be relatively unimportant.

members of the larger society for that reason lack interest in exacting penalties. Unrelated individuals may consider it unfortunate that the deviators are injuring themselves and their kin, but refuse to stop or punish the acts. A third possible reason for the predominance of supernatural sanctions is that unborn or infant children are frequently the ones thought to be hurt by the offenses. Since such youngsters lack human protectors other than the very parents who are injuring them, society nominates supernatural agents to serve as surrogate parents and additional protectors.

For the tabus in Group B, supernatural sanctions are important, but social sanctions also operate in almost every instance. Society concerns itself with preventing the violation of these tabus since members of *more than one family group* are affected (as in cases of infringements of mourning tabus, tabus on female homosexuality, and tabus on the seduction of a prenubile girl), or since, as in cases of incest and bestiality, the whole society is believed to be hurt by the acts.

In tabu Groups C and D, where supernatural sanctions are secondary, injury is frequently done to other individuals by the offender(s). Often a third and innocent party is affected. Supernatural sanctions seem insufficient here, and human agents become of prime importance in penalizing the culprits. Both where the injury is flagrant and where the act is considered trivial, there apparently is no need for recourse to supernatural sanctions.

SUMMARY AND CONCLUSIONS

The purpose of the present study has been to discover if and why specific types of sexual behavior are tabued more strongly than others. Following a compilation of a list of types of sexual behavior considered to be deviant by some or all of the 110 primitive societies comprising the present sample, the relative strengths of the tabus applied to the deviant types of behavior were measured in two ways. First, the percentages of the total societies which punished each specific type of behavior were tabulated. Second, the degree of the severity of the punishment for each type of behavior was estimated through the application of ratings of punishment-severity made by seventeen judges. When statistical tests were applied to the data, the following conclusions appeared to be justified.

1. A high positive correlation exists between the frequency with which a given type of behavior is tabued and the severity of the punishment.

2. Incest, abduction and rape are the forms of behavior most frequently tabued and most severely punished. Adultery is punished less frequently, and premarital indulgence, particularly if with a betrothed partner, is the least frequently and most lightly punished. These general tendencies to

punish certain forms of sexual behavior more severely than other forms persist despite differences in culture of individual societies and presumably derive from sociological factors common to human groups in general.

3. There appears to be a tendency for individual societies to be generally lax, moderate, or severe in their attitudes toward sexual activity. Significant positive correlations between the values of punishments accorded pairs of offenses within the same societies lend support to the view that the sexual mores of any given society tend to integrate.

4. Punishments tend to be more severe for those sexual deviations which involve greater numbers of individuals, transgress marital bonds, and contain elements of aggression, than for deviations which involve fewer individuals, concern single persons, and lack aggressive content.

5. In the great majority of cases the mores are actively upheld by human agents. Supernatural sanctions ordinarily supplement, rather than supplant, social sanctions.

6   ERIC WOLF

New Perspectives in Comparative Anthropology

[One] . . . postwar shift in outlook [among anthropologists] has been the retreat from the position that human nature was characterized by unlimited flexibility to a re-emphasis on the enduring features of the human psyche and sociality. Prewar anthropology had been concerned — nay, obsessed — with the discovery of human diversity. Ruth Benedict had given poetic voice to this concern in her *Patterns of Culture* (1934), in which she wrote of "the great arc" of human behavior, from which each culture selected only a limited number of possibilities. This thought she expressed beautifully in the image of the Californian Indian chief who spoke of a time when "God gave to every people a cup, a cup of clay, and

Eric R. Wolf, *Anthropology*, © 1964 by the Trustees of Princeton University. Reprinted by permission of the author and Prentice-Hall, Inc., Englewood Cliffs, New Jersey.

from this cup they drank their life." There were as many cups as there were peoples; Benedict saw the common humanity of men precisely in their unlimited variability.

But where the anthropologists of the 1930's emphasized the free play of the human disposition, the anthropologists of the postwar period have returned to the question of cultural universals, to a renewed emphasis on the enduring features of the human psyche and sociality. Perhaps the temper of the 1930's — the temper of the New Deal and the Soviet "experiment" — favored the view that human nature was inherently flexible and, therefore, changeable. Perhaps the colder realities of the postwar world, which has seen the abortion or early demise of many a cherished utopia, have discouraged such optimism. The silhouette of the City of Man is seen in bleaker outlines against a colder sky. Human nature seems less malleable. It is the apparently inherent dilemmas of human existence that strike our consciousness, not the hope of their transcendence. If human nature has set limits, then it also appears changeable only within such limits. Periods of this kind render deliverance less tangible. They also set a mood in which men wish to escape from the relentless march of events they cannot control into a mythology that stresses the stable and the enduring. Men seek to define unchangeable archetypes, in the hope that behind the illusion of change they may discover a basic repetitive reality.

. . .

[This] . . . shift [is] from an interest in the gamut of human variability as expressed in the multiplicity of human cultures to the attempt to define some underlying reality beneath the ever changing surface of human phenomena, to delineate the common psychobiological structure of man, to specify the common blueprint of the human animal. In prewar anthropology, the psychobiological design of man seemed irrelevant. The design was open; it could be made to subscribe to any culture. Cultural variability, unhampered by limitations of physique or psyche, seemed endless. In the postwar period, the design appeared closed. Much as the inherited genes are thought by some to dictate our adult characteristics, so the inherited design of man forced men over and over again to seek answers to the same questions, solutions to the same innate needs. At best, these answers might be seen as varying slightly from cultural setting to cultural setting, secondary variations upon the same basic themes, sounding with monotonous regularity.

No better indicator of this change can be found than the innovative work of Margaret Mead. A student of Boas at Columbia University, she first went into the field to investigate adolescence in Samoa and returned to emphasize the cross-cultural variability of the adolescent period in her *Coming of Age in Samoa* (1928). Her emphasis on the cultural variability of human nature reached its peak in her comparison of three New Guinea tribes in *Sex and Temperament in Three Primitive Societies* (1935). Among the first of these, the Arapesh, both sexes were shown as equally nurturant; among the second, the fierce Mundugumor, both sexes were equally aggressive. Among the third, the Tchambuli, the relation between the sexes stereotyped in Western culture appeared reversed. In these portrayals, as in her portrayals of many other cultures, the uniqueness of each culture was stressed and vividly presented through great skill in research and description. Yet in *Male and Female*, written in 1947, there appeared a renewed emphasis on the irreducible differences between the sexes. And in recent years, as she has shown in her self-evaluation entitled "Retrospects and Prospects" (1962), she has returned to the consideration of a layer of human behavior so basic and universal that cultural modification is minimal. Specifically, this reappraisal has involved a return also to the consideration of Sigmund Freud's *Totem and Taboo*, his inspired fantasy on the origin of the incest taboo.

. . .

Where the older anthropology . . . tended to see variability, postwar anthropology has tended to see a uniform plot, modified in particular instances only by a particular cultural "phrasing." The basic plot is that of a suffering humanity, forever living under the shadow of a painful and regressive infantilism. The cultural phrasings of this plot form the particular code through which a particular group of fellow-sufferers communicate both their fellow-suffering and their defenses against it. This view implies a new version of the old theory of the social contract. According to the old theory, human actors contract among themselves to maintain a social order for their mutual benefit. The current theory reproduces this contractual paradigm, but the times have changed and the original versions of the contract have suffered metamorphosis.

It is no longer a Hobbesian compact that is envisaged, according to which men lay down their arms, lest each man's hand be raised against every other. Nor is it a Lockean compact to guarantee the integrity of each man's property and maximal liberty. Today, rather, the contract is seen as an agreement to communicate, each man not a keeper of his fellow's safety or property, but of his social and emotional integrity. Thus, for example, Erving Goffman has, in his "The Nature of Deference and Demeanor" (1956), painted a billiant picture of how the self is delineated continuously anew, as it presents an appropriate image of itself to others, who, by paying the image deference, complete it. He sees the self as a ceremonial thing, a sacred object that must be treated with proper ritual care and that in turn must be presented in proper light to others. Hence no man is an island, and society is forever engaged in the ceremonial labor of undoing and shoring up these individual fragile selves. For the self is seen as a fragile reed, easily broken when the appropriate ceremonial communication is brought to a standstill.

I V

Historical Perspective

7   FRED EGGAN

Anthropology and Comparative Studies:
Some Early Developments

The early developments in American cultural anthropology have been delineated by Lowie[1] and parallel in many respects those which were occurring in England. In addition to Morgan, Bandelier, Cushing, J. O. Dorsey,
Alice Fletcher, and others were among the pioneers whose work is today
largely forgotten in the United States. For with the advent of Franz Boas
a major break was made with the past, resulting not so much from his
program for cultural anthropology as in its selective implementation. Boas

Reproduced by permission of the author and the American Anthropological
Association from the *American Anthropologist*: Vol. 56 (1954), pp. 748-755 and
763. The original title of the article was "Social Anthropology and the Method
of Controlled Comparison."

[1] Robert H. Lowie, *The History of Ethnological Theory* (New York: Farrar
& Rinehart, Inc., 1937).

in "The Limitations of the Comparative Method"[2] outlined a program which included two major tasks. The first task involved detailed studies of individual tribes in their cultural and regional context as a means to the reconstruction of the histories of tribal cultures and regions. A second task concerned the comparisons of these tribal histories, with the ultimate objective of formulating general laws of cultural growth, which were psychological in character.[3] This second task, which Boas thought of as the more important of the two, was never to be fully implemented by his students.

Boas formulated this program in connection with a destructive criticism of the comparative method as then practiced in England and America. After stating as a principle of method that uniformity of processes was essential for comparability, he goes on to say: "If anthropology desires to establish the laws governing the growth of culture it must not confine itself to comparing the results of growth alone, but whenever such is feasible, it must compare the processes of growth, and these can be discovered by means of studies of the cultures of small geographical areas."[4] He then compares this "historical method" with the "comparative method," which he states has been remarkably barren of results, and predicts that it will not become fruitful until we make our comparisons "on the broader and sounder basis which I ventured to outline." The requirement that only those phenomena can be compared which are derived psychologically or historically from common causes, valuable as it may have been at that time, has had the effect of predisposing most of Boas' students against the comparative method — except in linguistics where genetic relationships could be assumed — and hence against any generalizations which require comparison. And the processes which Boas sought in a study of art and mythology on the Northwest Coast proved more difficult to isolate than was anticipated. Kroeber notes that though Boas was "able to show a multiplicity of processes in culture, he was not able — it was impossible in his day and perhaps is still — to formulate these into a systematic theory."[5]

In the "Formative Period" of American ethnology, from 1900 to 1915, these were minor considerations. There were the vanishing Indian cultures to study, and it was natural for the students of Boas to concentrate on the first portion of his program. They wrote theses, for the most part, on specific problems, or to test various theories which had been advanced to explain art, or myth, or ritual, generally with negative results. This

[2] *Science*, 4 (1896), pp. 901-8.
[3] Franz Boas, *Race, Language, and Culture* (New York: The Macmillan Co., 1940), pp. 278-79.
[4] *Ibid.*, p. 280.
[5] Alfred L. Kroeber, "Concluding Review," in Sol Tax (ed.), *An Appraisal of Anthropology Today* (Chicago: University of Chicago Press, 1953), p. 368.

clearing of the intellectual air was essential, but it also led to excesses, as in Goldenweiser's famous study of totemism.[6] It also resulted in the ignoring of earlier anthropologists and even contemporaries. Alice Fletcher's *The Hako: A Pawnee Ceremony*[7] excellently describes and interprets a ritual but was never used as a model.

The major attention of the early Boas students was devoted to the task of ordering their growing data on the American Indian in tribal and regional context. During this and the following periods many important monographs and studies were published, which formed a solid base for future work. The climax of this fact-gathering revolution was reached with the culture-area concept as crystallized by Wissler,[8] and in the studies by Boas on the art, mythology, and social organization of the Northwest Coast.

The period which followed, from 1915 to 1930, was a "Florescent Period" in American ethnology. The culture area provided a framework for the analysis and interpretation of the cultural data in terms of history and process. Sapir opened the period with his famous *Time Perspective*,[9] which began: "Cultural anthropology is more and more rapidly getting to realize itself as a strictly historical science. Its data cannot be understood, either in themselves or in their relation to one another, except as the end-points of specific sequences of events reaching back into the remote past." Wissler, Lowie, Kroeber, Spier, Benedict, and many others provided a notable series of regional studies utilizing distributional analyses of cultural traits for chronological inferences — and for the study of culture process. Wissler developed the "law of diffusion" and then turned his attention to the dynamic factors underlying the culture area itself. In *The Relation of Nature to Man in Aboriginal America*[10] he thought that he had found them in the relationship of the culture center to the underlying ecology. The great museums dominated this period, and American anthropology shared in the general prosperity and optimism which followed the first World War.

One result of these distributional studies was that chronology tended to

[6] A. A. Goldenweiser, "Totemism: An Analytic Review," *Journal of American Folklore*, vol. 23 (1910), pp. 1-115.

[7] 22nd Annual Report, Bureau of American Ethnology, Washington, D.C., 1904.

[8] Clark Wissler, "Material Cultures of the North American Indian," *American Anthropologist*, 16 (1914), and *The American Indian* (New York: Oxford University Press, 1922).

[9] Edward Sapir, "Time Perspectives in Aboriginal American Culture: A Study in Method," Canada, Department of Mines, Geological Survey, Memoir 90, Anthropology Series 13, 1916.

[10] Clark Wissler, *The Relation of Nature to Man in Aboriginal America* (New York: Oxford University Press, 1926).

become an end in itself, and some ethnologists became so preoccupied with seeking time sequences that they did not pay much attention to culture as such. The analysis of culture into traits or elements and their subsequent treatment often violated principles of historical method by robbing them of their context. The normal procedure of historians of basing their analysis on chronology was here reversed — the chronology resulted from the analytic study. The generalizatiòns as to process which were formulated were used as short-cuts to further historical research.

Another important result of these studies was the conception of culture which gradually developed. Culture came to be viewed as a mere aggregation of traits brought together by the accidents of diffusion. Here is Benedict's conclusion to her doctoral dissertation: "It is, so far as we can see, an ultimate fact of human nature that man builds up his culture out of disparate elements, combining and recombining them; and until we have abandoned the superstition that the result is an organism functionally interrelated, we shall be unable to see our cultural life objectively, or to control its manifestations."[11]

The revolt against this mechanical and atomistic conception of culture came both from without and from within. Dixon[12] criticized both Wissler's procedures and his conceptions of the processes of culture growth, as well as his formulation of the dynamics of the culture area. Spier[13] renounced historical reconstruction as misleading and unnecessary for understanding the nature of the processes of culture growth, advocating in its place a consideration of the actual conditions under which cultural growth takes place. Benedict was soon engaged in the study of cultural patterns and configurations, and her *Patterns of Culture*[14] represents a complete reversal of her earlier position — here superstition has become reality.

During this period there was little interest in social structure as such, even though Kroeber, Lowie, and Parsons all studied Pueblo life at first hand. The shadows of Morgan, McLennan, Spencer, and Maine still loomed over them, and sociological interpretations were generally rejected in favor of psychological or linguistic ones. Lowie, however, began to develop a moderate functional position and sociological orientation with regard to social organization, perhaps best exemplified in his article on "Relationship Terms."[15]

[11] Ruth Benedict, "The Concept of the Guardian Spirit in North America," *Memoirs of the American Anthropological Association*, No. 29, 1923, pp. 84-5.
[12] R. B. Dixon, *The Building of Cultures* (New York: Scribners, 1928).
[13] Leslie Spier, "Problems Arising From the Cultural Position of the Havasupai," *American Anthropologist*, 16 (1929), pp. 222.
[14] (New York: Houghton Mifflin Co., 1934).
[15] Robert H. Lowie, "Relationship Terms," *Encyclopedia Britannica*, 1929.

The "Expansionist Period" which followed, 1930-1940, was a time of troubles and of transition for American ethnology. The old gods were no longer omniscient — and there was an invasion of foreign gods from overseas. The depression brought the great museums to their knees and temporarily ended their activities in ethnological research; the center of gravity shifted more and more to the universities, as the social sciences grappled with the new social problems. This was a period of considerable expansion for cultural anthropology, much of it in terms of joint departments with sociology. Archeology also experienced a remarkable expansion during the decade, partly as a by-product of its ability to utilize large quantities of WPA labor. The chronological framework that resulted, based on stratigraphy and other techniques, further emphasized the inadequacy of the reconstructions made from distributional analyses alone.

In the meantime *Argonauts* and *The Andaman Islanders* had been published but had made relatively little impression on American scholars. Malinowski's field methods were admired, and his functional conception of culture struck some responsive chords; as for Radcliffe-Brown, his "ethnological appendix" was utilized but his interpretations of Andamanese customs and beliefs were largely ignored. Soon afterwards, however, Malinowski began developing social anthropology in England on the basis of the functional method and new techniques of field research. Brief visits by Malinowski to the United States, including a summer session at the University of California, plus the work of his early students in Oceania and Africa, led to a considerable increase in his influence, but during the 1930's he was largely preoccupied with developing a program of research for Africa.

In 1931 Radcliffe-Brown, who had been first in South Africa and then in Australia, brought to this country "a method for the study of society, well defined and different enough from what prevailed here to require American anthropologists to reconsider the whole matter of method, to scrutinize their objectives, and to attend to new problems and new ways of looking at problems. He stirred us up and accelerated intellectual variation among us."[16]

As a result of these and other forces American ethnologists began to shift their interests in a variety of directions. Kroeber re-examined the relationship between cultural and natural areas in a more productive way and formulated the concept of culture climax to replace Wissler's culture center. He also explored the problem of culture elements more thoroughly, in the course of which he organized the Culture Element Survey; at the other end of the cultural spectrum he wrote *Configurations of Culture*

[16] Robert Redfield, "Introduction," Fred Eggan (ed.), *Social Anthropology of North American Tribes* (Chicago: University of Chicago Press, 1937), p. vii.

Growth.[17] Herskovits, who had earlier applied the culture-area concept to Africa, developed a dynamic approach to the study of culture[18] which has had important results. Redfield, in the meantime, was beginning the series of studies which resulted in *The Folk Culture of Yucatan*[19] — a new and important approach to the study of social and cultural change.

During this period, also, Steward was beginning his ecological studies of Great Basin tribes, Warner was applying social anthropological concepts and methods to the study of modern American communities, and Sapir was shifting his interests in the direction of psychiatry. Linton, with his perception of new and important trends, had put them together with the old, but his interests also shifted in the direction of personality and culture. Acculturation became a respectable subject with the Redfield, Linton, and Herskovits' "Memorandum on the Study of Acculturation,"[20] and applied anthropology secured a foothold in the Indian Service and in a few other government agencies.

In England cultural anthropology got off to a fine start through the efforts of Tylor, Maine, McLennan and other pioneers of the 1860's and 1870's, but their attempts to construct universal stages of development ultimately fell afoul of the facts. The nineteenth-century anthropologists in England were "armchair" anthropologists; it wasn't until Haddon, a zoologist by training, organized the famous Torres Straits expedition of 1898-1900 and converted an assorted group of psychologists and other scientists into ethnologists that field work began. But from this group came the leaders of early twentieth-century British anthropology: Haddon, Rivers, and Seligman. According to Evans-Pritchard, "This expedition marked a turning point in the history of social anthropology in Great Britain. From this time two important and interconnected developments began to take place: anthropology became more and more a whole-time professional study, and some field experience came to be regarded as an essential part of the training of its students."[21]

During the next decade a gradual separation of ethnology and social anthropology took place, culminating, according to Radcliffe-Brown,[22] in an agreement to use "ethnography" for descriptive accounts of nonliterate peoples, "ethnology" for historical reconstructions, and "social anthropology" for the comparative study of the institutions of primitive societies.

[17] (Berkeley: University of California Press, 1944).
[18] Melville J. Herskovits, *Man and His Works, The Science of Cultural Anthropology* (New York: A. A. Knopf, 1950).
[19] (Chicago: University of Chicago Press, 1941).
[20] *American Anthropologist*, 38 (1936), pp. 149-52.
[21] E. E. Evans-Pritchard, *Social Anthropology* (London: Cohen & West Ltd., 1951), p. 73.
[22] A. R. Radcliffe-Brown, "Historical Note on British Social Anthropology," *American Anthropologist*, 54 (1952), p. 276.

The institutional division of labor also took a different organization which has led to different views as to how anthropology should be constituted.

Sir James Frazer dominated social anthropology in the early decades of this century, and the conceptions of evolution and progress held sway long after they had given way in American anthropology. But Fortes notes that, while anthropologists had a magnificent field of inquiry, the subject had no intrinsic unity: "At the stage of development it had reached in 1920, anthropology, both in this country and elsewhere, was a bundle-subject, its data gathered, so to speak, from the same forest but otherwise heterogeneous and tied together only by the evolutionary theory."[23]

Ethnology flourished for a period under Haddon, Rivers, and Seligman, but with the advent of Malinowski and Radcliffe-Brown "social anthropology has emerged as the basic discipline concerned with custom and social organization in the simpler societies."[24] From their predecessors the latter received their tradition of field research and the principle of the intensive study of limited areas — a principle that Malinowski carried to its logical conclusion.

Beginning in 1924 Malinowski began to train a small but brilliant group of social anthropologists from all parts of the Commonwealth in the field techniques and functional theory that he had developed from his Trobriand experience, but his approach proved inadequate for the complex problems encountered in Africa.

. . .

If each anthropologist follows the Malinowskian tradition of specializing in one, or two, or three societies and spends his lifetime in writing about them, what happens to comparative studies? Evans-Pritchard recognizes this problem: "It is a matter of plain experience that it [the comparative study] is a formidable task which cannot be undertaken by a man who is under the obligation to publish the results of the two or three field studies he has made, since this will take him the rest of his life to complete if he has heavy teaching and administrative duties as well."[25]

In place of the comparative method he proposes the "experimental method," in which preliminary conclusions are formulated and then tested by the same or other social anthropologists on different societies, thus gradually developing broader and more adequate hypotheses. The old comparative method, he says, has been largely abandoned because it seldom gave answers to the questions asked.[26]

This concentration on intensive studies of one or two selected societies has its own limitations. The hypotheses advanced on such a basis can

[23] Meyer Fortes, "Social Anthropology at Cambridge Since 1900," an inaugural lecture, Cambridge University Press, 1953, p. 14.
[24] *Ibid.*, p. 16.
[25] *Op. cit.*, p. 89.
[26] *Ibid.*, p. 90.

often be modified in terms of studies easily available for comparison. Thus Schneider[27] points out that some of Evans-Pritchard's generalizations about the Nuer could well have been tested against the Zulu data. The degree to which comparison may sharpen hypotheses is well illustrated by Nadel's study of "Witchcraft in Four African Societies."[28] There is a further reason for this lack of interest in comparative studies on the part of Evans-Pritchard in that he thinks of social anthropology as "belonging to the humanities rather than to the natural sciences"[29] and conceives of his task as essentially a historical one of "descriptive integration."

·   ·   ·

I . . . [suggest] that there may be some virtues in combining the sound anthropological concepts of structure and function with the ethnological concepts of process and history. If we can do this in a satisfactory manner we can save the "ethnological baby" from the fate to which Kroeber has consigned it — what we call the infant when it has matured is a relatively minor matter.

8   STEIN ROKKAN

Recent Developments in
Cross-National Research

The history of international efforts in the social sciences offers a series of paradoxes. The nineteenth-century pioneers in the fields of statistics, sociology, and anthropology were almost without exception ardent advo-

---

[27] D. Schneider, "Review of Kinship and Marriage among the Nuer," *American Anthropologist*, 55 (1963), pp. 582-84.
[28] *American Anthropologist*, 54 (1952), pp. 18-29.
[29] *Op. cit.*, p. 60.

From *Comparing Nations*, edited by Richard L. Merritt and Stein Rokkan, pp. 3-20. Copyright © 1966 by Yale University. Reprinted by permission of the author and the publisher. The original title was "Comparative Cross-National Research: The Context of Current Efforts."

An early version of the first half of this contribution has been printed as part of the Introduction to a special issue of UNESCO's *International Social Science Journal* on "Data in Comparative Research," 16 (1964), 7-18.

cates of the comparative method and endeavored to establish an internationally and interculturally valid body of knowledge about variations and regularities in the functioning and development of human societies. But this aim proved difficult to reconcile with their other aims: to establish strict canons of evidence and inference in the social sciences and to ensure a high level of analytical precision. The very efforts made by the early pioneers to gain academic recognition for the new disciplines tended to force their disciples to abandon universal comparisons and to focus their inquiries on the local, the concrete, the specific. The social sciences had to establish their methodological status and win recognition in the academies of each nation. In this struggle it proved more and more difficult to maintain the initial worldwide perspective. The disciplines gained their academic honors through increasing attention to methodological rigor and through deliberate concentration on well-delimited local and national inquiries. The very success of the new sciences discouraged cross-cultural and cross-national generalization. The disciplines gained in methodological precision but in this process lost sight of the original aim: the development of systematic knowledge of the world's societies through comparisons.[1]

The result was that the social sciences were largely unprepared for the onrush of demands for concrete comparative research in the 1950s. The many efforts of international economic and political integration, the numerous programs of aid to the poorer countries of the world, the campaigns to fight illiteracy, to improve agriculture, to introduce basic industrial skills — all these varieties of efforts increased the demand for knowledge of social, economic, and cultural conditions throughout the world and accentuated the need for systematic comparative research. But the social sciences were not ready for these tasks. The theoretical underpinnings of any effort of cross-cultural or cross-national comparison were poor and fragmentary. Very little, if anything, had been done within each discipline to develop the tools of analysis and the testing procedures required in handling data at such different levels of comparability. And, what was to prove even more important, only a few scattered beginnings

[1] There is no comprehensive history of the vicissitudes of the comparative method in the social sciences. Among the most insightful contributions are F. J. Teggart, Theory of History (New Haven: Yale University Press, 1925); A. Köbben, "A New Way of Presenting an Old Idea: The Statistical Method in Social Anthropology," Journal of the Royal Anthropological Institute, 82 (1952), 129-46; E. H. Ackerknecht, "On the Comparative Method in Anthropology," in R. F. Spencer, ed., Method and Perspective in Anthropology (Minneapolis: University of Minnesota Press, 1954), pp. 117-25; Sol Tax, "From Lafitau to Radcliffe-Brown: A Short History of the Study of Social Organization," in F. Eggan, ed., Social Anthropology of North American Tribes (enlarged ed. Chicago: University of Chicago Press, 1955), pp. 443-80; K. E. Bock, The Acceptance of Histories (Berkeley: University of California Press, 1956).

had been made to ensure adequate data bases for systematic comparisons across the societies of the world.

We can roughly distinguish three categories of data for comparisons across human populations: (1) *"process-produced"* data, data generated through the very processes of living, working, interacting in the societies to be compared — from plain material evidence through all kinds of artifacts to the varieties of symbolic representations of ideas, activities, and events, whether drawings, tales, messages, or documents; (2) the data of *observations and descriptions*, whether by native historians or lawyers, foreign travelers or missionaries, academically trained linguists, ethnographers, or political scientists; (3) data from *standardized enumerations and sample surveys* of specified attributes of units within each territorial population, be they communities, work places, households, or individual subjects.

The ethnographic museums and the historical archives of the world are replete with process-produced data. The items assembled in these repositories, however, rarely lend themselves to analyses of regularities within and across societies: most of them are stored there because of their cultural or historical uniqueness, not because of their potential use in social science comparisons. To make such repositories useful for the testing of generalizations in the social sciences, efforts would have to be made to ensure representative coverage of each category of data for each society and period and to codify the items for systematic mass analysis. Important steps in this direction have been taken through the application of standardized procedures of textual analysis to such diverse process-produced data as folk tales, children's readers, and newspaper editorials. A remarkable rapprochement has occurred between the humanistic traditions of qualitative analysis in linguistic and folklore studies and the hardheaded frequency counting pioneered in the study of political communication and mass persuasion by Harold Lasswell and his associates.[2] A particularly promising example of a cross-national content analysis of cultural products is David McClelland's *The Achieving Society*.[3] The recent development

[2] The basic texts are Harold D. Lasswell, Nathan Leites *et al.*, *Language of Politics* (New York: G. W. Stewart, 1949); Harold D. Lasswell, Daniel Lerner, and Ithiel de Sola Pool, *The Comparative Study of Symbols* (Stanford, Hoover Institute Series, 1952); and Robert North *et al.*, *Handbook of Content Analysis* (Evanston: Northwestern University Press, 1963). The single most important volume on the trends toward a convergence of textual analysis techniques in linguistics, folklore, anthropology, and mass communications research is the one edited by Ithiel de Sola Pool on *Trends in Content Analysis* (Urbana: University of Illinois Press, 1959).

[3] David C. McClelland, *The Achieving Society* (New York: Van Nostrand, 1961). A curious example of the use of cross-cultural content analysis (jokes, cartoons) in the study of modal personality characteristics is Herbert Hendin's *Suicide and Scandinavia: A Psychoanalytic Story of Culture and Character* (London: Grune and Stratton, 1964).

of electronic computer facilities for content analyses of written documents[4] is bound to have a profound impact on such research, and we can in the near future expect accelerated efforts to store and codify data for such mass analyses.

Data from observations and descriptions of the institutions and peculiarities of different societies provide the basis for a rich literature of anecdotes and idiosyncratic interpretations but require detailed evaluation and codification if they are to serve the needs of comparative social science. The great pioneers in the study of primitive populations made important efforts to standardize the report taking of travelers and missionaries and to ensure the fullest possible coverage in each description. A number of attempts were made to store and codify the materials from such descriptions. Decisive progress was not achieved in this direction, however, until George Peter Murdock and his colleagues set up the Yale Cross-Cultural Survey in 1937 and later built up the Human Relations Area Files.[5] This extensive repository of coded information on a sample of the world's known societies[6] has proved an essential tool in the development of designs and techniques for the analysis of cross-cultural variations.[7] A large number of universities and research institutions subscribe to copies of the Files and more and more scholars have in recent years tried their hand at cross-cultural comparisons of this type. The Files aim at the fullest possible coverage of a representative sample of all the world's societies and will incorporate information on societies at all levels of development, from preagricultural tribes to highly industrialized nation-

[4] See Philip J. Stone et al., "The General Inquirer: A Computer System of Content Analysis and Retrieval Based on the Sentence as a Unit of Information," *Behavioral Science*, 7 (1962), 484-98; and the chapters by Scheuch and Stone, and North and Holsti in the present volume.

[5] George P. Murdock, "The Cross-Cultural Survey," *American Sociological Review*, 5 (1940), 361-70; cf. F. W. Moore, ed., *Readings in Cross-Cultural Methodology* (New Haven: HRAF Press, 1961).

[6] The code used in classifying information is given in George P. Murdock et al., *An Outline of Cultural Materials* (4th rev. ed. New Haven: HRAF Press, 1961). An up-to-date listing of the universe and the samples of the world's societies is given in George P. Murdock, *An Outline of World Cultures* (3d ed. New Haven: HRAF Press, 1963). Robert Textor is currently assembling a basic handbook of information on a sample of 400 societies; see his forthcoming work *A Cross-Cultural Summary*. Karl Deutsch and Carl Friedrich have recently launched a collective exploration of the possibilities of using HRAF data and HRAF techniques in the comparative study of political systems.

[7] See George P. Murdock, *Social Structure* (New York: Macmillan, 1949). For a host of subsequent analyses, cf. Oscar Lewis, "Comparisons in Cultural Anthropology," in W. L. Thomas, Jr., *Current Anthropology* (Chicago: University of Chicago Press, 1956), pp. 259-92; and W. J. McEwen, "Forms and Problems of Validation in Social Anthropology," *Current Anthropology*, 4 (1963), 155-83.

states. In practice, however, it has proved very difficult to apply the traditional anthropological techniques of data gathering and codification to
advanced nation-states, and most of the cross-cultural comparisons have
been limited to preliterate units.[8]

The comparative study of industrializing nation-states grew out of a
tradition of systematic observation by travelers, journalists, and itinerant-
scholars: the pioneering analyses of Montesquieu, Tocqueville, Marx,
Engels, Ostrogorski, Michels, Bryce, and Weber were all heavily influenced
by experiences of direct exposure to foreign manners and institutions.
Weber's ambitious attempt to build up a conceptual framework for the
comparative study of the growth of centralized bureaucracies and mass
democracies reflected more than a century of discussion of contrasts and
similarities among national developments in Europe and America and
between the West and East. The data for such ventures varied enor-
mously in reliability, precision, and coverage: from fairly well-researched
historical and legal evidence over crude official statistics to impressionistic
accounts of the workings of particular institutions. Scholars following in
Weber's path face a serious dilemma. If they decide to continue his
effort of theory construction, they will either find it impossible to establish an adequate data basis for their analyses or come under heavy and
justified attacks from historians and area specialists for ignorance and
distortions and for procrustean classifications of institutions and processes.
If, however, they concentrate their efforts on comparative data gathering
and data evaluation, they soon run into difficulties of conceptual integration and theoretical interpretation.[9] Shmuel Eisenstadt's gigantic effort
of comparative analysis of *The Political Systems of Empires*[10] exemplifies one possible research strategy: he develops an elaborate model of
processes of centralization, bureaucratization and debureaucratization, and
then seeks to test the consequences against evidence for five prebureau-

[8] A pioneering attempt to apply HRAF-type techniques to national polities
rather than societies is Arthur S. Banks and Robert B. Textor, A *Cross-Polity
Survey* (Cambridge, Mass.: M.I.T. Press, 1963).

[9] For discussions of the potentialities and the problems of comparative history,
see especially Marc Bloch, "Pour une histoire comparée des sociétés européennes,"
originally published in 1928, reprinted in *Mélanges Historiques* (Paris: S.E.V.-
P.E.N., 1963), *i*, 16-40; Sylvia Thrupp, "The Role of Comparison in the
Development of Economic History," *Journal of Economic History*, 17 (1957),
554-70; Fritz Redlich, "Toward Comparative Historiography," *Kyklos*, 11
(1958), 362-89; and D. Gerhard, *Alte und neue Wege in vergleichender
Geschichtsbetrachtung* (Göttingen: Vandenhoeck, 1960). Sylvia Thrupp has
made a pioneering effort to develop regular exchanges among historians and
social scientists interested in cross-national analyses through the organization of
the important international journal *Comparative Studies in Society and History*.

[10] Shmuel N. Eisenstadt, *The Political Systems of Empires* (New York: Free
Press, 1963).

cratic societies and 27 historical bureaucratic societies. The problems encountered in such attempts are twofold: first, are the categories precise
enough for effective analysis and are they meaningful across so many different areas of the world? second, does the evidence available allow some
measure of consensus among experts on the categorization of concrete
instances? To fit a large number of different cases, Eisenstadt's categories
had to leave a considerable margin of imprecision; but this very imprecision makes many of his one-man categorizations of concrete cases, despite
an extraordinary display of detailed historical erudition, highly debatable.
Reinhard Bendix's recent volume on *Nation-Building and Citizenship*[11]
exemplifies a more cautious approach: a number of theoretical distinctions
first set out by Tocqueville and Weber are worked out in greater detail
and then illustrated through the analysis of several concrete national
developments. Seymour Martin Lipset's early work exemplified the
empirical strategy: *Political Man* is essentially an outgrowth of a series
of efforts to assemble prima facie comparable data on society and
politics for a number of countries. His most recent contribution seeks to
achieve more of a balance between theory construction and empirical
analysis. *The First New Nation*[12] is essentially an attempt to bring
Tocqueville's interpretation of the uniqueness of American society up to
date through the development of a new analytical framework and through
the collation of illustrative quantitative comparisons. Although many
future "comparatists" will no doubt continue to pursue such "mixed"
strategies, substantial progress in this field does not seem likely unless we
reach a higher level of differentiation and specialization in research roles.
To meet the demands for evidence of those social scientists who will
continue to pursue theoretical refinements, we must also encourage the
formation of a broad phalanx of experts on a wide range of empirical data
across several countries.

To get a basis for detailed comparisons of rates of development within
new as well as established nation-states, it is essential to supplement the
information from historical documents and observers' reports with data
from *standardized counts and other efforts of systematic social, cultural,
and political map making*. Only in this way is it possible to approach
reliable estimates of changes over time and of within-unit variations in
the conditions and sequences of development.

The statisticians of the Western world can look back on more than
a century of cooperative efforts to standardize national bookkeeping and
census-taking procedures. The great Belgian pioneer Quetelet established
a network of contacts throughout Europe and, in 1851, took a decisive

[11] Reinhard Bendix, *Nation-Building and Citizenship* (New York: Wiley,
1964).
[12] Seymour Martin Lipset, *The First New Nation: The United States in
Historical and Comparative Perspective* (New York: Basic Books, 1963).

initiative in launching two International Statistical Congresses. The next generation went further and in 1887 set up the International Statistical Institute. The Institute provided a basis for continuous contact among experts and administrators of many nations and prepared the ground for the systematic efforts of comparison and standardization later taken up at the governmental level by the League of Nations, the International Labor Office, and, during the last two decades, by the United Nations and its specialized agencies.[13]

It took a long time, however, before the impact of these developments was felt throughout the social sciences. The demographers were the first to develop the tools of analysis required in mastering these vast quantities of data, the economists followed suit after the Second World War, but the sociologists have only recently faced up to the challenge of the increasing masses of cross-national data. The early fascination with comparative statistics for suicide and homicide and other items of *Moralstatistik* did not herald the advent of a comparative sociology of national development: Durkheim's work was of great methodological significance but was not followed up through broader comparative investigations of processes of change in industrializing and urbanizing nations. It is characteristic that the pioneering comparison of mobility data published by Pitirim Sorokin in 1927[14] left hardly a ripple in the scholarly world at the time and was only discovered as a true classic of cross-national research in the wake of the establishment of the Research Committee on Social Stratification and Mobility under the auspices of the International Sociological Association in 1951.[15] The decisive breakthrough toward quantitative comparisons

[13] The sheer mass of documentation produced by these efforts is overwhelming. A basic list of references to proposed standards is given in Statistical Office of the United Nations, *Directory of International Standards for Statistics* (New York: United Nations, Stat. Ser. M., No. 22, Rev. 1, 1960). This, however, gives little or no information on the concrete contents of the standards or on problems of application. UNESCO is currently attempting to remedy this lacuna through the compilation of a *Manual of International Standards of Classification in the Social Sciences* which will essentially cover the statistical indicators of cross-national differences presented in the UN *Compendium of Social Statistics, 1963*. For further details on UN statistical efforts see the chapter by Donald V. McGranahan in [Richard L. Merritt and Stein Rokkan (eds.) *Comparing Nations* (New Haven: Yale University Press, 1966).]

[14] Pitirim A. Sorokin, *Social Mobility* (London: Harper, 1927, reprinted Glencoe: Free Press, 1959). For a general bibliography of efforts to develop comparative sociology in the 1950s, see Robert M. Marsh, "Comparative Sociology 1950-1963," *Current Sociology, 14* (1966).

[15] Erik Rinde and Stein Rokkan, eds., *First International Working Conference on Social Stratification and Social Mobility* (Oslo: International Sociological Association, 1951); Seymour M. Lipset and Reinhard Bendix, *Social Mobility in Industrial Society* (Berkeley: University of California Press, 1958); S. M. Miller, "Comparative Social Mobility," *Current Sociology, 9* (1960), 1-89; David V. Glass and René König, *Soziale Schichtung und soziale Mobilität* (Cologne: Westdeutscher Verlag, 1961).

in fact did not occur until the 1950s, when economists finally came seriously to grips with the possibilities of precise analyses of rates and patterns of growth, when sociologists started to become concerned with comparative measures of processes of structural change, when even students of politics ceased to be exclusively absorbed in single systems and tried to work out schemes of comparison and to devise ways of testing their hypotheses quantitatively.

Two technical developments proved crucial in accelerating these movements toward greater boldness in tackling the problems of a cross-national comparison: first, the extraordinary improvements in the machinery for the handling of huge data masses; and, second, the organization in more and more countries of sample survey organizations gathering data on broader ranges of variables than normally covered in official statistical bookkeeping operations.

The development of the electronic computer has brought about a revolution in comparative research. Tasks of calculation previously judged beyond the reach of even the largest research institute can now be carried out quickly and at moderate cost at a number of academic computer centers. The very existence of these new machines has prompted a number of research organizations to build up extensive data archives on punch cards or on tape. Several archives now cover data from large numbers of countries throughout the world. The need for such data archives has proved most urgent in comparative studies of economic growth, and an impressive number of attempts has been made in recent years to apply complex techniques of computation to cross-national data on a variety of indicators of resources, production, income, distribution, etc.[16] The case for similar data archives has also been effectively demonstrated in a study of world urbanization through the work of Kingsley Davis and his group at the University of California at Berkeley[17] and more recently also in the study of political modernization by Karl Deutsch and his associates at Yale University.[18]

[16] An excellent source book on such indicators is Norton Ginsburg's *Atlas of Economic Development* (Chicago: University of Chicago Press, 1961); this also includes an example (by Brian J. L. Berry) of one type of correlational analysis now made possible on the basis of such data.
[17] The International Population and Urban Research Program at Berkeley has developed a systematic file of information on all of the world's cities and metropolitan areas of 100,000 inhabitants and more; cf. International Urban Research, *The World's Metropolitan Areas* (Berkeley: University of California Press, 1959).
[18] See especially Karl W. Deutsch, "Toward an Inventory of Basic Trends and Patterns in Comparative and International Politics," *American Political Science Review*, 54 (1960), 34-57, and the chapters on the Yale Political Data Program in [Richard L. Merritt and Stein Rokkan (eds.), *Comparing Nations* (New Haven: Yale University Press, 1966).]

The sociologists and political scientists developing such plans have of necessity been concerned with broader ranges of cross-national variables than the demographers and the economists. They have not only brought together data from censuses, national accounts, trade statistics, and other governmental bookkeeping operations but have also sought to accumulate the best available estimates of variations in the spread of education and culture, in the sway of religious, ideological, and political movements, and in the exposure of the population to the newer media of communication. UNESCO and such regional organizations as the OECD are doing magnificent work on the evaluation of the comparative statistics of education, a field in which sociologists and political scientists attempting to build up data programs can simply take over the country-by-country estimates produced by these organizations. The situation is less encouraging for mass media statistics. UNESCO has been making valiant efforts to accumulate information on mass media but has had very little opportunity to carry out detailed evaluations and analyses. On cultural, religious, and political variables the international organizations can deliver little or nothing; here the social scientist is pretty much on his own and will have to glean, from whatever national sources he can find, such data as seem worthy of comparison. Data on religious memberships, electoral turnout, and party strength can be assembled from official counts for a sizable number of countries, but to evaluate and interpret such data in any comparative analysis the social scientists will require detailed knowledge of the workings of each national system, and here the literature is often deficient.[19] Data on levels of participation, whether cultural, religious, or political, can only rarely be assembled from regular statistical sources but may sometimes be gathered through private counting operations (church attendance, party membership statistics) and ad hoc sample surveys. So far very little has been done to make use of such data in

[19] This is the essential rationale for the plan now under consideration within UNESCO for a series of *International Guides to Data for Comparative Research*. The first of these, the *International Guide to Electoral Statistics*, is already far advanced; the first volume will be published during 1965 by the International Committee of Social Science Documentation in cooperation with the International Social Science Council. In the United States the Social Science Research Council has supported an exploratory study by Walter D. Burnham on the possibilities of assembling a central file of historical election data by county for computer processing. The Inter-University Consortium for Political Research at Ann Arbor, Michigan, is currently following up this effort and is building up a large file of census and election data by county to facilitate ecological trend analyses. For a general discussion of the potentialities of such approaches to the comparative study of political ecology, see Stein Rokkan, "Electoral Mobilization, Party Competition and Territorial Integration," a paper to be published in Joseph LaPalombara and Myron Weiner, eds., *Political Parties and Political Development* (Princeton: Princeton University Press, 1966).

computer programs for cross-national comparison, but efforts are at least under way to establish a basis for such analyses through the development of archives of raw data from sample surveys for different countries.

The practice of interviewing samples of populations can be traced to several distinct historical roots. One line of development started out from the official census: sampling procedures were developed to cut down the cost of censuses of social conditions, particularly studies of poverty and sub-standard housing; and sampling also made it possible to gather information in greater detail than in official data gathering operations. Another line of development started out from the public referendum, the plebiscite: "straw polls" and opinion soundings serving as short cuts to information on the inclinations and the preferences of the general public. Up to the middle of the 1930s there were hardly any points of contact between these two traditions of inquiry. This changed radically, however, with the emergence of large-scale organizations conducting interview studies, first under commercial auspices and later also within government departments and universities. The mass interview was found to be a flexible instrument of social inquiry and soon proved its usefulness in a wide range of contexts. In fact, it combined within one unified operation at least six hitherto distinct models of social and behavioral data gathering: the census questionnaire, the standardized observation checklist, the informal reportorial conversation, the referendum, the election, and the psychological test. This flexibility proved the great strength of the interview as a research procedure but, at least in the initial phases, caused a good deal of confusion and controversy.[20]

International networks of interview organizations grew rapidly after World War II as more and more attempts were made to develop comparable procedures of opinion soundings and market studies across several different countries at the same time.[21] Only a handful of academic

[20] The sizable body of literature generated by these developments has never been systematically analyzed. Among the hundreds of articles and chapters produced in the course of the controversy these have perhaps proved the more significant: T. Harrison, "What is Public Opinion?" *Political Quarterly, 11* (1940), 368-83; H. Blumer, "Public Opinion and Public Opinion Polling," *American Sociological Review, 13* (1948), 542-65; H. Arbuthnot, "Democracy by Snap Judgment," *Listener* (March 4, 1948), pp. 367-68; Lindsay Rogers, *The Pollsters* (New York: Knopf, 1949); Hans Speier, "The Historical Development of Public Opinion," in his *Social Order and the Risk of War* (New York: Stewart, 1952); Herbert H. Hyman, *Survey Design and Analysis* (Glencoe: Free Press, 1955), Chap. 8; Paul F. Lazarsfeld, "Public Opinion and the Classical Tradition," *Public Opinion Quarterly, 21* (1957), 39-53.

[21] Stein Rokkan and Jean Viet are preparing an account of the development of *Comparative Survey Analysis*; a first version of the bibliographical part of this "trend report" was circulated in 1962 by the International Committee on Social Science Documentation.

social scientists took an interest in these international developments during the first decade or so, but at least a few imaginative beginnings were made. A pioneer in the use of these new techniques of cross-national research was the American psychologist Hadley Cantril. He showed how this machinery of data gathering could be used to throw light on central problems in the study of international communication. His UNESCO-sponsored study, *How Nations See Each Other*,[22] was the first in a series of attempts to make systematic use of national interview organizations in theory-oriented comparative research. He also pointed to the possibilities of drawing on the rapidly increasing production of interview data for comparative secondary analysis: his impressive compilation of findings through 1946[23] paved the way for subsequent efforts to assemble not only the press releases and reports from the many interview organizations of the world but also the raw data of their studies as recorded on punch cards or tapes.

Only a few academic social scientists have been able to command the resources required to organize comparative data-gathering operations of their own design. The number of full-scale studies following the pattern set by the UNESCO study of 1949 can still be counted on two hands.[24] The five-country study carried out in 1959-1960 by Gabriel Almond and Sidney Verba[25] demonstrates the immense possibilities for this line of research, but the cost of such ventures will for years to come keep them beyond the reach of most centers of research. The vast majority of academic social scientists will have to do what they can with data produced independently of their own interests and efforts, and seek to develop techniques for comparing such information ex post facto. To judge the comparability of such independently collected data, it is clearly essential to go beyond the simple tabulations generally given in the releases to the press or even in the reports given to sponsors and clients. This is the

[22] William Buchanan and Hadley Cantril, *How Nations See Each Other* (Urbana: University of Illinois Press, 1953).

[23] Hadley Cantril and Mildred Strunk, eds., *Public Opinion, 1935-46* (Princeton: Princeton University Press, 1951). The *Public Opinion Quarterly* listed "poll" results from 1940 to 1951 and again from 1961, but the coverage of these listings was not very systematic. Martin Brouwer at the University of Amsterdam has collected an important archive of releases and reports from polling organizations and has launched a journal registering questions and total response distributions in 1965: *Polls* (Amsterdam, Steinmetz Institute and Keesing's, 1965).

[24] A near-complete listing of such projects is included in the mimeographed bibliography by Stein Rokkan and Jean Viet; see note 22 above. A major comparative survey of the "modernization" of attitudes has recently been undertaken in six countries by Alex Inkeles of Harvard University.

[25] Gabriel Almond and Sidney Verba, *The Civic Culture* (Princeton: Princeton University Press, 1963).

essential rationale for the current efforts to assemble the raw data of a
variety of studies from different countries into archives for subsequent
secondary analysis by qualified scholars.[26]

In the early phase of commercial polling and market research the typical report simply gave for each question the per cent of all interviewed
responding one way or the other: so many X, so many Y, so many Z, so
many Don't Know. The underlying model of the public was plebiscitarian
and equalitarian. The "pollsters" started out from the basic premise of
full suffrage democracy: "one citizen, one vote, one value." They equated
votes and other expressions of opinion and gave the same numerical value
to every such expression, whether actively articulated independently
of any interview or elicited only in the interview situation. The sum total
of such unit expressions was presented as an estimate of "public opinion"
on the given issue. The aim was clearly not just elicitation, classification,
and enumeration; the essential aim was to establish the "will of the
people" through sample interviews instead of through elections and
referenda. To such pioneers as George Gallup and Elmo Roper, the
"poll" was essentially a new technique of democratic control; the interviews helped to bring out the will of the "inarticulate, unorganized
majority of the people" as a countervailing power against the persuasive
pressure of the many minority interests.[27]

By the late 1950s, however, there were more and more signs of change.
The "one citizen, one opinion" model was gradually given up and the
practices of even the most "cash-oriented" of the private pollsters began
to reflect the differentiated models of opinion formation developed by
social psychologists, sociologists, and political scientists. A series of
academic surveys of local communities and national cross-sections had
helped to establish the characteristics of the strata of opinion moulders,
opinion transmitters, and opinion receivers within our contemporary mass

[26] The first systematic report on such possibilities was prepared in 1957 by
Y. Lucci and Stein Rokkan in A *Library Center of Survey Research Data* (New
York: Columbia University School of Library Service). For further developments see the articles in the special issue on "Data in Comparative Research"
of the UNESCO *International Social Science Journal*, 16 (1964).

[27] The plebiscitarian assumptions of commercial polling have been analyzed
with great critical skill by the German philosopher Wilhelm Hennis in
Meinungsforschung und repräsentative Demokratie (Tübingen, Mohr, 1957).
This work is of particular interest as an attempt to bridge the gap between the
political theory of representation and democracy and the current controversies
about the assumptions underlying the practice of mass interviews. This theme is
discussed in a broader perspective of historical sociology in Jürgen Habermas,
Strukturwandel der Öffentlichkeit (Neuwied: Luchterhand, 1961). The position
of the "pollsters" has been ably defended by G. Schmidtchen, *Die befragte
Nation* (Freiburg, Rombach, 1959), and Manfred Kuhn, *Umfragen und Demokratie* (Allensbach, Verlag für Demoskopie, 1959).

electorates. Paul Lazarsfeld's pioneering studies of the "two-step flow of communication"[28] had a profound effect on contemporary theorizing about mass democracy. David Riesman and his associates developed this line of analysis further and emphasized the importance of the social context of the interview reaction: a lower-class response to a middle-class interviewer could not be analyzed in the same terms as an upper-class response to the same interviewer.[29] The Survey Research Center of the University of Michigan has added a number of further dimensions to this mapping of the hierarchies of "publics" within the mass electorate and provided perhaps the most telling demonstration of the deficiencies of the earlier arithmetic conceptions of aggregated national opinion. Philip Converse has recently presented a most revealing analysis of the reactions of a panel of respondents to identical questions asked three times over a period of four years.[30] On all three occasions filtering questions were used to sift out respondents definitely unfamiliar with the issue they were to express an opinion on. Nevertheless, responses on even basic issues of policy turned out to be highly unstable over the four years. Substantial proportions of those who offered opinions had clearly not given the matter any thought but only picked an alternative to please the interviewer. Only a small proportion of the panel proved stable in their responses and appeared to base their statements on information, experiences, and arguments which meant something to them personally. These "issue publics," normally only 20 to 40 per cent of the total electorate, will vary in composition from issue to issue but the citizens in the lowest of the strata of political actors would hardly ever be part of any such group of stable respondents.

Analyses along such lines are of obvious importance for an understanding of data for any single nation. They are crucial in any attempt to compare distributions of responses across several nations. How can one possibly compare one national distribution of responses with another without knowing anything about the levels of interest in the given issue in each country, the differences in education, in exposure, in knowledge?

[28] Paul F. Lazarsfeld *et al., The People's Choice* (New York: Duell, 1944); Elihu Katz and Paul F. Lazarsfeld, *Personal Influence* (Glencoe: Free Press, 1955). For a replication in Sweden see Bo Anderson, "Opinion Influentials and Political Opinion Formation in Four Swedish Communities," *International Social Science Journal,* 14 (1962), 320-36.

[29] See David Riesman and Nathan Glazer, "Social Structure, Character Structure and Opinion," *International Journal of Opinion and Attitude Research,* 2 (1948), 512-27; and particularly the special issue on the sociology of the interview of the *American Journal of Sociology,* 62 (1956).

[30] Philip E. Converse, "New Dimensions of Meaning for Cross-National Sample Surveys in Politics," *International Social Science Journal,* 16 (1964), 19-34; and "The Nature of Belief Systems in Mass Publics," in David E. Apter, ed., *Ideology and Discontent* (New York: Free Press, 1964), pp. 206-61.

The private networks of interview organizations in Europe and America
have in recent years found an expanding market for comparative studies,
and it is interesting to note how much more detailed the tabulations have
become as a result. To take a recent example, Gallup International, in
its study of *Public Opinion and the Europe of the Six*,[31] found that 62
per cent of the Dutch sample was strongly in favor of unification and only
36 per cent of the Italians. This difference, however, tells us very little
about the chances of strains between the two countries in the articulation of policies toward Europe. It turns out that the better educated
in the two national samples think practically alike: 70 per cent of them
were strongly in favor of European unification. The difference between
the two countries resulted almost entirely from a contrast in levels of education and information; most of the lower educated in Italy could not
articulate any opinion, and in the backward areas of the South and the
Islands two thirds to three fourths of those interviewed had never heard
of the European unification efforts.

Such checks by education and information exemplify only one line
of comparative evaluation. There are many more, some of which may
without much difficulty be explored further through secondary analysis of
the interview data directly from the punch cards, or when there are
doubts about the classifications of cases on such cards, even from the
original protocols of the field workers.

Systematic comparisons, however, must of necessity go beyond such
simple evaluation of estimates of cross-national similarities and differences.
The essential aims of cross-national analysis are "*micro*" replications and
the testing of "*macro*" hypotheses.[32] In replicative research the aim is to
test out in other national and cultural settings a proposition already
validated in one setting. Thus the social psychologist who has found for
one country that working-class adults are more authoritarian than middle-
class adults will want to replicate this analysis for as many countries as
possible to establish the generality of his finding.[33] This would be generalization at the *micro* level: the level of individuals, households, or other
component units of larger culturally and politically distinct systems. The

[31] Gallup International, *L'opinion publique et l'Europe des Six* (Paris, IFOP,
mimeo, 1963); and the special issue on these surveys of *Sondages*, 25 (1963),
3-58. Another comparative survey of great interest in this connection is reported
on in *Products and People: A Digest of the Marketing Survey of the European
Common Market, 1963* (London: The Reader's Digest Association Ltd., 1963).
[32] See the "paradigms" discussed in Stein Rokkan, "The Comparative Study
of Political Participation: Notes Toward a Perspective on Current Research,"
in Austin Ranney, ed., *Essays on the Behavioral Study of Politics* (Urbana:
University of Illinois Press, 1962), pp. 47-90.
[33] A proposition discussed in some detail by Seymour M. Lipset in *Political
Man* (Garden City, N.Y.: Doubleday, 1960), Chap. 4.

crucial tasks of cross-national analysis, however, lie at the *macro* level: the exploration of the interrelations of structural elements of total systems and the testing of hypotheses about structural influences on the behavior of component units. A social psychologist might want to explore the influence of childrearing practices and childhood experiences on the development of economic entrepreneurship in a variety of cultures,[34] but he would soon find it more fruitful to go beyond the mere replication of tests designed to get such information toward the exploration of "macro" conditions in the social and political structure — differences in educational systems, in opportunities for geographical and social mobility, in the legal status of entrepreneurs, etc. — which would increase or decrease the likelihood of such results of socialization. Although the distinction between "micro" and "macro" levels of analysis is essential in all cross-national research, the logical structure of these distinctions has not yet been worked out satisfactorily.[35]

[34] See McClelland, *The Achieving Society*, and E. Hagen, *On the Theory of Social Change* (Homewood, Ill.: Dorsey Press, 1962).

[35] An important basis for advances in this direction has been provided in Lazarsfeld's analysis of the properties of individual vs. group variables; cf. Paul F. Lazarsfeld and Morris Rosenberg, eds., *The Language of Social Research* (Glencoe: Free Press, 1955), Section IV; and Hanan C. Selvin and W. O. Hagstrom, "The Empirical Classification of Formal Groups," *American Sociological Review*, 28 (1963), 399-411.

V

Levels of Comparison

9   GLEN H. ELDER, JR.

Family Structure and Educational
Attainment: A Cross-National Analysis

Family structure is one of the more important determinants of achievement motivation and skills.[1] Many of the personal qualities and skills
that enable children to meet standards of excellence — self-reliance,
competent judgment, problem-solving ability, and a questioning mind —

From *American Sociological Review*, vol. 30, no. 1 (February 1965), pp.
81-96. Reprinted by permission of the author and the American Sociological
Association.

[1] David C. McClelland, *The Achieving Society*, Princeton, N.J.: D. Van
Nostrand, 1961, Ch. 9; Fred L. Strodtbeck, "Family Interaction, Values and
Achievement," in David C. McClelland, *et al.*, *Talent and Society*, Princeton,
N.J.: D. Van Nostrand, 1958, pp. 135-194; and Glen H. Elder, Jr., *Adolescent
Achievement and Mobility Aspirations*, Chapel Hill, N.C.: Institute for Research
in Social Science, 1962.

94

are acquired in parent-child relations providing guidance and yet allowing the child freedom to develop independent mastery and responsible decision-making.[2] Parental dominance, on the other hand, often produces passivity, rebelliousness, and dependency. Domination is characterized by "a rigidity or inflexibility of purpose, . . . an unwillingness to admit the contribution of another's experiences, desires, purposes or judgment in one's determining of goals which concern others."[3] Responsibility and confidence in independence are acquired through guided opportunities in independent problem solving and activity, and parental domination during late childhood and in adolescence largely denies these experiences.

Conjugal role patterns, affecting as they do family relations and climate, also influence the acquisition of self-confidence and mastery in children. The most negative effects are associated with wife-dominance. In a recent study, American adolescents who described their mothers as dominant in family decision-making tended to be relatively low on autonomy and academic motivation.[4] Devereux *et al.* found that American and West German pre-adolescent boys in extremely wife-dominated families were rated by teachers and peers as more selfish, incompetent, excitable, and dependent than boys from any other type of family.[5]

This paper reports a cross-national study of the effects of parent-child and conjugal role patterns on level of educational attainment. Most research on the effects of parental dominance on motivation and achievement level has been conducted in the U.S., so that the effects of family structure on educational achievement in other societies are to some

[2] W. D. Wall, F. J. Schonell, and Willard C. Olson, *Failure in School*, Hamburg: UNESCO Institute for Education, 1962; Bernard C. Rosen and Roy C. D'Andrade, "The Psychosocial Origins of Achievement Motivation," *Sociometry*, 22 (September 1959), pp. 185-218.

[3] Harold H. Anderson, "An Examination of the Concept of Domination and Integration in Relation to Domination and Ascendance," *Psychological Review*, 47 (January 1940), pp. 21-22.

[4] Glen H. Elder, Jr., *Family Structure and the Transmission of Values and Norms in the Process of Child Rearing*, unpublished Ph.D. dissertation, University of North Carolina, 1961. See also Murray H. Straus, "Conjugal Power Structure and Adolescent Personality," *Marriage and Family Living*, 24 (February 1962), pp. 17-25.

[5] See Edward C. Devereux, Jr., "Children of Democracy: On the Consequences for Children of Varying Patterns of Family Authority in the United States and West Germany," summary of a paper presented to the 7th International Seminars on Family Research, Washington, D.C., September 1962; Edward C. Devereux, Jr., Urie Bronfenbrenner and George J. Suci, "Patterns of Parent Behavior in America and West Germany: A Cross-National Comparison," *International Social Science Journal*, 14 (1962), pp. 488-506; Urie Bronfenbrenner, "Some Familial Antecedents of Responsibility and Leadership in Adolescents," in Luigi Petrullo and Bernard L. Bass (eds.), *Leadership and Interpersonal Behavior*, New York: Holt, Rinehart & Winston, 1961, pp. 237-272.

extent unknown.[6] The data for the present analysis are drawn from a
study of political behavior in the U.S., Great Britain, West Germany,
Italy, and Mexico.[7] Interviews were obtained from approximately 1,000
adults, ages 18 and over.

These nations represent considerable diversity of culture and of educational opportunity. Individual achievement and competition are core
themes in American culture, and are more prominent in Great Britain
and West Germany than in Italian and Mexican cultures.[8] On the
other hand, cultural support for male dominance in family, economic, and
political affairs is more pronounced in Italy and Mexico than in the
other countries. Italy and especially Mexico also stand apart from the
other countries in the development of human resources through education.[9] These variations define in part the general context in which I shall
assess the relation between family structure and educational attainment.

The control parents exercise over adolescent sons and daughters ranges
from complete subordination of the child to no regulation over the child's
behavior.[10] Both extremes have negative effects on the development of

[6] Studies in Japan, Brazil, Germany and Turkey have corroborated American
findings regarding the effects of paternal dominance on achievement motivation. . . .

[7] These data were obtained in 1959 and 1960 by Gabriel Almond and Sydney
Verba for a study of political behavior in these five countries. See *The Civic
Culture*, Princeton: Princeton University Press, 1963. . . .

Though the samples from each of the five countries are stratified multistage
probability samples, the design and execution of the survey varied substantially.
Each sample was intended to be a representative cross-section of the national
population, but this objective was not achieved in Mexico, and in the other
four nations it was only roughly approximated. Cost and technical difficulties
made it necessary to draw the Mexican sample from the population of persons
living in urban places of 10,000 or more and to weight the Mexico City interviews by a factor of 2.5 so as to make this portion of the sample equivalent to
its proportion in the national population. These conditions, as well as the high
rate of failure to obtain interviews at assigned addresses (40 per cent), seriously
weaken cross-national comparisons between Mexico and the other four nations.
Exclusion of the rural population tends to produce an underestimation of the
actual differences between Mexico and the other nations. One indication of the
quality of the other four samples is shown by the non-completion rates in interviewing: Germany, 26 per cent; Italy, 28 per cent; Great Britain, 41 per cent;
and the U.S., 17 per cent.

[8] On characteristic value patterns of the United States, Great Britain, and
West Germany, see Seymour M. Lipset, *The First New Nation*, New York:
Basic Books, 1963. See also Almond and Verba, *The Civic Culture, op. cit.*

[9] See Frederick Harbison and Charles A. Myers, *Education, Manpower and
Economic Growth*, New York: McGraw-Hill, 1964.

[10] Glen H. Elder, Jr., "Structural Variations in the Child-Rearing Relationship," *Sociometry*, 25 (September 1962), pp. 241-262.

achievement motivation and skills.[11] Among adolescents living in central areas of Ohio and North Carolina those who were dominated by their parents and prevented from acquiring decision-making experience lacked interest in school, academic motivation, and plans for additional education.[12]

To a lesser extent this pattern was characteristic of youth given little parental guidance and supervision. Girls and boys who participated, under parental guidance, in decisions concerning their own activities attained the highest levels of academic motivation and achievement.

These results suggest the following hypothesis: in each of the five nations, *educational attainment is negatively related to the degree of parental dominance in adolescence.*[13]

The effects of dominance on the development of ability and motivation to achieve are heavily contingent on which parent is dominant.[14] For boys, parental dominance and maternal overprotection have the most negative effects. Furthermore, in an authoritarian, father-dominated family boys seem to receive little achievement training from father. The authoritarian Brazilian father, according to Rosen,

> . . . tends to thwart his son's efforts to be self-reliant and autonomous. The child learns that toward a severely authoritarian father only revolt or submission is possible. And submission in the form of ingratiation and obedience is the dominant adjustment to authority in Brazil. . . . A pronounced concern with a son's achievement in "a father-centered" home may be perceived as a threat to the hegemony of the father. He . . . may indeed regard his son's competitive and achievement-oriented behavior (which normally tends

[11] Elder, *Adolescent Achievement and Mobility Aspirations, op. cit.*

[12] *Ibid.*

[13] The measure of educational attainment is the percentage reaching secondary school. An index of parent-youth relations was constructed from the following two items: "As you were growing up, let's say when you were around 16, how much influence do you remember having in family decisions affecting yourself?" (2, much influence; 1, some; 0, none at all. Other and "don't know" responses not scored.) "At around the same time, if a decision were made that you didn't like, did you feel *free* to complain, did you feel a little *uneasy* about complaining, or was it *better not* to complain?" (2, felt free; 1, felt a little uneasy; 0, it was better not to complain. Other and "don't know" responses not scored.) The index score, ranging from 0 to 4, is the sum of the two component scores. In the following analysis, scores 3 and 4 indicate *democratic* parent-child relations, and scores 0, 1, and 2 indicate authoritarian relations. (The data did not permit a measure of parental permissiveness.) The two component items are highly correlated; 3 x 3 tables based on the total sample in each nation yielded the following gamma coefficients. U.S., .61; Italy, .63; West Germany, .65; Great Britain, .56; Mexico, .46.

[14] Rosen and D'Andrade, *op. cit.*

> to have some aggressive overtones) as an expression of aggression. Since
> aggression against the father is perhaps the most heinous sin in the
> Brazilian family and ordinarily evokes harsh reprisals, children often
> learn to avoid even the appearance of aggressiveness which competi-
> tion suggests.[15]

The Brazilian mother in the father-dominated household tends to be
submissive and deferential toward her husband, and is both dominating
and excessively protective in relation to her children. Thus, self-reliance
is not encouraged by either parent.

In the present samples, father-dominance in parent-youth relations
tends to reflect husband-dominance in conjugal relations: the average
"Q" coefficient is .38. A similar positive association was obtained in most
age, sex and nationality subgroups. Respondents who reported being excluded from decision-making during adolescence were also more likely
to report that father was the chief decision-maker on matters pertaining
to discipline. To a limited extent, then, a parent-dominated home tends
to indicate father dominance in family relations generally.

Research on the effects of conjugal role patterns indicates that
achievement among American boys is highest in the "equalitarian"
household and lowest in wife-dominated homes.[16] Boys in a small
sample from a New England high school were most likely to have upwardly mobile occupational aspirations when mother and father shared
authority.[17] Similar results for boys have been observed in samples of
second generation Italians and Jews,[18] and a study conducted by Gill and
Spilka among Mexican-American youth indicates that in a "masculine"
culture, wife-domination has negative effects on academic achievement,
particularly for boys.[19]

These findings suggest that parent-youth and conjugal relations jointly
affect adolescent achievement. Accordingly, my second hypothesis is
that *high educational attainment is most prevalent among persons who
report democratic relations with their parents and equalitarian relations
between mother and father.* In his study of second-generation Italian
and Jewish boys in the Boston area, Strodtbeck found that those who
experienced democratic relations with their parents and reported equality

[15] Bernard C. Rosen, "Socialization and Achievement Motivation in Brazil,"
American Sociological Review, 27 (October 1962), pp. 623-624.

[16] Elder, *Adolescent Achievement and Mobility Aspirations, op. cit.*

[17] Donald G. McKinley, "Class, Resulting Family Structure, and the Socialized Child," a paper read at the American Sociological Association meetings,
Washington, D.C., September 1962.

[18] Strodtbeck, *op. cit.*

[19] Lois J. Gill and Bernard Spilka, "Some Non-intellectual Correlates of
Academic Achievement Among Mexican-American Secondary School Students,"
Journal of Educational Psychology, 53 (June 1962), pp. 144-149.

between parents were most likely to value independent mastery and achievement.[20] Variation in this relationship by sex is difficult to predict because most research has been conducted with boys, but both achievement pressures and educational opportunities are less commonly experienced by girls. Given educational opportunities and encouraged to take advantage of them, girls' achievement should be similarly affected by the same family structural patterns.

Power variations in the parent-child relationship should have a greater effect on adolescent achievement than role variations in the marital relationship. In a study of high school students, the joint effects of structural variations in parental and conjugal relations on academic motivation were assessed in an analysis of variance (with social class and sex controlled), and in three or four subgroups, variations in parent-youth relations accounted for substantially more of the variation in the desire to achieve.[21] The third hypothesis, then, is that *parent-youth relations have a greater effect on educational attainment than conjugal role patterns.*

Responses to the question, "How far did you get with your education?" ranged from no education to various types of higher education. For the present analysis, high educational attainment is defined as having reached secondary school. (Note that this does not necessarily imply *completion* of secondary school.) For Italian respondents, junior was distinguished from senior high school; I used the percentage reaching junior high school as the index of achievement, so that the percentage of Italian respondents reaching secondary school is slightly inflated. The proportion who reached 12 years of education was used as the index in the U.S., since it seems to be comparable to reaching secondary school in the other four nations.

Opportunities for secondary education vary substantially among the five countries in this study, and this variation is most notable among girls. In West Germany and Great Britain the percentages of 15-19 year olds enrolled in secondary school were 18.2 and 16.8, respectively, and slightly less than half of all students were girls.[22] In the U.S., the rate of secondary enrollment is about 90 per cent. In contrast, 7.8 per cent of the Italian 15-19 year olds were enrolled in secondary school, and less than

[20] Strodtbeck, *op. cit.* See also Elder, *Adolescent Achievement and Mobility Aspirations, op. cit.*

[21] Elder, *Adolescent Achievement and Mobility Aspirations, op. cit.*

[22] Statistics for Germany, Italy and Great Britain refer approximately to 1955 and were obtained from J. Frederick Dewhurst, *et al., Europe's Needs and Resources: Trends and Sources of Eighteen Centuries,* New York: Twentieth Century Fund, 1961, pp. 315-317. Statistics for Mexico and the U.S. were obtained from UNESCO *World Survey of Education, III: Secondary Education,* New York: International Documents Service, 1961, pp. 829 (Mexico) and 1380 (U.S.). Enrollment ratios were obtained from *ibid.,* pp. 580 (West Germany), 730 (Italy), 1171-1179 (Great Britain), 829 (Mexico), and 1380 (U.S.).

40 per cent of these students were girls. Secondary enrollment in Mexico was well below the Italian rate, and less than 33 per cent of the students were girls. Thus, the opportunity for secondary education is currently available to relatively few Mexican and Italian youth, though it was available to even fewer in the 1920's, 30's and 40's. Between 1950 and 1960, the secondary enrollment rate in Mexico doubled, yet less than 10 per cent of youth 15-19 years old are currently enrolled in secondary school.

These cross-national variations do not seriously limit the present analysis, since relations between the variables *within* each nation are of primary interest, not comparisons of single indicators across nations.[23] Of course, the strength of these relationships will itself vary with differences in the structure of education, and as a partial control for within-nation variations in educational opportunities, I have used socio-economic status and size of birthplace. Educational opportunities tend to be more available to urban and middle-class youth; rural residence, in particular, is a relatively accurate index of low educational opportunity.[24]

The influence of educational opportunity on educational attainment is illustrated in the recently completed Robbins Report on Higher Education in Great Britain. A multiple regression analysis indicated that persistence in school and entrance to institutions of higher education were most influenced by local opportunities to attend grammar school and parents' education. Persistence in school was measured by the number of the 17-year-olds at school in January, 1960 as a percentage of 13-year-olds at school in January, 1956 in each Local Education Authority. Zero-order correlation coefficients between this index and percentage in grammar school, father's education, and father's occupation were .82, .66 and .65, respectively. The degree of inequality of educational opportunity across the 145 Local Education Authorities in England and Wales is shown by the range in school persistence rates — 27.9 to 2.5.[25]

[23] Variations in the *quality* of secondary schools do present a serious problem, and it cannot be wholly remedied or controlled with the data at hand. Since a vast majority of persons in each nation attended a public primary school, over four-fifths of those who said they reached secondary school were probably referring to a public school, but qualitative variations among public schools are often as substantial as differences between public and private schools. In Italy, for instance, the difference between classical secondary schools and vocational schools, both public, is as great as the difference between high school and college in the U.S. Secondary schools in the U.S., however, are homogenous enough to permit a test of the effects of family structure on a level of educational attainment relatively free of these qualitative variations.

[24] Glen H. Elder, Jr., "Achievement Orientations and Career Patterns of Rural Youth," *Sociology of Education*, 37 (Fall 1963), pp. 30-58.

[25] Lord Robbins' Committee on Higher Education, *Higher Education: The Demand for Places in Higher Education*, London: Her Majesty's Stationery Office, 1963, App. 1, Sec. 3.

Value-orientations also influence the relation between family structure and educational attainment. American studies have found that individual-istic, competitive achievement is valued highly by urban, middle-class, and Protestant or Jewish families.[26] Familism, acceptance of social po-sition, and a belief that events affecting oneself are externally determined tend to be more prevalent among rural, working-class, and Catholic families. Parental dominance also tends to be more common in the latter categories, and evidence in several countries indicates that the educational attainment of youth from these families is relatively low. In the present analysis, place of birth, religious affiliation, and social class will be used as indicators of cultural orientation.[27]

RESULTS[28]

Birthplace, Parent-Youth Relations, and Educational Attain-ment. Educational attainment in part reflects the availability of schooling and in part, the motivational and intellectual capacities of the child. Since

[26] For social class and religious variations, see Gerhard Lenski, *The Religious Factor*, New York: Doubleday, 1961; and Herbert J. Gans, *The Urban Villagers*, New York: The Free Press of Glencoe, 1962. For rural-urban differences, see Elder, "Achievement Orientations and Career Patterns of Rural Youth," *op. cit.*

[27] Present religious affiliation was used as a substitute for childhood religious affiliation, and in lieu of a measure of childhood social class, the interviewer's four-point rating of adult social class is used. (Information on occupation was not available for all respondents.) A rating of 1 or 2 was defined as middle class, 3 was defined as working class and 4 indicated lower class. Interviewers were instructed to classify each respondent according to his economic status in the community or area in which he resides. The most commonly used criteria for this classification were housing, occupation, family status and size, income, and comforts and luxuries. To standardize the proportions of respondents rated 1, 2, 3, and 4 in each area, 1's and 2's were to equal the top 16 per cent of the community, the 3's the middle 52 per cent and the 4's the bottom 32 per cent.

[28] In appraising the significance of these findings, it is essential to consider the technique used to measure family structure. The two-item index of parent-youth relations (see note 13) is based on the interviewee's recall of perceived relations in his family when he was 16 years old. Since error due to lapses in memory is probably in part a function of age, age as well as sex is controlled throughout this analysis. The size of errors due to recall and perception is un-known but the direction of bias seems unlikely to favor the hypotheses as stated. On the value of using perceived parental behavior, see David P. Ausubel, *et al.*, "Perceived Parent Attitudes as Determinants of Children's Ego Struc-ture," *Child Development*, 25 (September 1954), pp. 173-182. For an attempt to compare various techniques used to measure family structures, see Robert D. Hess and Judith V. Torney, "A Comparison of Methods Used to Measure Family Power Structure," a paper read at the Biennial Meeting of the Society for Research in Child Development, University of California, Berkeley, April, 1963.
Percentage differences are used throughout the analysis to indicate the size, direction and consistency of the relation between parent-youth patterns and the percentage reaching secondary school. To estimate the main effects of each of

both the quality and availability of educational facilities differ substantially between rural and urban areas, the relation of parental dominance to achievement is evaluated with place of birth controlled. Places of birth defined as "rural" include communities of 5,000 population or less, and urban birthplaces include all larger communities. (Exceptions to this classification will be noted.) The most meaningful and practical age groups included persons 18 to 40 years of age in one and those older in the other. With larger samples at least three age groups would have been preferable to control for extraneous variations in memory and educational opportunity. As it is, the dichotomy employed leaves enough cases to analyze within each age group and also controls adequately for the extraneous effects.

Parental dominance is inversely related to the likelihood of reaching secondary school in each of the five countries, with age, sex, and birthplace controlled (see Table 1). Of the 36 possible comparisons, 33 are in the predicted direction. The degree of association between parent-youth relations and education is quite similar in each of the five nations: average percentage differences range from 13 per cent for Great Britain to 19 per cent for Italy.

The effects of parental dominance tend to be most pronounced among the urban-born in every nation except the U.S. Although these differences are frequently neither large nor entirely consistent, the data generally conform to other data showing that educational opportunities are much more favorable in urban places.[29] Not only do rural residents in each of the five nations have less access to primary and secondary education, but, typically the education they receive is lower in quality. Table 1 shows that entrance to secondary school is more common among the urban-born, especially in Mexico. Very few rural-born Mexicans, male or female, have reached secondary school. Yet even under these conditions parent-youth relations have some effect on educational attainment. The fact that the effect of parent-youth relations is markedly stronger among urban-born Mexicans indicates that in a favorable social and educational context a motivating family environment substantially encourages social advancement.

---

the independent variables I shall use a multivariate technique permitting the use of categorical independent and dependent variables such as religion and education in a regression analysis. For a description of this technique, see Alan B. Wilson, "Analysis of Multiple Cross-Classifications in Cross-Sectional Designs," revision of a paper presented to the American Association for Public Opinion Research, Excelsior Springs, Missouri, May 1964. See also J. W. Morgan, et al., *Income and Welfare in the United States,* New York: McGraw-Hill, 1962, Appendix E.

[29] UNESCO, *Rural Education,* Vol. 14, No. 3, 1962.

TABLE 1. PERCENTAGE WHO REACHED SECONDARY SCHOOL,
BY AGE, SEX, PARENT-YOUTH RELATIONS, AND
PLACE OF BIRTH

Place of Birth	Type of Parent-Youth Relations	Men 18–40	Men 41+	Women 18–40	Women 41+
United States					
Rural	Authoritarian	46 (26)	22 (75)	58 (24)	26 (92)
	Democratic	66 (41)	39 (48)	67 (49)	49 (74)
Urban	Authoritarian	82 (22)	44 (39)	60 (35)	41 (39)
	Democratic	88 (69)	42 (43)	77 (58)	51 (47)
Great Britain					
Rural	Authoritarian	*	19 (32)	*	16 (31)
	Democratic	48 (29)	32 (20)	48 (23)	15 (41)
Urban	Authoritarian	50 (58)	31 (82)	41 (59)	22 (101)
	Democratic	60 (102)	48 (91)	57 (112)	30 (91)
West Germany					
Rural	Authoritarian	11 (35)	10 (71)	2 (40)	2 (88)
	Democratic	27 (37)	19 (32)	20 (36)	9 (23)
Urban	Authoritarian	24 (45)	15 (59)	10 (59)	11 (70)
	Democratic	47 (60)	33 (43)	32 (53)	25 (52)
Italy					
Rural	Authoritarian	38 (48)	20 (45)	22 (49)	3 (60)
	Democratic	51 (39)	38 (37)	50 (32)	17 (30)
Urban	Authoritarian	54 (61)	22 (58)	28 (60)	26 (58)
	Democratic	60 (50)	58 (26)	60 (40)	29 (24)
Mexico					
Rural	Authoritarian	11 (45)	4 (45)	9 (127)	5 (82)
	Democratic	*	12 (34)	12 (25)	*
Urban	Authoritarian	19 (126)	7 (58)	20 (217)	8 (118)
	Democratic	63 (57)	42 (33)	31 (93)	8 (40)

*Fewer than 20 cases.

The combined influence of age, sex, birthplace and parent-youth relations is best revealed by comparing the educational attainment of persons with the most and least favorable characteristics, i.e., compare young democratically-reared, urban-born men with older authoritarian-reared, rural-born women, in Table 1. Percentages reaching secondary school are: U.S. 88 vs. 26 per cent; Great Britain, 60 vs. 16 per cent; Italy, 60 vs. 3 per cent; and Mexico, 63 vs. 5 per cent.

Social Class, Birthplace, Parent-Youth Relations, and Educational Attainment. Substituting adult social class for childhood social class involves several assumptions. Youth who experience democratic relations with parents as well as achievement training are likely to be achievement-oriented, and therefore are apt to be upwardly mobile. Youth who are dominated are likely to be non-mobile or downwardly mobile. Thus, lower- and working-class youth who experience achievement training in childhood and adolescence should be more apt to move into the middle class than youth of comparable status who are dominated. According to this reasoning, the relation between parent-child relations and education should be weakest among lower-class adults, slightly stronger among working-class adults, and strongest among middle-class adults, in part because of the assumed relation between dominance and vertical mobility, and in part because educational opportunities improve as one ascends the class hierarchy.

These expectations are generally confirmed. The relation between parental control and educational attainment is generally stronger in the middle than in the working class. No consistent relationships were observed in the lower class because only an extremely small proportion reached secondary school, and in the Mexican sample the number of Mexicans rated middle-class was too small to permit analysis. Among working-class persons in all five nations, dominance appears to have had pronounced effects on educational achievement.

The West German sample contained enough respondents at all class levels to permit analysis with age controlled, and these data are shown in Table 2. Percentage differences are substantially larger among middle-class than among working-class Germans: 53 vs. 13 percentage points for the younger age group and 20 vs. 12 percentage points for the older age group. The effects of parent-youth patterns are essentially the same for both sexes.

TABLE 2. PERCENTAGE OF WEST GERMANS WHO REACHED SECONDARY SCHOOL, BY TYPE OF PARENT-YOUTH RELATIONS, AGE, AND SOCIAL CLASS

Social Class (as rated by the interviewer)	Type of Parent-Youth Relations	Ages 18–40	Ages 41 and Over
Middle	Authoritarian	33 (21)	35 (40)
	Democratic	86 (35)	55 (33)
Working	Authoritarian	11 (130)	6 (172)
	Democratic	24 (127)	18 (96)
Lower	Authoritarian	3 (38)	1 (76)
	Democratic	4 (24)	0 (21)

Analysis of the relation between parental dominance and achievement, with birthplace and social class controlled, is restricted to the U.S., Great Britain, and West Germany, due to the paucity of middle-class Mexican and Italian respondents (Table 3). The index of parent-youth relations is related to educational attainment in the expected direction in all but one of the 18 subgroups. As in Table 2, the relationship is generally stronger in the working class and particularly in the middle class than it is in the lower class. Among rural-born, lower-class adults, the effects of authority patterns tend to be weakest and the likelihood of reaching secondary school least.

Extremes in both support and opportunity for education occur in

TABLE 3. PERCENTAGE WHO REACHED SECONDARY
SCHOOL, BY TYPE OF PARENT-YOUTH RELATIONS,
BIRTHPLACE,[a] AND SOCIAL CLASS

Type of Parent-Youth Relations	Rural			Urban		
	Middle Class	Working Class	Lower Class	Middle Class	Working Class	Lower Class
United States						
Authoritarian	54 (35)	31 (130)	27 (48)	77 (30)	54 (86)	16 (19)
Democratic	72 (39)	55 (143)	32 (28)	88 (57)	65 (143)	31 (16)
Great Britain						
Authoritarian	35 (23)	30 (61)	12 (58)	57 (70)	34 (83)	20 (93)
Democratic	62 (39)	39 (70)	19 (64)	72 (147)	39 (99)	28 (89)
West Germany						
Authoritarian	29 (35)	2 (142)	0 (67)	42 (26)	14 (160)	2 (47)
Democratic	67 (15)	16 (92)	0 (21)	72 (53)	25 (130)	4 (24)

[a]In Great Britain, birthplace communities of 20,000 or less are defined as rural to provide enough cases for analysis; in the U.S. and West Germany birthplaces of 5,000 or less are defined as rural.

rural lower-class and urban middle-class environments. This contrast is most evident in the Italian and Mexican samples. Almost none of the rural-born lower-class Italians and Mexicans reached secondary school, compared with over half the Italians and over one-third of the middle-class Mexicans who were born in communities larger than 5,000 in population. In addition to low educational opportunity, data reviewed above show that authoritarian parent-child relations are also more prevalent in rural, lower-class environments, and least common among urban middle-class families. The fact that lack of educational opportunity and parental dominance both characterize rural lower-class environments constitutes an imposing problem for the development of human resources.

Another negative factor in these rural areas is the prevalence of *countervailing conditions* that thwart the development of abilities and achievement motivation. The early induction of children into the farm labor market is one such factor, and frequent absence from school is one consequence of the intensive use of child labor.[30] In the U.S., child labor means absence from school most prominently among children in migrant farm families.

Relation between Parent-Youth Patterns and Educational Attainment in Protestant and Catholic Families. Analysis of the effect of religious affiliation on the relation between parental dominance and

[30] In Sicily, "there are children of eight or ten years old who are already working as laborers when they should be at school." Danilo Dolci, *Waste* (trans. R. Munroe), London: MacGibbon and Kee, 1963, p. 179. On child labor standards and school attendance laws pertaining to rural youth in the U.S.; see William E. Amos, *Child Labor Standards and School Attendance Laws as They Relate to Rural Youth*. Paper prepared for the National Conference of Rural Youth in a Changing Environment, September 1963.

educational achievement is possible only for the U.S. and West German samples. Parental dominance is negatively related to educational attainment among Americans and Germans of both Protestant and Catholic faiths (Table 4). The largest percentage difference occurs among urban-born Protestants in both nations, and the effects of parental dominance are stronger among Protestants than among Catholics, especially in West Germany. The relation between religion and educational achievement in the five nations is extremely complex, and a critical assessment is well beyond the resources of this study. The influence of religious beliefs on educational and occupational achievement should be examined in relation to particular sociocultural and economic environments.[31] In West Germany, for instance, Catholic and Protestant religious affiliation is not associated with ethnicity nor with attendance at private religious schools, as it is in the U.S.

TABLE 4. PERCENTAGE WHO REACHED SECONDARY SCHOOL
BY AGE, BIRTHPLACE, RELIGIOUS AFFILIATION AND
PARENT-YOUTH RELATIONS

Age	Type of Parent-Youth Relations	Birthplace and Religious Affiliation			
		Rural		Urban	
		Protestant	Catholic	Protestant	Catholic
United States					
18—40	Authoritarian	41 (34)	*	65 (31)	67 (18)
	Democratic	71 (75)	*	82 (67)	83 (40)
41+	Authoritarian	27 (132)	14 (28)	36 (36)	29 (27)
	Democratic	48 (105)	*	45 (53)	37 (26)
West Germany					
18—40	Authoritarian	8 (38)	7 (43)	17 (60)	15 (40)
	Democratic	23 (40)	21 (30)	46 (63)	30 (43)
41+	Authoritarian	8 (71)	2 (83)	13 (69)	17 (46)
	Democratic	16 (30)	14 (22)	37 (57)	13 (30)

*Fewer than 20 cases.

In his *The Protestant Ethic and the Spirit of Capitalism*, Max Weber characterized the Protestant personality type as individualistic, inclined to assume responsibility for personal deeds, ascetic in the use of time and money, and committed to productive work as the highest calling in life.[32] McClelland suggests that the Protestant personality may have resulted

[31] Seymour M. Lipset, "The Study of Jewish Communities in a Comparative Context," *The Jewish Journal of Sociology*, 5 (December 1963), pp. 157-166.
[32] Max Weber, *The Protestant Ethic and the Spirit of Capitalism* (1904), trans. by Talcott Parsons, New York: Scribner, 1958. Weber's hypothesized relation between the Protestant ethic and the rise of capitalism is demolished by Kurt Samuelson in *Religion and Economic Action*, New York: Basic Books, 1961.

from changes in child-rearing practices and in family structure which, in turn, could plausibly be considered an outcome of the Protestant Reformation.[33] According to McClelland, the Protestant Reformation could have produced a family environment highly conducive to the development of achievement motivation. "It stressed perfection (high standards of excellence) in every detail of performing one's duty in the world, tending to be anti-authoritarian at least in its initial impulse."[34] More recently, such differences between Catholics and Protestants as the value Catholics attach to familial over other relationships, their stress on obedience, their anti-intellectualism, and their opposition to physical monism have been used to explain the presumed "disaffection" of American Catholics with the scientific movement.[35] Social class and ethnic variations account in part for these differences, which have been attributed to religious affiliation.[36]

In the present data, German Catholics were less likely than Protestants to have reached secondary school (16 vs. 25 per cent), but no difference appeared in the American sample. When place and region of birth, adult social class, and family structure simultaneously controlled, however, American Catholic men ages 18-40 were somewhat more likely to have reached secondary school than their Protestant counterparts (see Table 7). No difference was found for German men on the same age group.

Religious differences in educational and occupational achievement in the U.S. clearly favored Protestants for generations born before 1940, but third- and fourth-generation Catholics have evidently achieved a status equal to that of Protestant youth (at least on a quantitative basis).[37] In a recent study of over 30,000 American college seniors, Greeley found little or no statistical difference between Protestant and Catholics in career interests and educational plans.[38] In Germany, on the other hand, propor-

[33] McClelland, *The Achieving Society, op. cit.*, Ch. 2.

[34] *Ibid.*, p. 357. In the absence of firm empirical evidence, however, it is equally probable that Lutheran families in Germany were more authoritarian than families remaining within the Catholic fold.

[35] See R. H. Knapp and H. B. Goodrich, *Origins of American Scientists*, Chicago: University of Chicago Press, 1959, and *The Younger American Scholar*, Chicago: University of Chicago Press, 1953; Lenski, *op. cit.*; and for a self-critic's view, see Thomas F. O'Dea, *American Catholic Dilemma*, New York: Sheed and Ward, 1958.

[36] Andrew M. Greeley, *Religion and Career*, New York: Sheed and Ward, 1963.

[37] *Ibid.* Catholic adults with parochial education do not seem to differ from Catholics with a non-parochial education in economic values and on indices of achievement; see Marvin Bressler and Charles F. Westoff, "Catholic Education, Economic Values, and Achievement," *American Journal of Sociology*, 69 (November, 1963), pp. 225-233.

[38] Greeley, *op. cit.*

tionally larger numbers of Protestants than Catholics enter schools more
advanced than the *Volkschule*, in both blue- and white-collar classes.[39]
If these latter data are accurate indicators of Protestant-Catholic differences in educational achievement, it appears that American Catholics have
gradually adopted the achievement ethic. A thorough exploration of the
relation between religion and educational achievement in the two nations,
however, requires a carefully controlled comparative study of American
and German families.

　　　　*Conjugal Relations, Parental Authority and Educational At-
tainment.* Since most relevant studies have found that equalitarian conjugal relations are associated with high occupational achievement among
boys, I hypothesized that adults who report democratic relations with
their parents *and* equalitarian relations between parents during adolescence are most likely to have reached secondary school. To assess conjugal decision making patterns, answers to the following question were
used: "We're interested in how decisions were made in your family when
you were a child, let's say when you were 16. Here's a list of ways of
making family decisions. By and large, how were decisions made in your
family?" Response categories were: "By and large, father made the decisions"; "By and large, mother made the decisions"; "Both parents acted
together"; and "Each parent acted individually." (If mother and father
were not present, the response was coded "other.") Since responses other
than father-dominance and the equalitarian pattern were too few to
permit analysis, these cases have been excluded, leaving four possible variations in perceived family structure: families are father-dominated or
equalitarian and parent-youth relations may be recalled as either authoritarian or democratic.[40] [See Table 5.] To distinguish the effects of family
structure, birthplace is held constant.

　　In all nations except Italy, adults who report equalitarian relations between their parents and democratic parent-youth relations are indeed most
likely to have reached secondary school. And in all five nations the likelihood of reaching secondary school is consistently low among persons
with authoritarian parents regardless of the pattern of decision making
between mother and father. The index of parent-youth relations is more

---

[39] McClelland, *op. cit.*, Ch. 8.

[40] The relative prevalence of each type of conjugal pattern in each nation is
difficult to determine because the proportion of respondents who gave "other"
and "don't know" responses varies. Among respondents who are 18-40 years old,
the percentages indicating a husband-dominant pattern in the U.S., Great
Britain, West Germany, Italy and Mexico are, for men: 23, 24, 42, and 26;
and for women: 14, 19, 26, 33, and 22. On wife dominance, the percentage
reporting wife-dominance are, for men: 11, 15, 12, 16, and 6; and for women:
11, 18, 19, 21, and ·11. The percentage giving the equalitarian response is
around 50 in each sample.

TABLE 5. PERCENTAGE WHO REACHED SECONDARY SCHOOL BY BIRTHPLACE AND FAMILY STRUCTURE

Type of Parent-Youth Relations	Rural Conjugal Pattern		Urban Conjugal Pattern	
	Husband Decides	Both Decide	Husband Decides	Both Decide
United States				
Authoritarian	34 (77)	29 (91)	50 (38)	61 (43)
Democratic	55 (39)	59 (117)	60 (32)	76 (111)
Great Britain				
Authoritarian	28 (36)	25 (67)	36 (54)	40 (75)
Democratic	33 (24)	38 (106)	47 (62)	53 (169)
West Germany				
Authoritarian	8 (73)	5 (135)	19 (83)	14 (108)
Democratic	11 (38)	26 (68)	26 (57)	44 (106)
Italy				
Authoritarian	18 (88)	26 (72)	32 (111)	29 (78)
Democratic	47 (62)	37 (53)	58 (45)	53 (63)
Mexico				
Authoritarian	5 (79)	7 (132)	13 (137)	12 (243)
Democratic	4 (27)	14 (35)	32 (54)	39 (132)

strongly and consistently related to educational attainment than the two conjugal patterns; of 20 possible comparisons between authority patterns, 19 show percentage differences in the expected direction. The only relatively consistent effects of conjugal relations appear among democratically-reared persons, with the percentage reaching secondary school tending to be largest among persons reporting equalitarian relations between parents. The weak effects of the conjugal pattern may reflect various flaws in the data; it is also reasonable to suppose that in fact conjugal relations have relatively little effect independently of parent-child relations. Recent American research suggests, however, that "either wife-dominance in the family or autocratic parental control in child-rearing, or both in combination, are relatively unlikely to promote high educational aspirations among boys."[41]

As noted, family structure has a different effect on the probability of reaching secondary school among Italians. Among both rural and urban respondents, those who describe their fathers as dominant in conjugal relations, and report democratic relations with their parents, are most likely to have reached secondary school. A similar reversal occurred among Mexican men. This slight reversal may be due in part to a cultural pattern of male dominance in which submission of husband to wife is considered evidence of weakness. From his intensive study of five Mexican families, Oscar Lewis concludes ". . . that in the strongly male-oriented Mexican

[41] Charles E. Bowerman and Glen H. Elder, Jr., "Variations in Adolescent Perception of Family Power Structure," American Sociological Review, 29 (August 1964), pp. 551-567.

culture, only men who are aging, impotent, homosexual, or "bewitched" are unable to carry out the authoritarian role of the husband."[42]

Parental Dominance and Tendency to Yield to Adolescent Requests. The present index of parent-youth relations refers to the extent to which the parents permitted involvement in decision-making during adolescence. The psychological significance of exclusion from decision-making probably depends on the extent to which it is coupled with rejection of complaints, requests, and suggestions.[43] If no consideration is given to the adolescent's desires, he is left with only two alternatives, blind submission to parental authority or rebellion.

Parental willingness to yield at times to adolescent requests and complaints was measured by answers to the following question: "If you complained, did it make any difference in your parent's decision?" This is an indicator of parental resistance to adolescent requests, whereas the two-item index of parent-youth relations measured the opportunity to exercise self-reliance in decision-making. In the case of authoritarian parent-youth relations, for instance, lack of decision-making opportunity coupled with strong parental resistance defines a markedly different type of relationship than one in which lack of opportunity is softened by parental receptivity and consideration of adolescent requests and complaints. Coercive authoritarian best describes the former relationship, while the latter seems to indicate a benevolent autocracy.

Table 6 shows that in the three nations for which the sample was large enough to permit analysis, the likelihood of reaching secondary school is greater among persons who described their parents as democratic and yielding. Authoritarian-reared persons in each nation who indicate that their parents yielded at times to their requests are more likely to have reached secondary school than those who describe their parents as unyielding. Parental yielding to adolescent requests is also associated with a higher likelihood of achievement among democratically-reared youth. Note, however, that relatively few authoritarian-reared persons described their parents as yielding.

Family Structure and Educational Attainment: A Summary Assessment. The analysis up to this point has indicated that the relation between family structure and educational attainment depends heavily

[42] Oscar Lewis, *Five Families,* New York: Basic Books, 1959, p. 17. See also William Madsen, *The Mexican-Americans of South Texas,* New York: Holt, Rinehart & Winston, 1964.

[43] In a recent study, adolescents with autocratic parents who explained rules were more apt to submit and to depend on parental guidance than were those with autocratic parents who did not provide explanations. The latter showed a greater tendency to make their own decisions even though they lacked confidence in their ability to do so. Glen H. Elder, Jr., "Parental Power Legitimation and Its Effects on the Adolescent," *Sociometry,* 26 (March 1963), pp. 50-65.

Family Structure and Educational Attainment   111

TABLE 6. PERCENTAGE WHO REACHED SECONDARY SCHOOL,
BY TYPE OF PARENT-YOUTH RELATIONS, PARENTAL
RESPONSE TO REQUESTS, SEX, AND BIRTHPLACE

	Birthplace	Type of Parent-Youth Relations	Parents Yielded at Times to Adolescent Requests	Parents Did Not Yield to Adolescent Requests
United States				
Men	Rural	Authoritarian	35 (29)	26 (73)
		Democratic	53 (68)	46 (22)
	Urban	Authoritarian	71 (24)	49 (37)
		Democratic	72 (95)	*
Women	Rural	Authoritarian	48 (29)	28 (87)
		Democratic	62 (98)	40 (25)
	Urban	Authoritarian	58 (26)	46 (48)
		Democratic	63 (87)	*
Great Britain				
Men	Rural	Authoritarian	*	19 (52)
		Democratic	45 (65)	*
	Urban	Authoritarian	42 (52)	41 (64)
		Democratic	60 (131)	40 (30)
Women	Rural	Authoritarian	20 (25)	21 (48)
		Democratic	32 (69)	29 (24)
	Urban	Authoritarian	39 (41)	26 (89)
	Democratic	46 (47)	44 (27)
West Germany				
Men	Rural	Authoritarian	13 (39)	9 (67)
		Democratic	23 (62)	*
	Urban	Authoritarian	23 (40)	18 (63)
		Democratic	31 (96)	*
Women	Rural	Authoritarian	2 (41)	1 (97)
		Democratic	15 (53)	*
	Urban	Authoritarian	12 (57)	8 (72)
		Democratic	28 (90)	*

*Fewer than 20 cases.

on educational opportunity and values. Among rural-born Mexicans and Italians, for instance, educational achievement is extremely low and conjugal and parent-youth relations have very little effect on achievement.

A summary assessment of the effects of conjugal and parent-youth relations, with all test factors simultaneously controlled, would be helpful at this point, but limited sample sizes seriously restrict the number of variables that can be simultaneously controlled in tabular cross-classifications. To surmount this limitation, a multiple regression analysis with dummy variables was used (see footnote 28). This procedure permits simultaneous control of all test factors by statistically adjusting subclass percentages for the effects of all other variables together. No assumptions concerning the linearity of the effects of each factor are required, but the technique does have the sizable disadvantage, for our purposes, of ignoring interaction and estimating only the main effects. For example, this procedure assumes that the effects of parent-youth relations are the same for each size of birthplace, though the data previously shown clearly indicate that this assumption is false. Nevertheless, an overview of the main effects of perceived family structure with residence, social class, and religion controlled is valuable at this point. Table 7 shows the adjusted percentages derived from this analysis for American and West German men ages 18 through 40. (Region of birth was included in the analysis because some regions, such as the American South, offer less educational opportunity.) Variations in the percentage reaching secondary school are generally small for all variables except adult social class, which is obviously closely related to educational attainment.

Conjugal patterns do not affect educational attainment appreciably, particularly in the U.S. sample. In the German sample, men from equalitarian homes are more apt to reach secondary school than are men from husband-dominant homes, while those who report mother-dominance are least likely to have reached secondary school. This finding corresponds to research findings reported earlier, but results from the U.S. sample tend to run in the opposite direction. In either case, however, the number of respondents reporting wife-dominance is simply too small to obtain reliable estimates of variation. Parent-youth relations have considerably more influence on achievement in both samples, but the percentage differences are relatively small.

Social class and size and region of birthplace reflect both educational opportunity and the value attached to education; thus, their effects on achievement are naturally greater than those of the index of parent-youth relations. Religious affiliation, however, has very little effect on achievement in the West German sample. American Catholics, on the other hand, are slightly more likely to have reached secondary school than Protestants; the difference is larger and in the same direction as the one shown in Table 4 for younger respondents. Even with social class and region controlled, educational attainment varies markedly by size of birthplace; conditions relevant to educational achievement are strongly linked to community size, even in highly industrialized nations.

The principal conclusion to be drawn, then, is that the independent influence of culture and the opportunity-structure on educational attainment exceeds that of perceived family structure among younger American and West German men. This result suggests feasible strategies in the development of human resources.

PARENT-YOUTH RELATIONS AND ECONOMIC DEVELOPMENT

When educational opportunities are available, as in the urban U.S., development of motivation and ability to achieve in school is reduced by parental domination. This pattern occurs in each of the five nations considered.

Comparison of the oldest and youngest persons in each of the five samples — those who were 16 before 1916 and between 1950-57 —

Family Structure and Educational Attainment 113

TABLE 7. PERCEIVED FAMILY STRUCTURE AND PERCENTAGE
WHO REACHED SECONDARY SCHOOL, WITH PLACE AND
REGION OF BIRTH, SOCIAL CLASS AND RELIGION
CONTROLLED: ADJUSTED PERCENTAGE FOR SUB-CLASSES
IN A MULTIPLE CLASSIFICATION ANALYSIS[a]

Categorical Variables	U.S. Men Ages 18–40		West German Men Ages 18–40	
	N	Adjusted Percentage	N	Adjusted Percentage
1. Family Structure				
A. Conjugal Role Pattern				
1. Father dominant	37	72.2	46	27.8
2. Mother dominant	19	76.9	23	13.4
3. Equalitarian	80	73.4	103	32.5
B. Parent-Youth Relations				
1. Authoritarian	47	65.6	80	23.7
2. Democratic	107	77.7	97	34.0
2. Educational Opportunity and Values				
A. Region of Birth				
1. United States				
East	51	78.9		
Central	59	71.6		
South	37	63.4		
West	9	*		
2. West Germany				
Schleswig-Holstein			24	32.2
N. Rhine Westphalia			56	16.9
Hesse			38	23.1
Bavaria			22	31.6
B. Place of Birth				
1. Less than 5,000	69	62.8	78	15.8
2. 5,000 to 100,000	52	78.1	55	36.1
3. 100,000 and over	42	78.8	57	33.9
C. Adult Social Class				
1. Middle	32	86.0	33	64.9
2. Working	112	74.8	129	24.4
3. Lower	19	30.4	29	0.0
D. Religion				
1. Protestant	104	68.5	100	27.7
2. Catholic	37	75.2	83	26.5
	Total N[b]	Grand Percentage	Total N[b]	Grand Percentage
	168	71.8	191	27.2

*Fewer than 10 cases. In this table adjusted percentages for two sub-classes are based on 19 cases each, despite the 20-case rule applied in all preceding tables except Table 3.

[a]The rank of each of the six variables was not computed because primary interest was in examining the effects of the two family-structure indices with the four test factors simultaneously controlled.

[b]Total N refers to the total number of respondents in the two subgroups. Summation of the cases in each response class of each variable will result in smaller totals due to non-response and omitted responses (e.g., Jews, under Religion).

suggests that the prevalence of parental dominance has decreased appreciably over the last 50 years.[44] The decline is very pronounced in the U.S., Great Britain, and in West Germany, less marked in Italy, and negligible in Mexico. These trends are consistent with the historical patterns of social and economic change during this period in each nation and there is little evidence that these trends are a result of age variations rather than an indication of changing parental authority patterns. For instance, a comparison of these two age groups among Italians shows a much larger change among those who were born in the North. Very little change was evident among Southern-born Italians, which reflects the slower rate of social and economic change generally in the South.[45] Decline in cultural support for parental dominance in the U.S., Great Britain, West Germany, and Northern Italy can be ascribed to increasing urbanization, technological advance, and rising levels of education. Equalitarianism between the sexes as well as between youth and parents is making inroads, even in rural Mexico, as communication, and transportation, and educational and economic opportunities improve.[46] Among persons in each sample who were 16 between 1950 and 1957, 70 per cent reported democratic patterns in the three more industrialized nations, compared with 31 per cent in Mexico and 48 per cent in Italy.

Parental domination is but one factor determining achievement; educational and vocational opportunities, as well as the expectations of significant others outside the family, are also important. "The key to the unlocking of potential is always found in the first instance in the widening of opportunity."[47] And yet, full utilization of opportunity is also contingent on ability and motivation. To elevate educational attainment, whether among youth in the American South or among rural Italians, not only must educational facilities be improved and made more widely available, but the kind of family relations conducive to achievement, and the value attached to education relative to other goals must be encouraged as well. Many patterns are possible: in one, changes in educational and economic opportunities may alter ideology, values and aspirations, and these newly acquired orientations may, in turn, change traditional family patterns.

The introduction of schools and industries to rural areas frequently

[44] Glen H. Elder, Jr., "Sociocultural Patterns and Parent-Youth Relations," unpublished manuscript, Spring 1964. For additional evidence of change in family systems during the 20th century, see William Goode, *World Revolution and Family Patterns*, New York: The Free Press of Glencoe, 1963.

[45] See Margaret Carlyle, *The Awakening of Southern Italy*, New York: Oxford University Press, 1962.

[46] See Goode, *op. cit.*, and Lewis, *Five Families, op. cit.*

[47] Eli Ginzberg, *The Negro Potential*, New York: Columbia University Press, 1956, p. 12.

initiates a whole series of improvements in the development of human potential.[48] The influx of technicians and managerial personnel, and their families, adds a more educated element and a source of potential leadership to the community. As non-agrarian employment opportunities increase, schooling is apt to acquire greater relevance and importance in the minds of youth and their parents. More and better education may develop a tradition of going to school and, ultimately, ideological support for education. These and other changes resulting from social and economic development directly widen the life opportunities of youth and should eventually alter family relations, in both present and future generations, creating family environments more conducive to the development of achievement motivation and skills.

Oscar Lewis has described how education, accompanied by other aspects of modernization, generated greater interest in schooling for children, elevated aspirations, and fostered changes in child-rearing practices in the Mexican village of Tepotzlan. "Younger and more educated parents," according to Lewis, "punish more lightly, permit more play, and send their children to school for as long as possible."[49] Even where traditional family organization and values inhibit social change, educational and economic opportunities can be manipulated *directly* — a form of intervention that is seldom possible in family and other social relations.

[48] Carlyle, *op. cit.* See also Charles J. Erasmus, *Man Takes Control*, Minneapolis: University of Minnesota Press, 1961, for a description of social, cultural, and economic change in Northwest Mexico.

[49] Oscar Lewis, *Tepotzlan: Village in Mexico*, New York: Holt, Rinehart and Winston, 1962, p. 101. For an interesting account of the genesis and effects of support for formal schooling in a small Mexican barrio inhabited by Mazahua Indians, see Alicza Iwanska, "New Knowledge: The Impact of School Upon the Traditional Structure of a Mexican Village," *Sociologus*, 13 (1963), pp. 137-150. The withdrawal of children from the full-time agrarian labor force increased markedly the work burden for adults in the village, yet this burden was willingly assumed because the villagers wanted their children to be people who "know."

Marital Satisfaction and Instability:
A Cross-Cultural Class Analysis
of Divorce Rates

Because family experiences arouse so much emotion and social philosophers continue to believe that the family is a major element in the social structure, the field has for over two millennia attracted more ideologists than theorists and has been the object of much speculation but little rigorous research. Personal acquaintance with a family system has usually been confused with valid knowledge, and journalistic descriptions of the past have been the main source of information for the analysis of family changes.

The past two decades have witnessed important changes in this situation. We have come to agree that theory is not opposed to fact but is a structure of interrelated empirical propositions.[1] Good theory not only orders known facts; it also leads to new ones. In this sense, good theoretical work on the family has been rare,[2] and the younger generation of theorists does not enter the field.[3] However, we have at least come to

From *International Social Science Journal*, vol. 14, no. 3 (1962), pp. 507-526. Reprinted by permission of UNESCO and the author.

[1] See the clear statement of this position by Robert K. Merton, "The Bearing of Sociological Theory on Empirical Research," in: *Social Theory and Social Structure*, 2nd edition, Glencoe, Ill.: The Free Press, 1957, pp. 85-101.

[2] Three serious monograph attempts may be noted here: George P. Murdock, *Social Structure*, New York: Macmillan, 1949; Claude Levi-Strauss, *Les Structures Élémentaires de la Parenté*, Paris: Presses Universitaires de France, 1949; and William J. Goode, *After Divorce*, Glencoe, Ill.: The Free Press, 1956. Various reviews of the research over the past decade are now available: Robert F. Winch, "Marriage and the Family," in: Joseph B. Gittler (ed.), *Review of Sociology*, 1945-55, New York: John Wiley, 1957; Reuben Hill and Richard L. Simpson, "Marriage and Family Sociology, 1945-55," in: Hans L. Zetterberg (ed.), *Sociology in the United States*, Paris: Unesco, 1956, pp. 93-101; and Nelson Foote and Leonard S. Cottrell, *Identity and Interpersonal Competence*, Chicago: University of Chicago Press, 1955. See also William J. Goode, "Horizons in Family Theory," in: Robert K. Merton, Leonard Broom and Leonard S. Cottrell (eds.), *Sociology Today*, New York: Basic Books, 1959.

[3] Theorists of the rank of Talcott Parsons, Kingsley Davis, Robert K. Merton, and George C. Homans have all written theoretical papers on the family, however.

understand the necessity of adequate theory even in this field. In addition, anthropologists — whose work is all too often neglected by sociologists — are no longer content to report that a tribe prefers some type of cross-cousin marriage but attempt to find out how frequently such marriages occur.[4] Moreover, the ideologist who sermonizes for or against some family behaviour, such as egalitarianism for women, is no less free to pursue his taste, but we no longer believe that his value-laden expositions should be given the same respect we pay to responsible research.

These changes do not imply that we should ignore ideological writings about the family. On the contrary, they are phenomena — like political or economic changes or public attitudes about morality — that affect family behaviour, and therefore must be taken seriously without being regarded at all as scientific reports. Moreover, an ideological position may determine a man's choice of the scientific problem he investigates. Nevertheless, we must keep clearly in mind that the ideological bases from which a scientific problem is chosen are essentially irrelevant to the truth of the research findings. We are properly suspicious when the author's aim seems to be to persuade us of his ideology, rather than to demonstrate, by a precise exposition of his methods, the accuracy of his data. On the other hand, the work itself is to be judged, not the motives of the researcher. We evaluate the importance of the research by its fruitfulness, and its validity and reliability by methodological canons; if it is adequately done, it is a contribution to science even if we deplore its policy sources and implications.

Finally, it is obvious that ideological positions can sometimes point to good research problems. For example, egalitarianism is certainly one motive for investigating how culture determines sex roles.[5] In general, however, ideology is a poorer compass than good theory for discovering important facts, and is at times successful only because it may happen (in the social sciences at least) that what is at the centre of ideological debate is also a key to understanding how a social pattern operates.

In any event, we are now better able to distinguish what is from what ought to be, and even the ideologist may gradually understand that without good science, policy is inevitably misguided.

Marital Adjustment and Happiness

Salon sociologists have talked and written much about the modern "right to marital happiness," but it is not clear that spouses even in the United States really accept such a norm. Society does not seek to create the

[4] See Meyer Fortes, "Kinship and Marriage among the Ashanti," in: A. R. Radcliffe-Brown and Daryll Forde (eds.), *African Systems of Kinship and Marriage*, London: Oxford University Press, 1956, p. 282.

[5] See Margaret Mead, *Sex and Temperament*, in: *From The South Seas*, New York: Morrow, 1939.

conditions which would assure its achievement, or punish anyone who fails to make others happy. On the other hand, all societies recognize the desirability of marital contentment and the intimate misery of marital discontent. The scientific problem of studies in marital adjustment was to try to predict whether certain types of couples were more or less likely to be content in their marriages. The ideological impulse was simply, as in the field of medicine, that it would be good to advise couples beforehand not to marry if they seemed ill-suited to one another. The pragmatic basis was simply that the wisdom of elders, who have in all societies made such predictions, might be systematized, standardized, and made more precise. The first published predictive instrument in this country was developed by Jessie Bernard,[6] but at that time Burgess and Cottrell had already begun (1931) their larger study, growing out of Burgess' creation of an instrument for parole prediction. The psychologist Lewis M. Terman utilized some of their findings in a similar study, but the Burgess-Cottrell work remained the most sophisticated attempt at developing a marital prediction instrument until the Burgess-Wallin study in 1953. Locke tested its discriminative power, and various men have tried the instrument in one form or another on other populations (Chinese, Swedes, Southern Negroes).[7]

Unfortunately, this line of research seems to have come to a dead end. Widely used by marital counsellors in this country, the instrument has not improved so as to achieve greater predictive power and its power was never great. Successive studies have confirmed the relevance of only a few items: for example, most show that if the couple's parents' marriages were happy, if the couple have been acquainted for a long time, and if the engagement was long, there is greater chance for marital success; but most other items are not confirmed by various researches. Most of the variance is not accounted for by the items that have been singled out as important.[8] In short, no new, and only few corroborating, findings have emerged in recent years.

[6] "An Instrument for Measurement of Success in Marriage," *Publications of the American Sociological Society*, No. 27, 1933, pp. 94-106.

[7] The major publications noted here are Ernest W. Burgess and Leonard S. Cottrell, *Predicting Success or Failure in Marriage*, New York: Prentice-Hall, 1939; Lewis M. Terman *et al.*, *Psychological Factors in Marital Happiness*, New York: McGraw-Hill, 1939; Harvey J. Locke, *Predicting Adjustment in Marriage*, New York: Henry Holt, 1951; Ernest W. Burgess and Paul W. Wallin, *Engagement and Marriage*; and Georg Karlsson, *Adaptability and Communication in Marriage*, Uppsala, Sweden: Almqvist & Wiksells, 1951. For a convenient summary of the meaning of various parts of the instrument, see Ernest W. Burgess and Harvey J. Locke, *The Family*, 2nd edition, New York: American, 1953, Chapters 14, 15.

[8] For a summary of the main findings, see: *ibid.*, pp. 408-29, and Clifford

The Theory of Complementarity

The primary key to this sterility can be found in the picture of the contented couple which emerges from these studies: it is the conventional bourgeois couple, meeting for the first time under respectable auspices, coming from non-divorcing families, not venturing far toward intimacy during acquaintanceship, holding steady jobs, enjoying a relatively higher education, and so on. Since, to a perhaps increasing degree, modern couples do not always come from such backgrounds, the instrument cannot estimate their future success relative to one another. To a considerable extent, the instrument in its various forms merely discriminates the old-fashioned from the modern couple, but does not discriminate from within the population of modern couples those who will be more or less successful.

One line of theory has emerged which might be helpful in gauging which men and women might live in harmony with one another, after granting that "modern" couples are less prone to be happy in marriage. The "Theory of Complementarity" was developed by Robert F. Winch to explain why, within a given pool of marital eligibles (leading to homogamy), certain people fall in love with one another and marry.[9] No one, unfortunately, has attempted either to verify this theory on a substantial random population, or even to extend it to other areas of courtship and marriage.[10]

This theory, developed with considerable rigour, accepts the wide range of findings which show that couples who marry are usually of the same religion, ethnic group, occupational background, education, and so on. However, the specific attraction between socially homogamous couples[11] is the heterogamy of their basic psychological needs.[12] For example, those who need to show deference are attracted by those who wish to achieve; those who seek abasement by those who seek dominance, and so on. Whether X falls in love with Y seems a trivial enough scientific issue, but precisely because this is a theory, it has further implications, pragmatic, sociological and psychological. It suggests, for example, why some di-

---

Kirkpatrick, *What Science Says About Happiness in Marriage*, Minneapolis: Burgess Publishing Co., 1947.

[9] Robert F. Winch, *Mate Selection*, New York: Harper, 1958.

[10] Several studies claim to have tested it, but they have not used the same measures for each important factor, or an appropriate population.

[11] Burgess and Locke, *op. cit.*, p. 369, note that over one hundred studies exist to show that married couples are homogamous with respect to a wide variety of traits.

[12] Winch developed his categories from the work of Henry A. Murray, *Explorations in Personality*, New York: Oxford University Press, 1938.

vorcees continue to marry precisely the kind of spouses who will make them unhappy. It points to the structurally determined misperceptions of others in the courtship situation — the Western male should, for example, exhibit a relatively dominant personality, seeking achievement and autonomy, but the woman who is attracted to him may find later that he is quite different in his real needs. Winch himself denies that the theory applies to marital happiness,[13] but such an application seems worthwhile. Essentially, it is the pleasure that the young man and woman give to one another by the mutual satisfaction of their basic personality needs which determines their serious emotional involvement and commitment. To the extent that this need-satisfaction continues after marriage, the union should have greater stability and happiness (other things being equal). That is, if need-satisfaction continues, then so should the attraction between spouses. A further implication is that the new situational elements of marriage may be very different from those of courtship, and thus frustrate (or perhaps enhance) the satisfaction of each other's needs. In addition, it is of psychological importance to ask, with reference to both courtship and marriage, just how much need-satisfaction of what kind (abasement, autonomy, deference, achievement, etc.) may outweigh a failure to get satisfaction of other needs. Next, one or the other spouse may eventually obtain some of these satisfactions outside marriage, e.g., in his or her work, thus posing a new set of questions to be answered. Finally, the theory seems to elucidate to some extent the attraction between very close friends.

Marital Instability

I have suggested elsewhere that happiness is probably not a strategic variable in the analysis of marital institutions. Marital strain and instability, however, or the stability of the family as a boundary-maintaining social unit, may well be because at such points the individual has an option and must decide among several sets of consequences (mostly difficult for him to predict) on the basis of a complex set of value and situational elements. By contrast, there can be no problem of moral choice as between happiness and unhappiness, or "happiness and duty." Happiness would always win. Moreover, happiness cannot be built into the structure of any marriage and kinship system as a statistical likelihood or a moral norm. Again by contrast, the stability of the family unit can be, and often is.

As fruitful as the view that marital instability is the failure of boundary-maintaining forces, is the view that the family is made up of role relations. Then instability can be defined as the failure of one or more individuals

[13] Personal communication, 22 July 1961.

to perform their role obligations.[14] The major forms of instability or disorganization could thereby be classified as follows:[15]

1. The uncompleted family unit: illegitimacy. Here, the family unit did not come into existence. However, the missing individual obviously fails in his "father-husband" role-obligations as defined by society, mother, or child. Moreover, a major indirect cause of the illegitimacy is likely to be the role-failure of both mother and father.

2. Instability when one spouse willfully departs: annulment, separation, divorce, and desertion. Instances of "job desertion" might also be included here, when the individual stays away from home for a long period of time on the excuse of a distant job.

3. The "empty-shell" family: in which individuals interact instrumentally, but fail essentially in the role-obligation to give emotional support to one another. Here, of course, there is no public dissolution or instability but the unit is in effect dissolved.

4. The crisis and strain caused by "external" events such as the temporary or permanent unwilled absence of one of the spouses because of death, imprisonment, or some impersonal catastrophe such as flood, war or depression.

5. Internal crises which create "unwilled" major role-failures: mental, emotional, or physical pathologies; severe mental retardation of a child, psychoses, chronic and incurable physical conditions.

Such a conception poses nearly impossible problems of data collection under present conditions, but does offer one way of conceptualizing the strains and options in certain kinds of marital instability. Indeed, precisely because at the present time we have no way of knowing, in any country, how many families fall into one or another of these categories at a given time, I shall in a moment limit my perspective somewhat and consider only certain problems of divorce rates.

For the moment, however, it is at least useful to keep in mind certain distinctions in this area of analysis. A primary distinction is that between the instability of the family unit and the instability of the family system in a given society. Both of these in turn must be distinguished from

[14] Winch has commented on this point in *Mate Selection, op. cit.*, pp. 202-10, 300-3. For some of the consequences of such actions in general terms, see the author's two related papers, "Norm Commitment and Conformity to Role-Status Obligations," *American Journal of Sociology*, No. 65, November 1960, pp. 246-58; and "A Theory of Role Strain," *American Sociological Review*, No. 25, August 1960, pp. 483-96; as well as the use of this theory in "Illegitimacy in the Caribbean Social Structure," *American Sociological Review*, No. 25, February 1960, pp. 21-30.

[15] This classification is developed and applied in my article, "Family Disorganization," in: Robert K. Merton and Robert A. Nisbet (eds.), *Contemporary Social Problems*, New York: Harcourt Brace, 1961, pp. 390 ff.

social change in the family system, as well as from disorganization. With respect to the first distinction, it is evident that all families do end, but this need not affect the family system. It is likely that high divorce rates have been common in Arab countries for many generations, as they are now, but there is no evidence that this has been until recently a changing family system. That is, the Arab family system creates — and, within limits, copes with — the problems of a high divorce rate and its essential structure remains unchanged. As we shall note in a moment, this may also be said of the Japanese Tokugawa family system. With respect to change, it is evident that if the rates of occurrence of major family happenings, such as the percentage eventually marrying, percentage married at certain ages, divorce rates, fertility, patterns and so on, are changing, then it may be that the family system is also changing and that at least some parts of it are dissolving or undergoing disorganization. On the other hand, some of these changes may actually reduce the rates of occurrence of some phenomena classically called "disorganization," such as divorce, separation, illegitimacy or desertion. Thus, for example, the rate of desertion has been dropping in the United States. In Latin American countries in process of industrialization, with all its predictable *anomie*, the rate of illegitimacy has been dropping. Japan's family system has been undergoing great changes over the past generation and thus by definition certain parts of it must have been "dissolving," but the divorce rate has steadily dropped. Finally, even though the old family patterns may be dissolving, they may be replaced by new ones which control as determinately as the old.

Returning for the moment to a publicly recognized form of marital instability, divorce, we ought at least to ask the ideological question of whether a high divorce rate is "good" or "bad." Doubtless, there is more marital disharmony in a period of great social change than in periods of stability (assuming one can find such periods). However, marital disharmony is probably ubiquitous, and one may ask the sociological question, what are the institutional patterns that cope with that potential or real strain? All family systems include some mechanisms for keeping the hostilities between spouses within limits. A primary pattern is, of course, to lower expectations of emotional performance on both sides, so that neither side expects great happiness or love but does expect a minimal set of behavioural performances. A second obvious pattern noted by many is to place the greatest social value on the kin network and to reduce the importance of the husband-wife relation. As a consequence the tensions between the two are less likely to build to an intolerable level. Thirdly, all groups have patterns of avoiding marital tensions, by suppression, by defining certain types of disagreements as unimportant, and by seeing to it that husbands and wives have similar social backgrounds so that the areas of disagreement will be fewer.

Nevertheless, despite such mechanisms of prevention, disharmony is bound to arise. Societies differ, however, as to how much strain should be tolerated, just as they also differ in their solutions of problems when the level of tension seems intolerable.

Of course, divorce is one of the major solutions for an intense degree of marital disharmony and is to be found in most societies and nations. Yet I know of no contemporary society, primitive or industrialized, in which divorce is actually valued.[16] Divorce has its consequences for the society, the kin networks, and the individual; and these are tedious when not awkward, and burdensome when not destructive. On the other hand, we cannot say as yet why one society develops the pattern of divorce rather than separation or taking on an additional wife or concubine. Its primary difference is that it permits both partners to remarry. In societies without divorce, it is ordinarily the man who is permitted to enter a new union. Thus in Western nations such as Brazil, Italy, Spain, and Portugal, the public attitudes opposing a wife's entering an unsanctioned public union are very strong while the husband is usually permitted to have a mistress outside his household. Viewing these alternatives, it seems false to speak of divorce as a "more extreme" solution than other patterns. We do not know at present whether the introduction of a concubine into a Japanese or Chinese household created more unhappiness than a divorce might have done. And whatever the answer might be, the judgement as to its desirability would still remain a matter of personal or social evaluation.

THE OBJECTIVE AND IDEOLOGICAL
EVALUATION OF MARITAL INSTABILITY

One's ideological position primarily determines the evaluation of marital instability, and evidently the "rising tide" of divorce in Western nations arouses dismay even among objective social scientists — the dismay arising mainly from the peculiar historical place of divorce in Church dogma. Adequate assessment of the costs of marital instability, by any ideological standards, is hampered by the lack of a good measure of "total marital instability" in even the most statistically sophisticated countries, if we are to include in such a rate all the five major types of instability listed above. In fact, we know neither of the total rate nor the psychological or social costs of any one of the five types.

We do not even know the effects of divorce although more analysts have busied themselves with this than with any other form of marital instability.[17] Moreover, such costs must always be assessed by reference

16 George P. Murdock notes that among the Crow a man might be ridiculed if he stayed too long with one woman ("Family Stability in Non-European Cultures," in: *Annals*, No. 272, November 1950, p. 198).

17 For example, I have been unable to locate in any Western country a monograph study comparable to my own *After Divorce*, dealing with the consequences of divorce in the lives of 425 young urban mothers.

to the genuine alternatives open to the participants. For example, children of divorce suffer many disadvantages compared to those who live in a happy home. But the divorcing couple cannot choose between creating a happy home and getting a divorce. They can will a divorce or not; they cannot will (and achieve) marital harmony. And, unfortunately, at least in the United States, the best opinion and data insist that children of discord or separation suffer greater disadvantages than those whose parents actually divorce.[18]

DIVORCE DIFFERENTIALS

Lacking a total rate of marital instability, I should like to explore further a question which I dealt with some years ago and which seems to relate the family in several interesting ways to the larger social structure: class differentials in the divorce rate. A fuller inquiry would be introduced by an analysis, which I am attempting elsewhere, of the broader social-structural concomitants of divorce rates. At present, we have no good study of the problem. Instead, current writers seem to be guided by the clichés, partly wrong in important theoretical and empirical respects, that urbanization and industrialization necessarily increase the divorce rates and that low divorce rates are only to be found in pious, peasant, patriarchical family systems. In addition, a good inference from anthropological data may be noted, that matrilineal societies are prone to a high divorce rate.[19]

CLASS DIFFERENTIALS: UNITED STATES

Postponing such a necessarily extended discussion of the structural conditions creating high divorce rates, let us confine ourselves instead to class differentials in the divorce rate, beginning with the United States which seems to foreshadow so many of the changes which later take place in other countries.

Prior to the first world war, social analysts had guessed that the social relations of certain occupations created a greater proneness to divorce: the travelling salesman because he lived much of the time away from the social control of his neighbours; the bartender and entertainers because of the temptations to which their lives exposed them; the physician because

[18] See Sheldon and Eleanor Glueck, *Unraveling Juvenile Delinquency*, Cambridge, Mass.: Harvard University Press, 1950, Table VIII-19, p. 91; Paul H. Landis, *The Broken Home in Teenage Adjustment*, Pullman, Washington: Institute of Agricultural Sciences, State College of Washington, 1953, p. 10 (*Rural Sociology Theories on The Family*, No. 4); and Raymond Ilsey and Barbara Thompson, "Women from Broken Homes," *Sociol. Rev.*, No. 9, March 1961, pp. 27-53.

[19] Although in earlier drafts he does not deal systematically with the problem of divorce, David L. Schneider in his excellent analysis of matriliny shows some of the inherent strains in such a system. See "The Distinctive Features of Matrilineal Descent Groups," Chapter 1 of his larger book, *Matrilineal Descent*

of the emotional responses ("transference phenomenon" in the modern psychodynamic vocabulary) he aroused; and so on. Occupational data were indeed collected at that time although registration procedures were poor.[20] Most American textbooks that dealt with the topic in succeeding decades repeated these findings in one form or another. But though predictions could be made from a few specific occupations (clergymen, physicians, teachers, dancers) our knowledge of most occupations permitted no prediction at all, and occupation was soon dropped from most records.

By contrast, it seems likely that class position, with its concomitant patterning of social relations and styles of life, might affect divorce rates in at least a rough fashion. Popular belief, and to some extent that of social scientists, supposed until recently that United States divorce rates were higher among the upper strata and lower among the lower strata, where desertion was and is a common occurrence. However, a summary of the available data extending over half a century, together with new calculations from national surveys and censuses, shows that in fact there was an inverse correlation between class position and divorce rates. These findings may be summarized briefly:

1. The findings do not negate the hypothesis that specific occupations in any class position may have high or low divorce rates. Thus clergymen and professors will have relatively low rates, while psychiatrists, surgeons, and perhaps general practitioners may have higher rates.

2. Negroes have a higher divorce rate than whites.

3. When occupation is used as an indicator of class, roughly following the Alba Edwards system used by the Census Bureau, the upper occupational groups have lower rates of divorce.

4. When income is used as an indicator, the upper income groups have lower rates of divorce.

5. When education is used as an indicator, the upper groups have lower rates of divorce.

6. However, the relationship between the education of non-whites and divorce rates is positive: the higher the education, the higher the proneness to divorce.

CLASS AND A MODEL OF DIVORCE DECISION

If we avoid the pitfall of attempting to analyse divorce through so-called "cause" and focus instead on rates, a simple model of divorce decision

Groups, Palo Alto: Center for Advanced Study in the Social Sciences, 1959, mimeographed. See also his "A Note on Bridewealth and the Stability of Marriage," in: *Man*, April 1953, No. 75.

[20] *Marriage and Divorce*, 1867-1906, Washington, Bureau of the Census, 1909. See my critique of these items in *After Divorce*, pp. 52 ff.

clarifies the inverse correlation between class and divorce. We would need at least these items:

1. Predispositions in the economic and social stratum in favour of or against divorce: values and attitudes.
2. Internal strains in, or satisfactions from, the marriage.
3. Alternatives outside marriage.
4. Supporting or dissolving pressures on the part of relevant social networks.

It seems likely that ideologically the upper strata in the United States are more tolerant of divorce than the lower strata. However, the following factors would seem to create a somewhat lesser propensity to divorce toward the upper socio-economic strata:

1. The network of social relations and of kin relations is more extended, more tightly organized, and exercises greater control over the individual.
2. The income differentials between the wife and husband in the upper strata are greater than in the lower strata; consequently the wife has more reason to maintain the marriage if she can.
3. Toward the upper strata, far more of the husband's income is committed to long-term expenditures, from which he cannot easily withdraw to support an independent existence.
4. The husband in the lower strata can more easily escape the child-support payments and other post-divorce expenditures because his life is more anonymous and legal controls are less effective.
5. The strains internal to the marriage are greater toward the lower strata: marital satisfaction scores are lower, romantic attachment between spouses is less common, the husband is less willing to share household tasks when the wife is working, and so on.

CLASS DIFFERENTIALS IN OTHER SOCIETIES: PHASES OF DEVELOPMENT

The relationship between social structure and divorce seems general enough to apply to other societies. Let us explore the matter. Where there is a well-developed stratification system it would seem likely that the lower class does not count on the stability of the marriage, that the marriage itself costs less, less is invested in it than in the upper strata, the kin ties are less important and therefore the ambiguity created by divorce would not be taken so seriously as in the upper strata.

In the past, on the other hand, without any questions the divorce rate (as distinguished from the general rate of instability) was higher in the upper strata of the United States. In some states' jurisdictions, an act of the legislature was necessary to obtain a divorce and generally divorce was costly. Consequently at some unknown point in American history, the lower strata began to surpass the upper strata in the divorce rate, just as happened with respect to the Negro-White divorce differential. Thus a fuller exploration must at some point introduce the notion of phase in these considerations. In other words, the lower strata may generally have a higher rate of marital instability, but their divorce rate may not always be higher until some stage of development in the marriage and divorce system occurs.

This general theory of the relationship between the larger social structure and class divorce rates may correctly apply to the Western culture complex where Church dogma with respect to the family was translated into State laws in every nation, and where the administration of these restrictive laws was until recently in the hands of the *élite*. However, those laws have been altered greatly over the past half-century in most Western States. Moreover, if the theory is to be generalized, it must be modified to fit those cultures such as China, India, Japan and Arab Islam where marriage and divorce were not generally under the jurisdiction of State officials (except for extreme cases) and where marriage was not primarily a sacred affair (Japan, China).

Finally, the use of occupation as a class index, perhaps the best in view of the necessarily crude data available for cross-national comparisons, may at times introduce a new variable into the analysis, the peculiar style of life of certain occupations. For example, clergymen and teachers (in the West) will have low divorce rates but physicians and artists will have high ones — yet in most national tabulations of divorce these will all be classified together. In the West, farmers have lower divorce rates, but in Japan a special pattern of "trial marriage" creates high divorce rates among agriculturists — though many of these are never recorded.

If these necessary modifications are integrated, several inferences can be tested. (a) In the pre-industrial or early industrialization period of Western nations the upper classes will have higher divorce rates. Indeed, there may be almost no lower class divorces. (b) As a Western nation industrializes, its divorce procedures are gradually made available to all classes. Since family strain toward the lower strata is greater, the proportion of lower strata divorces will increase, and eventually there should be an inverse relation between class and divorce rate, as in the United States. (c) In China, India, Japan and Arab Islam, where the power to divorce remained in the hands of the groom's family, no such set of phases will occur. Indeed — though very likely precise data do not exist — I hypothesize that the relation between class and divorce rate moves in the opposite direction: that is though the lower strata will continue to furnish more than their "share" of the divorces, the class differential will narrow somewhat as the upper strata begin to divorce more. (d) Finally (though here again the data will very likely never become available) since the dominant pattern of respectability was set by the urban *élite,* and the rural marriage and divorce patterns seem to have been looser, it is likely that in China, Japan, India and Arab Islam any modern changes would be toward a decline in the divorce rate of agriculturists.

New Zealand. The ratio of divorced to married by income distribution shows clearly that toward the lower strata the divorce rate is higher. [See Table 1.] The same relationship shows by occupation; the ratio of comparative frequency of divorce to numbers in each of various occupational groups . . . [is shown in Table 2].

TABLE 1. RATIO OF PERCENTAGE OF DIVORCED TO PERCENTAGE OF MARRIED, WITHIN INCOME GROUPS, [NEW ZEALAND]

Income Group	Ratio[a]
Under £100	1.78
£100−£149	1.84
£150−£199	1.86
£200−£249	1.50
£250−£299	1.10
£300−£349	.96
£350−£399	.87
£400−£449	.67
£450−£549	.58
£550−£649	.56
£650−£749	.48
£750 and over	.34
Not specified	2.01

[a]Figures higher than 1.00 indicate that the income group concerned contributes more than its numerical "share" to the total number of divorces.
Source: A.J.Dixon, *Divorce in New Zealand,* Auckland, Auckland University College Bulletin No. 46, 1954, p. 42 (Sociology Series No. 1).

TABLE 2. PRONENESS TO DIVORCE BY OCCUPATION, NEW ZEALAND

Occupation	Ratio[a]
Architect, dentist, lawyer, lecturer, doctor	.07
Engineer	.72
Farmer	.17
Manager (not company)	.32
Carpenter	.78
Butcher	1.05
Mechanic	.96
Railway employee	.80
Clerk	.55
Salesman	1.17
Barman	4.73
Labourer	2.30

[a]Figures higher than 1.00 indicate that the occupation concerned contributes more divorces than its numerically proportionate "share" within all occupations.
Source: ibid.

United States. Although an extensive summary of the relevant data is available for the United States,[21] it may be relevant to note that a more recent summary has corroborated these findings, and from one of these [Table 3] has been taken.

Australia. In Australia, too, the relationship holds [as seen in Table 4].

TABLE 3. RATIO OF DIVORCED TO 1,000 OF EVER-MARRIED MEN BY OCCUPATION OF CIVILIAN LABOUR FORCE, 14 YEARS AND OVER, 1950 UNITED STATES CENSUS

Occupations	Number Divorced per 1,000 Ever-Married Men
Professional, technical and kindred workers	18.49
Managers, officials and proprietors (excluding farm)	16.59
Clerical and kindred workers	25.70
Craftsmen, foremen and kindred workers	24.15
Operatives and kindred workers	26.18
Farm labourers and foremen	40.76

Source: Karen G. Hillman, *Marital Instability and Its Relation to Education, Income and Occupation: An Analysis Based on Census Data,* Evanston, Illinois, Northwestern University, 1961, p. 19, mimeographed.

TABLE 4. RATIO OF DIVORCED TO 1,000 MARRIED MALES BY OCCUPATIONAL CLASS, 1947 CENSUS OF AUSTRALIA[a]

Occupational Level	Number Divorced per 1,000 Married Males
Employer	9
Self-employed	9
Employee (on wage)	15
Helper (not on wage)	23

[a]Calculated from: *Census of the Commonwealth of Australia, 30 June, 1947. Statistician's Report,* Canberra, 1952, p. 268.

Sweden. A similar ratio may be found in the 1950 Swedish census. [See Table 5.]

Belgium. In [Table 6], calculated from the 1947 Belgian census, a similar relation appears, although here the differences are very small.

France. The relationship also holds here. [See Table 7.]

England. A special study of the occupational structure of the divorcing and the "continued married relations population" in England and Wales in 1951 reveals that the proportions of the divorcing population in the selected occupational categories were almost exactly those of the proportions in the continued married population. Thus the "profes-

21 *After Divorce, op. cit.,* pp. 52 ff. *et passim.*

130   WILLIAM J. GOODE

TABLE 5. RATIO OF DIVORCED PER 1,000 MARRIED MEN, BY
OCCUPATIONAL CATEGORY, [SWEDEN]^a

Category	Number Divorced per 1,000 Married Men
Employers	12
Salaried employees	21
Wage-earners	28

^aCalculated from: Personal correspondence, Central Bureau of Statistics, Sweden.
Statistiska Centralbyran, Folkräkningen, Den 31 December 1950, V, VI, Totala
Räkningen, Folkmängden Efter Yrke. Hushall. Utrikes Födda Och Utlänningar: Tab.
8., "Förvärvsarbetande befolkning efter näringsgren (huvudoch undergrupper) och
yrkesstallning i kombination med kön, alter och civilstand den 31 december 1950"
[Economically active population by industry (divisions and major groups) and
occupational status, and by sex, age and marital status], pp. 162-3 (males only).

TABLE 6. RATIO OF DIVORCED PER 1,000 MARRIED MEN, BY
OCCUPATIONAL CATEGORY (EXCLUDING AGRICULTURE,
FARMING AND FISHING), [BELGIUM]^a

Category	Number Divorced per 1,000 Married Men
Employers	13
Salaried workers	14
Skilled and unskilled workers	15
Auxiliary personnel	31

^aCalculated from: Institut national de Statistique, *Recensement Général de la
Population, de l'Industrie et du Commerce au 31 Décembre 1941.* Vol. 8:
Répartition de la Population d'après l'Activité et la Profession. Tableau 19 –
Répartition de la population active masculine de nationalité belge d'après l'État Civil,
l'État Social et les Sections d'Activité, pp. 34-5.

TABLE 7. RATIO OF DIVORCED PER 1,000 MARRIED MEN,
BY OCCUPATIONAL CATEGORY, [FRANCE]^a

Category	Number Divorced per 1,000 Married Men
Liberal professions and senior cadres	17
Intermediate cadres	20
Salaried workers	21
Skilled and unskilled workers	24
Domestic servants	78

^aCalculated from: *Résultats du sondage au 1/20e, Institut National de la
Statistique et des Études économiques,* Presses Universitaires de France, 1960
(Recensement général de la Population de Mai 1954), p. 61, p. 62, p. 63.

sional and managerial class" accounted for 13.5 per cent of the divorcing
sample and 13.9 per cent of the continuing married.

Much more instructive, however, and strongly confirming our second
hypothesis is the change in the distribution of the husband's occupation
at divorce. Such a comparison is presented [in Table 8], showing how the
"gentry, professional and managerial workers" dropped from 41.4 per cent

of the total divorcing population, to 11.4 per cent between 1871 and 1951. During the same period, the proportion furnished by the manual workers increased from 16.8 to 58.5 per cent.

TABLE 8. HUSBAND'S OCCUPATION AT DIVORCE,
1871 AND 1951, ENGLAND AND WALES[a]

Year	Gentry, Professional and Managerial Workers	Farmers and Shopkeepers	Blackcoated Workers	Manual	Unknown Occupation	Total of Occupations
	%	%	%	%	%	
1871	41.4	12.7	6.3	16.8	22.8	285
1951	11.4	6.7	7.6	58.5	15.8	1,813

[a]Calculated from: Griselda Rowntree and Norman H. Carrier, "The Resort to Divorce in England and Wales, 1858-1957", in: *Population Studies,* No. 11, March 1958, p. 222.

South Africa. Up to the time of writing, I have been unable to make a similar comparison for South Africa because the categories used for occupation and divorce do not correspond to one another in the sources available to me.[22]

Netherlands. The data from the Netherlands do not fit the hypothesis because of the extremely high divorce ratio among the free professions, which include both the established professions of medicine and law, and such occupations as musician, artist, writer and so on. Teaching is separate and of course has a low ratio. Unfortunately, skilled workers seem to be classified with manual labourers. Thus, although the extreme categories in the Netherlands do not fit our thesis, "free professions" do fit. [See Table 9.]

TABLE 9. RATIO OF DIVORCE PER 1,000 MARRIED MALE
HEADS OF HOUSEHOLDS, NETHERLANDS 1955-57
(EXCLUDING AGRICULTURE)[a]

Categories	Number of Divorces per 1,000 Male Household Heads
Heads of enterprises	18
Free professions	50
Civil Service and office employees	21
Teaching	15
Other bureaucrats	37
Manual workers	30

[a]Calculated from: Number of households taken as of 30 June 1956; divorces as of 1955-57.
Source: Eehtscheidingen in Nederland, 1900-57, Central Bureau Voor De Statistiek, Zeist, W. de Haan, 1958, Appendix II, Table D, p. 63.

[22] See the table on divorce and occupation in *Egskeiding in Suid-Afrika* by Hendrik Johannes Piek, Pretoria Ph.D., 1959, p. 262.

Yugoslavia. Yugoslavia has recently begun to industrialize, and our hypothesis would suggest that the divorce ratio would be higher towards the upper strata. If education is used as an index, this appears to be so as of 1959. [See Table 10.] However, the ratios by occupation are puzzling. Here the technical problem of the ratio itself is important: if the ratio used is actual divorces and marriages in one given year, the result may be an anomaly: e.g., a high divorce-marriage ratio among pensioners because they do experience some divorces, but very few marriages on account of their age. However, this result is a function of age level rather than of a high propensity to divorce.

In any event, with this warning, [Table 11] presents data comparable in part to the previous tables. These figures are also somewhat different from those which Milič has calculated, apparently from the same sources.[23]

[TABLE 10.] RATIO OF DIVORCE TO 1,000 MARRIED MALES, BY EDUCATION, [YUGOSLAVIA]

School Achievement of Husband	Number of Divorced per 1,000 Married
Without school	124
Primary school	124
Secondary school (incomplete)	144
Secondary school (completed)	148
Faculty, high and higher school	144

Source: Statistical Yearbook of the Federal People's Republic of Yugoslavia, Federal People's Republic of Yugoslavia Federal Statistical Institute, Belgrade, August 1961. Calculated from: Table 202-23—Contracted Marriages by School Qualifications of Bridegroom and Bride in 1959 (preliminary data), p. 83; Table 202-27—Divorces by School Qualifications of Husband and Wife in 1959 (preliminary data), p. 85.

[TABLE 11.] RATIO OF DIVORCES TO MARRIAGES BY OCCUPATION OF HUSBAND, [YUGOSLAVIA][a]

Occupation of Husband	Number of Divorces per 1,000 Marriages
Unskilled	144
Workers in manufacturing industries, arts, crafts	140
Administrative and managing personnel	256
Professional and technical occupations and artists	132

[a]Calculated from: *Statistical Yearbook of the Federal People's Republic of Yugoslavia,* Federal Statistical Institute, Belgrade, August 1961. Data calculated from: Table 202-21—Contracted Marriages by Occupation of Bridegroom and Bride in 1959 (preliminary data), p. 83; Table 202-28—Divorces by Occupation of Husband and Wife in 1959 (preliminary data), p. 85.

[23] Vojin Milič, "Sklapanje I Razvod Braka Prema Zanimanju," in: *Statisticka Revija* No. 7, March 1957, pp. 19-44, especially p. 38.

Egypt. Egyptian data on such a matter raises the problem, common to all countries in which divorce has been a limited concern of the State, of how adequate the coverage of divorces is, and whether the more literate or better educated couples who divorce are more likely to record their divorces. As can be seen in [Table 12], the divorce/married ratio predicted holds good primarily for the distinction between employers on the one hand and all other occupations on the other. However, one comparison of illiteracy and divorce shows no difference in the literacy of bridegrooms and divorced males in 1956 (47 and 45 per cent).[24]

[TABLE 12.] RATIO OF DIVORCES TO MARRIAGES BY OCCUPATION OF HUSBAND (EXCLUDING AGRICULTURE, FISHING AND HUNTING), [EGYPT][a]

Categories	Number of Divorces per 1,000 Marriages
Employers	9
On own account	18
Directors and sub-directors	12
Employees	11
Labourers and artisans	18
Unemployed	117

[a]Calculated from: *Population Census of Egypt,* 1947, General Tables, Ministry of Finance and Economy, Statistical and Census Department, Government Press, Cairo, 1954. Table XXIX (concluded) —Working Status for Persons engaged in Industries by Sex, Age Group and Civil Status (excluding children below 5 years). Table refers to males and excludes occupations in agriculture, fishing, and hunting, pp. 362-3.

Ratios calculated for those engaged in agriculture, fishing and hunting in Egypt follow the pattern presented above for occupations outside these categories.[25]

Jordan. Corresponding data do not exist for Jordan, but it is at least possible to calculate that in 1959 75 per cent of the males who married were literate, but only 59 per cent of those who divorced; and 25 per cent of the females who married were literate, but only 5 per cent of the divorcees.[26] Therefore we can conclude that the better educated

[24] United Arab Republic (Egypt), Presidency of the Republic, Statistics and Census Department, *Vital Statistics, 1956,* Vol. II, Table XXIII, p. 340 — Classification of Divorced Males by Locality according to Literacy for year 1956; Table VI, pp. 274-5 — Classification of Bridegrooms by Locality according to Literacy (and Marital Condition) for the year 1956. Perhaps the literate are more likely to record their divorces officially.

[25] Population Census of Egypt, 1947, General Tables, *op. cit.,* Table XXIX, — Working Status for Persons engaged in Industries by Sex, Age Group and Civil Status (excluding children under 5 years). This table refers to those engaged in agriculture, fishing and hunting only.

[26] *Statistical Yearbook,* 1959. Hashemite Kingdom of Jordan, Jerusalem, pp. 45-50.

134   WILLIAM J. GOODE

divorced less than the less educated. This general conclusion also emerges
from many non-quantitative analyses of divorce in Arabic Islam. Specifically, it is sometimes asserted that divorce and remarriage are the
"poor man's polygny."[27]

Finland. Allardt found that in 1947 the divorce rate per
100,000 of the main supporters of the family was higher toward the
upper strata, which would fit our first hypothesis. Using these three
classes, labouring, middle, and upper, he found rates of 527, 543, and
1022.

However, most of the *élite* are to be found in Helsinki, where the
divorce rates are higher than elsewhere in Finland and a comparison of
the divorce applications in different classes in 1945-46 showed no statistically significant differences among them, i.e., in the more industrialized
areas, the older class pattern had already changed. Allardt notes that the
differences among the classes were greater at the beginning of the century
but that there is now very little difference (second hypothesis).

Hungary. As a newly industrializing nation, Hungary would be
expected to have a somewhat lower divorce rate toward the lower strata.
Our data [see Table 13] suggest caution but do conform.

[TABLE 13.]   RATIO OF DIVORCES TO MARRIAGES,
[HUNGARY] 1958

Occupation	Number of Divorces	Number of Marriages	Number of Divorces per 1,000
Agricultural workers	1 827	25 154	72
Manual workers	9 133	51 017	179
Intellectuals	3 481	15 156	223

Source: Statisztikai Evkonyv, 1958, Kozponti Statisztikai Hivatal, Budapest,
1960. Table 20—Marriages by the Professional Status of Husband and Wife, p. 20.
Table 26—Divorces by Professional Status of Husband and Wife, p. 22.

India. The Indian pattern is, of course, very well known though
no quantitative data exist. Divorce has been impossible for Brahmans
until very recently (1955). On the other hand, the lower castes and the
outcasts, as well as tribal groups, have long permitted divorce. As a
consequence there is no doubt that the general relationship presented
earlier fits at least the observed differences among the strata — though

[27] Lester Mboria, *La Population de l'Égypte,* University of Paris Faculty of
Law Thesis, Cairo: Procaccia, 1938, p. 68. Erik Allardt, *The Influence of Different Systems of Social Norms on Divorce Rates in Finland,* Columbia University, 1954; mimeographed. These data are taken from Allardt's *Miljöbetingade
differenser i skilsmässofrekvensen i Finland 1891-1950,* Helsingfors, Finska Veten-
skaps-Societeten, 1953.

in this instance it is perhaps not possible to make a strong case for differential strain.[28]

China. The case of China is similar to that of Japan. Though China has permitted divorce from at least the T'ang period, divorce has not been a respectable step in Chinese culture and thus would tend to be more common towards the lower strata. Indeed among the *élite*, other solutions were open to the dissatisfied husband.[29]

Japan. The divorce rate in Japan has been dropping over the past half century, though at the same time divorce has been much more completely recorded than formerly. Again, our hypothesis is confirmed. [See Table 14.]

[TABLE 14.] THE RATIO OF DIVORCE PER 1,000 MARRIED MALE WORKERS 15 YEARS AND OVER, JAPAN, JULY 1957[a]

Occupation	Number Divorced per 1,000 Male Workers
Technicians and engineers	7
Professors and teachers	3
Medical and public health technicians	5
Managers and officials	4
Clerical and related workers	8
Farmers, lumbermen, fishermen and related workers	10
Workers in mining and quarrying	18
Craftsmen, production process workers, and labourers not else where included	18
Domestic	238

[a]Calculated from: Japan, Bureau of Statistics, Office of the Prime Minister, *1955 Population Census of Japan,* Vol. II: *One Percent Sample Tabulation,* Part III, "Occupation, July 1957," Table 3—Occupation (Intermediate Group) of Employed Persons 15 Years Old and Over by Marital Status and Sex, for all Japan, all *Shi* and all *Gun,* pp. 136-7 (Males only).

THE "EASY DIVORCE" PHASE: FURTHER INFERENCES

Fully to resolve all of these irregularities would require an institutional analysis of each country. Our earlier analysis seems to be correct, that there is likely to be more marital instability towards the lower strata than towards the upper. But whether this set of forces is exhibited in actual divorce proceedings depends on the extent to which divorce itself has become easy, that is, has come to "cost" little — these costs being calcu-

28 See *India: Sociological Background,* HRAF-44 Cornell 8, Vol. 1 (M. Opler, ed.) New Haven: Yale University Press, 1958, p. 25; P. V. Kane, *Hindu Custom and Modern Law,* Bombay: University of Bombay Press, 1950, p. 82; Mohindar Singh, *The Depressed Classes,* Bombay: Hind Kitebs, 1947, p. 168.

29 A good historical analysis of divorce in China is Wang Tse-Tsiu, *Le Divorce en Chine,* Paris: Lovitow, 1930.

lated necessarily by reference to the available resources of the family, and including both monetary and social costs. We also noted that in a country with "easy" divorce (Japan, Arab Islam), industrialization would reduce the divorce rate of the lower strata relative to the upper. In a country moving toward the easy divorce phase, the upper strata begin to furnish a smaller proportion of total divorces. Let us consider the further implications of these notions.

First, where divorce costs little, there will be a high divorce rate. This is a reciprocal and reinforcing relationship. Easy divorce means in effect that there are fewer strong factors to maintain the boundaries of the family unit. Moreover, in that type of situation, the peers of any individual are likely to have had similar experiences, that is, divorce, and therefore have less basis on which to chide or deprecate anyone who gets a divorce. And the ubiquitous strains in all marriage systems will ensure a high number of individuals who seek this way out and who are also available as potential mates.

Where divorce is difficult and costly, it is primarily an upper-class privilege. There are rarely special laws for the lower classes, other than those which prevent the lower classes from attacking the privileges of the élite. On the other hand, if and when there are upper-class family difficulties that have to be solved in a social structure posing barriers against divorce, there must be at least a few mechanisms for handling them, such as annulment and migratory divorce. The property stakes and problems of lineage are too important to permit the merely informal solutions which the lower classes may enjoy.

In a family system permitting easy divorce and thus having a high divorce rate, there will also be a very high rate of remarriage.[30] In the United States, this rate of eventual remarriage among divorces is roughly as high as that for the unmarried population, about nine in ten. No such figures exist for Arab Islam, but the few data available, including observations made in specific studies, suggest that there is an extremely high rate of marital turnover. The percentage married in the upper age groups in Japan has been over 95 per cent for decades, while the divorce rate was extremely high, thus showing that the rate of remarriage was high. Irene Taeuber has in addition used demographic techniques to show that the divorced as well as the widowed "disappear" in successive age groups.[31] In such a high-divorce system, divorce creates no social stigma, there are many available divorcees to marry, and divorce is no longer likely to be a deviant in many psychological or social respects.

Indeed the divorce system then becomes in effect part of the courtship

[30] Jesse Bernard, *Remarriage*, New York: Dryden, 1956, Chapters 2, 3.
[31] Irene Taeuber, *The Population of Japan*, Princeton: Princeton University Press, 1958, pp. 226 ff.

and marriage system: that is, it is part of the "sifting out" process, analogous to the adolescent dating pattern. Individuals marry, but there is a free market both in getting a first spouse, and in getting a second spouse should the individual not be able to create a harmonious life with the first one. Indeed, to the extent that marriage becomes a personal bond between husband and wife, and they marry after they are formed psychologically, there would seem to be at least some ideological arguments for their being free to shift about in order to find someone who fits better.

Finally, as such a system becomes established, heavy investments in bride-price or dowry will decline. These are never individual investments in any family system, but represent the commitment of an extended family network to the marriage. Where the likelihood is great that the marriage will be unstable, and undoing it expensive, then neither side is likely to be willing to make a large, long-term investment in it.

Some but not all of these hypotheses can be tested by available data, and in some of my current research I am attempting to assemble such materials from many countries — a formidable task! The present paper has aimed at presenting a small theoretical perspective, developing hypotheses from that theoretical position and then testing them.

11   AMITAI ETZIONI

Power and Alienation in a
Comparative Perspective

THE DILEMMA OF POWER

To use power, to overcome resistance, entails the generation of some resistance. The dilemma of power is how to increase the capacity to act without generating counter-currents so that the very movement forward will not reduce the capacity to move on this and future occasions. As this dilemma can never be fully resolved, the realistic question becomes one of which kind of power produces relatively weak counter-currents? The resistance generated by the use of power takes many forms and has many expressions. The term which most inclusively describes the various kinds of resistance is "alienation." It increases when power is exercised, adding to alienation which has other sources.

The term "alienation" serves to emphasize that the issue is not only one of the overt hostility of those subject to power, for their reactions may also express themselves in the victimization of others, neurosis, alcoholism, and so on. Secondly, the term reminds us that varying applications and kinds of power create different kinds of subject-and-power-wielder relationships and affect the totality of social organization. Thus, if one kind of social organization relies to a greater extent on force to advance its goals than another, this will affect not only the psychic states of those subjected to the exercise of power but also the pattern of the relevant social structure and most social relations within it. For instance, the application of power is expected to increase the distance between the members of the social unit and the fruits of their labor, render their social world less meaningful, and make the social structure less responsive. Thus, alienation has both subjective and objective facets — the psychic states of the subjects and power-wielders and the patterns of the societal unit.

The exercise of power can be observed without manifest signs of alienation. However, we still would hold that some new resistance is an inevitable outcome of the use of power, even though the focus of the alienation thus generated might be deflected from the sources of power. Actually, when alienation is very high, especially in situations in which the power applied is brute force and there is little hope of neutralizing it, the subjects are quite likely to deflect their psychic responses. Inmates in concentration camps, for instance, seem more often to have attacked each other than their guards. To demonstrate the validity of our proposition, we would have to demonstrate either that the brutal exercise of power is the cause of the victimization orientation which the subjects exhibit toward each other and/or that a significant weakening of the power-wielders will lead to the focusing of alienation on them; i.e., alienation is latent and becomes manifest when circumstances allow. In less extreme and more common power relations, we expect that at least part of the alienation will tend to be directed manifestly toward the wielders of the power.

While all actors face the dilemma of power, the need to minimize its self-contradictory consequences (or costs) is particularly evident on the macroscopic level. On the personal level, the application of the more alienating forms of power may satisfy sadism, vanity, or exhibitionism —

i.e., fulfill a "need." The same phenomenon may occur on the microscopic level in which personalities play a relatively large role. But on the macroscopic level, this seems less common; while some leaders may harbor such tendencies, the control of macro-units is usually mediated through other personalities, organizational arrangements, and structural constraints, each of which tends to dissociate power to a great extent from personality traits and to˙ rationalize it in the sense of making it *relatively* more goal-oriented. (The less a societal structure is responsive to the personality of one leader, the less the macro-unit is like a micro-actor from this viewpoint.) Finally, most macro-actors seem to be consciously concerned with applying the kinds of power that will gain the desired results while generating little new resistance. Therefore, this is the key problem in the *societal* application of power: On the one hand, there is often the fear of alienating, which slants the societal unit toward inaction; on the other hand, there is often the unnecessary use of power or use of the "wrong" kinds of power, which generates unnecessary alienation. The level of activeness attained depends on the balance which is achieved between these tendencies.

ALTERNATIVE MODES OF
SOCIAL ORGANIZATION

We now review briefly the major sociological responses to the question of the bases of social organization, in order to place our endeavor in relation to these responses. Past efforts pointed chiefly to two bases of social organization. According to the first, men are related to each other through emotional and moral bonds which form natural social groupings subject to natural leadership. These traditional social units, it is widely agreed, were being undermined by the impact of industrialization, and the second principle of social organization was increasing in importance. According to this principle, actors are related by shared interests and the interdependence emanating from the division of labor, specialization, and exchange. Since this mode of social organization is based on self-interest, no need for leadership was recognized. In short, man was not predatory to man either because he believed in a value that supported social organization (including the value of the other) or because it was profitable to be sociable and organized.

Despite the fact that this opposition between the normative and the utilitarian bases of social organization appears in many guises, a common element is found in almost all of its expression: An analytic preference for normative bonds over utilitarian ones. Weber viewed traditional authority as inherently more stable than the rationalist, bureaucratic type. Durkheim suggested that every contract has a pre-contractual foundation; that is, the containment of the centrifugal forces which utilitarian relations generate depends on their normative underpinnings. Weber made the same point in his study of stock exchanges. De Toqueville, Maine, Tönnies, Redfield, Mayo, Schmalenbach and numerous others saw the transition from a normatively-based social organization to a more utilitarian one as a decline in social organization if not an outright disintegration of the social fabric.

Even Marx, who in many ways is outside this tradition, shared in this basic perspective in that he saw history as a series of conflicts of interest to which man was subject from the time he was expelled from the harmonious, normative garden of the primitive commune until his eventual return to the conflictless, normative life of the classless society. Marx's disapproval of the utilitarian principle is evident in that he saw in it a foundation for the organization of a transforming conflict but not a basis of a stable society; it was not to be a basis of the classless one. Actually, the main difference between his and other socio-political theories on this point is that while Marx separated the two modes of societal relations into different periods and assumed a sharp transition from one to the other, most of the other theorists viewed modern society as a mixture of the two modes with only gradual changes in the mix.

For the Parsonian theory of action, the foundation of social organization is still the internalization and institutionalization of normative symbols which bind the actors into social groupings. Utilitarian interests might support the normative order, but they cannot be relied upon because at any point, actors who seek to maximize short-run interests at the cost of long-run ones or actors whose long-run interests differ might undermine the social order. Stability, continuity, and order rest on normative foundations.

If the normative principle took precedence almost unanimously in Western social philosophy over the utilitarian one as a basis of social organization, coercive relations were widely treated as chiefly destructive. As early as Plato, force was relegated to the relations of a polity to nonmembers, to barbarians and foreigners, and to the anarchy of interstate relations. The internal life of the *polis*, in which order reigned, was to be based on education and persuasion.

Hobbes' social philosophy is often represented as one in which violence plays a key role; this is true, but it is not as a foundation of social organization. It is the *escape* from the anarchy of violent life which Hobbes views as so desirable that it takes priority over all other values and leads man to bind himself into the protection of an absolute state. But the order of this state is based on a contract, or an understanding of the value of the institutions, and on a political formula — i.e., on legitimacy. In short, it is a part utilitarian, part normative order.

In Marxist theory, force has a more ambiguous status but, in balance, a destructive one. So far as the state is concerned, force is used for subjugation, an instrument of the propertied classes which contains the seeds of its own destruction: It is not an order but a preparation for and an element of warfare. Insofar as force is used by the proletariat, "violence is the midwife of history," the birth cry of the new society but not part of it. It destroys the old regime, the world of conflict, in a violent showdown, but — as the state withers away — force has no place in the new world, the truly ordered one.

A small group of Italian writers, among which Mosca and Pareto are the best known, saw in the use of force an organizing principle similar in status to the normative and utilitarian principles found in other theories (as well as in their own). Mosca saw in the protective function a foundation of a social order (though, again, the relations between the knight and the peasants were of mutual interests, an exchange of protection for services and goods, with the force aimed toward outsiders). Pareto's circulating elites used force not only for unseating an elite whose removal was overdue but also as a source of the power of the "lions" who rigidly enforced their rule. He came close to recognizing force as a permanent foundation of social organization.

The main lines of sociological thought, however, continued either not to treat force at all or to view it as largely destructive, generating a need for social organization rather than as a source of such organization. Authority, Weber stressed, is the legitimate use of power, and force is one source of power. But it is the legitimacy that makes for the order; naked power leads to disorder. In Parsons' writings, force without legitimacy has a destructive status similar to that of sex without love. It is a sign of anomie, of unsocialized or desocialized behavior, of the animal in man emerging from under the social super-structure. It is a threat to the social fabric and needs to be channeled into legitimate outlets: Just as sex is channeled into love, so force is channeled into authority. In political science, one of the most widely held propositions is that governments that rely on force are not firmly established (or "stabilized"). "You can do everything with bayonets but sit on them."

We suggest that the three organizational principles — the normative, the utilitarian, and the coercive — are equal in theoretical status. There are no a priori or empirical grounds on which to hold that one of these serves as a more general principle of social organization than the others. The relative distortive effects of the three principles of social organization cannot be examined without relating the kind of power used to the goals served.

In the following discussion, our treatment of power is analytic: We ask about the effects of changes in the kind of power used if all other factors remained unchanged.[1] The actor who is deciding which of the alternative kinds of power to use is faced with a problem which is analogous to the analytic model; he might attempt to affect other elements of the situation outside the power matrix, but he will be likely also to consider the differential consequences of forcing his way, of ensuring pay-offs to those who might otherwise hinder his action, of trying to convince others of the justice and wisdom of his course, or various combinations thereof.

We first classify the kinds of power, and we then examine their relationship to other abstract factors (or variables). We first relate the kind of power used to the level of alienation generated, then relate these two factors to the kinds of goals advanced, and then relate these three factors to various features of the social organization, such as the social distance (and the distribution of the access to power) among the member status-groups. When these factors are considered altogether, toward the end of the chapter, ideal types of societal organization emerge. *We find that the kind of power used tends to be associated with different kinds of societal organization.* Where force prevails, a terror regime is likely to prevail, with its concomitant factors — fear, hate, and a sharp differentiation between those in power and those subject to it. Where exchange is the prevailing mode of gaining one's way, where each person is a means to the other and the accounting and calculative orientations dominate, market relations prevail. Finally, where appeals to values, consensus, education, and debate are prevalent, members are more committed to each other and to the shared societal goals.

Even these three principles of organization are highly "ideal–typical" (or, analytic) in that any actual societal control mixes, to varying degrees, these types. . . . This approach allows for considerable economy. By using three ideal types and varying degrees of approximation to and mixing of them, we can characterize by the use of a few concepts the large variety of regimes which we encounter and their continual changes. It also serves to stress that societies are not simply totalitarian or democratic but use varying "mixes" of power, and that each regime may and frequently does change its mix.

Finally, it should be emphasized that while we begin our exploration of the relationships among the various factors by comparing the effects of the use of various kinds of power, we do not wish to suggest that power is the determining factor and that the level of alienation and the kinds of

---

[1] Analytic in two senses: (1) concrete power might be a combination of two or more kinds of power as seen from the viewpoint of the analytic classification. (Which kinds are combined and which kind prevails in the combination, if any, can be empirically determined.) (2) Variables used for classification belong to an analytic scheme — in this case, a theory of compliance.

societal goals to which the actors are committed are determined by it. As we see it, these three factors interact and tend toward "typical" constellations; none of them has a clear primacy.

A CLASSIFICATION OF POWER

The conversion of assets into power generates a variety of sanctions, rewards, and instruments to penalize those who resist, to reward those who assist, to remove those who block, and to provide facilities for those who implement a collectively-set course of action. These sanctions, rewards, and instruments differ in their substance: They are either physical, material, or symbolic. This makes for a threefold classification of assets and power: Power is either coercive (e.g., military forces), utilitarian (e.g., economic sanctions), or persuasive (e.g., propaganda). The classification is exhaustive. Each concrete application of the use of power is either one of the three or is composed of their various combinations. The classification covers both "real" and "ideal" elements, mechanical and symbolic elements, and elements representing the three sociological orientations reviewed above. Threats and promises are classified in terms of their asset base, though they are all symbolic and, in this sense, similar to persuasive power. Thus, a threat to bomb is coercive, a promise to provide foreign aid is utilitarian, and a threat to excommunicate is persuasive. In general, threats and promises are "milder" in their effects than the actual exercise of the same kind and amount of power.

Utilitarian assets include economic possessions, technical and administrative capabilities, manpower, etc. Utilitarian power is generated when these assets are applied or exchanged in such a fashion as to allow the unit which possesses them to bring other units to support its line of action.[2]

Coercive assets are the weapons, installations, and manpower which the military, the police, or similar agencies use. There is a thin line between utilitarian and coercive assets; civilians may be inducted into the military and factories might be converted to military use. But so long as such a conversion has not occurred, these means will not be viewed as coercive assets. Coercive power (or force) results when one unit uses coercive assets to impose its preferred course of action on others. Note that coercion refers here to the employment of violent means and not to pressure in a more generic sense. Or, to put it differently, coercive power refers to the use of force and not to other means of enforcement.

Persuasive power[3] is exercised through the manipulation of symbols,

[2] *Utilitarian power* is preferred over "economic power" because administrative and technical assets as well as economic ones are included.
[3] We used "normative" or "identative" power in previous publications. Our reason for this change of terminology will become evident in the following pages.

such as appeals to the values and sentiments of the citizens, in order to mobilize support and to penalize those who deviate (e.g., by excommunicating them). Unlike utilitarian and coercive power, two concepts which are frequently applied, the concept of persuasive power is not widely used and raises several analytic problems which need to be discussed briefly, especially since the relations between assets and power are less evident in regard to persuasion than with respect to the other two categories.

The normative bonds of societal units, the bases of persuasive power, are often perceived as either resting on personal attitudes and interpersonal relations or as having no structural and organizational base at all. Actually, the capacity to persuade is not randomly distributed in social systems. For instance, in societies in which the church is a main source of persuasive power, the power-holders themselves constitute a hierarchy with a variety of goals, in the pursuit of which the hierarchy brings its power to bear. And the secular authorities which have the church's blessing possess access to a source of power that other secular authorities do not. In the Spanish civil war, for example, Franco was granted such support and the Republicans were undermined. Similarly, in democratic societies, access to the mass media is a source of persuasive power that is more available to potential incumbents than to the opposition; in totalitarian societies, this source of persuasive power is largely monopolized by the establishment. In short, persuasive power is structured and organized, allocated and applied, in much the same ways as other kinds of power.

The capacity to persuade is a power; like other kinds of power, it enables those who have it to reduce the resistance to the course of action they prefer — that is, initially the actors subjected to persuasive power were not supportive of the action advanced by the power-wielder, but they suspended their preferences in the face of the power. Had they been fully convinced that the course of action to be followed was in accord with their preferences but that they did not have sufficient information to be aware of this or had their preferences been altered without residue rather than suspended, information would have been given or influence would have been exercised but no application of power would have occurred. The indication that power has been exercised is the remaining latent resistance of the actors who suspended their preferences. Persuasive power differs from information and influence in much the same way that suppression differs from specification (or respecification) and full substitution.

The socialization of a people, the values to which they subscribe and the intensity with which they hold them, largely determines the scope and limits of persuasive "assets." At each point in time, we suggest, the values to which actors are committed cannot quickly be changed because these commitments are the result of slow processes. These commitments are assets to those who can appeal to the values and to a power potential not available to those who seek to promote a course of action outside the context of the possible courses of action which these values approve. While commitment to a new value can be developed and then used to support a line of action, this is a much more costly process than appealing to a value that has already been internalized. Hence, the existing distribution of values almost invariably provides an advantage for some lines of action — and of persuasion — over others. The amount of these assets can be measured either in terms of the costs and efforts that were necessary to create and reinforce the relevant commitments (or those which would be required to alter them) or in terms of the scope and amount of action that can be generated by drawing upon them.

The greater the potential appeal of these values and symbols, the larger will be the amount of the persuasive assets of the unit under examination. Persuasive assets are transformed into persuasive power when a member unit or a system-elite succeeds in demonstrating that a particular course of action which it seeks other units or all member-units to follow is consistent with or an expression of those values and symbols to which the other units are committed.

POWER, INFLUENCE, AND AUTHORITY

Influence and power are often used synonymously. We suggest, however, that it is useful to keep these two terms separate in order to express a significant conceptual distinction. An application of *power* changes the actor's situation and/or his conception of his situation — but not his preferences. Resistance is overcome not because the actor subjected to the use of power changes his "will" but because resistance has been made more expensive, prohibitive, or impossible. The exercise of *influence* entails an authentic change in the actor's preferences; given the same situation, he would not choose the same course of action he favored before influence was exercised. While from the power-wielders' viewpoint, the difference between the two might be relatively small (the exercise of influence also consumes assets though it produces fewer or no countercurrents), from the subjects' viewpoint, it is more significant in that influence involves not suspension or suppression of their preferences but a respecification of their commitments.

Of the three kinds of power, persuasive power is the most similar to influence, since both are symbolic and draw on values and sentiments. The difference between them rest in the depth of their effects; persuasion suppresses the actor's preferences without changing them; it, hence, resembles influence on the surface, but there is really an exercise of power beneath. The difference between persuasion and influence is analogous to the difference between propaganda and education. When persuasive power is very effective and influence is superficial, the two are very similar, but, in general, it is not difficult to distinguish one from the other. Persuasive power works more quickly and is less costly in assets than influence,[4] but is more alienating and less commitment-inducing and has an impact that is more superficial and temporary.

Many individuals and collectivities do not have a fully developed "will" or position in regard to many issues. When they consent to a course of action, is this influence or persuasion? Assisting them to specify their positions — by helping them to articulate what they earlier only diffusely sensed they wanted — is an exercise of influence and not of power, so long as the subjects view the course of action finally followed as consonant with their needs, interests, and values. When this is the case, no resistance is overcome. When, on the other hand, people are "talked into" a course of action and have an unarticulated uneasiness about having been pressured or cheated, persuasive power has been exercised, resistance is being overcome, and alienation is being generated. The fact that the borderline between a weak exercise of influence and the competent exercise of persuasive power is blurred does not mean that the two categories are indistinguishable.

Both concepts are related to the concepts of authority and legitimation. *Authority* is defined as legitimate power — that is, power that is used in accord with the subject's values and under conditions he views as proper. But even power that is completely legitimate may still support a course of action that is not desired by the subject and is therefore alienating. This is because the course of action, legitimate or not, is still not an expression of the subject's preferences. Army officers who take their men into battle have the right to do so, a right which the subjects may acknowledge, but this does not necessarily make combat a course of action preferred by the subjects. Illegitimate power is doubly alienating, because the action is both undesirable *and* violates the sense of right and wrong. But if an authorized individual orders the same act, this still would not make the act desirable. Paying taxes to a rejected government, such as a colonial one, after the peoples' consciousness has been aroused by a national independence movement as compared to paying taxes to one's own government when identification with it is high illustrates the difference. Legitimation and satisfaction are not to be confused. On the other hand, when influence is exercised, the act does not become *desirable* even if the influence were illegitimate (although, as a rule, a full measure of influence would require that it be legitimate in terms of the subject's values).

---

[4] When we seek to deal with influence and persuasive power together, we refer to *normative control*.

KINDS OF POWER AND
LEVELS OF ALIENATION

Actors applying power have a degree of choice among the various kinds of power which differ in their alienating effects. We suggest that the application of persuasive power tends to be the least alienating (e.g., when the United States succeeds in persuading a country that not trading with Cuba is in line with values the particular country and the United States share). The application of force is the most alienating (when, for example, American military forces assume control of a foreign country). The exercise of utilitarian power, such as reducing the sugar quota or foreign aid, is less alienating than the use of force but more alienating than persuasive power.

Since societies are highly complex social systems which rely in various areas on all three kinds of power in intricate combinations, it is useful to consider the relations between the kinds of power and the corresponding levels of alienation and the social organizations associated with them first in a context less intricate (but far from trivial) than that of a total society — that is, in complex organizations. The instruments which the elites of complex organizations use to control the lower participants (e.g., students in schools, workers in factories, inmates in prisons) differ greatly in terms of their power composition. Elites which rely heavily on force to control their lower participants tend to have highly alienated lower participants; prisons are the archetype of the resulting mode of social organization. Elites which rely heavily on persuasive power and other normative controls[5] tend to have the least alienated or even committed lower participants; progressive schools are the archetype of this mode of organization. Elites which rely heavily on utilitarian power tend to have lower participants who are "in the middle" — less alienated than those subject to force but more alienated than those subject to normative control; factories are the archetype of this kind of organization. While organizations tend to mix two or three kinds of power, most "specialize" in their reliance of one kind. There is some empirical evidence to support the proposition that the varying mixes of the three kinds of power used are associated with varying degrees of alienation, as the preceding discussion implied. For instance, when the elites of an organization rely on a mix of power that is less coercive and more utilitarian than that which is found in prisons — e.g., in company towns — the alienation of those subject to control is lower and the social structure is less "distorted" by the uses of power than in prisons.

Attempts to apply these and other findings on compliance structures in

[5] We examine these points in more detail in A *Comparative Analysis of Complex Organizations* (New York: The Free Press, 1961), pp. 14-16.

complex organizations to the exploration of the foundations of societal control and organization have often proceeded by treating kinds of complex organizations as direct analogies to types of societies. Societies have been loosely characterized as prisons (for instance, totalitarian ones), as factories and market places (in particular, capitalist societies), or as giant bureaucracies. Comparisons to normative organizations are used when utopian societies are depicted.

The analogies are not without value. Some general and some specific points learned about compliance relations on one level can be transferred to the other and found to be valid. Thus, for instance, if the elites of one society rely on coercion to a greater extent than the elites of another society, or more so than the elites of the same society in an earlier period, or more to control one sub-society than others, this is expected to generate more subjective and objective alienation in the relevant societal units; we expect other specific propositions to hold as well. In prisons, it was found that the guards, themselves unable to control coercively the large numbers of inmates, grant a small number of inmates privileged positions and, thus, gain their cooperation in imposing a particular regime on the rest. In South Africa, the white police are reported to be lenient, even encouraging, toward African gangs who victimize and keep in a state of terror and suppression African neighborhoods. In concentration camps, a few Jewish "councilmen" played a role in preventing the uprising of the Jews. Similar analogies have been drawn concerning the relations between the workers and the management in industry and among the classes in the industrial society, and for other kinds of organizations and societies as well.

The direct analogy of one organizational type to one societal structure, however, is limited in the sense that societies are more complex and varied if for no other reason than that they contain organizations of all the three main types. Hence, there is a need to draw on organizational analogies other than a direct, isomorphic one; societal controlling overlayers differ in their relative reliance on coercive, utilitarian, and normative organizations, which, in turn, is expected to affect the societal level of alienation in accord with what we know about relations in these organizations.

In this context, it is fruitful to view alienation as a continuum ranging from high to low and not to assume a sharp dichotomy between alienating and non-alienating societal structures. Some modes of control are more oppressive than those of the most capitalistic industry — i.e., control by force; on the other hand, there may be a considerable degree of alienation even when there are few market relations and the role of the state is minimal, as when a societal order relies on persuasion. A guidance mechanism which is not alienating can be theoretically depicted; it is one in which action will be limited to that which is approved in a process of authentic consensus-formation in which nothing closer to power than influence is used to promote concensus among actors who differ in their needs, viewpoints, interests, and values. This, however, is likely to be a very passive society. In such a society, the lack of societal action and realization of societal goals may be more alienating than more intensive societal controls.

Alienation, it is here assumed, is generated by all users of power and not only by economic ones. Coercive power is not merely an instrument to protect property relations but a general base of power which appears more extensively in societies in which the principal means of production have been nationalized by the state than in market economies. Similarly, persuasion has alienating effects. In the sociological literature, much has been written about the directly alienating effect of work relations and the indirectly alienating effects of the societal structures based on such a work world — about the alienating impact of bureaucratic societies. Much less attention has been devoted to force and terror as modes of societal organization and the resulting distortions. Of course, the role of force in totalitarian societies is widely discussed, but there has been much less analysis of its scope in other societies. Some scant data and personal observation lead us to suggest that in developing and undeveloped nations, the fear of the use of force by the police, a gang, or the local power elite constitutes a major mode of societal control. It is easy to imagine that when hundreds of thousands of men are killed in a country in a relatively short period of time, as they were in Colombia between 1948-1962 and in Indonesia in 1966, millions of others live in great fear, and this greatly affects their relations to each other and to the power-wielders. The role of force in "undeveloped" sectors of post-modern societies has been given less attention. Whenever the subject is raised — Spanish Harlem, Negroes in Mississippi, working-class neighborhoods, the Mafia in New York — the roles of the fear of force and the actual use of force stand out as major components of societal control. Consequently, the question of the conditions under which force is curbed and milder forms of power are used is a central rather than a marginal subject for a theory of societal guidance.

We refer to *compliance* structures as the typical patterns of relations between power-wielders and their subjects; these are affected to a considerable extent by the kinds of power used and the orientations of the subjects. The main compliance structures are based on force and high alienation (coercive compliance), remuneration and comparatively lower alienation (utilitarian compliance), and normative control and commitment or low alienation (normative compliance).

Before we proceed with our main argument, it seems worth noting that, insofar as the largely qualitative and secondary data we have used allow the drawing of a conclusion, the data suggest that the same associations between the kinds of power used and the levels of alienation generated seem to hold for relations within societal units (e.g., among ranks within complex organizations), among parts of the societies. For instance, to the degree that the United Kingdom succeeded in persuading the West Indian elites that a federation was an expression of their values, its pressure to federate the islands was least alienating; to the degree that Britain used the allocation of development funds to promote support for the federation, resistance was intensified. No force was used in the case of the West Indies, but it was used elsewhere — for example, in attempts to keep the federation of Nyasaland and Northern and Southern Rhodesia intact and, for a short while, in attempts to keep Syria as a part of the United Arab Republic. In both instances, force was found to be highly alienating.

CONGRUENT AND NON-CONGRUENT
TYPES OF COMPLIANCE STRUCTURES

The association between the kinds of power employed and the amount of alienation generated can be explained in part by self-enforcing processes built into the relationship: When force is used, those subject to it tend to become highly alienated (with the exception of extreme force, as discussed above), and those who are highly alienated can hardly be controlled except by the use of force. Or those who are highly committed can readily be guided by normative means, and the reliance on normative guidance tends to build up commitment (or, at worst, to generate comparatively mild alienation). Of the nine possible combinations of the three kinds of power and the three levels of subject involvement (high alienation, high commitment, middle to low in both), only three types of compliance structure seem to be congruent: force and high alienation, normative control and commitment (or low alienation), and utilitarian power and middle to low alienation. We expect that the other six combinations are inherently unstable in that when they do occur, pressure is generated to move toward one of the three congruent combinations. When corporal punishment is introduced into a school system which has committed students, because, let us say, a new generation of teachers is not sure that it can maintain discipline in any other way, the system's compliance structure will soon shift from a coercive-committed combination to a coercive-alienated one. When a change of personnel in a prison system brings about an attempt to move from a custodial to a therapeutic orientation and, thus, to rely on normative controls rather than on force, this initially makes for a normative-alienated non-congruent compliance structure. But either the inmates will alter their orientations, leading to a congruent normative-committed pattern (as in some rehabilitation centers), or the staff will tend toward more coercive forms of control, thus restoring the coercive-alienated balance. This seems to hold on the societal level as well, with reference to the relative reliance on police forces, full employment and welfare policies, and normative leadership or opportunities for authentic participation — and the level of citizens' alienation. (There are, of course, significant differences in the ways in which various groups of participants in organizations and citizens are controlled and in the expected levels of their alienation.)

Non-congruent types occur because the orientations of those subjected to power and the kinds of power that elites employ are only partly determined by each other. The subjects' orientations toward the power-wielding elites are partly determined by the socialization, association, and mobilization of the subjects themselves. These factors might, for instance, keep a prison's inmates highly alienated even if the prison increases its reliance on normative guidance.

Similarly, the power which the elites of a societal unit employ is determined in part by such factors as the unit's market position which affects the elites' ability to rely on utilitarian power, the elites' societal license to use force, and their normative standing (e.g., endorsement by the church) which affects the elites' ability to appeal to the values of the subjects. In other words, supra- and inter-unit system factors affect both sides of the intra-unit compliance relationship: The orientation of those subject to power toward those who wield it, and the ability of the elites who wield power to exercise the various kinds of power.

The interplay between collectivistic system factors and the controlling overlayer is evident here. On the one hand, both power and the subjects' orientations, as we have seen, are affected by various system relationships (e.g., the members' affiliations with collectivities other than the one under study or the collectivity's position in the society's stratification structure). On the other hand, each societal unit has a degree of freedom — for instance, in terms of the ways in which it internally allocates whatever assets it commands. Does the unit, for example, allocate a high proportion of its utilitarian assets to the higher ranks and rely on coercion for the control of the lower ranks, or does it allocate its utilitarian assets more evenly among the ranks? Similarly, although the subjects' orientations to the elites in power are in part determined by factors external to the relationship (which, let us assume, make their predisposition a hostile one), they still are in part affected by the kinds of power used in the relationship itself. This is not to suggest that the power composition of the controlling overlayers is not affected by system factors — e.g., by what the overlayers of other units are drawing upon and by what is culturally acceptable — but to suggest that the system, in turn, is also affected by the controlling overlayers of the various member-units in that their actions help to stabilize or transform it. Hence, at each point in time, it is best to view separately the compliance (power and alienation) relationship and other relationships in the same system, and to study their reciprocal effects over a period of time.

Non-congruent types of compliance structures may persist despite internal strains for two major reasons: (1) system constraints (e.g., the lower the GNP level of a society, the more difficult it is for the society to rely on utilitarian rewards), and (2) limitations of the controlling overlayer — for instance, in its knowledge of the system (e.g., those higher in rank often have erroneous conceptions of the values, interests, and outlooks of those lower in rank). The proposition that these are non-congruent types can be tested, in that we expect the compliance structures to move in a congruent direction when the system constraints "untighten" or when a controlling overlayer's effectiveness is increased.

NEUTRALIZATION, MIXING, AND DUAL STRUCTURES

So far, we have analytically explored the patterns of compliance; we have illustrated them by pointing to those concrete units which approximate the compliance ideal-types, for in these units, one pattern of compliance is unusually predominant (e.g., coercion in prison systems). It should be noted, however, that even in those units in which one pattern is predominant, other patterns are operative (e.g., in prison systems, some inmates cooperate with the guards in exchange for goods and services). Second, several important units combine patterns of compliance much more evenly. We refer to these as dual-compliance structures.

It might at first seem that the ability of an elite to draw simultaneously on two or even three kinds of power would simply increase its capacity to control its subjects. If the subjects can be influenced *and* paid *and* forced, would the power-wielders not establish maximum control? The problem here is that each kind of power tends to slant compliance in its own direction which is partially incompatible with that of the others, and that, hence, the various kinds of power tend to have neutralization effects on each other. In particular, force and influence seem to be incompatible if relied upon *in the same control relation*; the combining of other means of control, we suggest, will also generate neutralizing effects. To illustrate, a study of mass persuasion showed that when utilitarian and normative appeals were combined to urge that the purchase of federal bonds during World War II was both a good investment and a patriotic act, this combination was less effective than when the campaign stressed normative themes alone.

However, the controlling overlayers of several societal units do mix various kinds of power without giving clear priority to one kind. In part, this is because they are unaware of the neutralization effect, and, thus, some of their power is lost. In part, the neutralization effect is minimized by segregating the application of different kinds of power, in the sense that initial attempts rely on one kind of power (usually one of the less alienating kinds), and only when they fail is the other, more alienating kind of power exercised. Thus, during a war, the population is first exhorted to increase its productive efforts before more coercive measures are introduced. And those who violate laws for the first time are more likely to be reprimanded or to have their sentences suspended (normative controls) or to be fined, and only repeated offenders are likely to be jailed (including those who did not pay their fines or heed the conditions of their suspended sentences). In addition, societal units shift controls from predominantly one pattern to another; e.g., peacetime armies change their compliance patterns as they go to war, and labor unions shift as they move from nonstrike to strike periods. Thus, various divisions — through time, between ranks, between groups of participants of the same rank — allow a dual compliance structure to be maintained with more effectiveness than when the patterns are "mixed" in the same control relation.

At the lower alienation end of the compliance continuum, utilitarian and normative controls seem to be "dissonant" when mixed, which is one reason that educators object to parents paying their children for doing their homework. Similarly, in societies, voluntary and paid services are segregated: When workers are asked to work for a cause and are given low pay, this tends to be ineffective except for limited, usually crisis, situations. (This proposition could be studied in situations in which labor unions were urged to hold down wages in time of war, to prevent inflation, or to help a labor government.)

Moving further toward commitment, we expect a strain between pure normative control and social power. Social power rests in the interpersonal ties which bind the members of a unit to each other, in terms of symbolic sanctions against leaving the unit (or secession) and against violating its norms (or changing its structure). Thus, social power rests in horizontal, associational relations and, as such, is not available for downward, hierarchical control. Normative control, on the other hand, tends to be hierarchical, to work down a rank structure, however informal it is. While social power is not hierarchical, it can be mobilized for downward control purposes, as, for instance, when leaders (who elicit normative commitments) appeal to their sub-collectivities rather than directly to the subjects. Thus, the President, like a teacher appealing to a class not to support disorderly students, may ask the nation not to support the inflationary wage demands of labor unions. In this way, normative controls are linked to horizontal networks and make the power built into these networks available for control purposes. (This is approximated by the colonial method of indirect rule using the tribes and tribal chiefs, as opposed to the more direct control of the subjects.)

While social power supports normative control under the circumstances just depicted, it tends to neutralize normative control when those circumstances are not present, despite its similarity to normative control in that they are both symbolic and relatively committing. This occurs macroscopically when a collectivity or a sub-collectivity is mobilized against societal leadership (or elites). Actually, this often entails a conflict between two normative elites of which one mobilizes the social power of the unit. A purer form of this normative versus social power conflict appears when those who seek to mobilize an unmobilized unit (or its unmobilized segments) are confronted not by a counter-elite but with apathy institutionalized in social bonds and reinforced by expressive associational activities.

The strain between normative and social power has been observed in religious movements, in which, in recent decades, increased emphasis has been placed on associational-social activities to induce people who otherwise would not do so to participate in normative activities. These social activities have grown in scope and have, thus, created a serious conflict over the amount of time which is to be devoted to religious (normative) activities as opposed to recreational (social) ones. Similarly, nuns are warned not to become too friendly toward each other lest their prime commitment to the service of God be diluted. And members of radical movements are expected to maintain their primary normative commitments to the movements rather than to other members. In addition to conflicts concerning time and the primacy of commitments, strains arise from those normative activities which, like producing activities, have an instrumental aspect (though the instrumental aspects of activities tend more often to be collectivistic than individualistic). When the instrumental aspect is stressed, man is viewed as a utensil; this is as true of totalitarian social movements as it is of the ideal-typical capitalistic corporations. It is only in egalitarian social relationships that alienation is reduced to its lowest level and man is treated as a goal unto himself. In these relationships, however, the capacity for directed collective action, for the realization of goals, is low.

THE CORRELATES OF COMPLIANCE

Many socio-political factors tend to co-vary with changes in the prevailing compliance pattern. It is not our purpose to review all or even the most important of these factors but rather to highlight the significance of compliance patterns for the understanding of the complex relationships among societal factors and their dynamics. For instance, the *internal divisions* of societal units and the *relationships among them* (both in the stratification structure and in the level of system-integration) are greatly affected by the prevailing compliance pattern. Where coercion is the rule, a caste system with sharp and rigid divisions between those in power and those subject to it tends to evolve. The divisions are sharp because there tends to be very marked social distance between the associational networks of those who are in control and those who are not (though there are always some power differences among those in control and among those who are not in control but command some power by virtue of their contract with those in control or their influence over the powerless caste). The divisions are rigid because there are little upward or downward mobility between the castes and few opportunities for gradual change in the stratification structure or polity. Such caste relations are approximated in the relations between inmates and guards in prisons, occupation forces and native populations, and racially divided societies.

Where normative controls prevail, stratification is likely to be flat — that is, there are few ranks, ranking is informal, mobility is common, and associational gradations are mild and continuous. The "ideal type" is approximated to varying degrees in therapeutic mental hospitals, in progressive schools (in the original *Kibbutzim*), and, above all, in social and political movements. Utilitarian compliance tends to be associated with a "middle" score on most of these dimensions — sub-units are less sharply segregated than they are in coercive units but more so than in normative ones; mobility is of an intermediary range, etc. Many established corporations in contemporary Western societies approximate this ideal-type.

Societal units that differ in the ways and means by which they maintain discipline also differ in their *leadership patterns*. In relatively pure coercive units, the ruling caste in its control of the subjugated caste cannot rely on leadership, for the subjugated caste tends to follow its own leaders. Inmate communities and "harsh" colonial situations, as in Algeria during the war between the French and the National Liberation Front, are cases in point. (This societal pattern is not to be confused with the pattern of control which draws on a combination of coercion and persuasion; in the latter case, the caste in power is more likely to provide some leadership to the subjugated caste. Also, early colonial situations, in which the subjugated caste does not act as a collectivity, should be kept separate.) In units that use relatively exclusively normative compliance, much of the leadership comes from the higher ranks, not only because it is accepted by the lower ranks but also because there are relatively few barriers to the promotion of informal leaders from lower to higher ranks. Social movements are a case in point. Units in which compliance is largely based on an exchange of remunerative rewards by the elites for the work of the subjects show little leadership on either level; they either never had an internal expressive life, or, so to speak, it ran "dry." To the degree that these units maintain associational-social bonds among the members, leadership emerges, but compliance also tends to move from the highly utilitarian pattern toward the normative (or normative-social) direction.

Other features of societal units are related to their respective compliance patterns, including the shapes of the intra-unit communication networks, the degree to which there is consensus among the various sub-units, and the degree to which the unit encompasses the life of the members ("scope" and "pervasiveness"). These and other related factors need not be discussed here; our purpose was only to illustrate the importance of differences in compliance patterns for societal structure. The main point is evident: The more alienating usages of power tend to split the societal units, increase the distances among the divisions, increase the instrumental or manipulative orientation, and lessen the opportunity for authentic leadership and participation — in short, decrease the possibility of an active society.

GOALS, POWER, AND ALIENATION

Assuming that our basic proposition is valid — that normative controls incur the least costs (in terms of the alienation and resistance generated), and influence is even less costly than persuasive power — the question arises: What prevents societal units from limiting their projects to those on which there is a consensus or to those which can be guided by norma-tive controls? If existing societies, distorted in various ways, are unable (or perhaps not committed) to do so, could an active society be thus designed and guided?

The study of complex organizations casts some light on both the limits and the possibilities of moving toward more normative and less coercive societal control. The limits are inherent in the variety of goals served, since the goals differ in the services which their realization requires — that is, in their ability to rely on the three major kinds of power. *Cultural* (or symbolic) *goals*, it seems, are, in general, most readily implemented by normative controls. That is, if the goal is education, socialization, re-habilitation, the reinforcement of normative commitments, or tension re-lease (as in entertainment), little other power is needed and the alienation generated is comparatively low. When other kinds of power are employed to advance cultural goals, alienation is increased and effectiveness is reduced. Paying subjects to be socialized tends to generate a calculative orientation which undermines identification with the agents of socializa-tion, an identification which is a prerequisite for the effective implementation of cultural goals.[6] Force undermines even further the conditions under which socialization succeeds; this is one of the principal reasons that rehabilitation efforts in custodial prison systems tend to be unsuccessful, or, when they are successful, they follow or are accompanied by a reduction of the prisons' use of force. This also partially accounts for the fact that totalitarian regimes, with an abundance of force at their command, invest a good deal in persuasive controls.

Production goals, including not only the manufacture of goods but also the provision of services, white collar work, and monetary activities, are served more effectively by utilitarian power as compared to both coercive and normative controls. Production is a "rational" activity in that it requires a systematic division of labor and responsibilities, a considerable amount of comparatively precise coordination, and a relatively detailed and close control (schools, churches, and prisons, it is widely agreed, can be run much more loosely than a bank or an assembly line and can still function quite effectively, probably even more effectively than if they were more "orderly"). Therefore, production requires sanctions and rewards that can be readily measured and allocated in relatively close association to performance, and utilitarian assets can be precisely applied as compared to prestige, force, or other sources of rewards and sanctions. Coercion will not suffice because most kinds of work require some degree of initiative, responsibility, and commitment on the part of even the lower participants. Only work which is routine and easily supervised, such as carrying loads or rowing in the galleys, can be controlled effectively by a reliance on coercion. Studies of forced labor camps and of societies similarly organized show that if any other kind of work is to be accomplished, either coercion is reduced or effectiveness is low.

Symbolic rewards and sanctions are quite adequate for limited, intermittent work; especially when the effort is dramatic and the relation of the project to societal goals and values is highly observable; thus, fire and flood control brigades can rely quite effectively on normative controls so long as the demands for service are infrequent and only insofar as the effort itself is concerned, as distinct from the less rewarding requirements of long alerts. The more routine, continual, and instrumental a project, the less it is able to rely on symbolic rewards and the greater the need for utilitarian ones. Nursing was a voluntary, highly normative mission when it was limited and sporadic, as in its early, Florence Nightingale days; when it became a profession, the utilitarian element in its control was greatly increased. A comparison of peacetime armies with combat troops further highlights this point: Utilitarian power is much more necessary and normative control is much less effective in the routine situation.

[6] This statement should be viewed as a proposition that needs to be supported; we shall assume that it is valid for the sake of our analysis.

Order goals involve the control of deviants by segregating them from the body of society, by punishing as well as segregating them, or by eliminating them. For all of these goals, the task involved is one of protecting the society as a system and the particular societal mold that the elites in power favor. Organizations that implement the order aims of a society tend to see the maintenance of control as their major task since the confinement of deviants, as a rule, is involuntary and punitive. Thus, it is not accidental that most prison systems are not very effective agents of resocialization, for the resocialization goal is secondary and partially incompatible with the primary goal of keeping the inmates confined. This makes reliance on controls other than coercive ones highly ineffective in terms of these organizations' primary societal goal.

The kind of power used and the nature of the compliance maintained are closely associated with the kinds of societal goals pursued as well as with the degree to which these goals are shared by elites and subjects. If the purpose of those in power is to educate and if those subject to control wish to be educated, normative control can be quite effective. If the purpose of those in power is to render ineffective those subject to power, as the subjects seek to escape, rebel, or subvert the power-wielders, violence is to be expected from both sides. If production is the goal of those in power and if those subject to power seek to exchange their labor for income, utilitarian power will serve.

This relationship also holds for more subtle differences between power-wielders' and subject-populations' goals, in terms of the kinds of power used, the alienation incurred, and the extent to which the goals are implemented. Thus, if the administration of a prison is less concerned with suppressing all deviance and more concerned with output, less force will be employed and less alienation incurred than when the prevention of escapes is the only goal and whatever the inmates produce is considered a bonus.

. . .

In exploring the relationships among power, alienation, and goals, it must be taken into account that: (1) We are dealing with relative weights; that is, no society or government ever gives up completely the use of any of the three instruments of power. Rather the differences and trends are in the mode of compliance and the related societal organization which are relatively emphasized. (2) In the same society or collectivity, the mode of compliance varies from one sub-unit to another; for instance, the "purging" of one collectivity (i.e., increased coercion and alienation) might be accompanied by "liberalization" for another, although there seems to be some pressure to follow unit-wide patterns (a) to change the controls of various sub-units in the same general direction, and (b) to treat higher strata less coercively than lower ones (note, for example, stratified law enforcement in the Western societies, in which offenders from higher classes are more likely to be controlled with a reprimand or a suspended sentence or are committed into the custody of the family, while offenders from lower classes are more likely to be incarcerated).

A COMPARATIVE PERSPECTIVE ON COMPLIANCE

The final answer to the question of how much counter-current a particular mode of societal organization generates rests in the goals pursued, because these differ in their intrinsic requirements in terms of the kinds of power their effective service demands. And in turn, these kinds of power differ in terms of the relative amounts of alienation they generate. The significance of the relative emphasis a society places on order, production, or cultural goals is further magnified in that such differences in commitment affect not only the compliance relationship between the elites and the non-elites, but also the whole societal structure and organization, from the degree to which collectivities are segregated from each other to the level of conflict among them.

Our position differs from those who see the main source of alienation in the economic or political structure (expecting capitalist societies to be and socialist ones not to be alienating), as well as from those who view "modernization" as generating alienation because of the rise of large-scale societal organizations or bureaucratization. We do recognize that the shape of the distributive patterns and the level of political responsiveness of a society are affected by the ownership of the means of production and by the size and complexity of the societal organization, and, these factors, in turn, affect the level of alienation and the power relations. We suggest, however, that although societies do differ considerably in the general levels of alienation which they generate, there are also significant differences *within* each society with respect to the goals which the particular societal sector serves and the control mix employed in that particular sector. And since all societies devote portions of their activities to cultural, production, and order goals, all societies — whatever their stratification structure and political organization — are expected to have respectively a relatively less alienating and a relatively more alienating sector. Thus, inmates of American and Soviet prison systems are expected to be more subjectively and objectively alienated from their respective societies than children in the more successful school systems in these societies, despite the important differences between the stratification structures, polities, and cultures of the two countries. Similarly, we expect factory workers in both societies to be less alienated than inmates and more alienated than students in successful schools.

To shift to another comparative dimension, we expect some important similarities in the reactions of factory workers to their role in the organization of production in developed, developing, and underdeveloped societies, despite large differences in the size and complexities of their societies as well as in their stratification and political structures and cultures. The same would hold for inmates of the respective prison systems and for members of normatively controlled organizations — let us say, non-violent ideological political parties. To put it differently, against the backdrop of *differing societal structures*, there are *sectoral similarities* due to similarities in the goals served, in their intrinsic needs, and in the "typical" means of control used. Actually, there is repeated surprise expressed in some social science literature about the similar ways in which organizations that are similar in their societal goals are managed, since the societies in which they are located differ considerably in their cultural, societal, and political life — e.g., similarities in factories in Poland, India, West Germany, the United States, and Britain. The theoretical framework presented here may help to account for this similarity.

Secondly, the cross-societal differences themselves are due, in part, to differences in the relative emphases given to goals and means of control and in the scopes of the respective sectors rather than to differences in overall societal structures. Thus, if society X is less alienating than society Y, this is in part because society X produces less and is more supportive of associational-social activities (which are classified here as "cultural") as well as because of differences in the ownership of the means of production or in societal complexity. Thus, for instance, if inmates of Norwegian prisons are less alienated than inmates of American ones, this is not because Norway's means of production are more nationalized or Norway is a less complex or modernized society, but because there is a *relatively* greater emphasis placed on rehabilitation and on normative means of control in Norwegian prisons than in American prisons. The fact that those prisons in the United States in which the compliance mix is similar to that in Norwegian prisons seem to have less alienated inmates supports this statement.

Societal structures are relevant in that they affect the degrees to which the various goals are emphasized and the various means of control are favored. For instance, modernization tends to entail an increased emphasis on production and a greater reliance on utilitarian controls; market economies are more tolerant of utilitarian controls than centrally regulated economies. But there are limits, all too often ignored, to the degree to which (a) the services to the same basic goal can be differently controlled in terms of the kind of power employed; and (b) societies can reduce their emphasis on order and production goals and increase their emphasis on cultural ones, which is the primary way of reducing alienation resulting from the means of control. (The secondary way of reducing such alienation is to use less alienating means of control within each category — e.g., to control prison systems with as little coercion as possible.) The active society, hence, will be neither without power nor without alienation. Their scope will depend on the extension and acceleration of . . . various historical trends. . . .

12   RUTH C. YOUNG AND
       JOSE A. MORENO

d✓

Economic Development and Social Rigidity:
A Comparative Study of the
Forty-eight States

A number of cross-national studies have discriminated poor nations from rich. A cluster of attributes has been demonstrated to be closely associated with poverty, defined commonly as per capita income. Among these are illiteracy, low industrialization, degree of urbanization, energy consumption, mass media use, and the like. Indeed, all of these are so closely associated as to preclude the possibility that they are separate and causally related factors. Schnore has shown that among some eleven such measures a single factor explained a large part of the variation.[1] Perhaps now we should back off from this approach and view the general problem of national development from a different perspective. If we compare societies with a similar level of economic development, is there any theoretical framework that might enable us to discriminate among them and predict which has the best long range potential for future survival and development?

Among societies with a similar level of economic development, it is pro-

From *Economic Development and Cultural Change*, Vol. XIII, 1965, pp. 439-451, © 1965 by The University of Chicago. Reprinted by permission of the authors and The University of Chicago Press.

[1] Leo F. Schnore, "The Statistical Measurement of Urbanization and Economic Development," *Land Economics*, XXXVII, No. 3 (August 1961). At the state level see F. W. Ogburn and Francis R. Allen, "Technological Development and Per Capita Income," *American Journal of Sociology*, LXV, No. 2 (September 1959), 127-31.

posed that those with economic and political potential are those with flexible social structure. All known societies have some type of class system and are divided into some types of specialized, relatively segregated groupings. By a flexible social structure we mean one in which such classes and other groupings are highly intercommunicative; they have a rational and non-ascriptive basis for recruitment of members; they have permeable boundaries and interchange members freely; and indeed, when the situation which brought a particular grouping into existence changes, the group itself merges with another or goes out of existence readily.

We are predicting that societies with a flexible social structure will have a flexible political structure and a flexible economy. By a flexible political structure we mean one in which many ideas can compete for a hearing and decisions can be made among them in a peaceful manner. Such a political structure can handle new information and adapt to it effectively.

By a flexible economy we mean one which is optimally organized to gather new information and make use of it. Such an economy is, by definition, innovative. But the handling of information efficiently requires also great technical specialization. Such specialization requires complex integrating organizations. To make use of information requires, one might say, great adaptability on the part of the economic sector, which is organized to allow for all types of talents, which can handle a diversity of specialized problems in a diversity of types or organizations. These in turn are integrated into a functioning sub-system of such mechanisms as professional associations, trade unions, research organizations, patent systems, marketing organizations, advertising, and the like. A flexible economy finally requires a system that allocates its rewards rationally so as to encourage the necessary technical development and innovative participation on the part of its labor force. This practice is especially necessary in a flexible system, because the labor force is important not only physically but as essential units in the acquisition of information, as social beings who feed new information back into the system, both innovative and critical. For a flexible system to maintain its efficiency, new information must be fed not only into constructive channels from the top and work its way to the bottom, but the bottom must report critically to the top of the organizational hierarchy so that the system may be continually self-correcting.

A flexible social system as a whole is one which can receive, sort, evaluate, and act upon a wide array of information and make any adjustment that might help maintain its favorable position relative to other societies, from additional specialization to radical change. By its essential openness, it has institutionalized innovation in a variety of ways so that it is not haphazard or serendipitous, but it is valued, regularized, and built into the entire social structure.

It is assumed that the class structure, the economy, and the political structure of a system are relatively separate but closely interacting sub-systems. The social structure has often been termed the integrative and the economy the adaptative sub-system. We might say here that in a society in which all of these sub-systems are flexible, they are loosely co-ordinated in such a way that change can enter the social system through any channel, and that channel can act with some degree of autonomy apart from other sectors which adapt later. Such terms as dynamic equilibrium suggest our conceptual intent, even though they are difficult to define precisely.

The closed or rigid society, in contrast, is a static equilibrium, where a *status quo* is highly institutionalized and all the forces of the system are focused on the prevention of change. New information is prevented from entering channels and endangering its static state. The rigid or closed society requires a class system based on ascriptive or traditional criteria such as race, religion, caste, or ethnicity, in which mobility is severely restricted and boundaries are tight. It has a centralized political and power system, and both institutions are protected by a traditional ideology and a view of the truth passed on unchanging. Its economic structure also tends to be monolithic in nature, so as to prevent alternate sources of power from arising. Its industry requires a low level of technical training, and this lack of personal competence reinforces the class system and discourages critical feedback. It is not innovative, for sanctions are exercised against theories that challenge the traditional view of the truth. It is simpler or less differentiated in organization. The sub-systems of a rigid society are tightly interlocked, and the pressures exerted on each by the others tend to make all throw up barriers to an outside stimulus which could endanger the whole rigid system. One might go so far as to say that any change in a rigid system, for this reason, will tend to be a violent one. In sum, it serves and preserves the *status quo*. In the long run of history it is less resilient than the open social system and is subject to obsolescence, corruption, and revolt from within, and economic, political, or military conquest from without.

From this theory we derive the following hypothesis: in social systems with similar levels of industrialization, a flexible or open society will tend to have a more innovative and change-oriented economic structure than a closed one, and it will have a more intercommunicative, competitive political structure. While this synchronic hypothesis lacks the time prediction implied by the early statement, a truly diachronic hypothesis would require going back to the early period in the United States before any interaction between dependent and independent variables would have been possible.

Flexibility of the social system will be indexed by the openness of the social class structure, a *sine qua non* of the flexible, communicative society. An innovative or change-oriented economic system will be indexed in terms of amounts of innovation, by degree of technical competence, by organizational complexity, productivity, and the extent to which it allocates its rewards widely among its labor force, which we have claimed to be essential to the development of a technically superior and a self-correcting economic structure. Innovation is a primary characteristic of a flexible economy and its most direct indicator, but the other attributes are closely implied by the theory. Political flexibility will be measured in terms of the degree to which the political sub-system is competitive.

The general level of industrial development is treated as a control variable and will be measured in a variety of ways: proportion of workers in industrial work, per capita income, and degree of urbanization.

RESEARCH METHOD

A methodological difficulty of cross-national studies has been the paucity and unreliability of data. But there is an abundance of data on the 48 (now 50) United States. These units are very different in their social, political, and economic structure. It is true that their participation in a strong federal union mitigates economic differences, at least, by way of federal aid, lack of tariffs and sanctions, price supports, and the like; hence, any results obtained should have great credibility. The fact that they are not wholly independent units of analysis works against the hypothesis of this study. While states are undoubtedly different from nations in many respects, it must be acknowledged that they are similar in many others and act as autonomous units in many respects. Likewise, few nations are wholly autonomous but have international interaction and constraints through participation in all manner of alliances, from the bonds of former colonialism to the Common Market.

Thus, the former forty-eight United States of America comprised the universe studied. Although no tests of significance are required in such a case, degrees of association among variables are of interest, and levels of significance which would obtain for samples of similar size are given for purposes of comparison. The standard hypothesis relating rigid social structures to low levels of industrialization, urbanization, and per capita income has also been tested as part of the background of the study, though this is of lesser importance in the present context. On other tests, the level of industrialization was controlled. In most cases such control meant using a ratio, the denominator of which was not total population of a state, but rather population employed in manufacturing. In one case where this procedure was not possible, the level of industrialization was partialled out.

It might be emphasized again that this is a study of group structure, of social systems acting as units. It does not hypothesize about individual people as actors nor study them as units of analysis. The unit of analysis is the state, with its highly institutionalized social, political, and economic structure developed over a long period of time.

MEASUREMENT OF SOCIAL RIGIDITY

The openness of the class system was indexed by a scale of institutionalized white supremacy developed by Shapiro,[2] H. D. Price,[3] and Williams.[4] Though a rigid and nonrational class structure might be based on criteria such as religion, caste, ethnicity, regionalism, or any other ascriptive rule, the most prevalent and most pervasive expression of such rigidity in the United States seems to be discrimination against Negroes. The scale used by Williams covered only the Southern states and involved only discriminatory laws or state-level discriminatory practices. Therefore it was necessary to extend it to the rest of the forty-eight states by adding items based on anti-discrimination laws in the more socially progressive states.[5] The fourteen items in Table 1 represent a demonstration of cumulative institutional barriers to general social mobility. Items are all phrased in terms of fluidity and each represents a law or, in a couple of cases and explicitly phrased as such, state-wide practices. Of course, the items might have been phrased in terms of rigidity. At the top of the scale, only ten percent of the states have laws forbidding discrimination in the civil service, while at the bottom the last scale items cuts off 91 percent of all states, and only nine percent had any vote for Thurmond in 1948. These nine percent constitute a last step in the scale, although it is not indicated as such. The items tap in various ways the institutionalized, publicly known and supported barriers to mobility appear in the civil service, schools, and voting practices. It is not simply a measure of interpersonal relations, but taps the way a state is organized to determine these relationships, regardless of variations among individuals. Table 1 also shows the errors, marginals, and source from which each item was derived. The coefficient of reproducibility is .99, and the coefficient of scalability[6] is .97. A few items which were candidates for the scale did not qualify. These consisted of

[2] G. Shapiro, "Myrdal's Definition of the South: A Methodological Note," *American Sociological Review* (1948), 619-21.

[3] H. D. Price, *The Negro and Southern Politics* (New York: New York University Press, 1957).

[4] Robin M. Williams, *Strangers Next Door: Ethnic Relations in American Communities* (Englewood Cliffs, N.J.: Prentice-Hall, 1964). Ranking of states on this scale and other indicators used are available on request to the authors.

[5] Edwin S. Neuman, *The Law of Civil Rights and Civil Liberties* (New York: Oceana Publications, 1957), pp. 83-93.

[6] H. Menzel, "A New Coefficient for Scalogram Analysis," *Public Opinion Quarterly*, XVII, No. 2 (September 1953), 268-80.

166 RUTH C. YOUNG AND JOSE A. MORENO

TABLE 1. GUTTMAN SCALE OF SOCIAL FLUIDITY OF THE FORTY-EIGHT STATES[a]

	Errors	Marginals	Source
1. No discrimination in the Civil Service.	1	.10	Newman, 1957, 86
2. No discrimination in Public Housing and Veterans Administration.	1	.12	Newman, 1957, 90
3. No discrimination in National Guard.	0	.17	Newman, 1957, 92
4. No discrimination in city zoning.	1	.20	Newman, 1957, 90
5. No discrimination in public works, and/or Fair Employment Practices.	0	.42	Newman, 1957, 83-85
6. No discrimination in "public places," hotels, and travel facilities.	1	.44	Newman, 1957, 79
7. No school segregation in 1948 or 1954.	0	.64	Williams, 1964
8. No slave state in 1860.	1	.64	Williams, 1964
9. No Jim Crow laws in railways.	0	.69	Williams, 1964
10. No Jim Crow laws in street cars.	0	.75	Williams, 1964
11. No white primary part.	0	.77	Williams, 1964
12. No white primary total.	0	.83	Williams, 1964
13. No vote for Democrats in both 1924 and 1928 elections.	0	.88	Williams, 1964
14. No vote for Thurmond in 1948.	0	.91	Williams, 1964

[a]Coefficient of reproducibility = .99; coefficient of scalability = .97.

two main types: first, items such as restrictions on the sale of liquor to minorities that applied in only one or two states and may be considered random error; second, certain items, like additional aspects of school segregation, that probably reflect the present state of abnormal fluctuation in response to integration pressures.

MEASUREMENT OF POLITICAL RIGIDITY

A similar cumulative scale of political competitiveness was developed using recent studies of interparty competition in the states.[7] It is identical in form with the first scale, except that here the items are phrased in terms of increasing rigidity. The first step, high competition for offices both of

[7] See Table 3 and bibliographic references to V. O. Key, Jr.; A. Ranney and W. Kendall; and J. A. Schlesinger.

governor and president, is found in only 19 percent of the states and represents high interparty competition. The nature of the scale tells us that those 19 percent of the states had all the other items as well. The theme of interparty political competition and multiplicity of representation runs through the whole scale. The last step, possessed by all but nine percent of the states, is that the minority party gets at least 30 percent of the votes in at least ten percent of the elections, and these nine percent again form a last step in the scale. All items were devised by political scientists as measures of interparty competitiveness. One item was used in both scales, item 9 in this scale, no white primary total. In the first scale it represents a racial barrier; in the second it represents a political maneuver. But in neither case would its omission materially change the correlations, since it cuts off so few states. The coefficient of reproducibility is .99, and the coefficient of scalability is .94. Table 2 presents the scale steps, the errors for each item, the marginals, and the source from which it was derived. The correlation between the scales of social rigidity and political competitiveness is .51, using Kendall's tau,[8] confirming part of the hypothesis. One might argue that the reason for this close correlation is that these scales really represent different measures of the same thing, that the rigid social class system implies a social system that fills roles according to the same criterion, rational or otherwise, in its hierarchies of wealth, prestige, and power. Or one might argue that a political system cannot be considered a system that lacks some definition of the selection process for its various positions of leader, citizen, etc. Actually, we consider these all to be closely interrelated sub-systems of a single social system, which can only be relatively separated for analytic purposes, and one might define these sub-systems variously for different purposes of strategic attack. Since revolutions, wars, etc., of a government can lead to changes in a political system independent in the first instance of prior changes in the class system, and since changes in a class system can be initiated by means other than re-organization of the political structure, some focusing on these as relatively separate sub-systems seems justified. Even if it were not, however, we wish to offer different measures, in order to relate this research to what

[8] M. G. Kendall, *Rank Correlation Methods* (London: Charles Griffin, 1948), p. 26.

$$tau = \frac{S}{\sqrt{\frac{1}{2} N (N-1) - T} \cdot \sqrt{\frac{1}{2} N (N-1) - U}}$$

where S = the total score, N = number of subjects, $T = \frac{1}{2} \Sigma t (t-1)$ (t = the number of ties in X), and U similarly allows for the number of ties in Y. For a test of significance see S. Siegel, *Non-Parametric Statistics for the Behavioral Sciences* (New York: Maple Press, 1956), pp. 221-47. Coefficients which would be significant in a random sample of this size at the .01 level are .21, and at the .05 level .16, respectively.

TABLE 2. GUTTMAN SCALE OF POLITICAL COMPETITIVENESS OF THE FORTY-EIGHT STATES[a]

	Errors	Marginals	Source
1. States are highly competitive for office of governor and president; there has been a change in party in power in 40 percent or more of the elections from 1870 to 1950 for both offices.	0	.19	Schlesinger, 1955, 1122 and 1127
2. Governor's office is competitive; in non-competitive states the minority party is unable to win elections often and "when it wins it is likely to be by default."	0	.44	Schlesinger, 1955, 1122
3. State is classified as a two-party system; the minority party has won at least 25 percent of all elections, from 1914 to 1952.	2	.54	Ranney and Kendall, 1954, 482
4. President's office is competitive; same rule as item 2.	2	.60	Schlesinger, 1955, 1127
5. There is minimum partisan division of power between the governor and legislature; the office of governor and the legislatures were not controlled by the same party for at least 2 years between 1931 and 1952.	1	.69	V. O. Key, 1956, 55
6. Minority party gets at least 40 percent of the vote in most elections.	0	.75	Ranney and Kendall, 1954, 483
7. There is no run-off primary; held when no candidate receives a majority in the first polling, and the two high candidates compete in the run-off.	0	.77	V. O. Key, 1950, 417
8. Minority party gets at least 30 percent of the vote in most elections.	0	.81	Ranney and Kendall, 1954, 483
9. No white primary total.	0	.83	Williams, 1964
10. Minority party gets 30 percent of the votes in at least 10 percent of the elections.	0	.91	Ranney and Kendall, 1954, 484

[a]Coefficient of reproducibility = .99; coefficient of scalability = .94.

have been, with or without justification, quite separate lines of research and theory.

MEASUREMENT OF ATTRIBUTES OF ECONOMIC FLEXIBILITY

Tables 3, 4, and 5 show the economic attributes, the indicators used to measure them, and sources from which they were taken. Table 3 gives general measures of economic development, per capita income, urbanization, and industrialization. Table 4 shows measures of economic fluidity or flexibility. Innovation is measured in terms of new construction, rapidly growing industries, and patents filed. The single best measure of technological development available was the number of engineers in the state. To measure organizational complexity, we used the number of plants in a state with over 100 workers and the distribution of the 500 largest corporations, banks, transportation companies, and the like. General productivity was measured by value added by manufacture. Table 5 lists a number of measures of "distributive economic development" (or the extent to which the state's wealth is spread over the populace). In Table 4, all the tests were made with industrialization controlled, and in Table 5, subgroups of workers with similar occupations were compared, in order to nullify the effect of any disproportion of certain occupational categories, like professional jobs, that arises from a high level of industrialization.

Table 3 establishes the expected relations between social rigidity and the general level of economic and industrial development and urbanization. While this was not an hypothesis of this study, it is nonetheless of

TABLE 3. RELATION OF URBANIZATION AND
INDUSTRIALIZATION TO SOCIAL FLUIDITY

	Value t_b	Source of Data
1. Percent total population of state urban.	.42[a]	U.S. Census of Population, 1960, U.S. Summary, Table 107
2. Percent of labor force in manufacture.	.19	*Ibid.*, Table 106
3. Percent of labor force in white collar occupations.	.41[a]	*Ibid.*, Table 106
4. Percent of labor force professional.	.39[a]	*Ibid.*, Table 128
5. Total value added as a ratio of total number of people in state.	.35[a]	U.S. Census of Manufacture, 1958, Table 6, U.S. Census of Population, 1960. U.S. Summary, Table 1, Item 3.

[a]Significant at the .01 level.

RUTH C. YOUNG AND JOSE A. MORENO

TABLE 4. RELATION OF ECONOMIC FLUIDITY
TO SOCIAL FLUIDITY

	Value t_b	Source of Data
1. Innovation		
a. Construction of industrial plants (private) in millions of dollars as a ratio of number of industrial workers in the state.	−.14	U.S. Statistical Abstracts, 1963, Tables 1060 and 1094.
b. Number of workers employed in rapidly growing industries as a ratio of total number of industrial workers in the state.	.47[a]	Perloff, 1960, 68 ff., 304
c. Average number of patents and designs issued in state for every 10,000 workers, three years totals centered on 1900, 1920, 1930, 1940, and 1950.	.65[a]	Smookler, 1957, 327 ff.
d. Same indicator as c., partialling out number of workers employed in manufacture in each state.	.63[b]	Ibid.; and U.S. Census of Population, 1950, U.S. Summary, Table 82
2. Technological development Engineers in state per every 10,000 workers in manufacture.	.37[a]	U.S. Census of Population, 1960, U.S. Summary, Table 126
3. Organizational complexity		
a. Ratio of plants with more than 100 workers in state to total number of plants of same size in country, divided by ratio of workers in manufacture in state to total number in country.	−29[a]	U.S. Census of Population, 1960, U.S. Summary, Table 1, Item 88.
b. Percentage distribution of the 500 largest corporations, the 50 largest banks, merchandizing, transportation, utility, and life insurance companies in the country, divided by number of workers in manufacture in state as percentage of total in country.	.26[a]	Fortune: The Largest 500, 1962; and U.S. Census of Population, 1960, U.S. Summary, Table 1, Items 89 and 94
4. General productivity Value added by manufacture as ratio of total number of workers in manufacture in the state.	.15	U.S. Census of Manufacture, 1958, Table 6; U.S. Census of Population, 1960, U.S. Summary, Table 1, Items 89 and 94.

[a]Significant at .01 level.

[b]See Kendall, op. cit., for formula for partial rank correlation, p. 97. No tests of significance are available for the partial rank correlation.

importance in the general understanding of the results. Percent of the labor force in manufacture, which we used repeatedly as a control variable in later tests is not significant at the .05 level, and it was among the lowest relations discovered in the study. That is, despite social rigidity differences, states are somewhat more comparable in this respect than in some other aspects of economic functioning that we have considered more critical.

Tables 4 and 5 test the essential element in the hypothesis, the relation between social rigidity and economic structure. Two of the three tests relating social fluidity to innovation were confirmed, and these probably

TABLE 5. RELATION OF DISTRIBUTIVE ECONOMIC
DEVELOPMENT TO SOCIAL FLUIDITY

	Value t_b	Source of Data
1. Median per capita income for males by states.	.61[a]	U.S. Census of Population, 1960, U.S. Summary, Table 139.
2. Median family income by states.	.59[a]	*Ibid.,* Table 137.
3. Average hourly earnings of workers in manufacture.	.40[a]	U.S. Statistical Abstract 1963, Table 307.
4. Median earnings of male farm laborers by states.	.39[a]	U.S. Census of Population, 1960, U.S. Summary, Table 10.
5. Median earnings of male professional, managerial, and kindred workers by states.	.48[a]	*Ibid.*
6. Difference between observed and expected per capita income by states, as a percentage of expected income.	.44[a]	Perloff, 1960, 529 and 530
7. State relatives of U.S. per capita income, 1920-54 (state per capita incomes a percentage of the national per capita income).	.57[a]	Hanna, 1959, 37
8. Measure of intersectoral inequality (difference between the share in the labor force of the three sectors of industry: manufacture, agriculture, and services).	.39[a]	Kuznets, 1963, 74-76, and Appendix Table 3.
9. Concentration ratio by states.[b]	.50[a]	*Ibid.,* 74-77, Appendix Table 3.
10. Federal tax burden per capita by states (state per capita income as a percentage of the national per capita income).	.54[a]	Facts and Figures, 1962, Table 139.

[a]Significant at .01 level.

[b]The ratio of the area between the Lorenz curve and the diagonal representing full equality, to the area under the diagonal which measures the departure of the Lorenz curve from complete equality, expressed as a ratio to the complete inequality. It ranges from 0 for complete equality to 1 for maximum inequality.

represent the most direct measures of this attribute. The test which was not confirmed involved construction of industrial plants. This test probably failed because of errors of measurement. New construction is only a small part of innovation. Similarly, not all construction represents innovation, but rather simple replication or expansion of already well established types of industry.

The test of technological complexity, as indexed by engineers per state, was confirmed.

The test of organizational complexity ran into some unexpected results. While the relationship involving the distribution of the 500 largest corporations was confirmed, the one regarding the distribution of plants with more than 100 workers was not. Moreover, the ratio of plants with over 100 workers was negatively related to social fluidity, in contradiction to the hypothesis. However, a later section will argue that this result, although requiring a revised and more penetrating explanation of the economic structure of rigid societies, does not call for a rejection of the general hypothesis.

The test of the relation between social fluidity and productivity was unsuccessful. Value added by manufacture is a somewhat mysterious measure which must take into account, among other things, the state of the market. Its lack of clarity makes explanation of its failure to relate more difficult, but this again might fit into a revised explanation.

Table 5 shows the relationships between what we have termed distributive economic development and social fluidity. All ten tests were successful. These results have more significance in terms of the present theoretical approach than the associations of a structural measure with indices of well-being, welfare, or levels of consumption. In terms of this approach, they represent the fact that the economic strength and skill is spread over the populace, rather than being confined to a narrow sector of society. Societies which have such a spread are investing profits in building a well-trained, flexible work force which, under conditions of rational mobility, can be expected to make great positive contributions to the strength of the rest of the economic structure.

Finally, Table 6 gives the relations between the scale of political competitiveness and representative indicators of economic development and fluidity. All tests were confirmed, except that involving the 500 largest corporations.

DISCUSSION

Social rigidity and political rigidity have been shown to be related to attributes of a stagnant economic structure; they are inversely correlated with innovation, risk-taking, technical proficiency, organizational complex-

TABLE 6. RELATIONS OF POLITICAL FLUIDITY TO
SELECTED INDICATORS OF ECONOMIC FLUIDITY[a]

	t_b
1. Number of engineers per 10,000 workers in manufacture, by states.	.41[b]
2. Number of patents and designs per 10,000 workers in the state.	.50[b]
3. Ratio of the 500 largest corporations, the 50 largest banks, merchandising, transportation, utility, and life insurance companies in the country, divided by number of workers in state as percentage of total in country.	.18
4. Percent of people in state urban.	.34[b]
5. Median per capita income, by states.	.57[b]

[a]Sources are the same as those in Tables 3, 4, and 5.
[b]Significant at .01 level.

ity, and distributive economic development, over and above the expected value of these attributes based on the general level of industrialization of the states. They are also related, of course, to the general levels of industrialization, urbanization, and income.

Although the socially flexible states had the highest proportion of the 500 largest plants in the United States, they also had significantly higher proportions of the smallest plants (as demonstrated by the negative correlation with proportions of plants with over 100 workers). They have also been shown to be highly innovative, and we might posit that innovation is characteristic of small and new industry. Additionally, what do these facts suggest? The fact that the flexible states have a disproportionate share of the largest as well as the smallest industries suggests a revision of, rather than rejection of the theory.

The largest industries relate as expected, since they are the most complex. But the disproportionate number of small plants in the socially flexible states may also be interpreted as a measure of diversity of type of industry. While the largest industries represent great resources for adaptation and research operations, the smaller industries probably represent innovative activity of a different type. This certainly has been thought to be the case in American society. Similarly, perhaps the reason that the rigid states have disproportionally more plants with over 100 employees can be explained by hypothesizing that these states develop a type of industry different from other states and consonant with their social structure. We might characterize this pattern as a "plantation" type of industry, depending on simple processing operations which exploit natural resources with a ready market, involving work of simple skill, requiring little innovation and little development of the skills of workers, all of which have been shown here to be related to this type of industry. This "plantation" type of industry, we propose, supports a highly centralized, non-rational, and unchanging political power structure which remains unchallenged over the years by new ideas or developing expectations. The maintenance of this *status quo* involves the avoidance, of course, of free social mobility; and a non-rational class structure serves admirably to keep the same positions over time.

The reason that it is possible to maintain this anachronistic type of industrial organization with its obvious limitations is that it does not differ from the more progressive and flexible organizations in "value added" and, with a labor surplus and a non-competitive market, in profit to the controlling financial investors. It is functional in terms of ordinary business criteria, but it is not functional in terms of a contribution to national strength. The truth of this analysis follows from the fact that "value added," representing as it does the difference between cost of materials and market value of a product, includes labor costs, industrial costs, and costs of capital and also considers the state of the market. Since the flexible states have more technically involved operations, and since they invest more in labor, the implication is that rigid industries make their profit in two ways: by taking advantage of a relatively monopolistic market situation with great present demand for a product that is subject to change in a changing world, or by using a technically simple operation for processing primary products like iron or steel that, once set up, is all that is required to make it valuable in a competing market. But because of its diminished research operations, its less adventurous nature, its lesser technical resources, and its low-skilled labor force, such industry is extremely vulnerable in the face of change.

That is, the difficulty and danger in this type of operation lies not, as economists have suggested, in its failure to make immediate profit, but in its failure to develop a skilled labor force, a ready supply of new ideas, a supporting scientific structure, and a modern industrial organization, for it is these that enable it to survive the challenge of inevitable change in the world around it and avoid extinction as a system. This danger is enhanced by the obvious ability of certain types of "plantation" industry to compare in "value added" with more progressive types. This point has been unclear up to now, because many persons who have discussed the differences in value added between, for instance, the North and South,[9] have discussed value added per capita of the populace, rather than relative to the amount of industry. The present analysis suggests, however, that

[9] See, for instance, William H. Nicholls, *Southern Tradition and Regional Progress* (Chapel Hill: University of North Carolina Press), p. 177.

in certain instances with a special market situation, plantation agriculture or industry is competitive, in terms of value added, with agriculture or industry superior in innovation, technical competence, organization, or development of the labor force. This fact enables such an economy to maintain the society in which it exists as stagnant and backward in every other way. But again let us note that "value added" is here and now, is highly dependent upon a certain type of market, and is linked to a certain present stage of scientific development. It can be quickly threatened when nylon is invented to compete with cotton, or tobacco is shown to cause cancer. Moreover, the profit is distributed mainly to stockholders and not to the wider populace who, when educated and skilled in industrial and political participation, are a social system's chief hope for survival.

SUMMARY

Societies with socially rigid structures have been shown to have less competitive political structures and economic structures different from open societies. Even when similar with respect to level of industrialization, they are less innovative, are less technically complex, and have less of both extremely large and very small (and new) types of industry. They are similar to open societies in value added, but appear to maintain such comparability partially, at least, by a poorly paid, low-skilled, relatively immobile labor force, combined with a special type of market situation. Therefore, we have characterized them as having industry similar in social structure to plantation agriculture, with a few persons at the top and many low-skilled workers at the bottom, limited in its technical complexity and producing a simple marketable product in a manner that changes little over time. It is of "plantation size," does not allow room for small industry, and does not maintain the gigantic innovative organization of the very large. Many hands make dull work but reasonable profits.

Do we have a tautology here, in the sense that social, economic, and political rigidity are all simply ways of characterizing rigid societies and are so closely related as to preclude the possibility that they are separate factors that vary separately? An answer involves a number of considerations. First, the correlations range from .14 to .65. The relationships are not so strong as to indicate a redundancy. But even if all the variables were simply components of a more general rigid dimension, we have still shown that they are at least quite different from a nonetheless related factor, level of industrialization. However, this study did not claim to be a causal analysis, and we do not pretend to have evidence on this point. Future studies hopefully will replicate results cross-nationally and also develop time perspective. The most likely hypothesis about causal relations among the three factors, however, is that in response to the system's interaction with other social systems in the wider world, one of these sets of institutions can undergo some change. But this change, since all of the institutions are closely linked in an interacting social system, reacts on the other two sets of institutions. However, the persistence of the essential nature of these systems over a long period of time in our history argues that such change is not easily effected. The internal interaction among these institutions, and especially in a tightly interlocked, rigid society, probably results in common reinforcement such that, failing important outside pressure, the rigid structures get more so over time.[10]

13   EDWARD T. SILVA

A Note on Cross-Societal Propositions
and American State Data

. . . Young and Moreno ask: "If we compare societies at a similar level of economic development, is there any theoretical framework that might enable us to discriminate among them and predict which has the best long range potential for future survival and development?" (p. 161). They then develop such a framework and use data referring to the experiences of the American states to test it. This immediately raises questions as to the appropriateness of such data in the testing of cross-societal propositions. It is the purpose of this note to suggest that, in general, a research strategy involving comparisons among the 48 (now 50) states to test cross-societal propositions rests upon certain untenable assumptions. Therefore, it will be argued, such a research strategy cannot be fruitfully employed to this end. Finally, it will be said that only under certain conditions is 48-state data of fundamental utility to the student of societal change.

[10] See Gunnar Myrdal, *Rich Lands and Poor: The Road to World Prosperity* (New York: Harper, 1958), who observes that rich nations appear to get richer and poor poorer, a similar cyclical point of view.

From *Economic Development and Cultural Change*, Vol. XIV, 1966, pp. 355-360, © 1966 by The University of Chicago. Reprinted by permission of the author and The University of Chicago Press.

I

The ability of data that reflects the experiences of the American states to represent the experiences of national societies rests upon the assumption that each of these states is a reasonable approximation of such a society. Young and Moreno are aware of considerations of this sort. They remark:

> It is true that their [i.e., the states'] participation in a strong federal union mitigates economic differences, at least, by way of federal aid, lack of tariffs and sanctions, price supports and the like; hence, any results obtained should have great credibility. The fact that they are not wholly independent units of analysis works against the hypothesis of this study. While states are undoubtedly different from nations in many respects, it must be acknowledged that they are similar in many other and act as autonomous units in many respects. Likewise, few nations are wholly autonomous but have international interaction and constraints through participation in all manner of alliances . . . (p. 164).

This statement avoids a defense of the assumption that states approximate national societies, substituting for it the impression that the data will somehow enter a brief. It must be pointed out that the question of whether or not "any results obtained should have great credibility" — and thus vitiate the lack of formally specified similarities between states and societies — is an open one. The answer to this question is dependent upon a myriad of factors, including the epistemic correlation of each measurement device utilized. For example, the scale of social fluidity developed by Young and Moreno does not appear to be epistemically correlated with "class structure." Rather, most of the scale items refer primarily to Negro-white structural arrangements and thus to caste, and not class, barriers to social mobility. Hence, unless the notion of social fluidity is to be restricted to caste considerations, which is clearly not the authors' intention, the measure appears to be devoid of logical validity. However, quite aside from considerations of empirical credibility and epistemic validity, the demonstration that the American states are generally similar to national societies seems unlikely, for two sets of structural reasons which are particular to the American situation (1) as a federated political unit, and (2) as a national, economic entity which is not structured with respect to the states.

Politically, the several American states are structurally embedded in a federated nation state. It is true that this structure of association among the states, and between the states and the central government, is a variable attribute, as was demonstrated by the American civil war. Yet it seems of overriding importance that the legal and political structures of each state are significantly and continuously affected by the bargaining and decision behavior of federal level actors, at least some of whom represent other states. Thus, for example, several of the items in the Young-Moreno scale of social fluidity, notably, discrimination in public accommodations and school segregation, were previously permitted and are currently prohibited by federal-level rule-making and enforcement units acting, at least in part, at the behest of the agents of other states. Additionally, the several states are constitutionally excluded from a large number of activities that one usually associates with national societies. Specifically, the states may not maintain a separate coinage; nor may they enter into treaties, alliances, or confederations with national societies. Further, they may not maintain a standing peacetime military force, nor levy import or export duties, nor enter into interstate compacts without the express consent of the national congress. Finally, all state legislative, executive, and judicial officers and all state agents in the national congress are bound by the federal constitution, and all laws and treaties made under it, notwithstanding the constitutions and laws of any individual state. Thus, although the individual states do possess sufficient autonomy to exercise certain kinds of rule-making and enforcement,[1] they do not appear to possess a sufficient monopoly of these features to be considered analogous to politically autonomous societies.

Similarly, the American states are subjected to an economic environment that is nationwide in character. This is to say that the territorial boundaries of the several states appear to bear little relationship to the distribution of either production or consumption among the states. Although some state legislatures do attempt to influence the "business climate" of their state by offering permissive tax structures, and the like, the contribution of these efforts to the economy of the state remains problematic. This is because state legislatures can do little to influence the distribution of raw materials and markets. Indeed, it seems more reasonable to suggest that the territorial aspects of the American economy are better understood on the basis of regional or metropolitan considerations,[2] rather than with respect to state boundaries.

Therefore, by reason of the particular structure of both the American polity and economy, the American states cannot be said to be analogous

[1] For a comprehensive treatment of this relative autonomy, see Herbert Jacob and Kenneth Vines, ed., *Politics in the American States* (Boston and Toronto: Little, Brown, 1965).

[2] For an example of a regional treatment (of the American south), see Arthur Goldschmidt's essay in *Technology and Economic Development* (New York: Knopf, 1963). For a treatment of the metropolitan considerations, see Don J. Bogue, *The Structure of the Metropolitan Community* (Ann Arbor: The University of Michigan, 1950); and Amos Hawley, *Human Ecology: A Theory of Community Structure* (New York: Roland, 1950).

to national societies, in the usual senses of that term. Hence, a research strategy which rests upon such an analogy, as does the Young-Moreno methodology, is invalid when used to illuminate cross-societal propositions.

It is possible to argue that this discussion of the relative autonomy of the 48 states is not relevant to the Young-Moreno thesis, because their strategy rests upon the assumption that each of the American states, and all national societies, are social systems and therefore are by definition comparable units. This argument cannot be maintained. If we are agreed that the logic of social system analysis implies that each system exhibits the capacity to maintain its own boundaries, then the discussion above can be read to mean that the American states differ significantly from all national societies in this capacity. In the rhetoric of social systems: the 48 states more closely approximate open systems than closed systems, while the reverse is true for national societies. The matter then pivots on the comparability of relatively open systems with relatively closed systems. The logic of such comparisons is as yet undeveloped, and the burden of its development would seem to rest upon those who would make such comparisons.

II

It should not be inferred from the above that data from the American states is uninteresting to the student of economic development and cultural change as the cross-societal level. What is of fundamental interest about the 48 states is that they are instances of a more general class of political units, *viz.*, those that are sub-units within politically federated national societies. Several general problems are of interest here. First, comparisons among the several sub-units of one federation are possible. I believe that the Young and Moreno paper is a sparkling example of the possibilities of such comparisons. Second, the contributions of sub-units to national patterns of integration and change can be evaluated. Third, comparisons among several federated states as to the role of the sub-unit in patterns of stability and flux may be made. In particular, data from the 48 states offer a unique mode of *entré* into questions concerning the development of cultural institutions in politically federated societies that exhibit capitalistic economies. In general, the best questions that can be asked may be those in which the individual states have some range of autonomous decision potential, while at least some of the eco-cultural attributes associated with capitalistic economies are relatively constant and hence, in a sense, controlled.

For example, one may inquire into the developmental relationship between citizenship and social class within each of the American states both before and after the several instances of federal-level intervention. This would provide one with material to compare with the experiences of other capitalistic federated states. The experiences of the sub-units of the Canadian and Australian federations should be especially germane here, because both also share Anglo institutional origins. The results obtained might then be fruitfully contrasted with T. H. Marshall's findings on this relationship in the mother country,[3] and with other federated national societies which do not exhibit similar capitalistic eco-cultural institutions. In the opinion of the writer, it is by comparative studies such as these that the relatively abundant data on the American states will prove to be most useful to the student of cross-societal economic development and cultural change.

RUTH C. YOUNG

Reply

I was very glad to see Mr. Silva's note and take the opportunity to comment on it. In general, I believe that the paper paints in clear blacks and whites issues that have a great deal more greyness. I am now engaged in cross-national research and wish wholeheartedly that these issues were so simple and clear. It would make this task a great deal easier. As this type of research is still relatively new and rare, it seems particularly important not only to have a debate about important issues, but for that debate to bring out some of the complexity of the situation for the sake of those unfamiliar with this type of research. I shall try to point out some of the complexity in the points which seem so unequivocal to Mr. Silva.

.   .   .

Mr. Silva's main issue . . . is the question of whether states and nations are the same or different and in what respects. If one has tried to draw up a universe of autonomous nations, it immediately becomes apparent that there are many respects in which nations can be interrelated or independent and many degrees of autonomy in each of these respects. Whether a thick black line may be drawn between nations and states becomes a less clear question.

Then a second issue arises. Are the respects in which nations and states differ germane to the research hypothesis?

One difference Mr. Silva points out is that of economic independence,

[3] T. H. Marshall, ."Citizenship and Social Class," Chapter V of his *Sociology at the Crossroads* (London: Heineman, 1963).

especially ability to coin one's own money. Let us take some examples. Panama uses mostly U.S. dollars for its currency. Is it independent? This is very close. Let us take another degree of control over money. Let us consider the nations whose money is pegged to the British pound or to the U.S. dollar. Let us consider those nations which entered into the Bretton Woods agreement on monetary exchange rates. Are they independent? Let us consider the world in 1929; the collapse of the stock market in the U.S. had repercussions as great in Europe as it did throughout the United States; in fact all over the world. Let us consider the European common market or the Central American Common Market. Let us consider the satellite countries. All of these are examples of close economic relations, in which countries have surrendered, willingly or of necessity, a measure of economic control or independence, have aligned themselves in a social organization with other nations and differentiated this organization from the rest of the world. Are such associations different in kind or in degree from the relations prevailing among the states? I would opt for degree; Mr. Silva may be of another opinion. I think only a test of hypotheses based on this assumption would be convincing, and this will have to wait until a later date.

Similar examples and arguments could be made, obviously, on the basis of military alliances, troop occupation, bases held, or simply superior might. And similar relationships based on political relations or other types of distinctions could be shown to exist. On the basis of what happens every day, it is far easier for me to see nations as interrelated than autonomous. But does it not depend on what one means by autonomy? Mr. Silva chooses federalism and economic autonomy. He points out that this nation has shown that it can abrogate state laws, including those in the scale. Again this seems a black and white issue. But the nation has been at least a hundred years in standing for integration, during which segregation laws as well as customs have prevailed; and even now such laws and customs have not been easily or totally abandoned. States may not have what Mr. Silva would call autonomy in this respect, but they do have power, even if they lack authority.

There does indeed seem to be a trend toward increasing control on the part of the federal government in this country, but this fact does not negate the value of studying the states at this point in time with respect to their differences. In this case, I believe the proof of the pudding is in the eating.

There are many types of autonomy, or rather, many areas of national life with respect to which the nation may be more or less autonomous: money and economic life in general; military power; political government; external relations of an official nature; cultural relations; etc. These are not the same thing. They can and obviously do vary independently. The research question is: what aspects of national autonomy are relevant to one's hypotheses?

One might carry the argument to extremes by questioning whether the several states of the union or, for instance, the nations of Latin America have greater autonomy or more influence in this hemisphere on U.S. policy. Robert Kennedy can object to our national policy in the Dominican Republic and carry the weight of a state with votes in Congress and with citizens who vote in national elections. Mexico, one might argue, is in a poorer position to differ with the president of the United States, since it does not have representation in congress, where many of the important decisions of this world are made. But one need not go to such extremes.

However, all national or state systems are open systems. None are completely closed. The "one-world" assumption seems to me a more realistic one. Nations differ greatly in degree of openness, of course; and I think this characteristic of national systems is an extremely important one. I have built it into my cross-national studies. But in the case of the United States hypothesis, the degree of openness of the various state systems, in my theoretical terms, increases internal national communication and therefore should reduce rigidity and economic stagnation. While this assumption is not subject to test in the U.S. study, I intend to test it as a researchable hypothesis on nations. Meanwhile, I do not hear any counter-theory as to why the openness of the social system of the states should increase rigidity or any counter-proposal for testing this counter-hypothesis.

To me, the most important respect in which states and nations differ is with respect to their external relations. I think this type of autonomy is important and has repercussions. The diversity of external relations maintained by the United States as a whole again increases communications for the rigid states over and above relations they would have for themselves and therefore puts them in a superior position to controlled economies in other parts of the world. Again, this is not subject to test on the data herein, but I do not understand what counter-theory Mr. Silva presents.

As for the point that states do not influence the economy: if so, they are the only type of legislative or governing elite in the world which does not have close ties to the economy and a great deal of influence on it. This influence does not have to be in terms of laws passed, but in terms of laws not passed, of positions filled, of representations in congress, of informal controls and pressures of all types. If state legislatures are not economically significant, why do so many interest groups lobby before them? The power elite of the rigid states is clearly a tight oligarchy. In every city, state, or national study of a power elite that I can think of, we have evidence of the influence of such a group on social life, the economy, political life, in all ramifications. This would indeed be the great exception, and I do not think that it is. At any rate, the study has demonstrated a correlation, at least between society and economy, and causal relations are notoriously difficult to establish.

But again, this is a question which can be researched further and to which insufficient attention has been devoted. To dismiss it summarily appears to me to be a mistake.

In short, I do not feel in a position to controvert Mr. Silva's statements in the same strenuous tones in which he presents them. Rather, I think these are all still open questions, with many facets, many nuances, much complexity. If only they could be settled so easily. But alas, they cannot.

In summary, I am glad to see the argument opened so that some of the real complexity of state or cross-national research can be brought out. The field is a difficult one with which we all need help and open discussion of such questions.

14   TERENCE K. HOPKINS AND
      IMMANUEL WALLERSTEIN

*The Comparative Study of
National Societies*

. . . In our view, comparative studies involving national societies, whether only as the research sites or also as the theoretical units in comparisons, comprise one major class of comparative inquiries. We need a term to refer to this comprehensive subcategory and shall use the term "pluri-national" studies. Similarly, there is another major class of studies in which other kinds of societies (and even more comprehensive entities such as civilizations and the world religions) figure as the sources of observations or the units of comparisons, and these can be collectively

From *Social Science Information*, 6(5), October 1967, pp. 27-33, 44-58. Reprinted by permission of the publisher and the authors. This abbreviated version of the article omits caveats and statements of unresolved issues which the authors included in the original.

referred to in an analogous way, as "pluri-cultural" studies. That is one broad distinction we shall draw. A second is among three main kinds of pluri-national studies according to the "level" or kinds of units used in comparisons: the societies themselves (societal-level), individuals or collectivities within societies (sub-national level), and groups or networks of societies (supra-national level). We shall denote these respectively as cross-national, multi-national, and international studies. (Correlatively, there are cross-cultural, multi-cultural, and inter-cultural studies, but we do not concern ourselves with them here.)

We develop first the distinction among the three kinds of pluri-national research because its logical basis applies very generally. Then we shall try to defend limiting our concern to national societies.

VARIETIES OF
PLURI-NATIONAL RESEARCH

What makes a study pluri-national is simply that its design involves observations in or on two or more national societies. The national societies or the nation-states are not necessarily the units compared, however. They may be, and are in some inquiries, but that is only one kind of pluri-national study. In another kind, the comparisons are among smaller-scale, sub-national units, such as individuals or groups; in these the national societies serve only as the contexts or settings of their respective "members." In still a third variety, the comparisons are among international networks or systems; and in these the national societies or nation-states are themselves only "members" of the larger-scale units being compared. More generally, in our view every complex social unit exists in three forms or at three levels: it is an entity in its own right; it is a context for its constituent members; and it, in turn, is a member of larger contexts. Corresponding to these three possible positions of the national society in analysis are the three kinds of pluri-national research to which we have assigned the names respectively of cross-national, multi-national and international.

The distinction is not always easy to make in practice, for researchers have phrased their hypotheses and findings in a wide variety of ways which sometimes obscure the units being compared or about which generalizations are being made. Nevertheless, a careful reading of the main propositions of a given study with the distinction in mind will usually permit one to characterize it in terms of our categories.

To classify studies systematically, it is useful to consider the main characteristics of what Lazarsfeld has labeled "generalizing propositions." These are as follows:

> a. They [the propositions] say something about a set of *elements* ("cases," "units of observation").
> b. For the research purposes at hand, these elements are considered

comparable. This means that the same set of *properties* is used to
describe each of the elements.

    c. Each element has a certain value on each property (these values
may be quantitative or qualitative).

    d. The *propositions* assert interrelationships between these proper-
ties.[1]

1. *Cross-national Studies*

In these studies the units (or elements) are national societies or "parts"
of such societies (polities, economies, stratification systems, occupational
structures, and so forth); the properties are predicated of societies or
their "parts"; and the propositions state relations among these societal-
level properties. A good illustration of the kind of proposition characteristic of such studies is the following hypothesis drawn from Lipset's
well-known essay on democracy and economic development:

> The more well-to-do a nation, the greater the chances that it will
> sustain democracy.[2]

Or, more pointedly (if less guardedly),

> For any national society, the more developed its economy, the more
> democratic its polity.

The units (or elements or subjects) here are "nations" or national societies; the properties are, one, level of well-being or economic development and, two, degree of democracy; and the proposition asserts a positive
qualitative relation between these two properties.

Some other propositions drawn from recent work are the following:

    a) Economic expansion varies directly with an increasing ratio of eco-
nomically productive persons to the total population.[3]

    b) Given an increase of productivity in a capitalist national economy,
the working class gains less than do the capitalists, and may lose abso-
lutely.[4]

    c) The greater the degree of social integration in the national com-
munity, the lower the illegitimacy rate.[5]

    d) At a given per capita income level of a country, the amount of emi-

[1] P. F. Lazarsfeld, "Evidence and Inference in Social Research," in D. Lerner,
ed., *Evidence and Inference*, Glencoe, Ill.: The Free Press, 1959, p. 118.

[2] S. M. Lipset, *Political Man*, Garden City, N.J.: Doubleday, 1960, pp. 49-51.

[3] A. Gongedo, "La struttura demografica dei tre paesi, Francia-Italia-Spagna,"
Quaderni di Sociologia 5, Summer 1955:105-124.

[4] C. T. de Padua, "Productividade, instrument de mistificação," *Revista
Brasiliense* 3, January-February 1956:144-164.

[5] W. J. Goode, "Illegitimacy, Anomie, and Cultural Penetration," *American
Sociological Review* 26 (6), December 1961:910-925.

gration will vary directly with the rate of natural increase of the population.[6]

2. *Multi-national Studies*

This kind is quite different, although perhaps no less common. In these, the units of the generalizing propositions are not national societies or any large-scale parts of societies (such as their economics, polities, kinship system, etc.) but individual persons, small groups, complex organizations, and so forth. The distinguishing feature of the focal unit here is that it is *not* conceived to be an integral "part" of a society. It is, as it were, an ultimate unit in its own right. The national society in which the unit is located enters this case only as the unit's setting, sometimes in the form of the nominal contextual property, nationality, and sometimes in the form of a more general contextual property designating the kind of society the unit is in (e.g., developing vs. developed). The properties in these studies are thus predicated of individuals (or of groups or organizations); and the propositions state relations between these individual-level (or group-level) properties.

For example, Murphy, and others, conducted a survey of schizophrenic symptomatology in a large number of countries throughout the world.[7] They found that certain symptoms are more likely to be found in certain sub-cultures; for example, urban middle-class individuals are more likely than others to exhibit paranoid symptoms. The findings are reported by culture area (more or less, continent), religion, and residence (rural/urban).

Verba reports on a survey conducted by him and Gabriel Almond in the United States, Great Britain, Germany, Italy, Mexico.[8] He finds, among other things, that the more education an individual has, and the higher his social group, the more likely he is to report himself as capable of influencing his local government.

Banton notes differences among migrants to the United Kingdom.[9] West Africans come because they are attracted to the "glamour" of the U.K. whereas Jamaicans and others from the Caribbean come primarily because economic conditions at home motivate them to seek employment abroad.

[6] R. A. Easterlin, "Influences in European Overseas Emigration before World War I," *Economic Development and Cultural Change* 9 (3), April 1961: 331-351.

[7] H. B. Murphy, and others, "A Cross-cultural Survey of Schizophrenic Symptomatology," *International Journal of Social Psychiatry* 9 (4), Autumn 1963: 237-249.

[8] S. Verba, "Political Participation and Strategies of Influence: A Comparative Study," *Acta Sociologica* 6 (1-2), 1962:22-42.

[9] M. Banton, "Recent Migration from West Africa and the West Indies to the United Kingdom," *Population Studies* 7, Part I, 1953-1954:2-13.

Van den Berghe describes the similarities and differences of the Indian community in Fiji and Natal (Rep. of South Africa).[10]

Melikian surveys a group of Egyptians and compares his results with surveys of Americans.[11] He finds that despite differences between the two societies, if the family is permissive, individuals tend not to be authoritarian, as measured by F-scale scores.

In all of these cases the propositions are not about national societies. They might of course be converted into such, as we shall demonstrate below. But as they stand, the units being compared are individuals and the independent variables in each case are properties predicated of individuals: family background (Melikian), socio-economic class (Murphy, and others, Verba), ethnic group membership (Banton: West Africans as United Kingdom minority group; van den Berghe: Indians as Natal and Fiji ethnic group). The studies are thus instances of multi-national but cross-individual research.

What, of course, is striking about these is that their multi-national character is, strictly speaking, incidental. It is not, in any sense, required by the hypothesis being tested, nor is it reflected in the findings as stated. Indeed, if a pluri-national design is called for at all, it is simply because the hypothesis in each case is stated as a universal and hence should apply in principle to any individual, no matter in what particular society he happens to live. Indeed, most often, the point of the multi-national design is to demonstrate that differences among national societies do not in any important way affect the truth affirmed.

One kind of pluri-national study is at first glance difficult to classify in our categories and deserves special attention. In this kind one of the *variables* in the main finding or hypothesis is the highly concrete characteristic of "nationality." The propositions are substantively similar to those in multi-national studies, in that the subjects appear to be individuals, the properties are predicated of individuals, and the propositions state relations between these seemingly individual-level properties. They differ in the important respect, however, that the nominal classes which constitute the values of "nationality" as a variable are not theoretically relevant categories in any of the behavioral sciences. They are only various proper names, such as American, Thai, German, Turkish, Argentinian, etc.

Scheuch,[12] rightly in our view, calls into question the worth of these "nationality" studies, or at least the value of phrasing the results so con-

[10] P. Van Den Berghe, "Indians in Natal and Fiji: A Controlled Experiment in Culture Contact," *Civilisations* 12 (1), 1962:75-82.

[11] L. H. Melikian, "Authoritarianism and Its Correlates in Egyptian Culture and the United States," *Journal of Social Issues* 15 (3), 1959:58-68.

[12] E. K. Scheuch, "Society as Context in Cross-cultural Comparisons," *Social Science Information*, 6 (5), October 1967:7-23.

cretely, on three grounds: theoretical — the (implicit) explanatory inferences are unsound more often than not; methodological — the designs are frequently weak; and social — the reported findings may well be pernicious (since they lend themselves to being misused as "scientific" facts to support ethnic and national stereotypes).

At present it is his first objection that concerns us, for we think the causal inferences being (implicitly) made must take one or the other of two forms. Either the researcher assumes that, say, authoritarianism is correlated with some other psychological disposition and this happens to be more frequent in some national populations than in others, in which case he should specify the disposition, and the proposition would be multi-national in form. Or he assumes it is correlated with some societal-level characteristic, in which case the true generalizing proposition is cross-national in form and should be explicated as such. For example, assume that people from the U.S.A. register a higher average set of scores on authoritarianism scales than do people from Norway. This correlation may result, one, because authoritarianism is commonly correlated with psychological rigidity and such rigidity happens to be more common among U.S. residents than among Norwegians (multi-national) or, two, because in the U.S., popular culture values traits of an authoritarian nature more highly than does Norwegian popular culture (cross-national). In the first case the proposition reads,

> For any individual, the more psychologically rigid he is, the more authoritarian he is.

The second kind of proposition reads,

> For any society, the more its popular culture emphasizes traits 1, 2, ...n, the higher the average level of authoritarianism in its population.

In short, pluri-national studies using nationality as a variable are either multi-national, cross-individual studies or cross-national studies, depending upon the analyst's (usually implicit) theoretical presuppositions.

We might add here, with respect to Scheuch's concern about the theoretical, methodological, and social value of such studies, that if analysts were more explicit about the explanatory sketches they work with, some of his misgivings would presumably be allayed. For if one wants to invoke psychological rigidity as an explanation (or resultant) of authoritarianism, it is necessary to measure it as well. The same holds for whatever traits of a cultural nature are allegedly causally relevant: they, too would have to be independently measured, i.e., measured independently of "nationality." The sample designs, moreover, would have to be equal to the task of giving reliable estimates on all properties for each national population as a whole. Finally, the results would presumably be phrased using the terms of the theoretical ideas guiding the research, and thus without reference to "nationality" and its highly concrete nominal classes.

3. *International Studies*

This is the third kind of pluri-national research. Here the unit under study is either some network or bloc of countries — such as a common market, a political federation, a regional association, or a world-wide organization whose members are nation-states — or a substantive relationship between two or more particular countries (Anglo-American relations, East European trade, etc.). In these studies observations are usually made on or in the countries involved, but the properties they measure, are, usually, properties of the inter-national network(s) or international relations under investigation. Although research in several countries is usually required for these studies, their theoretical focus is not societies but inter-societal events and relations.

Three examples, all dealing with the European Economic Community (EEC), will suffice to illustrate this. Deutsch discusses some obstacles to integration of the EEC, comparing the EEC to other "federations" and measuring it on certain scales he has developed.[13] Bochet discusses the problems presented to various Latin American countries by the creation of the EEC, analyzing the relationship of one country or a group of countries to another group which has a common market.[14] Vladislav argues that the creation of the EEC has resulted in increased inequalities both among the members of the common market and between them collectively and less developed nations as a whole.[15] In each case, it is the larger system, the EEC or the world, that is the focus of the analysis, nations entering only as "members" of these larger systems.

To sum up, then, empirical studies making use of pluri-national research designs, in the very specific sense that each uses observations made on or in two or more countries, are of three major kinds — studies of national societies, studies of individuals, and studies of international networks. Only one of these, studies of societies, is properly called cross-national, it seems to us. For only in studies where societies are the subjects of the generalizing propositions (hypotheses or findings) are the principal comparisons made "across" or among national societies. Because all three

[13] K. W. Deutsch, "Supranational Organizations in the 1960's," *Journal of Common Market Studies* 1 (3), n.d.:212-218.

[14] B. Bochet, "Les produits primaires, l'Amérique latine, et la Communauté Économique Européenne," *Tiers-Monde* 5 (19), July-December 1964:403-426.

[15] P. Vladislav, "Strukturnye sdvigi v ekonomičeskih svjazjah stran EEC: Statističeskoe issledovanie" [Structural improvements in the economic relations of the EEC countries: Statistical investigations], *Mirovaja ekonomika i mezdunarodnyh otnošlenij*, Feb. 1963:889-896. (From the translation by J. D. Zagoria.)

kinds make use of observations in or on two or more countries, they may at times run into similar technical problems associated with the collection and processing of data from several societies. These can be protean problems, as the numerous programmatic and *post mortem* articles on the difficulties of multi-national sample surveys alone testify, and nothing said here is intended to suggest they are not. But these occasional technical similarities among three kinds of studies that are otherwise different seem to us too slight a ground on which to base a field of study. Were this delimitation of the field to prove acceptable, cross-national research would come to refer, relatively unambiguously, to the various kinds of empirical inquiries that bear on the plausibility of the many interpretations and theoretical sketches which depict the processes and structures of national societies.

We are not arguing that multi-national and international studies are irrelevant to the comparative study of national societies. Often, societal-level properties can be derived from properties of individuals or groups (construed as members or parts of societies) or from properties of the international settings of societies. It may thus be possible sometimes to incorporate findings from multi-national or international researches into generalizations about national societies by using these "derived" societal properties. But the generalization must imply *cross*-national comparisons in order to be relevant to the comparative study of national societies.

. . .

A CLASSIFICATION OF SOCIETAL PROPERTIES

. . . [W]e wish to outline a taxonomy of societal properties which, in our view, clarifies and facilitates the use of findings from multi-national and international research in cross-national studies. We shall first illustrate the "translation" of statements from multi-national and international studies into statements about national societies; then briefly outline the classification; and then comment on its uses and limitations.

1. *Two Illustrative "Translations"*

Consider the common finding in political social psychology that among the electorate in industrialized capitalist societies, the people with larger incomes, higher social standing, more education, and so forth are more likely than others to vote for right-of-center parties, while those with smaller incomes, lower social standing, less education, and so forth are more likely than others to vote for left-of-center parties. That is,

For any individual (in an electorate), the higher his social position, the more likely he is to vote conservatively.

The unit is the individual, the properties are individual-level properties (social rank and direction of one's vote), and the proposition states a simple positive probability relation between the two. Moreover, the usual explanation of the finding, in terms of vested interests, elaborates the argument on the individual-level: the higher a person's position in society, the more his interests are vested in present social arrangements and also the more likely he is to be aware of this; the more aware he is, the more likely he is to act to preserve his interests, which actions include his voting for conservative or right-of-center parties.

No comparison among societies occurs here, nor can any generalizing proposition about societies be inferred (at least none that does not entail a host of dubious assumptions). The universality of this finding may well be in doubt, however, and so an enterprising analyst designs a multi-national study to see how frequently it recurs. Relevant observations on individuals from several countries are compiled, and the data are arrayed for each country separately (the measurements being relative to each setting, that is, "the more well-to-do" people are more well-to-do in relation to others in the same country). The results can then be summarized by describing how often one observes, over the several sets of data from the several countries, the relationship between an individual's social position and his vote-direction. (A very clear instance of this procedure occurs in a recent article by Lenski, who reports a multi-national test of the hypothesis that a person whose several statuses are differently ranked, that is, who is characterized by "status inconsistency," is more likely to vote for liberal or left parties than one whose several statuses are similarly ranked.[16]

Again, nothing is said about the various countries *per se*. They remain no more than so many empirical settings or sites for the research. Any other units that circumscribe electorates would do as well. If the analysis ended here we would have a conventional multi-national finding.

The analyst may take notice, however, that the probability of correctly "predicting" an individual's vote-direction from a knowledge of his social position is higher in some settings than in others. (Lenski, for instance, in the article just referred to, observes that, in 21 of the 25 "tests" of the hypothesis, the results were in the predicted direction but "that two of the four faulty predictions occurred in the case of Britain, and there was only one correct prediction in the British samples."[17]) He may then turn to the question of why the relationship between social position and vote-direction is "stronger" in some settings or electorates than in others. He is not concerned with the strength of the relationship

---

[16] G. E. Lenski, "Status Inconsistency and the Vote: A Four Nation Test," *American Sociological Review* 32 (2), April 1967:298-301.

[17] *Ibid.*, p. 299.

as indicating anything about the setting itself but only with the observed variation in its strength from one setting to another. He then follows the usual procedures in survey analysis of introducing "third" variables serially.[18] Among these "test factors" may be properties that, although predicated of an individual, are in fact derived from or directly reflect characteristics specific to the settings or contexts the individual is in. This sort of "contextual analysis" may generate the following kind of finding: the low-income individual in an electorate with a highly unequal personal-income distribution has a much higher likelihood of voting for left-of-center parties than does the low-income individual in an electorate with a less skewed income distribution. Let us assume a parallel contextual effect influences the vote-propensity of the higher-income person, that is, the more skewed his electorate's income distribution, the more likely he is to vote for right-of-center parties. The unit remains throughout the individual, the properties remain properties predicated of individuals, and the proposition continues to have the form of a (qualitative) probability relation between individual-level properties.

But now let us assume that the electorates in question are national electorates and that the correlation over individuals, between class-position and vote-direction, measures a societal property, "class voting." It then is possible to restate the finding as a proposition about national societies. That is,

For any national society, the more unequal the distribution of personal income, the greater the extent of class voting.

Here societies are the units, the properties are societal-level properties (income distribution and class-voting), and the proposition states a relation between these two societal attributes. (More exactly, it states a relation between inequality of income-distribution and degree or strength of class-voting.)

To convert a finding from a cross-individual study (that uses a multinational design) into a generalizing proposition about national societies, then, it is obviously necessary to construe the original observations as telling us something about national societies in addition to telling us something about individuals. This can be done in a variety of ways. A simple aggregate measure might be used (% of population voting for left-of-center parties); or a measure of distribution (inequality of income-distribution); or a more complex measure such as one characterizing a joint distribution (strength of correlation over individuals between their

[18] Actually, in this example, he would be introducing "fourth" variables, because he has already used three characteristics of individuals, namely, their social position, their vote-direction, and, in grouping his materials, their "nationality."

income-level and vote-direction); and so forth. We shall say more about this shortly.

It should be noted, however, that sampling considerations are paramount in determining the validity of such operations. For what one is doing, in effect, is estimating a society's "value" on a societal property from observations on the society's individual members. To the extent that the sample of individuals one happens to be working with is not relevantly representative of the society's population, the measurement is unreliable and consequently invalid as well. The point is important because whether or not, or the extent to which, a set of subjects is representative of its national population may be a relatively minor consideration in attempts to extend the "universality" of an individual-level generalization. Studies of the correlates of authoritarianism, n-achievement, social distance, familism, and the like, for example, often seem to use whatever nationals of various countries happen to be at hand — students, refugees, migrants, traveling businessmen, and so on. The measurement errors likely to be involved in such cases, were one to convert the findings from these cross-individual, multi-national studies into statements about societies, are so substantial that it is probably best not to use them at all for this purpose.

In addition, it is also usually necessary to have more information about the societies being studied than is contained in the initial, individual-level finding. In the example above, it will be recalled, the two original pieces of information about individuals, their social position and vote-direction, were combined to form one piece of information about a society, namely its degree or strength of class-voting. In order to formulate the proposition about societies, additional information had to be introduced, in this case about income-distribution. This may not always be necessary, however. It may sometimes be possible to convert each of the individual-level characteristics into a societal property, so that virtually the same proposition is stated at both levels, as the following prepared statements illustrate:

For any individual, the more strictly he was raised as a child, the higher his n-achievement level.
For any society, the stricter its child-rearing practices, the higher its population's mean n-achievement level.

But such simple conversions may well result in highly erroneous macro-level propositions, because of the various "compositional" errors that can occur. For example, it is generally the case that an individual who receives an increase in his income saves proportionately more of his income following the increase than he saved before; but it is apparently not the case that as the national income of a society increases over time, proportionately more of it is saved. The difference here may be owing to the different time-scales at the two levels, to price-level changes in the second case but not in the first, perhaps to different methods of measurement, and so forth. Simple conversion must thus be done very carefully. Furthermore, when it is done carefully, it may well provide little more than a trivially true proposition, to the effect that if an individual-level proposition is true of a population, then it is true of that population. Hence, as was suggested, it is generally necessary to use more information in the derived proposition about societies than was contained in the original proposition about individuals.

Much more briefly, let us consider an example of a translation from an international study. In the generalizing propositions characteristic of such studies, it will be recalled, the subjects are international networks, the properties are predicated of the networks, and the propositions state relations among these network-level properties. The proposition stated earlier may serve as our example:

> For any international network, the greater the inequality of well-being among the national units, the less likely is the network to stay intact.

(We assume "international network" refers here to some formal organization or union whose participants or members are nation-states.)

Perhaps the most important observation to make here is that no derived generalization, about the societies in such a network, can be obtained from such a proposition other than a trivially true one which merely rephrases the assertion (for instance, for any national society, if it is a member of an international network whose member states are highly unequal in their levels of well-being, it is likely to be a member of an unstable network). This is so because the network forms the same context for each of its constituent societies. Therefore, while any of its properties may with ease be converted into a contextual property of the countries involved, each country will necessarily have exactly the same "value" on the derived property. If a particular common market, for example, is marked by a low volume of trade (compared to other common markets), each of its participants may be characterized by the contextual property, "volume of trade in the common market in which a participant"; but they will each also have exactly the same "value" on that property, namely, "low."

The same data may allow one to formulate a societal-level proposition, however, if the initial network-level assertion is based on observations about the substantive relations among the participating societies. The illustrative proposition above, for example, permits a restatement along the following lines:

For any national society, the greater the gap between its level of well-being and that of other societies with which it shares membership in an international organization, the more likely it is to withdraw from membership in the international organization.

This proposition does not logically follow from the other because it requires an additional assumption, to the effect that the nations most likely to withdraw are those at either end of the well-being continuum. But it is not unreasonable to say it derives from the other (with some help). The difference between this example and the preceding one is that here a society is characterized by its position *in relation* to the other societies in the network. Whereas all societies in the same network are equally in that network and therefore have the same "value" on any derived contextual property, each society is likely to occupy a relatively distinct relational position within the network, compared to the others, and hence to have a somewhat different "value" from the others on these relational properties.

Before proceeding to the classification of societal properties, we should give one more illustration of the conversion of a relational proposition into a unit proposition. Consider the statement:

For any bilateral relation between countries, the more unequal the balance of payments, the lower the volume of trade.

The more strictly that generalization holds, the more likely it is that the following derived proposition is also warranted:

For any country, the more unequal its balance of payments with another country, the lower its volume of trade with that other country.

If the original proposition is but weakly supported by fact, however, the "derived" assertion may well be more often wrong than right. For example the first might hold only for the bilateral relations in which one partner is one of the highly-developed countries; but because these countries trade with about everyone, the relations they are in make up a majority of the bilateral trade relations at any given time; hence the first statement is factually warranted. But the second might well be untrue; for the countries that are not highly developed are in the majority, and each may well have a developed country as its major trading partner and also have, in that particular relation, a highly unfavorable balance-of-payments position.

Translations can be made, then, but, as before, only with care and often only by adding some additional information or an assumption.

2. The Classification

We turn now to some of the assumptions and general principles underlying and governing this sort of translation of findings from one level
of discourse to another. In developing these ideas we have drawn heavily
on the work of Paul F. Lazarsfeld and his colleagues, who, in a series of
papers over the last decade or so, have worked out various logical relations
between individual- and collective-level measurements.[19] In particular,
they have spelled out various ways in which one can use either data on
individuals to measure characteristics of collectivities or data on collectivities to measure characteristics of individuals. We are not concerned here
with measurement but with conceptualization, and so instead of summariz-
ing their ideas we shall simply draw freely on them in developing an
analogous ordering of several kinds of properties of national societies. The
line between conceptualization (concept-formation) and measurement is
of course a thin one, but it does exist. Specifically we do not consider
here the operations one actually performs on data in order to measure
whether or to what extent one society differs from another in some respect. Rather, we only sketch various ways in which one may conceive of
or formulate these respects or properties.

For present purposes we need to have in mind the three levels of social
organization we have discussed — individuals, national societies, and international networks. And we need to assume that these stand in a relation
of progressive inclusiveness: individuals are included within or compose
national societies; and societies are included within or compose international networks. Alternatively, the networks form the social contexts
of societies; and societies form the social contexts of individuals. Finally,
as already noted, we realize that each one of those may serve on occasion
as a theoretical or focal unit in its own right, which makes each capable
of having properties predicated of it, but here we take only national
societies as the focal units.

We can now distinguish several rather different kinds of *societal-level*
properties. One, there are properties that are *integral* or specific to national societies as wholes, properties which designate states or conditions

[19] P. F. Kendall and P. F. Lazarsfeld, "Problems of Survey Analysis," in R. K.
Merton and P. F. Lazarsfeld, eds., *Continuities in Social Research: Studies in
the Scope and Method of "The American Soldier,"* Glencoe, Ill.: The Free
Press, 1950, pp. 133-196; P. F. Lazarsfeld and H. Menzel, "On the Relation
between Individual and Collective Properties," in A. Etzioni, ed., *Complex Or-
ganizations,* New York: Holt, Rinehart and Winston, 1961, pp. 422-440; A. H.
Barton, *Organizational Measurement and Its Bearing on the Study of College
Environments,* Princeton, N.J.: College Entrance Examination Board, 1961;
A. H. Barton, "Methods of Research on Organizations," in *International Ency-
clopedia of the Social Sciences,* forthcoming.

of the society *per se,* and which can be formulated without reference either to the society's component units in their severalty (here, individuals) or to any of the contexts in which the society may be situated (here, international networks or settings). For example, "the productive capacity of a nation" is usually formulated as an integral property; "degree of democracy" may be; "whether or not a country is a nuclear power" is an integral property; Durkheim used "organic solidarity" and "the tendency to anomie" as integral properties; and so forth.

Two, there are societal-level properties that specifically designate something about the social composition of a society. These, in effect are constructed from the characteristics of a society's *individual* members and therefore are usually so formulated that they refer explicitly in their definitions to one or more properties of the society's component members (here, individuals). These we call *compositional* properties. They are of several kinds, depending on the way they are mentally "constructed" (i.e., depending on the kinds of logical operations or combinations their formulation implies or suggests). These are simple aggregate properties: by the way they are defined these imply some sort of summing over the units, such as the size of a country's population or of its labor force. We include here "distributions" of the population over nominal, unordered categories and hence simple proportions (a "black" society, a "Christian" society, an "English-speaking" society). There are also simple distributive properties. These imply by their definitions a frequency distribution of the individual members with respect to some ordinal or higher-order characteristic. They differ in the way the imagined distribution is depicted, usually in terms of either some kind of central tendency (*per capita* income) or some kind of dispersion or bunching (concentration of ownership of means of production). And, there are various complex compositional properties, more complicated combinations of individual-level properties (extent of religious- or class-voting, the income-elasticity of demand for imports).

A third kind of societal-level property we call *structural,* for want of a better term. To introduce it we need to add to our initial picturing and assume that individuals in societies stand in various substantive relations with one another (relations of marriage, buying and selling, working together, etc.). We thus view individuals as linked to one another within a society through various sub-national groups (formal organizations, local communities, families, ethnic groups, etc.). Now, just as individuals in societies have properties which, when combined in various ways, give rise to societal-level properties, so also do networks and groups. That is, these groups and networks are also elements or components of societies, and their properties, combined or related in some fashion, also form societal-level properties. Thus we speak of "kinship-organized" societies, "bureaucratized" societies, "multi-party" polities, "dual" economies, "plural" societies, and so forth.[20]

In addition to integral, compositional, and structural properties there are at least two main kinds of societal-level properties that derive from the international settings of countries, that is, that reflect something about the international networks in which countries are implicated. These two differ in an important way, as was pointed out above. For one of them, *contextual* properties, a country is characterized by those features of a network that are common to all the countries in that network or context (a North Atlantic state, a Soviet-bloc country, a Common-Market country). Necessarily, then, all the countries in a given setting or network have the same "value" on the overall network or "contextual" property in question — all Latin American countries are equally "Latin American"; all countries today are equally "Atomic-Age" countries.

But a country may also be described in terms of properties referring to its relative position within a network. On this positional or *relational* property, different countries in the same network may very well have rather different "values." Predicates like "metropolitan," "colonial," and "post-colonial" are all "values" of a country-level relational property, reflecting a country's relative position within a network; so too are "primary exporting," "capital exporting," and so forth. The picture underlying each of these sets of terms is some sort of substantive link or relationship between or among two or more countries, and the terms themselves ("values") depict one country's position vis-à-vis the others. Two countries may both be in or of an empire, for example, and hence have the same "value" on the contextual property, "in or of an empire"; but within the empire they may occupy quite different positions, or stand in rather different relations to the rest, in which case they would have different "scores" or "values" on the relational property depicting position (e.g., "metropolitan" vs. "colonial").

These five kinds of properties may be briefly summarized as follows:

Kind of societal-level property	Source	Examples Initial description of property	Derived property
Compositional	Individual members	Whether or not person works	Size of country's labor force
Structural	Groups (including subnational relational networks)	Whether relations among people in an organization are formally defined, etc.	Extent of bureaucratization in country

---

[20] It should be noted that such terms usually refer to qualitative "values" on societal-level properties, not to the properties themselves.

Integral	Societies	Whether a society is land-locked or not	
Relational	Supra-national networks of relations among societies	Characterization of overall balance-of-payments within a common market	Country's balance-of-payments position within network
Contextual	International or world settings	Level of world industrialization	Country in world with few industrial nations (vs. one in world with many industrial nations)

3. *Problems in the Analysis of National Societies*

As was noted above, the formal or logical differences among the foregoing kinds of societal properties derive directly from work by Lazarsfeld and his colleagues on some of the measurement procedures used in survey analysis. The choice of the focal unit of analysis, however, involves substantive considerations as well, and these substantive differences have a quite different source. Specifically, they derive from a particular theoretical orientation or approach to the study of national societies. It will prove helpful in the following discussion of the limitations and uses of the classification to have in mind one or two features of this particular approach. (It is perhaps unnecessary to add that the features of the approach we mention here are only those specifically relevant to the present topic, and the discussion is in no way intended to convey in some general sense the nature of the approach, which it would take an essay devoted to the topic to do.)

We remarked earlier that the basic formal picturing we work with entails viewing any complex focal unit as simultaneously an entity in its own right (or *sui generis*, to use the phrase Durkheim preferred), a context for the smaller-scale entities or units of which it is composed, and a part, in turn, of various larger-scale contexts in which it is but one unit among several. This formal picturing of course applies quite generally and may be used in analysing many kinds of focal units, not just national societies. All it does in this general sense is direct the analyst to pay systematic attention not only to the processes he considers integral to the focal unit in question but also to the processes he thinks may be going on both within the component parts of the unit and within the larger settings of which the unit itself is a part. When we take the national society as our focal unit, then, we are directed to view it as 1) an entity in its own right, 2) a setting for its component members, and 3) a part of various more comprehensive settings. And that of course is what we did in developing the classification, the corresponding three kinds of properties being

1) integral properties, 2) compositional properties, and 3) contextual properties.

At the same time, in order to develop a classification which catches the main differences among the kinds of properties actually used in cross-national research, we evidently had to go beyond the paradigmatic three levels. Specifically, we had to introduce a "structural" level between the compositional and integral levels and a "relational" level between the integral and contextual levels. These five — the focal units (national societies), their individual members, their groups or relational parts, the substantive relations among societies (the international networks), and the world or subportions of it as a whole (international contexts) — were enough for our purpose, since with them we could depict the most important and familiar kinds of societal properties. Quite clearly, however, the number of levels, or the complexity of the picturing in that sense, could well be increased. The basic paradigm calls for three; we found five necessary. There would seem to be no reason why for other purposes several additional levels, and hence, possible kinds of properties, might not be distinguished. Our "structural" category, in particular, would seem to be an extremely simplified, and quite possibly over-simplified, way of handling the societal-level counterparts of properties of units as different as marriage relations and friendship pairs, on the one hand, and political party systems and sectors of national economies, on the other. Here, surely, is one important limitation of the present version of the classification.

Another limitation comes from a somewhat different source, namely, our assumption about simple "inclusion." It will be recalled that we assume progressive inclusiveness to occur as one goes from the individual-level through to the global or contextual-level. This too, may turn out to be a simplification which cannot be justified, in which case an alternative assumption that permits "interpenetration" or overlap would have to be introduced in its place. Individuals, for example, may not be "simply located" in one national society but be simultaneously in or of two national societies (students, migrants, alien residents, etc.). Analogously many international non-governmental organizations are by no stretch of the imagination usefully construed as inter-societal.

These two qualifications of the taxonomy as a whole (and they by no means exhaust the possible list) make it very important that it be seen as no more than a provisional sketch intended mainly to suggest a method of classifying societal properties.

Much the same kind of disclaimer attaches to our descriptions of the categories severally. We have only tried to suggest in a very broad way how each kind of property differs logically from the rest. The differences, quite clearly, are neither depicted in depth nor illustrated at length. Nor have we tried to distinguish varieties of properties within each category, although a step indicative of what might be done along these lines was taken in the paragraph on compositional properties. More generally, what we said above about the probably heterogeneous nature of the "structural" properties probably applies to some extent to the other categories as well.

So much, then, for limitations. There are others, of course, but these should be enough to alert the reader to the highly provisional nature of the scheme. Let us now turn to some of its uses.

One, as we pointed out earlier, is in enlarging the range of empirical materials brought to bear on societal-level propositions. The classification, because it depicts logical bridges between characteristics of societies, on the one hand, and characteristics of individuals, groups, international networks, and intergovernmental structures, on the other, provides one systematic way in which comparative studies of national societies can make use of the results of multi-national and international research. Used in this way the schema functions as a labor-saving device. In virtue of it the student of societies can sometimes transform findings from studies that are not about societies in such a way as to use them in statements that are about societies. This use has already been exemplified.

A second way in which the schema is useful is in connection with the kind of complex, multi-level analyses that are becoming increasingly frequent in cross-national studies, especially in studies of social and economic development. For example, several people have set forth explanatory sketches that link 1) variations (mainly downward) in world price-levels of primary products to 2) variations in a developing country's structure of income-distribution and through this to 3) patterns of market behavior, 4) tendencies toward class formation and action, and 5) overt political-military activities. In analyses making use of such theoretical sketches, frequent shifts in the level of discourse are virtually unavoidable. Analysts almost of necessity move back and forth among individuals, groups, the societies in which both are located, the larger settings in which the societies are located, and so forth. But they do so in ways that frequently are difficult to follow and sometimes are simply bewildering. Were there space enough and time, we could show that, simple as it is, a schema of the sort presented above not only permits the analyst to shift his level of discourse clearly but also makes it possible for the reader to follow and work out such shifts even when the analyst has not. In this use the schema functions mainly as a device for organizing and clarifying complex analyses.

A third use pertains specifically to contextual properties. Currently many, perhaps most, of the "contextual properties" actually used are, at one and the same time, both specific and vague. They are specific historically or geographically; they are vague theoretically. Research reports abound with such terms as a "Soviet-bloc country," an "Anglo-American society," a "Latin-American" or a "French-speaking" nation; or, an "atomic-age society," "a country in the turbulent inter-war years," "a Renaissance state." Contextual properties, however, need not be so tied to continents, languages, and calendars. For example, the world-situation has been described as exhibiting more polarization at some times than at others. In such accounts countries can easily be characterized according to the degree of polarization of the world at one time or another, and this derived property can then be linked causally to other society-level features (e.g., level of internal mobilization). Or, it has been argued that a country industrializing when everyone else is mainly an agricultural country is in a very different position from one that is industrializing when one-third of the world is already industrialized. Such statements can be read as saying that "level of world industrialization" is an important contextual property and that if two countries gave different "values" on this property (i.e., the world is more industrialized at one time than at another), they are in consequence apt to differ in other ways as well, such as rate of industrialization, or sequence of sectoral development, or degree of democracy during and following industrialization. In this use the schema functions as a generalizing device, as a means by which concrete historical and geographical conditions can be transformed into variable theoretical properties.

The fourth, and for here the final, use of the schema is in our view its most important. This is its role in theory-construction. To indicate how it comes in here, we need to add to the discussion above something about the particular approach we take to the comparative study of national societies. Specifically, it seems to us useful to think of the national or society-wide level of social organization as continually subject to two fundamental kinds of disturbing influences, one of which emanates from sub-national levels of organization and one from supra-national levels of organization. Among the various local-level or more generally sub-national processes are some which continually exert centrifugal pressures on the society and which would eventually divide it into two or more smaller-scale entities if they were not countered. And among the various supranational processes are some which constantly exert incorporative pressures and which tend in the short-run to diminish a national society's autonomy or independence in some respect or another and in the long-run to absorb it completely into a larger whole.

Given this view or conception, it follows as a matter of course that we consider it useful when describing national societies, and necessary when explaining their features, to take into account the nature and effects of processes operating at sub-national and supra-national levels of social organization. Or, put somewhat differently, we think almost any theory about modernization needs to include variables and even propositions that refer to attributes and processes of both the sub-national units and the supra-national contexts.

The classification of societal properties materially aids in the construction of such multi-level theories. We assume the focus of any such theory is one or another kind of modernizing change (or lack thereof) and that the "dependent variables" depicting the change are all societal-level properties of one kind or another. We further assume that the "independent variables" used to account for the change or its absence are also depicted as societal-level properties. However, and this is the point we want to make, it is *not* necessary to decide *a priori* the levels of the processes to be included in the explanatory sketch or theory. On the contrary, not only is it quite possible to explain societal changes in terms of processes that operate at other levels of social organization and still keep societies as the focal units of the theory; it is often necessary to do so and always probably advisable to make room for such explanations.

It is one of the virtues of the schema depicting the several kinds of societal-level properties that it shows quite clearly how multi-level theories can be constructed. For example, let us assume we view the evolution of a country's national economy as likely to depend upon (among other things), one, a continuing loss of autarchy by the country's localities and, two, a progressive dimunition in the capacity of other countries to influence the way the economy of the country in question is organized or operates. Neither the degree of autarchy of a locality, however, nor the economic power of other countries, is, as it stands, a property of a national society or a national economy. The first is quite obviously a characteristic of a sub-national unit (a locality) and the other is no less obviously a characteristic of other countries (although only relevantly so in virtue of their presumed participation in some setting or other with the country under review). Nevertheless, they are both causally relevant to what concerns us (or at least so we have assumed) and we therefore need to include them among the variables of the theory being used to account for the development or non-development of a national economy. The resolution of the difficulty is by now presumably evident. So far as local autarchy is concerned, one constructs a structural property that reflects for a country as a whole the degree of autarchy of each of its component localities or regions. This societal-level property, "extent of local autarchy," can be used to characterize the national society as a whole, and the influence of local autarchy on the formation of its national economy can then be systematically assessed. Analogously, the extent to which geographically external events or actions (cessation of aid, world-price fluctuations) have effects that, transmitted via the international relations and contexts a country takes part in, induce direct and corresponding effects in the operation or organization of the country's national economy, can be treated as forming a societal-level property, "economic openness" (or, inversely, "closure") to outside influence. This *relational* property can be used to characterize the national society in question, and the causal relevance of other countries' economic power to the formation of a society's national economy can then be systematically assessed.[21]

CONCLUSION

Our aim has been . . . to discuss what seems to us the central issue raised at the session of the Sixth World Congress of Sociology devoted to "cross-national research." This is the question of the appropriate focus and scope of this field of study. We have proposed, and argued in support of, a doubly narrow view of the field. We believe it should focus on *national* societies and their modernization and thus should not include either comparisons of other kinds of societies or comparative studies of units other than societies.

We would like to reiterate that terms *per se* do not interest us. What does interest us is the delimitation of a field of inquiry around a core set of concepts in such a way that both new ventures in empirical research and new approaches in the constructing (and reconstructing) of theories are provided with overall guidelines. We have not of course tried to provide these guidelines here. Our intention instead has been the more modest one of offering some preliminary methodological distinctions designed to clarify discussions of comparative studies and in particular discussions of cross-national research.

[21] Lest there be misunderstanding, we should clarify the meaning of "closure." "Closure," in this sense of insulating an economy from untoward external influences, bears no necessary relation to such specific policy actions as closing borders, reducing the volume of foreign trade, altering its composition, and so forth. For example, increasing the volume of foreign trade, in conjunction with an increase in the diversity of trade partners or exports, may well increase an economy's "closure" to external influences.

VI

Types of Theorizing

15   JOHN STUART MILL

Two Methods of Comparison

The simplest and most obvious modes of singling out from among the circumstances which precede or follow a phenomenon, those with which it is really connected by an invariable law, are two in number. One is, by comparing together different instances in which the phenomenon occurs. The other is, by comparing instances in which the phenomenon does occur, with instances in other respects similar in which it does not. These two methods may be respectively denominated, the Method of Agreement, and the Method of Difference.

In illustrating these methods, it will be necessary to bear in mind the twofold character of inquiries into the laws of phenomena; which may be either inquiries into the cause of a given effect, or into the effects or prop-

From A *System of Logic* by John Stuart Mill (New York: Harper & Row, Publishers, 1888), pp. 278, 279-283, and 610-612. The original title was "Of the Four Methods of Experimental Inquiry."

erties of a given cause. We shall consider the methods in their application
to either order of investigation, and shall draw our examples equally from
both.

We shall denote antecedents by the large letters of the alphabet, and
the consequents corresponding to them by the small. Let A, then, be an
agent or cause, and let the object of our inquiry be to ascertain what are
the effects of this cause. If we can either find, or produce, the agent A in
such varieties of circumstances that the different cases have no circumstance in common except A; then whatever effect we find to be produced
in all our trials, is indicated as the effect of A. Suppose, for example, that
A is tried along with B and C, and that the effect is *a b c*; and suppose
that A is next tried with D and E, but without B and C, and that the
effect is *a d e*. Then we may reason thus: *b* and *c* are not effects of A,
for they were not produced by it in the second experiment; nor are *d* and
e, for they were not produced in the first. Whatever is really the effect of
A must have been produced in both instances; now this condition is
fulfilled by no circumstance except *a*. The phenomenon *a* can not have
been the effect of B or C, since it was produced where they were not; nor
of D or E, since it was produced where they were not. Therefore it is the
effect of A.

.   .   .

The mode of discovering and proving laws of nature, which we have
now examined, proceeds on the following axiom: Whatever circumstances
can be excluded, without prejudice to the phenomenon, or can be absent
notwithstanding its presence, is not connected with it in the way of
causation. The casual circumstances being thus eliminated, if only one remains, that one is the cause which we are in search of: if more than one,
they either are, or contain among them, the cause; and so, *mutatis mutan-
dis*, of the effect. As this method proceeds by comparing different instances
to ascertain in what they agree, I have termed it the Method of Agreement; and we may adopt as its regulating principal the following canon:

FIRST CANON. *If two or more instances of the phenomenon under investigation have only one circumstance in common, the circumstance
in which alone all the instances agree, is the cause (or effect) of the
given phenomenon.*

Quitting for the present the Method of Agreement, to which we shall
almost immediately return, we proceed to a still more potent instrument
of the investigation of nature, the Method of Difference.

In the Method of Agreement, we endeavored to obtain instances which
agreed in the given circumstance but differed in every other: in the present

method we require, on the contrary, two instances resembling one another in every other respect, but differing in the presence or absence of the phenomenon we wish to study. If our object be to discover the effects of an agent A, we must procure A in some set of ascertained circumstances, as A B C, and having noted the effects produced, compare them with the effect of the remaining circumstances B C, when A is absent. If the effect of A B C is *a b c*, and the effect of B C *b c*, it is evident that the effect of A is *a*. So again, if we begin at the other end, and desire to investigate the cause of an effect *a*, we must select an instance, as *a b c*, in which the effect occurs, and in which the antecedents were A B C, and we must look out for another instance in which the remaining circumstances, *b c*, occur without *a*. If the antecedents, in that instance, are B C, we know that the cause of *a* must be A: either A alone, or A in conjunction with some of the other circumstances present.

It is scarcely necessary to give examples of a logical process to which we owe almost all the inductive conclusions we draw in daily life. When a man is shot through the heart, it is by this method we know that it was the gunshot which killed him: for he was in the fullness of life immediately before, all circumstances being the same, except the wound.

The axioms implied in this method are evidently the following. Whatever antecedent can not be excluded without preventing the phenomenon, is the cause, or a condition, of that phenomenon: whatever consequent can be excluded, with no other difference in the antecedents than the absence of a particular one, is the effect of that one. Instead of comparing different instances of a phenomenon, to discover in what they agree, this method compares an instance of its occurrence with an instance of its nonoccurrence, to discover in what they differ. The canon which is the regulating principle of the Method of Difference may be expressed as follows:

SECOND CANON. *If an instance in which the phenomenon under investigation occurs, and an instance in which it does not occur, have every circumstance in common save one, that one occurring only in the former; the circumstance in which alone the two instances differ, is the effect, or the cause, or an indispensable part of the cause, of the phenomenon.*

The two methods which we have now stated have many features of resemblance, but there are also many distinctions between them. Both are methods of *elimination*. This term (employed in the theory of equations to denote the process by which one after another of the elements of a question is excluded, and the solution made to depend on the relation between the remaining elements only) is well suited to express the operation, analogous to this, which has been understood since the time of

Bacon to be the foundation of experimental inquiry: namely, the successive exclusion of the various circumstances which are found to accompany
a phenomenon in a given instance, in order to ascertain what are those
among them which can be absent consistently with the existence of the
phenomenon. The Method of Agreement stands on the ground that whatever can be eliminated, is not connected with the phenomenon by any
law. The Method of Difference has for its foundation, that whatever can
not be eliminated, is connected with the phenomenon by a law.

Of these methods, that of Difference is more particularly a method of
artificial experiment; while that of Agreement is more especially the resource employed where experimentation is impossible. A few reflections
will prove the fact, and point out the reason of it.

It is inherent in the peculiar character of the Method of Difference, that
the nature of the combinations which it requires is much more strictly defined than in the Method of Agreement. The two instances which are to
be compared with one another must be exactly similar, in all circumstances except the one which we are attempting to investigate: they must
be in the relation of A B C and B C, or of $a\ b\ c$ and $b\ c$. It is true that
this similarity of circumstances needs not extend to such as are already
known to be immaterial to the result. And in the case of most phenomena
we learn at once, from the commonest experience, that most of the co-
existent phenomena of the universe may be either present or absent without affecting the given phenomenon; or, if present, are present indiffer-
ently when the phenomenon does not happen and when it does. Still,
even limiting the identity which is required between the two instances,
A B C and B C, to such circumstances as are not already known to be
indifferent, it is very seldom that nature affords two instances, of which we
can be assured that they stand in this precise relation to one another. In
the spontaneous operations of nature there is generally such complication
and such obscurity, they are mostly either on so overwhelmingly large or
on so inaccessibly minute a scale, we are so ignorant of a great part of the
facts which really take place, and even those of which we are not ignorant
are so multitudinous, and therefore so seldom exactly alike in any two
cases, that a spontaneous experiment, of the kind required by the Method
of Difference, is commonly not to be found. When, on the contrary, we
obtain a phenomenon by an artificial experiment, a pair of instances such
as the method requires is obtained almost as a matter of course, provided
the process does not last a long time. A certain state of surrounding circumstances existed before we commenced the experiment; this is B C. We
then introduce A; say, for instance, by merely bringing an object from
another part of the room, before there has been time for any change in the
other elements. It is, in short (as M. Comté observes), the very nature of
an experiment, to introduce into the pre-existing state of circumstances a

change perfectly definite. We choose a previous state of things with which we are well acquainted, so that no unforeseen alteration in that state is likely to pass unobserved; and into this we introduce, as rapidly as possible, the phenomenon which we wish to study; so that in general we are entitled to feel complete assurance that the pre-existing state, and the state which we have produced, differ in nothing except the presence or absence of that phenomenon. If a bird is taken from a cage, and instantly plunged into carbonic acid gas, the experimentalist may be fully assured (at all events after one or two repetitions) that no circumstance capable of causing suffocation had supervened in the interim, except the change from immersion in the atmosphere to immersion in carbonic acid gas. There is one doubt, indeed, which may remain in some cases of this description; the effect may have been produced not by the change, but by the means employed to produce the change. The possibility, however, of this last supposition generally admits of being conclusively tested by other experiments. It thus appears that in the study of the various kinds of phenomena which we can, by our voluntary agency, modify or control, we can in general satisfy the requisitions of the Method of Difference; but that by the spontaneous operations of nature those requisitions are seldom fulfilled.

The reverse of this is the case with the Method of Agreement. We do not here require instances of so special and determinate a kind. Any instances whatever, in which nature presents us with a phenomenon, may be examined for the purposes of this method; and if all such instances agree in any thing, a conclusion of considerable value is already attained. We can seldom, indeed, be sure that the one point of agreement is the only one; but this ignorance does not, as in the Method of Difference, vitiate the conclusion; the certainty of the result, as far as it goes, is not affected. We have ascertained one invariable antecedent or consequent, however, many other invariable antecedents or consequents may still remain unascertained. If A B C, A D E, A F G, are all equally followed by *a*, then *a* is an invariable consequent of A. If *abc, ade, afg*, all number A among their antecedents, then A is connected as an antecedent, by some invariable law, with *a*. But to determine whether this invariable antecedent is a cause, or this invariable consequent an effect, we must be able, in addition, to produce the one by means of the other; or, at least, to obtain that which alone constitutes our assurance of having produced any thing, namely, an instance in which the effect, *a*, has come into existence, with no other change in the pre-existing circumstances than the addition of A. And this, if we can do it, is an application of the Method of Difference, not of the Method of Agreement.

It thus appears to be by the Method of Difference alone that we can ever, in the way of direct experience, arrive with certainty at causes. The

Method of Agreement leads only to laws of phenomena (as some writers
call them, but improperly, since laws of causation are also laws of phenomena): that is, to uniformities, which either are not laws of causation,
or in which the question of causation must for the present remain undecided. The Method of Agreement is chiefly to be resorted to, as a means
of suggesting applications of the Method of Differences (as in the last
example the comparison of ABC, ADE, AFG, suggested that A was the
antecedent on which to try the experiment whether it could produce *a*);
or as an inferior resource, in case the Method of Difference is impracti-
cable; which, as we before showed, generally arises from the impossibility
of artificially producing the phenomena. And hence it is that the Method
of Agreement, though applicable in principle to either case, is more
emphatically the method of investigation on those subjects where artificial
experimentation is impossible; because on those it is, generally, our only
resource of a directly inductive nature; while, in the phenomena which we
can produce at pleasure, the Method of Difference generally affords a more
efficacious process, which will ascertain causes as well as mere laws.

.   .   .

The first difficulty which meets us in the attempt to apply experimental
methods for ascertaining the laws of social phenomena, is that we are
without the means of making artificial experiments. Even if we could
contrive experiments at leisure, and try them without limit, we should do
so under immense disadvantage; both from the impossibility of ascertaining and taking note of all the facts of each case, and because (those facts
being in a perpetual state of change), before sufficient time had elapsed
to ascertain the result of the experiment, some material circumstances
would always have ceased to be the same. But it is unnecessary to consider
the logical objections which would exist to the conclusiveness of our experiments, since we palpably never have the power of trying any. We can
only watch those which nature produces, or which are produced for other
reasons. We can not adapt our logical means to our wants, by varying the
circumstances as the exigencies of elimination may require. If the spontaneous instances, formed by contemporary events and by the successions
of phenomena recorded in history, afford a sufficient variation of circumstances, an induction from specific experience is attainable; otherwise not.
The question to be resolved is, therefore, whether the requisites for induction respecting the causes of political effects or the properties of political
agents, are to be met with in history? including under the term, contemporary history. And in order to give fixity to our conceptions, it will be
advisable to suppose this question asked in reference to some special
subject of political inquiry or controversy; such as that frequent topic of
debate in the present century, the operation of restrictive and prohibitory

commercial legislation upon national wealth. Let this, then, be the scientific question to be investigated by specific experience.

In order to apply to the case the most perfect of the methods of experimental inquiry, the Method of Difference, we require to find two instances which tally in every particular except the one which is the subject of inquiry. If two nations can be found which are alike in all natural advantages and disadvantages; whose people resemble each other in every quality, physical and moral, spontaneous and acquired; whose habits, usages, opinions, laws, and institutions are the same in all respects, except that one of them has a more protective tariff, or in other respects interferes more with the freedom of industry; if one of these nations is found to be rich and the other poor, or one richer than the other, this will be an *experimentum crucis:* a real proof by experience, which of the two systems is most favorable to national riches. But the supposition that two such instances can be met with is manifestly absurd. Nor is such a concurrence even abstractedly possible. Two nations which agreed in every thing except their commercial policy would agree also in that. Differences of legislation are not inherent and ultimate diversities; are not properties of Kinds. They are effects of pre-existing causes. If the two nations differ in this portion of their institutions, it is from some difference in their position, and thence in their apparent interests, or in some portion or other of their opinions, habits, and tendencies; which opens a view of further differences without any assignable limit, capable of operating on their industrial prosperity, as well as on every other feature of their condition, in more ways than can be enumerated or imagined. There is thus a demonstrated impossibility of obtaining, in the investigations of the social science, the conditions required for the most conclusive form of inquiry by specific experience.

In the absence of the direct, we may next try, as in other cases, the supplementary resource, called in a former place the Indirect Method of Difference; which, instead of two instances differing in nothing but the presence or absence of a given circumstance, compares two *classes* of instances respectively agreeing in nothing but the presence of a circumstance on the one side and its absence on the other. To choose the most advantageous case conceivable (a case far too advantageous to be ever obtained), suppose that we compare one nation which has a restrictive policy with two or more nations agreeing in nothing but in permitting free trade. We need not now suppose that either of these nations agrees with the first in all its circumstances; one may agree with it in some of its circumstances, and another in the remainder. And it may be argued, that if these nations remain poorer than the restrictive nation, it can not be for want either of the first or of the second set of circumstances, but it must be for want of the protective system. If (we might say) the restrictive nation had prospered from the one set of causes, the first of the free-trade nations would have prospered equally; if by reason of the other, the second would; but neither has; therefore the prosperity was owing to the restrictions. This will be allowed to be a very favorable specimen of an argument from specific experience in politics, and if this be inconclusive, it would not be easy to find another preferable to it.

Yet, that it is inconclusive, scarcely requires to be pointed out. Why must the prosperous nation have prospered from one cause exclusively? National prosperity is always the collective result of a multitude of favorable circumstances; and of these, the restrictive nation may unite a greater number than either of the others, though it may have all of those circumstances in common with either one or the other of them. Its prosperity may be partly owing to circumstances common to it with one of those nations, and partly with the other, while they, having each of them only half the number of favorable circumstances, have remained inferior. So that the closest imitation which can be made, in the social science, of a legitimate induction from direct experience, gives but a specious semblance of conclusiveness, without any real value.

The Method of Difference in either of its forms being thus completely out of the question, there remains the Method of Agreement. But we are already aware of how little value this method is, in cases admitting Plurality of Causes; and social phenomena are those in which the plurality prevails in the utmost possible extent.

Suppose that the observer makes the luckiest hit which could be given by any conceivable combination of chances; that he finds two nations which agree in no circumstance whatever, except in having a restrictive system, and in being prosperous; or a number of nations, all prosperous, which have no antecedent circumstances common to them all but that of having a restrictive policy. It is unnecessary to go into the consideration of the impossibility of ascertaining from history, or even from contemporary observation, that such is really the fact; that the nations agree in no other circumstance capable of influencing the case. Let us suppose this impossibility vanquished, and the fact ascertained that they agree only in a restrictive system as an antecedent, and industrial prosperity as a consequent. What degree of presumption does this raise that the restrictive system caused the prosperity? One so trifling as to be equivalent to none at all. That some one antecedent is the cause of a given effect, because all other antecedents have been found capable of being eliminated, is a just inference, only if the effect can have but one cause. If it admits of several, nothing is more natural than that each of these should separately admit of being eliminated. Now, in the case of political phenomena, the supposition of unity of cause is not only wide of the truth, but at an immeasurable distance from it. The causes of every social phenomenon which we are particularly interested about, security, wealth, freedom, good government, public virtue, general intelligence, or their opposites, are infinitely numerous, especially the external or remote causes, which alone are, for the most part, accessible to direct observation. No one cause suffices of itself to produce any of these phenomena; while there are countless causes which have some influence over them, and may co-operate either in their production or in their prevention. From the mere fact, therefore, of our having been able to eliminate some circumstance, we can by no means infer that this circumstance was not instrumental to the effect in some of the very instances from which we have eliminated it. We can conclude that the effect is sometimes produced without it; but not that, when present, it does not contribute its share.

16   JOSEPH K. FOLSOM

Family Phenomena in Two Contrasting Societies

In the insular realm known as Melanesia are the Trobriand Islands, just northeast of Australia. The people of these islands live in a system of family relationships strikingly different from our own. This family system has been described in interesting detail by Malinowski in his *Sexual Life of Savages*. The title may be somewhat misleading, since the physical sex relations are only a small part of the total picture. Because this description is so much more adequate than most descriptions of primitive family life, it is chosen for our present study.

The Trobriand Islanders are a primitive, that is, a *pre-literate* people. Their culture is not, however, of the lowest order. They practice agricul-

From *The Family and Democratic Society*, by Joseph K. Folsom (New York: John Wiley & Sons, Inc.), pp. 1-6, 8-15. Reprinted by permission of the publisher.

ture and keep pigs, and are placed upon the second or middle agriculture level in the classification of Hobhouse, Wheeler, and Ginsberg. They are a black-skinned, woolly-haired people, classified physically under the Oceanic branch of the negroid race (geographically remote and somewhat different anatomically from African negroes). Considering the smallness of this population and the probability that it will sooner or later die off or be absorbed into the white man's society, what can be the significance of studying its family system?

The size and the geographic and historic importance of a primitive tribe are no indication of the sociological significance of their ways of life. Strange as it may seem, this study of primitives is one of the most valuable avenues to an understanding of society in general. In recent years sociology and cultural anthropology (ethnology) have come closer together and are now essentially one and the same science. In zoology we do not demand that attention be apportioned to the various animals according to their abundance and the frequency with which we have to deal with them. Such a "practical" zoology might confine itself largely to horses, dogs, and other domestic animals. But he who would really understand animal life can learn more in the zoological garden than in the barnyard, because of the much wider variety of species exhibited. *Primitive tribes are the "zoo" of sociology.*

Let us compare the family system of the Trobrianders with that of our own society. The description of our own society will have a certain naivete. It is the description which we might imagine would be given to it by a Trobriand sociologist, if such a person existed.

I. SPATIAL AND MATERIAL PATTERNS
Arrangement of Dwellings and Settlements

TROBRIAND ISLANDS. Practically all the people live in small villages. These are circular, with two concentric rings of buildings. The inner ring consists of storehouses and the outer of dwellings. Both face toward the center. Between the two rings is the "street," where everyday living goes on. Within the inner ring of storehouses is a circular space which contains the chief's hut, sometimes his storehouse, a burial ground, and a dancing ground. This is the area of public and festive life. Houses, except the chief's, are rather similar in size and quality. The storehouses, which are used mostly to store yams between harvest, are built more elaborately and decoratively than the dwelling houses. The gardens are outside the village.

AMERICA. About a fourth of the people live on separate farms, about a fourth in villages, a half in cities. Farms have their own barns and outbuildings near the dwelling. Houses vary tremendously in size and equipment, but the majority far surpass anything in primitive society.

The better houses are concentrated in certain areas of cities; their inhabitants do "mental" rather than "manual" work. A large area of suburbs with urban modes of work and play but lesser density of buildings and population surrounds the typical city.

Relation of Geographic to Social Patterns

TROBRIAND ISLANDS. One continuous arc of the village circle of dwellings is inhabited by the chief's wives and their children, another by his material kinsmen, and the remaining arc by commoners not related to the chief as kinsmen or children.

New dwellings are commonly erected in the village by newly married couples.

AMERICA. Proximity of dwelling has little or no relation to kinship or to friendship; it merely classifies people as to economic status and indicates mere chance in the availability of dwellings. People often become friends because they are neighbors, but contacts based upon neighborhood alone are weak, even in suburbs. With the help of the automobile and telephone people have their main contacts at some distance. The community population divides itself into groups based upon recreational interests, cultural similarities, and personal congenialities having little relation to geography, except that each such group is likely to consist of people having similar economic status and living in the same type of social-ecological area.

In cities and suburbs, change of residence is frequent (average every two years in some). The sentiment surrounding a specific "home" location is less than in the country.

Relation of Kinship to Geography

TROBRIAND ISLANDS. Each village community is owned by one sub-clan. It has its head man, commonly the oldest. If the sub-clan is of high rank, this head man also has power over a whole district and is called a chief.

AMERICA. There is no relation between kinship groups and possession of any village or locality. Small, isolated rural communities tend to intramarry and to have their social relationships somewhat associated with kin relationship.

Composition of the Household Group

TROBRIAND ISLANDS. In monogamous families, husband, wife, and their younger children live together in a hut. Other relatives sometimes live with them.

AMERICA. Husband, wife, and their children (until maturity) live in the same home. Other relatives may live with them but this is regarded as less preferable.

The Housing of Adolescents and Unmarried

TROBRIAND ISLANDS. At puberty children leave their parents' home, especially the boys. Boys go to live in bachelors' quarters, girls to live with older maternal female relatives except when living with boys in the bachelors' quarters.

Adolescents tend to be segregated in special quarters, the bachelors' houses, of which there may be several in a village. These are located in the inner circle of the village with the storehouses, apart from the huts of married couples. In these, unmarried youths, with some widowers and divorced men, live with their mistresses, whom they possess in temporary exclusiveness and do not share. These bachelors' houses are owned by groups of boys, the eldest being the titular owner. When liaisons break up, it is usually the girl who moves, to another bachelors' hut or to a home of her parents or maternal relatives.

AMERICA. Both boys and girls remain in the parental home till marriage or occupation takes them elsewhere. In the business classes boys leave sooner because their occupations more often take them away from home. In conservative groups it is regarded as desirable for the girl not to take an occupation which requires her leaving home, but to remain at home helping in housework and engaging in courtship with possible husbands under parental supervision.

There are bachelors' quarters for unmarried young people, but these everywhere involve rigid segregation of the sexes. They are normally used only by persons working or studying in communities away from their parental homes.

Home Ownership

TROBRIAND ISLANDS. The houses, garden land, livestock, and trees are owned almost exclusively by the men, who inhabit or use them, and not by women or families as such.

AMERICA. In rural areas, villages, and smaller cities, a majority of houses are owned by their inhabitants. This ownership, however, often involves carrying a debt. It is also common to rent houses, more especially in cities.

Pattern of the Dwelling House

TROBRIAND ISLANDS. The typical dwelling house has a symmetrical, steep roof of thatched material which may extend to the ground, giving the entire structure the form of a triangular prism resting on its narrowest side, with the two elevated sides slightly convex. The ground plan is thus a rectangle, with entrance at one end under a gable. The dwelling is built directly on the ground, with a floor of beaten earth; it is one-storied and, except for a small antechamber, consists of one room.

AMERICA. Most dwellings are single-family houses, but there are some large apartment houses, especially in large cities. The typical house is of box form, has two or three stories, no interior courtyard, and is divided into rooms. In most localities, porches are attached. Except near centers of cities, each house is surrounded by more or less ground used as a lawn, garden, playground, and space to dry clothes. The more elaborate and esthetic houses emphasize the decorative functions of their yards, but many of the poorer houses, especially in cities, have mainly "back yards" and conspicuous clothes-drying.

Technology and Furnishing of the Home

TROBRIAND ISLANDS. Along one side wall of the house is the fireplace, which is a ring of stones; along the opposite side wall and one end of the house are wooden sleeping bunks in two or more tiers. At the other end is the door, with shelves above and alongside of it for the storage of property. Water is carried in vessels from a distance. Bathing is done out of doors.

AMERICA. Although there is enormous variation, a typical American standard of living includes piped water in the home, electric light, central heating, a bath tub and frequent bathing, three cooked meals a day with a great variety of food (including animal and vegetable), elevated tables, seats, and sleeping surfaces, table and bed linen, eating utensils, frequent laundering and pressing of clothes.

There are four main forms of furniture: table, seat, bed, and storage box with drawers or shelves.

Numerous machines are possessed and used.

Occupations

TROBRIAND ISLANDS. There is little or no lifelong specialization of labor for any individual except that between the sexes. On any one day a person may be engaged principally in agriculture, fishing, construction, manufacture, or trading.

AMERICA. On the farms people produce food, most of it being sold to the rest of the population. Village and city people are engaged in trade, transportation, manufacture, planning, and paper work. Adult males and about 40 per cent of the adult females give full time to these occupations, which are broken down into thousands of specialties. About 60 per cent of the adult females give most of their time to homemaking and care of children.

Work in the Home

TROBRIAND ISLANDS. Most work of both sexes is performed out of doors near the dwelling or yam house, or in the gardens, although there are occasional distant expeditions, especially of men in canoes or on foot to other villages. Family groups work in close proximity much of the time. Men perform much of the care of children. In transporting food and other large tasks, helpers are commonly used; they are chosen largely according to customary kinship obligations with reciprocity according to custom.

AMERICA. Typically, cooking and serving of meals, minor clothing repair, laundering, and the care of young children still remain as work within the home, and occupy practically the full time of the homemaker. These tasks are sometimes shared by other members of the household group, but the great bulk usually falls upon one woman. If there are more than two adults in the group, the extra adult usually does outside work and earns money.

About a fourth of the families have part-time or full-time hired servants who participate in the work, but only to a minor degree in the consumption processes of the home. They retire for limited periods of time to their own homes, of lower standards, elsewhere.

. . .

II. THE STRUCTURE OF MARITAL AND SEXUAL RELATIONSHIPS

Recognition of Fatherhood

TROBRIAND ISLANDS. The "father" of a child is the mother's husband, who helps her to bring it up. Pre-marital pregnancy (though not intercourse) is shameful, and often leads to the abandonment of a girl by her fiancé, even though he has been the cause. As a matter of fact, pregnancy is a comparatively rare result of the free sex relations before marriage, for some reason unknown even to modern scientists. After marriage fertility is desired and actually quite adequate, but no child of a married woman is attributed to any biological father, even in cases of known adultery during prolonged absence of the social father.

AMERICA. The social father of a child is also the biological father. He should be married to the mother and live with her, exercising more or less authority over her and their children. All sexual intercourse before marriage or with other than the married partner is immoral, in varying degrees. Premarital pregnancy is shameful, because it is evidence of intercourse. But subsequent marriage of the sexual partners removes much of the shame, especially if it takes place before the child is born. Fertility in marriage is generally desired; deliberate infertility is immoral according to more conservative attitudes, though in most classes it is regarded as subject to personal choice. Any evidence that a child's biological father is other than his social father leads typically to anger of the husband and to investigation; if illegitimacy is found to exist, great moral condemnation falls upon the woman.

Social Control of Marriage and Divorce

TROBRIAND ISLANDS. Marriage and divorce are subject to no higher legal control than individual will, the approval of the girl's family, and sometimes informal group judgment.

AMERICA. Marriage and divorce are defined, licensed, and in certain respects regulated, by the governmental authority, which in these matters is supreme. The religious authority and the parental families may practically regulate marriage within still narrower limits through their disapproval, but cannot legally enforce such regulations. The adult is protected by law against coercion from any other power.

Monogamy and Polygamy

TROBRIAND ISLANDS. Marriage is monogamous except for men of high rank or great importance, who generally practice polygyny. The chief motive for this polygyny is to acquire extra wealth, which is necessary for power.

In polygynous families of chiefs there are three classes of wives: older ones inherited from the former chief, with whom there are few sexual relations; women married by the chief in his youth; and younger, attractive women married more recently. Political considerations and personal choice govern selection. There is usually a personal favorite among the second group of wives, and sometimes among the third, but the roles of the several wives are determined by their age and personality, and the chief's preference, rather than by law.

The several wives live in separate huts close to that of the chief, each with her own young children. There is no marked jealousy among them or need for them to be further separated. The chief may make his principal abode, outside his own hut, with one of them.

AMERICA. Marriage is monogamous without exception. A marriage to a second partner before the marriage to the first has been legally dissolved is not legally valid, and in addition is punishable under the criminal law, although it sometimes occurs secretely.

Through divorce, however, there exists a system which may be called consecutive polygamy for a certain minority, which is of intermediate rather than of high or low social approval.

Age Differences of Mates

TROBRIAND ISLANDS. In monogamous families the mates are of about the same age.

AMERICA. The husband is on the average about three years older than the wife. There is no moral taboo or legal restrictions, but marriages of great age difference are regarded as undesirable, especially when the woman is older.

Procedure of Choosing and Obtaining Mate

TROBRIAND ISLANDS. The great majority of marriages are based upon the initiative of the young people themselves, who choose one another freely.

A girl's father has the principal responsibility for guiding her to marriage. Her family usually consents to the marriage, and can usually prevent it by economic power, since it is their function to provide food for the young couple. The man's family exercises no control over the marriage.

Very rarely marriage takes place by elopement in defiance of the will of the girl's family.

There is no wife capture.

There are no matchmakers.

AMERICA. All marriages are based upon the initiative of the young people themselves, who choose freely, although not entirely without parental guidance.

Families, however, approve and disapprove marriages, but the limit of their power is to cut off social contacts and inheritance, which is rarely done even when there is disapproval of the marriage. The powers of families are seldom sufficient to prevent a marriage desired by both partners. Family influence upon marriage is somewhat greater from the girl's family. Cultural sentiments approve love marriages in defiance, if necessary, of the will of families, and the law sanctions and protects such marriages.

Elopements occasionally occur to avoid the hostile interference of families.

There is no wife capture.

There is no matchmaking save for some informal personal mediation, and some organized "services" used by a very few.

Personal Qualifications for Marriage

TROBRIAND ISLANDS. There are no formal trials or tests through which a young man must go before marriage.

People marry at an early age.

Defective persons usually cannot win mates.

AMERICA. There are no formal suitors' trials. The bridegroom is expected, however, to be able to support the bride economically without other than housework contribution from her.

There are legal age limitations upon marriage, most typically 21 for men and 18 for girls without parental consent, and 18 for boys and 16 for girls with parental consent. In many jurisdictions persons with certain defects and diseases are legally forbidden to marry.

The Rituals of Mate Finding and Marriage

TROBRIAND ISLANDS. The marriage is ritualized as follows: (1) The girl's parents signify consent by asking the boy (who has already been having sexual relations with the girl) for a small present. (2) After some interval the girl, instead of returning home, remains all day with her husband, taking meals at the home of his parents (this constituting the public declaration). (3) There is a series of complicated gift exchanges between the families, the larger gifts being exchanged after the next harvest, during which time the couple is "honeymooning" at the hut of *his* parents. (4) After the harvest comes the building of the new home, usually in the boy's mother's village.

AMERICA. The marriage procedure is: (1) The boy proposes marriage to the girl. He does this usually only after she has shown some evidence of fondness for him, but there is no disgrace if he proposes prematurely or unsuccessfully. A girl must not directly propose; the boy must take the initiative at each step toward closer relations. (2) The girl accepts, usually first making sure of the consent of her parents; in certain classes the boy formally asks the consent of the girl's parents. (3) The engagement is announced to friends; in the upper classes this is done with some ritual. (4) After the engagement the partners must be more or less exclusive in their comradeship. (5) After a certain length of time formal authorization of marriage is obtained from the government authority, and the marriage is soon thereafter consummated by a definite ceremony performed by a governmental or religious officer. Until this ceremony has taken place either party is free to break the relationship. After the ceremony it may be broken only through divorce or annulment procedure. The ideology of the ceremony is religious, the essential union of the patterns being regarded as an act of the Deity. (6) On the night after the marriage ceremony the partners sleep together for the first time. Before the ceremony they may not morally be alone together in any situation for a whole night, although they may eat and play and spend whole days alone together throughout courtship. (7) The partners then usually take a honeymoon of a week or more away from friends and relatives, indulging freely in all types of love behavior. This is supposedly the climax of romantic love. (8) The time and place of founding the new home are matters of individual choice and convenience. It is the bridegroom's responsibility to provide the new home, normally within a short time after marriage.

Status and Satisfactions of the Married and Unmarried

TROBRIAND ISLANDS. The unmarried men enjoy a lower social status and lesser economic advantages than the married. No persons remain unmarried except because of personal unattractiveness or defectiveness.

Women gain no economic advantages through marriage, but gain social status and supposedly the power to have children.

AMERICA. There is little or no difference in social status between married and unmarried. About 10 per cent of the people never marry, and this brings no moral condemnation. Many other causes than personal defectiveness or unattractiveness lead to non-marriage.

The desires for morally approved love satisfactions and for legitimate offspring are the motives for marriage; many women expect to get greater economic security.

Divorce: Frequency and Grounds

TROBRIAND ISLANDS. Divorce is permissible on the desire of either party, and is frequent. Usually it is the woman who seeks it, sometimes because of her husband's adultery. Any dissatisfaction with the other party may be the cause; there is no public control or formal adjudication, but informal group judgment has some controlling influence.

Childlessness of a woman is not given special weight as a ground for divorce.

Since divorce requires no formal procedure, an actual separation is equivalent to divorce.

AMERICA. Divorce is permissible only through formal legal procedure, upon specified causes which are practically the same for both man and woman; they must be judicially proved, and they vary from one territorial government to another. Adultery is the most universally accepted ground for divorce. Desertion for a term of years and physical cruelty are valid grounds in most jurisdictions but not in all. The permissibility of a given divorce depends upon technical specifications rather than upon group judgment of its desirability.

Childlessness is nowhere a ground for divorce.

Divorce is always a right obtained by a theoretically innocent party against a party proved guilty of a specific offense. Double guilt and collusive mutual consent render divorce non-permissible.

Married partners may and do freely separate without divorce, but their legal marriage obligations continue and they may not remarry.

Widowhood

TROBRIAND ISLANDS. Widows and widowers have about the same status and love privileges as the unmarried, except for a required period of mourning, which is more severe and more strictly supervised for widows, and is carefully ritualized. After this period they remarry readily.

AMERICA. Widows and widowers have the same social status and love privileges as the unmarried. A period of mourning for each is regarded as proper, but the ritual is very simple and not strictly enforced.

Illegitimacy

TROBRIAND ISLANDS. Illegitimate children are pitied because they have no father to nurse and love them. Only those born before marriage are regarded as illegitimate, regardless of biological paternity. Those recognized as illegitimates are readily adopted by kinsfolk and are not especially stigmatized.

AMERICA. Illegitimate children are socially stigmatized but have full legal rights, except as to inheritance. The chief stigma falls upon the unmarried mother, because she has broken an important sex taboo. The father, if he can be identified, can be compelled to furnish economic support. The illegitimate children of a married woman are treated variously; they may cause divorce or they may be accepted by the legal husband.

Extra-marital Sex Relations

TROBRIAND ISLANDS. Extra-marital intercourse of either a married man or married woman is regarded as improper and is typically reacted to by a display of anger by the injured party. How far this anger will go depends upon personalities and circumstances. It may lead to the killing of the unfaithful partner or paramour or his being driven by insults to suicide. Reconciliation is usual, however, and no special stigma fastens to the occasional adulterer, though the frequent adulterer may be publicly scorned.

Clandestine adultery is, however, frequent, especially during the absence of the mate. Female adultery is not so readily detected as among civilized groups because an untimely birth is never regarded as evidence thereof.

Extra-marital relations are probably more frequent, and less disapproved, on the part of married men than of married women.

Adultery with a chief's wife is especially desired and especially dangerous.

AMERICA. All such relations are taboo. Their legal consequences are the same for an unfaithful husband as for an unfaithful wife, except in some states which judge the wife somewhat more severely. The offended party, if innocent himself, may secure a divorce, but may not use physical violence upon the offenders. In the mores, however, such relations which involve a married woman are regarded as worse than those involving a married man and an unmarried woman. The man is often excused on the theory of his greater sexual need, whereas the woman is condemned on the theory that her adultery is pure wantonness. A basic motive is the man's fear of having children not his own in the family; a woman has no similar fear in case of her husband's adultery. A man's attitude toward his wife is outwardly more possessive than that of a wife toward her husband. There is also a code of personal "honor" or "respectability" which forces a husband to react dramatically to his wife's adultery regardless of his inner feelings. Meek toleration of it leads to his being held in contempt.

Here, too, a sharp moral line is drawn between completed intercourse and "petting," the latter being tolerated in greater degree in many classes even if extra-marital.

"Promiscuous" Classes

TROBRIAND ISLANDS. There is no special class of prostitutes, though some men and women are notoriously more promiscuous than others.

AMERICA. There is a recognizable class of women who for financial compensation and at the penalty of social degradation satisfy the purely sexual needs of a much larger number of men. Traditionally these prostitutes are sharply distinguished from "virtuous" married women and virgins, to whom they are socially inferior and yet whom they supposedly help to protect from the excesses of male passion. Yet there are always, and now increasingly so, many women whose concealed sexual life is intermediate between that prescribed by the mores and that which is "promiscuous." There are also some male prostitutes.

MARION J. LEVY, JR.

Contrasting Factors in the Modernization of China and Japan

INTRODUCTION

Whereas industrialization made little progress in China, it proceeded rapidly in Japan in the late nineteenth and the present century. To account for this difference, five hypotheses are advanced:

1. It was not differences in the new forces introduced to China and Japan that accounted for their different experiences in industrialization. It was rather differences in the social structures into which those new forces were introduced.

2. Differences in "nonsocial" factors such as raw material resources, etc., do not account for the differences. In so far as they are relevant they would indicate either an outcome opposite to that which occurred or no special difference in outcome.

3. One strategic factor in Japan's industrialization was the fact that the basis from which change took place in Japan was such that the transition did not undercut the system of control over deviance or the possibility of highly controlled direction of the members of the society, as was the case in China.

4. There existed in Japan a group of individuals relatively easily converted, particularly to the planning and administrative roles required by the conversion.

5. There existed in Japan a possibility of eliminating without internal breakdown the influence of those individuals not relatively well adapted to make the changes required by the conversion.

The material on which these hypotheses rest consists of findings presented in earlier studies relating to China[1] and of inferences drawn con-

From *Economic Growth: Brazil, India, and Japan*, edited by Simon Kuznets, Wilbert E. Moore, and Joseph J. Spengler (Durham, N.C.: Duke University Press, 1955), pp. 496-536. Reprinted with permission of the author and the publisher.
    [1] *The Family Revolution in Modern China* (Cambridge, Mass., 1949); *Some Problems of Modernization in China* (New York, 1949); and Shih Kuo-Heng

cerning factors present in Japan and their implications in terms of the Japanese social structure. Limitations of space have prevented elaboration either of the concepts employed or of the interrelationships found.

ABSTRACT

Statement of the Problem

This paper is concerned with strategic, necessary, but not sufficient conditions for Japan's apparent success in relatively rapid and peaceful conversion from a markedly nonindustrialized to a relatively highly industrialized society in so far as those conditions are to be found in the social structure of Japan and the new forces brought to bear on Japan.

Method

The method used has been that of a comparative presentation of the cases of China and Japan. This has been done because I have felt that the presentation of those features of China that were similar to those of Japan or offered China perhaps even greater advantages in the process would highlight and clarify those factors strategic in the case of Japan. The material presented in both cases has been deliberately oversimplified, particularly in the case of Japan. This has been done because space does not permit extended and carefully qualified elaboration of the interrelationships found, or of concepts developed for the analysis of the available materials.

The Stages of the Analysis

Any problem of social change is a problem in comparative social analysis. Three stages of a social system must be distinguished either explicitly or implicitly: (1) that from which change takes place, *the initial stage*; (2) that during which the change takes place, *the transitional stage*; (3) that of the system when the change under study may be considered complete, *the resultant stage*.[2] In the case of both China and Japan the initial stage is one of relatively little industrialization. For present purposes a system will be considered more or less industrialized to the extent that its system of allocation of goods and services (including in that allocation both consumption and production) involves tools that multiply or

and Marion J. Levy, Jr., *The Rise of the Modern Chinese Business Class* (New York, 1949), Part I.

[2] See M. J. Levy, Jr., *The Structure of Society* (Princeton, 1952), pp. 44-45, 71-76 (especially these pages), 83-88, 140-144, and 147-148 for a discussion of problems involved in the analysis of social change. (The treatment here is based on that discussion.)

magnify the effect of human energy offered and to the extent that inanimate sources of power are being utilized.[3] Elements of industrialization thus defined are encountered in the initial stages of both China and Japan as those stages are distinguished here — and probably in any society. But these elements are unimportant by comparison with those involved in "modern Western" nations such as the United States, Great Britain, and Germany, or Japan of the 1930's. It is in this sense that the initial stages of China and Japan distinguished here are spoken of as nonindustrialized or relatively little industrialized.

The period of Chinese society that will be considered its initial stage is that period of the Ch'ing Dynasty in the middle and latter part of the eighteenth century. The period of Japanese society that will be considered its initial stage is that of the reign of the Shogun Iyemitsu (1623-51). These stages will be referred to respectively as "traditional" China and "traditional" Japan. In both cases there are, no doubt, many elements of social structure for which an authentic pedigree can be traced further back in the history of the societies concerned. Here, however, we are concerned with the character of the initial stages and not with their origins.

These two particular stages have been chosen in order to accent two sources of change in the societies. The first has to do with sources that were indigenous to the societies concerned. The second has to do with the sources of change that came from social systems outside the two societies considered. The internal sources of change were markedly different, but the external sources of change as treated here were identical. In China the internal sources had to do with the breakdown of the Imperial bureaucracy. This was a breakdown of a sort that had been seen in many of its facets in the history of previous Chinese dynasties. In Japan the internal sources of change had to do with the breakdown of a feudal[4] social system — a breakdown in which a major role was played by the changing actual role of the merchants in the society. In both China and Japan the external sources were virtually identical. They were the factors involved in modern

[3] See the items cited as "industrial society" and "industrialization" in the index of *The Structure of Society* for a discussion of this concept and some of its general implications, etc.

[4] The term *feudal* is here applied to social systems with the following characteristics: (a) closed social classes, (b) a well-defined hierarchy of power-holders, (c) identification, at least ideally speaking, of each individual as responsible to some particular individual higher than himself in the hierarchy and related to others outside of that direct line by virtue of his overlord's relations to them, and (d) a distribution of goods and services, most especially land ownership and control, primarily on the basis of the ranks distinguished in the hierarchy of power and responsibility.

industrialization. Neither China nor Japan was responsible for the development of the highly industrialized social systems that provided the factors that were the external sources of change. If the changes described as internal sources are in fact internal sources of change, then it follows that these internal sources are themselves products of the operation of the systems that have been referred to as the initial stages of the societies concerned. This in turn argues that whatever differences we may find between China and Japan with respect to their resultant stages must be primarily a result of their differences in their initial stages. This would follow in so far as it is in fact true that their external sources of change were identical and their internal sources of change were different.

THE PROBLEM OF CHANGE IN CHINA

The Initial Stage

Perhaps the most significant feature of "traditional" China for present purposes is the fact that it was "family oriented" to an overwhelming degree.[5] Ideally speaking, it was expected that decisions be made primarily with reference to family interests. The individual owed loyalty first, last, and always to his family. This was true even in a conflict between one's family and the Imperial bureaucracy. The whole Confucian theory of order rested in considerable part on the theory that if family members were so well imbued with filial piety that they would never consider disloyalty to one another, the individual members could not possibly be the sort of people who would as individuals commit improper acts.

There were several organizations that brought pressure to bear on family groups and limited the extremes to which the individual might go in sacrificing the interests of others to the interests of his family. Especially noteworthy in these respects were such organizations as the neighborhood councils and the guilds. But even in these the pressure was often brought in family terms. The individual was constrained in effect by the threat that he would achieve only the short-run interest of his family and that in the long run his acts would so unite other families against his as to bring about its downfall. In such organizations families were represented by family heads, and pressure on individuals was usually brought to bear through the family head rather than directly.

The family in "traditional" China was not the only overriding focus for individual loyalties in the ideal case. It was also the basic unit in terms of which the economic aspects of life were carried out. The average Chinese family, and that means the ordinary peasant family in "traditional" China, was self-sufficient in both production and consumption to

[5] Only the sketchiest outline of points about "traditional" China will be given here. Greater elaboration of the points stressed here may be found in the sources cited in n. 1, above.

a degree that it is difficult for persons from highly industrialized societies to understand. Departures from this pattern in either direction were considered unfortunate. Even in gentry families in which such self-sufficiency was in fact much lower, the dependency on nonfamily members as producers was minimized, at least ostensibly, by the use of servants who were often quasi-family members and by cutting to a minimum the number of family members through whom these outside contacts were made.

Finally, the family was the basic unit in terms of which the allocation of power and responsibility took place. The individual was controlled primarily through pressure brought to bear on him by the family head. The hierarchy of power and responsibility with which he was most familiar was that of his own family. When he participated in groups outside his family group, these were likely to be organized on a pseudo-family basis, or he was likely to be controlled, in so far as he was controlled, on the basis of the implications of his deviance for the fortunes of his family.

There were, of course, organizations of considerable importance for Chinese society apart from the family organization. These often required decisions that were not in accordance with those that might have been made by unbridled family self-interest. Most notable among these was perhaps the Imperial bureaucracy. "Traditional" Chinese society was dependent in many respects upon some highly organized administrative machinery. This dependence was particularly marked with regard to problems centering about irrigation, but in most of the dynasties, whatever were the reasons, the production of certain strategic goods and services (e.g., certain metals, salt, communications, etc.) were also handled on this basis. The equipment and organization involved required considerable talent to devise, but they were also subject to extremely low rates of obsolescence, and apparently also to relatively slow rates of decay. This is true at least by comparison with the situation in a highly industrialized system in which the attention to equipment and organization must be unremitting in a sense and to a degree unnecessary in the Chinese case.

When the bureaucracy was working as it was "supposed to," individual family interests were rigidly ruled out. Nepotism in recruitment was banished by a most carefully worked-out examination system. During one's service in the organization every attempt was made to remove temptation for putting one's family interests above one's duties to the state. But no attempt was made to teach the members that such family interferences were bad. It was the responsibility of the system to insulate the individual from such pressures by properly conducted examinations, by refusing permission to serve in one's home area, and the like. The attempts to insulate the individual broke down in many cases through the years. The dynastic cycle in China for some two thousand years saw a continual breakdown and renovation of the Imperial bureaucracy. Any attempt at conversion as opposed to insulation would probably have been extremely difficult. It would have involved a radical departure from the tenets held good and true throughout the rest of the society and would have undercut many of the other aspects of the bureaucracy itself. As it existed, the Imperial bureaucracy did not ideally speaking provide an organization that took precedence over the family. The underlying theory of government was that a proper government could not be unjust to any family, that no filial son could have reason therefore for not obeying the government. A good family man could not be other than a good citizen.

Friendship groups of various kinds and degrees tempered family relationships, but here again in case of clear contradiction between the interests of one's family and one's friends, the family interests, at least ideally speaking, took precedence. The overwhelming significance of the family as a center of attention in the society was demonstrated in other ways than this matter of precedence, however. In groups outside the family the terminology of kinship was likely to be applied, particularly if the relationships involved were considered to be extremely close and binding. Thus close friends were likely to be referred to as "older brother," teachers assumed a role likened to that of "father" or "father's elder brother" relative to their students. Thus quite apart from the precedence taken by the family in case of conflicts, in the ordinary course of those relationships outside the family, family solidarities were continually being called to mind, simulated, and reinforced.

Organizations like the neighborhood ruling councils, the guilds, etc. have already been mentioned above. They often operated in such a way as to limit the pursuit of family self-interest, but as has been pointed out above, they operated frequently through the use of family pressures. The strong emphasis on continued family residence in a single locale enhanced this possibility in the case of the neighborhood groups, and the tendency of apprenticeships, particularly in the more lucrative fields dominated by the guilds, to be given on highly nepotistic bases enhanced this possibility in that field. The use of the family as the vehicle of governmental control as exemplified in the *pao-chia* system is too obvious to require further mention. But in these respects again the family priority was made clear in other ways. Here too there was the transfer of kinship terms to non-kinship relations. But the matter was highlighted by what happened when the patterns in these areas did not work out as they would have under conditions generally considered ideal in that society. When, for example, a given family in a neighborhood became so powerful that pressure could not be exerted on it successfully by the threat of its long-run disadvantage, family self-interest did take precedence over the neighborhood council, or more properly the neighborhood council came to be completely dominated by the members of that powerful family. When this happened, the interests of other families in the area were preserved only if their abrogation served no useful purpose for the family in power or if the family head of the family in power were a benevolent despot in the area and took an essentially paternal attitude toward those over whom he could in fact have exerted power.

The comparison of China and Japan in these and in other respects has often been confused by the use of the term *feudal* to denote both of these social systems. This can, of course, be done legitimately, depending on one's definition of the term. But its use in this connection has perhaps on the whole been more misleading than any other single term used in discussions of the industrialization of nonindustrialized areas. If the term is used to mean that from the point of view of the observer, the peasant had a difficult time of it in both societies, that individuals were not treated "democratically," that there was a great gulf between the "haves" and the "have nots," that most people made their livelihood from agrarian pursuits, that many of the "haves" lived on income secured by virtue of ownership of land, etc., then both cases may be described as feudal. But the connotations of the term *feudal* include as a minimum the factors listed above[6] as the defining elements in the term. Unless the term is redefined by the user, these connotations go along with it, and the term is not usually redefined. In the sense of the term *feudal* as defined explicitly above, "traditional" China was decidedly nonfeudal; in this sense China has not been truly feudal for the last two thousand years. In this sense Tokugawa Japan was feudal. It is the hypothesis here that the structural differences involved in this distinction are of primary importance in understanding the different experiences that these two systems have had with industrialization. If in fact the basis from which change is taking place today in China were feudal in the sense of that term as defined here and as rather generally understood, then China would present very different possibilities and probabilities of change than are in fact present.

"Traditional" China did not contain a closed class system. It is true that the paths of social mobility were frequently badly clogged, but it is doubtful that they were actually ever completely closed during the last two thousand years of Chinese history, and certainly they were never ideally closed during that time. It is true that some groups were at least in theory excluded from social mobility since their members were excluded from admission to the examinations, but the vast mass of the population was never so excluded. Ideally speaking a peasant family could always climb to the top of the tree if it could produce and educate a son of great talent.

[6] See n. 4, above.

The ideal type family in "traditional" China was the gentry type family. There was in fact mobility upwards, and there was also mobility downwards. Peasant sons did rise to the top of the bureaucracy. Wealthy gentry families not only lost their wealth and power in many instances, but they often returned to the status of peasant families or worse. In societies like those of medieval Europe and Tokugawa Japan, the expectations, both ideal and actual, of every member of those societies were that one and one's family would retain forever the class status into which one was born. However much the actual expectation may have been of a similar sort in China, the ideal expectation was not of this order. It is extremely doubtful that the actual closure of class membership in "traditional" China ever approached that of Tokugawa Japan, but even if it did, their differences in ideal patterns in these respects mark them as animals of a different species.[7]

The allocation of power and responsibility in "traditional" China was also quite different from that involved in a feudal society. There was a relatively well-defined hierarchy of power-holders, but this situation existed only in so far as each individual responded to the expected family controls and the relations among different families remained in equilibrium. In time of upset, change, or crisis one owed loyalty first to one's family and only secondarily to the power-responsibility hierarchy outside the family. When new situations arose, the family head decided whether he and the other members of the family would go along with orders from outside the family or not. When the individual was not in a position to decide such a question on the basis of family interests (either because of separation from or loss of his family members), he was in a position of "individualism by default." He would under such conditions go along with the rules of magistrates or princes or whatever if he felt his interest coincided with theirs or if he felt that the force at their command was such that he had no alternative, and if not, not.

Within the family the hierarchy of power and responsibility was clear-cut ideally speaking, but the position of a given family relative to other families and to organizations other than families was subject to considerable shifts. Hence the third condition of the definition of *fuedal* given above[8] was not met. The orientation of the family head was not to someone over him in the general social hierarchy of power and responsibility, but rather was owed to the organization of which he was the head. His

[7] There is little about which we may feel certain in the social sciences, but the importance for understanding social phenomena of the distinction between ideal and actual patterns is one of them. Systems with similar actual patterns but different ideal patterns in a given sphere cannot be without structural implications, of either a static or a dynamic sort, of these differences.

[8] See n. 4, above.

loyalty and submission to others outside that organization was ideally speaking primarily instrumental for the welfare of the organization that he headed. It was generally to be expected that he be ruthlessly rational in seeking to maximize that welfare. Last, but not least, if he could maximize the welfare of his own family at the expense of others in the society, the responsibility was not considered his but rather that of the sovereign.

It would be beside the point here to go into detail about the many ways in which those factors were interrelated with other aspects of the social system, or the roles they played both in adapting the system to its setting and in maladapting it to that setting. Actually under the circumstances it made for a system of control which was characterized by relatively long periods of stability and of gradual disintegration and which tended to be restored after a period of decay in a renovated rather than a revolutionized form. What is important from the present point of view is that it was a system of control that was peculiarly vulnerable to certain types of changes, that these changes, if introduced rapidly, could result in rather dramatic disintegration of control. The keystone of social structure in these respects was the family structure. For roughly two thousand years family structure does not seem to have been radically altered in these respects, and no genuine alternative was offered for it. But in the nineteenth and twentieth centuries there were forces elsewhere in the world that impinged on China and undercut the "traditional" family structure.

Turning for a moment from these problems of control, the special situation of the merchants in "traditional" China must be considered. Ideally speaking the merchants held roles of extremely low prestige in "traditional" China. They were ranked well below the peasants, who were, of course, ranked well below the gentry. There were even periods in which attempts were made to make a closed class of the merchants by forbidding them or their sons or grandsons from taking the Imperial examinations. For reasons that need not detain us here, these attempts were never successful in the long run. *In actuality* the merchants who were successful as merchants frequently became powerful politically and prestigious socially despite the ideal patterns of the society to the contrary. This sort of violation of the ideal patterns of a society should not seem strange to Westerners who are really quite familiar with the phenomena in the form of racketeers and the like controlling local and even state governments, amassing fortunes through corruption, escaping the punishment ideally decreed for such activities, and eventually in some cases becoming highly respected members of their communities. This again is a discrepancy between ideal and actual patterns which is of great importance for understanding the social phenomena of modern Chinese history.

It is probably true that the merchants in "traditional" China tended to be rather more emancipated from the traditional features of their social environment than were Chinese in the roles of gentry, peasants, artisans, etc. This is probably one of the reasons that attempts were made to restrict their power and influence. By and large the merchants made their fortunes by trading rather than production. As such, unlike the other members of the society, the self-sufficiency of their families was minimal. Frequently they produced neither what they sold nor what they consumed. Their contacts with persons outside their own family groups were therefore broader than those of most of the members of their society. They saw more of China and of other lands, as well as of people drawn from wider backgrounds. One would expect that these people with their greater perspective, their commercialism, and the like would have been the ideal people to break new ground when industrial influences were first felt, that they would convert easily to the roles played by members of the "middle class" in modern Western societies such as England and the United States. But this does not turn out to have been the case, and at least some of the explanation of this would seem to lie in factors already mentioned above.

Often when there are discrepancies between the ideal and actual roles of individuals, the pressure placed on those actually holding high positions to acquire the ideal ones as well is enormous. Many of the rising bourgeoisie in England sought to become landed gentry there. Many racketeers and political bosses in the United States seek to become businessmen. The transition is sometimes spread over several generations. In "traditional" China prestige par excellence lay in the roles of the gentry. The gentry were expected to depend for income on the perquisites of political office and the absentee ownership of land. The most aristocratic circles in the Western world have not for many decades denigrated the stain of participating in "trade" to the extent common even to the present day in China. The successful merchant, like all other Chinese, was under great pressure to secure the future of his family. This called for an education of sons directed to their entry into the bureaucracy, and hence a classical Chinese education, and the investment of capital in land rather than its continued reinvestment in the business. This investment of profits in land was further reinforced by the almost shady status of trade, and hence its vulnerability to exploitation could be prevented only by being able to buy and control officials or by having strong personal relations, preferably kinship relations with officials in positions of power. Land ownership, the major economic basis of the gentry, was also vulnerable to the pressures of the officials, but by virtue of its eminently respectable status and by virtue of the fact that an official threatening the income from absentee ownership of land simultaneously threatened all of the gentry in his area, income from land was not nearly so vulnerable in these respects as were both the income from and the capital invested in commercial pursuits.

There were other relevant factors, but these should suffice to indicate that there was a considerable source of motivation for a flight of both talent and capital from the merchant role. A merchant who got his sons a classical education, invested in land, and terminated his involvement in trade laid a firm foundation for gentry status for his family in the future. If he got a son or another relative into the bureaucracy, he established thereby connections that increased his security from exploitation. The emphasis on talent in the bureaucracy, even at its most corrupt, increased the motivation for sending the ablest of one's sons or male relatives into these roles rather than into merchant roles. These factors, combined with the open class structure of "traditional" Chinese society even as regards the merchants, made of the merchant role a transitory social status both ideally and actually. Merchant roles, if successful in a monetary sense, enabled one to accumulate the economic base necessary to guarantee, or make possible, gentry status for one's family in the future. A merchant was most fully successful to the extent that he and his ceased to be merchants and were enabled to do so by virtue of his commercial successes.

In this general background of "traditional" China, of which only some of the more strategic features for the present problem have been touched upon, there were several sources of stress and containment of stress that must be noted here. The factors of stress in this society have often been overlooked. The errors here have arisen largely from a presentation of the ideal rather than the actual picture of the facts of social life in China and from focusing attention on some phases of the life history of individuals to the exclusion of others. For example, the picture generally given of the "traditional" Chinese family is a picture of the ideal gentry type of family, a family type actually approximated by only a very small minority of Chinese. An example of the second source of error mentioned above is to be found in the frequent treatment of the role of women as "secure" by contrast with the uncertainties facing women in modern Western societies. However tenable this may be as a comparative statement, it gives a misleading view of the position of Chinese women. At some stages of their lives they have indeed a large measure of security, but at others they are to a rather remarkable degree in positions of considerable stress. One of the most intriguing aspects about "traditional" Chinese social structure is that virtually every individual in the society went through periods of great social stress, but could, in terms of the ideal patterns at least, and to a high degree in terms of the actual patterns as well, look forward to stages of greatly reduced stress.[9]

Some of the most fundamental sources of stress in "traditional" Chinese society were concentrated within the strongest unit of solidarity of that society, i.e., the family. There is not time to go into these sources

[9] This whole question is taken up in some detail in *The Family Revolution in Modern China*, cited above (n. 1).

in detail, but short of a theory holding the Chinese to be inherently masochistic, notable stresses must be granted as the result of relations between fathers and sons, mothers-in-law and daughters-in-law, and men and women. Less notable ones perhaps resulted from certain relations among brothers, brothers and sisters, women in the family apart from the specific roles already mentioned, etc. Suffice it to say that there is good reason to believe that there were sources enough for motivation to defy, desert, or modify the family patterns if opportunities to do so presented themselves.

There were many other notable sources of stress in the society. General economic conditions were close to a subsistence minimum for a large proportion of the members of the society in the best of times. In times of crop failures, despotic officials and the like, whatever margin existed could easily be and often was wiped out. Relations between the townsmen and the villagers were an important source of difficulty. Those whom the peasants often regarded as exploiters (i.e., landlords, usurers, officials, merchants, etc.) were typically town dwellers. The economic structure of "traditional" China was one in which the townsmen were supported by goods and services from both the towns and the villages, but the villagers were supported almost entirely by what they produced alone. The village economy was the keystone of the whole economy, but as far as most of the villagers were concerned the flow of goods and services was a one-way affair. When times were difficult, the townsmen were likely to be regarded as the source of difficulties by the villagers whether this was in fact justified or not.

Another source of stress in the society was, of course, the breakdown of the bureaucratic system. The insulation of that system from the family pressures on which the society was based was not in fact effective for long. Graft and corruption grew as the dynasties went their course. As the system decayed, the irrigation and communications systems also decayed. This had its implications in lowered productivity. More and more of a premium was placed on the officials squeezing all they could from whomever they could get hold of. Taxes were often collected years in advance. Combinations of officials, landlords, and merchants preyed on the peasants in many ways. In regions in which official power declined powerful families were often able to become the effective governing force in the area and exploit the rest of the population there. A popular saying in China held that it was better to live in a tiger-infested area than in one ruled by a bad government, and it is not without significance that the district magistrate's yamen was known frequently as a "tiger's mouth."

Despite these sources of stress and strain, the structure of "traditional" Chinese society seems to have been a remarkably stable arrangement for a nonindustrial society of the scale encompassed. It is the hypothesis of the present paper that the structure had built into it a very potent method of containing these strains. The family stresses in particular were contained by the fact that the possibilities for alternative employment for rebels were so restricted. As noted above, people were hired primarily on the basis of who they were, and the primary criterion of who a person was depended on his family status. A rebel from the family cut himself or herself off from this source of identification, and in doing so he or she was virtually certain to break the major ethical tenet of the society and to sin against filial piety. No respectable employer wanted such a person. The jobs open were those of extremely low status and jobs in which life was very likely to be "poor, nasty, brutish, and short." There were rebels, of course, but they were rather effectively disposed of by the opportunities open to them, and those who avoided these fates and who prospered were usually at some pains to disguise the fact that they had ever been rebels.

There were more positive sources of containment too. Each family head was emancipated from direct responsibility to other members of his family, but he was responsible to the ancestors for the welfare of the family. In so far as he continued sincere in these devotions, he was likely to try to prevent such stresses from getting out of hand. Nevertheless, it is hardly likely that this positive obligation did more than modify the extremity of these stresses.

Relative to the more general stresses in the society mentioned above, the overwhelming tendency for redress was via a refurbishment of the system rather than by revolutionary change. In the first place, the system, when relatively devoid of graft and corruption, was probably as effective and well-balanced a system of organizing and controlling a large scale highly decentralized system as the world has ever seen. This was particularly so since the units of the system were capable of such a high degree of economic self-sufficiency and hence, with the technologies available, so difficult to control in detail by a highly centralized governmental organization. In the second place, the relatively slow disintegration of the dynasties gave the people a relatively prosperous period to look back on. The lack of basic structural changes either from within or without the system tended in this context to focus attention on reform of the system and return thereby to things as "they should be" rather than on radical change of the system. This tendency was further reinforced by virtue of the fact that the intellectual and ethical authorities revered by the members of the system were well aware of such breakdowns and had counseled dealing with them via renovation.

The Transitional Stage

There were two sources of change in the transitional period of modern China, and indeed they continue to operate today. The resultant stage of China is phrased negatively for present purposes — she did not make much headway with industrialization. Those sources were on the one hand the disintegration of the typical patterns of "traditional" China, particularly those having to do with the imperial bureaucracy, and on the other those new forces that were introduced to China with the introduction from the West of social patterns pertaining to modern industrialization. The factors involved in the first have already been touched on above and are in general too familiar to require extended comment here. They involve the tremendous increase in graft and corruption in government to the point of virtual governmental impotence. In China the Ch'ing rulers fell and were replaced by a republic in name. This latter made a start in the direction of reform, but it had more to cope with than had past reformers. It had to cope with the sources of disintegration added by the new forces, and it did not succeed. The new forces precluded at least temporarily the return to the old situation, and the heritage of the old situation made the successful establishment of the new especially difficult — at least sufficiently so that none of the modern rulers of China have succeeded in coping with the situation in terms of the new forces. Certainly the Nationalist regime did not, and the Communist regime has not yet shown that it can do so.[10]

In so far as both China and Japan sought to industrialize (and one can make a good case for the fact that neither had much alternative given the general world situation), they were faced with certain common problems. They had with regard to industrialization certain advantages and certain disadvantages over those countries in which the development of industrialization in the modern sense was indigenous. Both countries had the advantage of starting with the latest available technological equipment without having to go through the process of developing the equipment with all the implications of that process in terms of obsolete equipment, etc. Both were in a position to take advantage of the lessons in terms of management and the like that Western countries had learned through costly experience. Finally both countries were in a position to use labor at much cheaper rates than were available to industry in the West. Each had considerable disadvantages as well. The stage at which they encountered industrialization required that the scale of modernization be relatively large, and the longer industrialization was delayed (as in the case of China), the greater was this problem. By the time each came to the process of industrialization, the type of capital equipment required was such that ready conversion of the prevailing economic resources into the required form of capital was not nearly so easy as it had been in those

---

[10] As regards the latter, there are indications that the fate of the former awaits it with relatively slight modifications unless it is able to find and adopt techniques quite at variance with present policies, but there is not time or space to go into this matter here.

countries which industrialized slowly over a relatively long period. In the West the transitions were gradual, and capital and labor at one stage were gradually shifted into the forms required for the succeeding one. Similarly the changes in aspects of the social system other than the economic ones proceeded gradually. The institutional basis for change had a long, unbroken pedigree in much of the West, whereas in both China and Japan, radical breaks with the past were involved. For present purposes it is necessary to ignore certain special problems faced by China and Japan. Most notable in these respects is the demographic problem. In kind this problem was similar for both East and West, but the differences in degree, timing, and alternatives open were enormous.

There is not space here to detail all of the special features of the new forces that were imported into these two societies. For present purposes brief mention of two will have to suffice. In the first place, the new forces placed a tremendous emphasis on an entirely different sort of social relationship than had been common in either China or Japan. In the second place, the development of industrialization when it became available to China and Japan, given their respective economic bases, had of necessity to be carried out on a large scale or none, at least with regard to many crucial areas.

In the sphere of relationships industrialization carried with it an emphasis hitherto unequaled in social history on what the sociologists speak of as highly rational, highly universalistic, and highly functionally specific relationships. For present purposes these terms may be explained as follows. In a highly industrialized situation a tremendous amount of action has to be based on what would amount to tenable engineering criteria of efficiency and the like, rather than on traditional arguments about the right and wrong way to do things. The individual has to think critically and in scientifically tenable terms about how to do things, what to buy, when to sell, where to locate, and the like. In regard to choosing people for jobs and the like he has to place great emphasis on what a person can do that is germane to the reasons for which he is chosen — on his abilities rather than on who he is. In this sense great emphasis must be placed on highly universalistic rather than on particularistic criteria. Finally, in many of the relationships in a highly industrialized situation the obligations, etc., involved in a relationship must be precisely defined and delimited regardless of how complex they may be. At least a tendency in this direction is extremely important. In this sense an emphasis is placed by modern industry on functionally specific relationships rather than on functionally diffuse ones.[11]

[11] For discussions of the relevance of these relationship aspects to industrialization, see Talcott Parsons, *Essays in Sociological Theory* (Glencoe, Ill., 1949), pp. 185-199; and M. J. Levy, *The Structure of Society*, pp. 238-298, 421-443, etc.

With regard to the special problems of scale involved in the industrialization of China and Japan, or of any late-comers to industrialization for that matter, the basic problem involved is, perhaps, the implication of these scale requirements for the problem of planning and control. Given the discrepancy between the basis of industrialization in these two countries and the stages of development it had reached in the West, it was necessary for these countries to import en masse what had been developed gradually elsewhere. Railroad systems and communications in general had to be undertaken on a large scale if they were to be of maximum usefulness or even to be useful at all. The lack of ready convertibility of the capital in private hands to uses of this sort virtually forced governmental involvement in these projects; certainly this was true if, as in the case of Japan, the members of the system were anxious to carry out such a program without permitting control of the program or of the country to fall into the hands of foreign individuals or foreign governments. It is perfectly true that industrialization grew up in countries like England and the United States with relatively little centralized planning, and it may even be true that it could not have developed had such planning been present, but China and Japan were not developing industrialization. They were taking it over after it had become rather highly developed. The gradual passing from a system of highly decentralized, highly self-sufficient units to highly interdependent ones could not be repeated in these countries. They were faced at the very outset with large-scale problems of co-ordination if they were to take advantage of their special situation as late-comers to industrialization. They could not even modernize methods of agricultural production without raising a whole host of other problems such as systems of roads, repair depots for equipment, agricultural stations for testing and growing special seeds, etc.

This problem of co-ordination involves a problem of control, by force if necessary, in cases in which deviance develops or threatens. More importantly it requires that there be patterns in operation that tend to minimize the development of deviance. In the last analysis it is the latter rather than the former that is crucial because of the limited effectiveness of the use of force and the fact that every effective use of force on a large scale implies the presence of patterns that motivate conformity without the actual invocation of force.

In the transitional period in China the internal sources of change provided motivation aplenty for individuals to try the new patterns introduced from the West. The family strains alone were capable of motivating many individuals to seek alternative roles if those were available. By the latter part of the Ch'ing Dynasty the disintegration of the Imperial bureaucracy was far advanced. This disintegration itself put pressures of many sorts on individuals. Tenancy rates were high, usury was extreme, graft and corruption were such as to subject individuals to the most capricious types of exploitation, irrigation systems were in bad repair — conditions had reached a state at which many were willing to try anything.

Into this situation which had been seen in China at the end of dynasties before, the new forces were injected. There was plenty of motivation for the injection of these forces by Westerners either on a peaceful or a forceful basis. China represented vast potential markets and also a vast potential source of production. The fact that the Chinese had little with which to buy foreign goods went along with the extremely cheap labor force, and the latter meant that China could be used by others as the scene of low-cost production for sale outside of China. The new patterns from the West were cast into the picture of dynastic decay, and they immediately began to disintegrate the central form of control in the society.

For the first time in modern Chinese history at least the strength of the family system was seriously undercut in these areas affected by the new forces. These new patterns wherever introduced offered the possibility of alternative employment on relatively objective grounds, and consequently they offered those subjected to strains by the prevailing system the possibility of a way out that did not depend upon a refurbishment of the old. The absolute amount of industry introduced was never great, but the effects of it spread far beyond the limits of the new ventures themselves. Jobs offered on the new basis attracted reservoirs of unemployed to the areas concerned, and these offered a radical price competition for the more traditional forms of employment and so threw these open to a greater degree of relatively objective employment opportunities. Family controls disintegrated in and around the most populous centers of China at the very time that the controls of the Imperial bureaucracy were in a state of disintegration. The individuals who either willingly or unwillingly were separated from their families as the major orientation of their decisions became radically individualistic by default, and thereby they compounded the difficulty of controlling and co-ordinating their activities. At the same time the introduction of extremely cheap goods competed with handicraft labor, lessened the self-sufficiency of the peasant families, and increased their vulnerability to exploitation by the townsmen.

At the same time the scale on which industrialization had to be carried out, if it was to be carried out at all, was such that a great deal of co-ordination and control was necessary. The groups from whose ranks officials had been drawn in the past were completely incapacitated by their training to do the sort of planning necessary in this situation, for they were above all trained to seek solutions in precedents (and there were no indigenous precedents for these requirements), to operate on the basis of extremely vaguely defined and delimited relations, and to select people on the basis of who they were rather than on the basis of what they could do.

The merchants were only to a slight degree convertible for the new requirements. They were used to thinking primarily in commercial rather than in industrial terms and to taking their capital out of such pursuits and putting it into land as soon as possible. They were as little oriented to the reinvestment of talent as they were to the reinvestment of capital. Furthermore, in a situation of extremely unstable governmental control, they had more to lose if they tried to set up plants and factories than if they depended primarily upon training. In the former case a turn of the political wheel could cost them not only their inventories but their capital investments as well, and these capital investments were more difficult to conceal or move than were inventories. The international settlements offered some protection in these respects, but nevertheless there was a tremendous motivation to seek profits on a commercial basis rather than on an industrial basis.[12]

The industrial development, however, was essential to solve certain other problems, if China could not return to a refurbished form of the "traditional" patterns. One of the great sources of strain between the towns and villages lay in the fact that the towns were supported almost entirely by income that had its origins in the villages. They produced for export to the villages almost nothing that was capable of increasing net productivity there and hence bettering the lot of the peasants. Modern industry could have produced goods and services cheaply enough to compete with handicraft labor and could have made available new tools and techniques, but only the former got anywhere for the profit in them was immediate and obvious. The net result of this was a further impoverishment of the peasants which increased their alienation and played a vital role in their at least passive support of a new change in government that overthrew the Republic that had replaced the Ch'ing Dynasty.

In those few areas in which modernization did make some headway the same sort of changes seen elsewhere in the world with such changes were begun. Again family change was prominent. The family changed in composition, type, role in the life of the individual, and all the rest, but what is important here is that it could no longer be used as a basis for control of individuals. And yet Chinese society had developed no other forms of control that would operate effectively and stably in the absence of family controls. For the last five decades or more China has been a sort of no man's land with regard to modernization. It has bits and parts of it, but it has not achieved any considerable level of industrialization. It also has not been able to regain a stable version of the "traditional" society it once had. The present rulers of China offer a picture of momentary stability, but so far they have not accomplished anything that

---

[12] This tended, of course, to drain off resources from China just when it was strategic that they be carefully husbanded.

indicates any basic alteration in the picture of Chinese social structure. They have not accomplished the changes necessary for industrialization. They have eliminated, at least for the time being, the usual forms of graft and corruption, but the prognosis is for their replacement on the basis of party membership rather than on the more usual nepotistic basis. If the present regime is not able to industrialize, its general prognosis would seem to be much the same as that of its predecessor.

The Resultant Stage

In the case of China the resultant stage is not different from the transitional one in respects relevant here. The most relevant characteristic of it for present purposes is that industrialization was unable to make any dramatic headway in China. It is true that many of the "traditional" patterns seem doomed, but the stage reached, at least prior to the Communist hegemony, was one in which there was an uneasy balance between the new and the old. The inheritance of the past stood out as a major obstacle to the firmer establishment of the new, and what in effect was established of the new by its direct and indirect effects undercut the possibility of the stable re-establishment of the "traditional" patterns. The situation was, of course, immensely complicated by the invasion by Japan and the internecine strife between the Nationalists and the Communists. Nevertheless, prior to the invasion and the effective threat of the Communists, China had shown no signs of competing with the rapidity and thoroughness of industrialization that were achieved by Japan in a corresponding period.

THE PROBLEM OF CHANGE IN JAPAN

The Initial Stage

The initial stage taken for Japan can be set up for the purposes relevant here by contrast with that of China. There were, of course, many similarities. Both of these societies were predominantly agrarian in their systems of economic production. In both cases the nonagrarian members of the society found their basic means of support in the goods and services produced by the peasants. The peasants in "traditional" Japan were also to a very high degree self-sufficient in the matter of production and consumption and received little in return for the portion of their production that was received by others. Certainly they did not receive goods and services from the nonfarmers in the society that permitted or accounted for a rise in the net productivity of agriculture. In the system of production of "traditional" Japan there were no elements of modern industrial production. As in China relationships in most spheres, and certainly in the economic aspects of action, were to a very high degree traditionally determined. People were selected for relationships primarily on the basis of who they were rather than what they could do, with certain peculiar and important exceptions, as will be seen below. The relationships between individuals contained many specific obligations and rights, but they were in strategic respects only vaguely defined and delimited. The great emphasis in relationships was not upon what was specifically covered but rather upon the question of to whom a given individual owed loyalty under any and all possible conditions. As in China, the vast majority of people lived very close to the margin of subsistence for the society, and a relatively small group lived on a comparatively luxurious basis. The family was a fundamental unit of solidarity in Japan as in China, and many of the decisions and activities of daily life were family oriented. As will be seen below, however, action in Tokugawa Japan was not in the last analysis nearly so overwhelmingly family oriented as in China. In fact family orientation took a clearly secondary position relative to another solidarity orientation.

As in China, the role of the merchant in Japan was an ambiguous one. Merchants were rated well below the ruling group, the peasants, and the artisans. Perhaps their only inferiors, ideally speaking, were two outcast groups, the Eta and the Ainu, although even here the picture was sometimes confused by the appearance of Eta in merchant roles. As in China, the ideal position of the merchants was definitely belied by their actual position, and in the transitional period (the degeneration of the Tokugawa Shogunate and the early establishment of modern Japan) the merchants of Japan assumed very prominent roles indeed. In the modern period (i.e., the resultant stage), of course, the roles of the merchants and their successors became both respectable and esteemed ideally as well as actually.

In "traditional" Japan there existed the sort of distinction between the towns and the villages that existed in China, though in Japan one must include in the category of towns the headquarters of the main feudal lords, the daimio. The feudal lords and their retainers, who formed the ruling class of Japan, depended primarily on the income from land, and hence on the labor of the peasants, as did the gentry of China, but their relation to the peasants was of quite another order. The artisans and merchants of Japan oriented their activities, particularly in their economic aspects, to those members of the ruling class, and of course to supplying their own needs. The peasants were not beset by usury in the same sense that the Chinese peasants were. Land was not ideally speaking held by the peasants, but they felt the weight of usury indirectly because their lords sought greater exactions from the peasants to meet their greater debts to the merchants and moneylenders. Taxes as such were hardly experienced by the peasants. The peasants were virtually all in the position of tenants or serfs, ideally speaking, and their lords exacted a portion of their produce as a matter of right. The Shogunate itself did not depend upon taxes as a source of income but relied on the income from the lands held by the Shogun as a feudal lord and upon such special requirements as he might from time to time exact directly or indirectly from the feudal lords (especially the daimio).

The exactions from the peasants were great. Early in the development of the regime the Shogun issued regulations requiring that the peasants be kept so busy on their farms night and day that they be unable to think of anything save agriculture. The attitude held that benevolence to peasants consisted in keeping them neither in extreme distress nor in a situation of prosperity. This policy toward the peasants was integrally related to the attempt by the regime to minimize the possibilities for social change, a policy that will be taken up below, but it certainly had its effects in setting the economic position of the peasants in the total scheme of Japanese social life as well. Economically the position of the peasants was likely to be judged from their point of view in terms of bad or worse rather than in terms of good or better. The social analyst is not beset by the problem of what the peasants did in "good times" but rather by the problem of what they did when things got particularly "bad." In the latter event some peasant revolts occurred, and these offer the social analyst one of his most revealing insights into the peculiar type of strength of the feudal regime in Japan.

As in China the governmental structure was a combination of highly centralized and highly decentralized elements. The system of controls set up by the Tokugawa rulers was certainly in its initial stages one of the most tightly and effectively controlled feudal systems the world has ever seen. The strong men of the Tokugawa regime were well aware of the sort of trouble nobles could give if they were permitted to get out of hand, and they set about deliberately to make this impossible, as will be discussed below. Nevertheless, in the local areas controlled by the daimio, the discretion of the daimio was virtually unlimited as long as it did not threaten in any conceivable way the precedence and power of the Shogun. Neither the centralized elements nor the decentralized ones were of the same sort as those in China however. One of the main differences in these respects lay in the fact that decentralization went all the way down the hierarchy in China, stopping in essence only with the family head, whose powers were not decentralized though they were sometimes delegated. In Japan the decentralization lay in the scope of power left to the daimio (as in the case of the scope of power left to the governors in China), but the daimio did not necessarily decentralize their control further. Certainly the system in Japan was not such that the position of family head was in general as strategic as in China.

As in China there was in fact a bureaucracy that conducted and was held responsible for major administrative functions, but it was not in anything like the Chinese sense a single bureaucracy for the country as a whole. As in China there was considerable need for and emphasis on ability on the part of the persons who fulfilled these administrative roles. Unlike the Chinese bureaucracy, that in Japan was not set up as a separate concrete organization with members chosen for ability and insulated, ideally speaking, from other concrete organizations in the society. In this sphere the Japanese resorted to a most interesting social device, and this device was one that had considerable adaptive value in the period of modernization. In Japan the family system was also a major focus of loyalty despite the fact that it did not take the same order or type of precedence as that taken by the Chinese family system. Unlike the case in China the major administrative posts were hereditarily determined. In China this was only true, ideally speaking, of the Emperor's position.

This situation also obtained among the merchants. Among the merchants of Japan there was not the possibility of leaving merchant roles that existed in China, as will be seen below, and since the rule of equal inheritance on the part of all sons that held in China was not characteristic in Japan, there was not the tendency for a man's successor in these roles to inherit something less than the estate that he had left intact. The Japanese worked out, either deliberately or not, a sort of civil service system by adoption. Sometimes these adoptions would even cross the ordinarily closed class lines. A daimio might adopt as his successor an exceptionally able young man from among his samurai, who in general performed administrative functions for him. He would ordinarily seek an able man from within his own family if possible, but he could and sometimes did go outside the family or the kinship structure as a whole. Furthermore he could and sometimes did supplant his actual eldest son with a person adopted as eldest son. Such adoptions were generally made only after the previously legitimate successor, if any, had shown himself to be conspicuously unable. When such an adoption took place, one had an administrator picked for ability. But one did not have to seek vainly to insulate this man from a sea of nepotistic and similar conflicting pressures. He was put in a role such that all of these pressures motivated him to use his abilities to the utmost for the administrative purpose for which he was chosen. Family, friends, feudal loyalties, everything he had been taught to respect, in both fact and ideal, required the maximum objective use of his talents in the role for which he was selected. The conflict between the betterment of one's family and the proper fulfilment of office so common in China was not to nearly the same degree a problem here because one's family and one's office were combined.

This was done by the merchants as well as by the feudal lords. Japanese merchants, unlike Chinese ones, were not preoccupied with the use of merchant status to abandon merchant roles. They were rather much concerned to recruit on the basis of competence family members who would in fact remain in merchant roles and preserve the welfare of the family thereby. This particular technique was continued by the successors of the merchants in the modernization of Japan. The zaibatsu, who in strategic numbers developed directly out of Tokugawa merchant families, were well known for this. These families instituted a sort of business civil service within their companies, and those men most successful in the competition and destined to become major figures in the various enterprises of the family were frequently brought into the family membership itself. It was, in a sense, the Japanese equivalent of giving a particularly important member of the administration of a stock company a major block of stock in the company, presumably tying thereby his self-interest and the interest of the owners of the company as tightly together as possible.

There were two major differences between Chinese and Japanese family structure that are relevant for present purposes: (1) the manner in which family considerations entered the total social picture and (2) the fact that there was not in Japan a single ideal type of family for the entire membership of the society. The first of these turned on the difference in manner of integrating the two societies; the second turned on the marked differences in class structure in the two societies.[13] Both will be discussed below.

A third difference that was probably strategic for present purposes lay in the emphasis on primogeniture in Japan. It was not always true that the oldest son in fact succeeded to the family property or rights. He could be and sometimes was replaced by someone adopted as an oldest son, or he could even be replaced by a younger brother, but the rule practiced in China of equal inheritance among all the sons was not followed in Japan. This made possible at one and the same time the continued concentration of wealth in a single family line and the creation of a cadet class. Both of these are closely related to the feudal social structure that will be discussed below.

Despite many similarities between "traditional" China and "traditional" Japan the total structures of the two societies were markedly different. "Traditional" Japan was a feudal society in the sense in which that term is used here, or at least a very close approach to one, and this was not true of "traditional" China. Furthermore, when one looks into the history of Chinese and Japanese experience one is struck by the contrast between Chinese and Japanese attitudes toward general social control and the maintenance of social stability. The Chinese had an attitude much like that attributed to Locke. The structure of society would function to the

[13] This had many implications. For example, in Japan the possibilities of alternative employment were even more restricted than in China because of the closed class situation and because of the relations of the peasants to their lords.

best interests of everyone if it were set up in accord with the Will of
Heaven and left as much alone as possible, with occasional interference
only to restore the Will of Heaven. The rulers of Japan, however, often
seem to have been preoccupied with the possibilities of manipulating social structure for purposes of control, and with the strategic role of those
who know how to plan and execute such manipulations. There is certainly
evidence that the strong men of the Tokugawa knew what they were about
in these respects, and there is at least good reason to suspect that those in
power during the modernization of Japan were up to the same sort of
thing.

The founder of the Tokugawa regime, Iyeyasu, and his followers, especially Iyemitsu and Yoshimuno, seem certainly to have been conscious
social engineers. The early Tokugawa (Iyeyasu and Iyemitsu) were well
aware of the vulnerabilities of social control in a feudal system. It was
one thing to order a power hierarchy and tie land distribution to it in the
feudal manner. It was quite another to retain control over the nobles
once great power had been allocated to them. Iyeyasu's predecessors and
colleagues, Nobunaga and Hideyoshi, had subdued just such a set of
nobles and thereby made the Tokugawa regime possible. Iyeyasu and
Iyemitsu had no intention of having to do it again. At a time when the
nobles were still relatively weak and they strong, the Tokugawa set up a
system intended to defy the decay so common in feudal systems. For one
thing they set up an official capital city in the form of a court at Yedo.
Then they made it clear that, although they were not the emperors of
Japan, they were not merely the first among equals as far as the nobles
were concerned. Each feudal lord of any consequence, the daimio in this
case, was required to spend a definite portion of his time at the Shogun's
court, and when he was not there, he had to leave members of his family
(preferably his wife and heirs) in his place. The only solidarity in Japanese
social structure that offered any threat to the primacy of the obligation to
one's overlord was the family bond, and by this hostage system the
Tokugawa tied the two together as far as the daimio were concerned.
One might, as will be shown below, meritoriously sacrifice one's family to
fulfil one's obligations to one's overlord, but to sacrifice one's family in
the attempt to defy one's overlord was sin itself in that society. Even
if one lord did attempt revolt, the pressures that the Shogun could bring
to bear upon the rest through their own feelings of loyalty and the hostage
system were enough to guarantee the Shogun overwhelming allies in addition to his own strength.

Having established their regime, the Tokugawa attempted to guarantee
its security into perpetuity. This was of course futile in the long run,
but the thoroughness of the attempt and the relative stability it achieved
for some two and a half centuries are illuminating. The Tokugawa at-

tempted in every way possible, at first, to prevent change. There were detailed regulations as to what was expected of virtually every type of person in the society. These regulations were made as minute as possible, the more so the more an individual's role was likely to be one in which deviance on his part could be significantly disruptive of order in the society. The regulations covered dress and deportment to such an extent that deviant activity was likely to be immediately and visually obvious. Individuals failing to offer the proper homage in a given situation could be and were on occasion cut down by the samurai without further question. On one occasion in the nineteenth century the automatic application of such measures involved the Japanese in a serious incident with the British — an incident that brought home radically to the Japanese their utter defenselessness before the Western powers.[14]

Whatever their methods or whatever the foundations on which they built, subjects of the Tokugawa both knew and, of their own will apparently, came to accept the tremendous emphasis placed on loyalty to the various positions in the feudal hierarchy. Every man's first duty was to his overlord. This obligation surpassed even the family obligation, and it was in considerable part because of this that the role of the family in Japanese social structure was so markedly different from that in China. The extreme emphasis placed on this sort of loyalty is well illustrated in the case of the nobility by the Tale of the Forty-Seven Ronin and in the case of the peasants by certain of the phenomena associated with the peasant revolts under the Tokugawa regime. In the case of the Forty-Seven Ronin the facts are perhaps not as important as the legend that immediately sprang up about them. Much was made of this legend in the transitional and resultant stage of Japan. In brief the legend has to do with a group of retainers who sacrifice all other goals to avenge the death of their immediate overlord. In order to throw their master's enemy off guard they are credited with virtually every act held evil, especially the ruination of their own families. After he has relaxed his guard, they slay him. Their vendetta, however, has been at least superficially in defiance of the Shogun's law against vendettas, so they fulfil their obligation to the Shogun by peacefully surrendering themselves with never a plea for

14 The Namamugi incident (1862) involved a British subject named Richardson, who was overwhelmed by the magnificence of an approaching daimio's retinue, remained mounted, and stared. It was gross insolence and lese majesty from the Japanese point of view, something every person of low social status knew better than to do. The daimio's samurai cut down the offender. The British in reprisal made their first punitive use of a breech loading naval rifle to pound to pieces certain Japanese forts which had, perhaps, the most modern artillery in Japan. The Japanese were most impressed. They learned far more from the incident than the fact that Westerners were not sensitive to the intricacies of feudal respect and the like.

mercy. The Shogun despite his own respect for their extreme regard for loyalty cannot let their breach of the law go unnoticed. Their fate is sealed, but the Shogun does permit them to atone for their crime by the honorable ceremonial suicide of the samurai. All of them commit *seppuku* and complete thereby all of the responsibilities they bear. Their master is avenged; their duty to the Shogun is fulfilled; and last their family obligations are satisfied because they leave their families a most honorable heritage. They have sacrificed everything to the ideal of feudal loyalty, and in so doing they have realized everything.

The peasant revolts sometimes furnished an equally impressive example of the emphasis placed on loyalty to one's masters. During the Tokugawa regime the exactions placed upon the peasants sometimes were such that the peasants took matters into their own hands and backed their demands for reform by a show of force. It was quite clear in some of these cases that they in fact commanded the force necessary to carry their points, and in fact their demands were granted. Even after their power had been clearly demonstrated, however, once their demands were granted, their leaders on more than one occasion either were taken by, or themselves surrendered to, the very authorities against whom their use of force had been successful. These leaders usually suffered most painful deaths apparently without ever becoming the cause for a further demonstration of force on the part of the peasants. The peasants seemed to feel that, while they had had no choice but to revolt, someone had somehow to pay for this violation of things as they "should be."

In Japan loyalty to the feudal hierarchy took clear precedence over loyalty to one's family. This did not mean that loyalty to one's family was unimportant. It was tremendously important. It did mean, however, that one had two means of control over the deviance of individuals, control as in the Chinese case through the family organization and direct control through the feudal hierarchy. One of the implications of this dual hold on the individual was that the possibility of individualism by default was minimized. Even if an individual were to lose or be separated from his family, he could not lose or be separated from the entire hierarchy of persons in positions of power over him. One of the most important arguments used in the amazingly peaceable deposition of the Shogun was, of course, to the effect that the Shogun had himself violated his loyalty to his overlord, the Emperor. The emphasis on loyalty was never denigrated. The people were simply told that this loyalty was due directly to the Emperor and his officials and hence to the Japanese nation and not to the Shogun.

The transition was facilitated by another aspect of the society. The higher up one was in the social scale and the greater his basis for power in the feudal system (under the Tokugawa the Emperor and the Kuge are exceptions to the fact that high social position and great basis for power went together), the more was expected from him in the form of careful indoctrination about loyalty to the hierarchy. In the Ronin tale, for example, the Ronin were in actuality forgiven their unintended transgression against the Shogun, but many other samurai were executed and disgraced for not having fought strongly enough to prevent their act. The leading daimio had been weakened in many ways by the end of the Tokugawa, but with rare exceptions they saw the whole basis of their position swept away in the name of the good of the nation without a protest or even with their aid. Those exceptions that did arise arose in a different conception of where the good of the nation lay and not in where the good of the daimio lay.

Some of the differences between the "traditional" Chinese social system and that of "traditional" Japan have already been mentioned in the preceding discussion. One of the most important that has cropped up above is the difference in class system in the two societies. As noted above, China had *ideally speaking* almost an entirely open class system.[15] In the Japanese case the picture was almost exactly the opposite with regard to the ideal patterns. Ideally speaking the class system was completely closed. One was born to the social position of one's parents. It was expected that one stay in that position and that one's children and children's children stay in it as well. Actually there was some mobility, but it was rather carefully hedged so as not to disturb the general or the ideal patterns. There was some mobility within the class distinctions. One could, for example, rise higher or fall lower in the scale of daimio or peasant families, for example. There were also occasional cases of families that were demoted, though these were more likely to be wiped out. There were cases of elevation in status by the Shogun, but again these were probably rare. Certainly the most strategic form of mobility as far as its bearing on the present problem is concerned is one that appeared to involve no interclass mobility at all. This was the mobility involved in the peculiar "family civil service" mentioned above. But it is the essence of the adoption procedure that one's past position is in theory wiped out; the adopted son is at least in fiction held always to have been what he has just been made. Furthermore such elevation was neither so frequent nor was it conducted in such a way that it could be made the goal of achievement by others generally in the society. It was a bonus that came occasionally; it was not something that could or should be striven for. This lack of general motivation to compete no doubt resulted in a failure to realize many human resources in the society, but at least in the Tokugawa period the strategic significance of relatively small differences in skill was not such as could be met only by large scale motivation of this sort. In the modern period

[15] See p. 231.

when such differences did assume importance, an embryonic pattern of mobility that could be adapted to new conditions was in existence. Furthermore, the basis for such mobility in Japan was specifically relevant to the position for which the person was chosen. This was in marked contrast with the system of China, which had more of the character of the old British Civil Service in which persons were selected primarily on the basis of examinations on a general intellectual background that was not necessarily germane to the roles that a person would fulfil after selection. For this purpose there was a sort of "on the job training" or none at all. In Japan those selected for advance by adoption were not selected until they had already shown the specific abilities for which their services were desired, and this in turn gave a precedent of sorts for later selection of persons on the basis of germane abilities in the modern period in which such a basis became so important. Furthermore, initially at least, it gave a basis for selection that would interfere with established family patterns to the minimum degree. Finally in the Japanese system the person so selected was specifically cut off from his past particular social connections with those in his old class position, at least ideally, and therefore it was not expected that in his new role the interests of these actual former family members, etc. would be a primary source of motivation for him and hence prejudice, unless properly insulated against, his performance of duties in his new role.

The significance of this emphasis on closed classes in Japan was widespread for the problem of Japan's transition. The accustomed lack of expectation or striving on the part of the vast majority of the population, the peasants, meant that at least in the initial stages of change, the expectations of the peasants would be modest, that they would be accustomed to sacrifice directed by a ruling group, and that comparatively small material improvements in their lot would make a comparatively big impression upon them. The upper classes were also specially prepared for control and sacrifices, and to some extent these latter, both by the adoption procedure mentioned above and the increasing role of the merchants, as will be discussed below, were prepared to have many roles performed by those most competent to take them over. This was of far-reaching importance because like the gentry in China the upper classes of Japan, ideally speaking, were as a whole almost completely unprepared and unadaptable to the requirements of the roles necessary if Japan were to modernize rapidly and thoroughly, especially given the fact that Japan was a late-comer to industrialization and was therefore involved in the problems of scale mentioned previously. Although they were ill prepared to assume such roles of leadership, they were beautifully prepared in Japan to step aside with relatively little disturbance, and this, of course, was conspicuously not the case in China. Neither warlordism nor a yearning for, and attempt at, the re-establishment of the "good old days," so prominent among the gentry of China, was a substantial problem in the transition of Japan. The "civil service by adoption" gave a pedigree to justify the transfer of those of the old upper classes who had strategic abilities to roles of importance in the new order of things, and the special role of the merchants offered another source of supply of more generally adaptable talent.

The general argument of this paper includes two points of special importance. The first is that the differing systems of control over individuals in China and Japan made for much of the difference in their respective experiences with industrialization. The second is that what on the surface in the early nineteenth century might have seemed like comparatively small differences in the roles of the merchants in the two societies was also of special importance in the different experiences of the two countries. This difference between the merchants was directly related to the general and the specific characteristics of feudalism in Japan. As regards the general characteristics the most important factor for present purposes is the closed-class character of "traditional" Japanese society in contrast with that of Chinese society. In both societies the merchant role was, ideally speaking, one of extremely low prestige. Actually in both societies, as has been noted above, the merchants were often powerful and even respected. But in Chinese society the open-class character of the social system held out to all merchants the possibility of achieving for their families, if not for themselves, the genuinely ideal social position of gentry status. Thus, as noted above, there was motivation aplenty in China for a flight of both talent and funds from the merchant field. These were not important features of the Japanese system. No matter how much he might wish to do so, a merchant could not become a member of the nobility. He might become the power behind the throne of a daimio, but he could not become one, nor could his family after him acquire that status. The best he might hope for would be the entrance of a daughter into such an upper-class family by marriage. Such marriages as this were in the nature of family foreign relations. They might increase the prestige and security of a merchant by allying him more tightly with members of the upper classes, but they did not make him or his family a member of that class.

There was another strategic difference from the Chinese. Power in the feudal hierarchy was tied to land ownership by the daimio. Even the daimio retainers, the samurai in general, were given rights to the income from land that was part of the overlord's domain rather than title to land itself. The feudal relationships of individuals to the land were an important part of social position in Japanese society, but land could correspondingly not be bought and sold with any general freedom, at least ideally speaking. This meant that many actual transfers of land were exceedingly vulnerable to confiscation. These limitations on the acquisition of land either as a symbol of social status or as a category of investment meant that one of the most prominent forms of capital flight from merchant uses in China was virtually out of the question in Japan. Talent could not be readily drained from the field because of the class system. Capital could not be readily drained from the field either, because of the closely associated restrictions on the holding of land. The merchants of Japan could not seek to minimize their vulnerability to the political hierarchy by either a personal or capital flight from merchant pursuits. Through no virtue of their own, perhaps, they were forced to think in terms of buying and selling and production and reinvestment. Their hope for security lay in being more and more successful merchants and in having their successors continue in that vein. Their abilities in exchange were vital to the upper classes. Their security and achievement lay in playing those roles well, and this they did so very well that by the end of the Tokugawa regime many of the most striking features of Japanese society were aspects of the activities of the merchants.

The potentiality of the merchants as a group was built up in still another way in "traditional" Japan. The early powers of the Tokugawa planned carefully and relatively well to minimize the possibilities of change of any sort and of a successful revolt by the daimio in particular. Here the peculiar qualities of Tokugawa feudalism came into play. The basic structure of the Tokugawa economy as in other feudalisms was the use of land, ownership and control of which was tied to the power hierarchy. Each major fief was to be in essence a self-contained and highly self-sufficient economy in addition to its other characteristics. But this carried with it, of course, the possibility of a rebellious noble developing a basis of power on which to stand in opposition to the Shogun. Iyemitsu or his advisers put a stop to this possibility by the special hostage system described above that tied feudal loyalty and family obligations together for the top power holders in the society. The elaborate ceremonial involved in the Shogun's court had its functions as a damper on change, but the requirements of this ceremonial plus the necessary expense of maintaining elaborate establishments in Yedo plus the requirements of graft that were a prominent feature of that court called for middlemen to convert the rice income of the daimio into a form of wealth useful and negotiable at court. The daimio themselves could not carry out those functions because it was socially degrading on the one hand and involved them in relationships outside of areas that they controlled on the other. The very techniques of the Tokugawa for tight control of the nobles guaranteed the merchants a vital role in the society. Furthermore their position as a class ideally beneath the notice of the nobles gave them a certain freedom of operation in meeting new situations that did not exist for the members of the upper classes. In tying the nobles down the Tokugawa unwittingly turned the merchants loose. At the same time the closed-class system prevented the powerful merchants from assuming the carefully restricted roles of the upper classes whom the Tokugawa had expected to be and to remain the sole foci of power apart from the Tokugawa themselves.

The Transitional Period

As in China the transitional period in Japan was compounded of the disintegration of the old order and the introduction of the new forces. The new forces were virtually identical, as has been pointed out above. The old order was different, however, and in the transitional stage in Japan industrialization made dramatic headway, which was not true in China. Furthermore the transition was made without the chaotic state of affairs that characterized China. Here we shall first examine the disintegration of the old order prior to the introduction of the new.

It is perhaps not an exaggeration to state that the disintegration of the old order is best mirrored for present purposes in the rise in actual power and importance of the merchants. They made their position, ideally a minor interstitial one, the kingpin of the whole system. The daimio relied upon them for their needs of exchange, and their reliance made the merchants powerful and the nobles dependent upon them. Outside of the peasant households and outside of the strictly agrarian pursuits all other aspects of production and consumption came to revolve around the merchants. The artisans produced for the wealthy and for other artisans. They depended for food on the production of rice and other staples by either the farmers or the fishermen of a given daimio. The upper classes depended upon the artisans for much of what they consumed. The scale of operations precluded barter as a daily means, and the merchants provided the facilities to make barter unnecessary. They not only traded; they financed production and consumption; they developed banks; they created commodity markets and dealt in futures as well as in concrete goods. They became in short general entrepreneurs for endeavors of all sorts. It is not a matter of chance that the zaibatsu of modern Japan who grew out of these merchant roles characteristically built industrial and economic empires of the most diverse sorts. In the modern West such great family enterprises as have grown up have tended to specialize to a much greater degree in, say, banking or insurance or even the industrial production of a particular sort of product with others added primarily if germane to that original one.

In their economic roles at least the merchants became a sort of middle class such as had developed in Europe. The term "middle class" is a dangerous one in this context, for there are those who would say that the appearance of a middle class solves virtually all problems of industrialization and that such a class was lacking throughout the Far East. This middle class was quite different from that of Europe in at least one respect. The relatively strictly maintained feudal distinctions tended to keep people from coming into the group as well as from getting out of it, so that in so far as it partook of the characteristics of a middle class it was a very restricted one in numbers. The merchants did not occupy such a role in China because the open-class nature of the system prevented the way of life of the merchants ever from becoming an ideal pattern in its own right, as it certainly did in both Europe and Japan.

As the merchants grew in power and wealth, the proportion of the goods and services of the total society that went to their maintenance increased. They developed a theater and a literature largely of their own. They maintained more or less elaborate establishments — not sufficiently elaborate to threaten their capital base as exemplified by the retainer system of the feudal lords, but costly none the less. Sir George Sansom in his *Japan, a Cultural History* (New York, 1938) gives a vivid picture of the world in which those merchants (*chōnin*) lived. This is mentioned because it is closely related to the major factor that undercut the power of the Shogunate and caused its future to be threatened quite apart from the blow to the Japanese of Perry's forced entry of Japan. Japan was like China in that the basic support of the entire economy came from the production of the peasants. The townsmen produced little or nothing that was essential to the farmers or that increased their net productivity and so enabled them to better their standard of living. It is true that the peasants were not accustomed to much, but the increasing amount of their production that came to be drained off into the pockets of the merchants and hence into support of the townspeople, let alone the amounts that went to support the feudal court proper, kept increasing the burden upon the peasants. The increase in peasant revolts as the Tokugawa regime aged has been commented upon and documented by many, especially by Professor Hugh Borton ("Peasant Uprisings in Japan of the Tokugawa Period," *Transactions of the Asiatic Society of Japan*, XVI, May, 1938). By the time of Perry's appearance, the whole society was ripe for some change of control at least, if not of the general social structure.

Most of the stresses and strains already mentioned in the case of China were also operative in Japan. These are sufficient to account for motivation to take up alternative ways. There were, however, more effective ways of restraining such motivation in Japan, especially in the form of the controls on the individual independent of his family structure. The remarkable thing about the transitional period in Japan, however, was that the new forces did not dribble into the society, being taken up by individuals here and there at their own wills. The process shows numerous signs of being carefully controlled and even planned from the very start. The actual opening of Japan that was forced by Perry was not of course a part of Japanese operations, but it was not totally unexpected, and its possible significance for the future of Japan was grasped at once. The closure of Japan was one of the techniques by which the Tokugawa hoped to hold back change and incidentally to forestall changes brought about by foreign contacts raising the possibility of foreign allies for rebellious nobles — a possibility that might have broken the rather thorough system of control devised by the Shogunate. But all through the period of closure the Tokugawa kept a window to the West in the carefully restricted Dutch trading concession. This was so restricted as to offer the Dutch no uncontrolled basis for influencing the people at large as existed in China even before the Opium Wars forced more contacts to be made available. One of the exactions placed on the Dutch was a periodic report on what transpired in the Western world. Scholars today may laugh at the naïveté of some of the ideas of the West held by the Japanese in power in those days, but the fact remains that they knew a great deal more about the West than the West knew about Japan. They were particularly impressed by the apparent ease and avidity with which the Western powers took over control of those parts of the world that lacked even the beginnings of industrialization and yet were strategic for it in terms of raw materials, markets, transportation, etc. The manner of Perry's appearance in Japan was to many of the Japanese a sign that their time had come unless they moved to prevent it.

They certainly moved to prevent it. How far back in Japanese social structure one could trace an authentic and intense desire to maintain "national" integrity is probably not known. But the devotion of the leaders, at least, to rule of Japan by Japanese was certainly intense in the middle of the nineteenth century, and apparently had been so for centuries past. The Japanese who seized control from the Tokugawa were determined to prevent the domination of Japan by outside forces. In the period between Perry's appearance and the restoration of the Emperor, the power of the West was studied in Japan, and Japanese went abroad to see for themselves. They were given conclusive evidence by the West of the importance of armies and fleets in these matters in a series of incidents in which victory went inevitably to the West.

The graft, corruption, and decay of the Tokugawa made it a relatively simple matter for a determined group backed by some of the major daimio to "overthrow" the Shogun and restore the Emperor. In fact the Shogun himself seems almost to have co-operated in the transition. All through the Shogunate the fiction had been preserved that the Shogun was simply the representative of the Emperor — that the Emperor was too honorific to be bothered with the day-to-day affairs of state. In the crisis that presented itself the reigning Shogun in fact vountarily turned over his power to the Emperor. Such bloodshed as had featured the reign of the previous Shogun was conducted in defiance of the Shogun but had

posed either as being directed against the chief minister of the Shogun
or as undertaken out of loyalty to the Emperor, whose court had been
permitted to gain increasing power toward the end of the Shogunate. The
new regime that took over, originally as a sort of regency for the young
Emperor Meiji, a boy of fifteen at the time, had a window dressing of
nobles from eminent families, but the actual executives of the new order
were a group of young samurai who had been in administrative positions
in the various powerful daimiates and who had been in close contact with
the merchants. The merchants themselves by this time through their
alliance with the samurai had become powers in many of these administra-
tions and in some cases had apparently even held offices as chamberlains
and the like. They had not, however, lost their merchant roles, because
their income-earning capacities were sorely needed and caused them to be
valuable to the upper classes, with whom they became allied.

Reforms followed the Restoration of the Emperor (formally dated
as 1868) quickly. The men in power understood that an army and fleet
of the modern sort were necessary if Japan were to escape absorption.
A conscript army of peasants was organized and trained — a radical departure for Japan, in which the right to bear arms was the prerogative par
excellence of the upper classes. Despite skepticism this army quickly
demonstrated its effectiveness by the defeat of the Satsuma rebellion, the
last gasp of the old feudal system. The samurai fighters of the Satsuma
were easily defeated by this conscript army organized and recruited in the
Western fashion. The Satsuma had from their point of view revolted
from motives of loyalty, and after their defeat they became immediate and
substantial supporters of the new regime. The leaders of the revolt even
became heroes of a sort in modern Japan by virtue of the fact that their
motivation by loyalty was accented even though their loyalty was misguided in the view of the modern rulers of Japan.

The new rulers understood that a modern army and fleet were minimal
requirements if Japan was to escape foreign domination. They also realized that a modern heavy industry was necessary if Japan was to be able
to support a modern military establishment without dependence upon
foreign powers. They understood even more. They understood that one of
the major avenues of encroachment by the modern Western nations in
other underdeveloped countries had been via the protection of their investments in those areas. The new rulers of Japan early faced up to the
problem of building up these necessary industrial facilities without resort
to financing from abroad with all the footholds that sort of a relationship
offered to foreign governments. The problem posed for them by this point
of view was a serious one. In the first place the scale on which these industries had to be set up precluded the easy transformation of capital
from prevailing forms to the modern ones. In the second place the Japa-

nese had initially at least to seek their capital equipment abroad, since they lacked the means of making it at home. Finally, and perhaps most difficult of all, the sort of heavy industry necessary to serve as a basis for the independent maintenance of a modern army and fleet was uneconomic in Japan. Because of the relative lack of good coal and iron deposits in Japan proper, it was cheaper for Japan to buy heavy industrial goods abroad than to produce them at home. But buying them abroad would make and would keep Japan more and more vulnerable to the interests of her foreign sources of supply of these commodities. National interest from the point of view of the Japanese required the subsidization of those industries at any cost. The maintenance of a modern army and fleet was another economic strain on Japan. Armies and fleets may be justified on many grounds, but they are always net drains on the effective material productivity for other uses of any country. Economically they are never justified save by a consideration of the spoils of conquest that they may make possible or by a consideration of the costs of the conquests they prevent. It was the prevention of conquest by outsiders that initially at least motivated the money and effort spent on army and fleet in Japan.

The Japanese feat came as close to being one of lifting oneself by one's bootstraps as the modern world has ever seen. They started close to bankruptcy, used almost no foreign capital, established uneconomic heavy industries, organized and maintained a modern military and naval establishment, changed their governmental system radically, altered their system of production and consumption of goods and services to one in which modern industry was strategic, erected and conducted many highly profitable modern enterprises, made literacy of a sort virtually universal, and taught their people to operate effectively in terms of types of relationships that had been relatively unimportant and unknown in the Tokugawa period. They did it all with virtually no internal bloodshed or disintegration of major proportions, and they were very far along with the job in no more than five decades. The problems they posed themselves required even tighter controls on the process than industrialization would have in another context in which the utilization of loans and other help from abroad would not have been excluded or in which natural resources furnished a better material basis for industrialization than they did in Japan.

A start could be made and was made by the export of raw silk and specie, but this could not carry the burden for long. To accomplish their aim Japan's leaders had to find a special sort of manufacture or service. As a latecomer to industrialization Japan could use what the world had already learned. She could start with the most modern machines available without the burden of obsolete machinery that still carried capital obligations; she could start without unnecessary capital expenditures to cover the developmental process; she could use the latest managerial techniques; and she had a source of labor that was abundant and very cheap. These advantages were necessary because out of those industries in which Japan had a comparative advantage the Japanese had to make enough not only to pay for those and for further development, but also to pay for those industries that had to be subsidized and for the military establishment. The lack of raw materials at home meant that Japan had to look for products that satisfied the following list of conditions: (1) the cost of raw materials and their transport plus the cost of transport of the finished goods to the markets would be small relative to the total value of the finished goods, (2) a great deal of the value of the finished goods could be added in fabrication, (3) large amounts of labor could be utilized in the manufacture of the goods, (4) the product would be largely produced for export, and (5) perferably other countries producing it for export would have large amounts of obsolete equipment and relatively high labor costs. Textiles were goods of this sort par excellence, and many other light manufactured goods fell into this category. The Japanese judiciously combined some modern manufacture with a system of domestic industry to produce certain goods that could not be produced on a domestic-industry basis in the West because of labor rates and were not adapted to or did not justify economically large-scale machine production. Shipping was a service industry in which the Japanese could have similar conditions. In the pursuit of development in those fields the Japanese were assiduous and successful, for they had unusual comparative advantages. But these comparative advantages depended in considerable part on tight co-ordination and control. For example, sale or use of manufactured goods within Japan proper as opposed to their production for export had to be very carefully controlled and had above all to wait until the net productivity of Japanese workers had risen by more than the cost of the new goods they were here permitted to buy. One of the major advantages that Japan had in international trade was that the standard of living in Japan was different and cheaper than that of the Western world, and hence Japanese labor costs were much lower. Consumption of the goods produced at home that did not wait on increases in net productivity would have wiped out that advantage. That advantage had to be kept large because some of it had to be wiped out to support the uneconomic heavy industries and the military establishment. This in turn posed a special problem of control. In their production roles Japanese had to be taught as rapidly as possible to use Western techniques, and this had to be done with those of their consumption roles that were directly reflected in increases in net productivity. But for the rest the total advantage of the society, as conceived by those in control, lay in retaining as many as possible of the features of the "Japanese way" that involved a standard of living different from and cheaper than that of the West. It is not a matter of chance that so many items showing Western standards of living and Western domestic habits were expunged from movies, literature, and the like and put in the category of "dangerous thoughts" along with such things as plots against the state, etc.

The transition had to be kept smooth. The Japanese were well aware that civil strife was a well understood fishing ground for foreign nations. Their own expulsion of Europeans some centuries before had been intimately tied up with the participation of these Europeans in Japanese domestic struggles for power. The Japanese also had China as a constant warning to them. China had all the obvious possibilities for industrialization that Japan had plus very much better raw material resources and even cheaper labor. But China lacked the ability to organize and maintain tightly a planned program for industrialization, and most of the things Japan's leaders feared for Japan happened to China. In fact, Japan herself in her initial tests of her progress was an outstanding participant in the exploitation of China's weakness.

One of the first problems faced by the new regime was reform that would secure the allegiance of the peasants for certain by improving their lot if possible, and another was to place at the disposal of those who could make effective modern use of it those capital resources that did exist and were not marshaled in such hands already. Both reforms involved the feudal lords and the land; wealth not in the form of land was pretty much already in the hands of the merchants. The way out was ingenious. The lands were taken over and turned over to the peasants by the national government. The feudal landholders were compensated with government securities. But these were matters that only the bankers really understood, and the new bankers were the old merchants who acquired thereby effective control for purposes of financial manipulation of virtually the entire finances of the society. There was hardly any opposition from the former nobles. Those who were already closely allied with the merchants went over into modern business and industrial roles. Some of the able ones went into professional roles, and some went into the government. But these adaptations were on the basis of germane abilities for the most part; when these were lacking, they lived out their lives on what income was left to them from their government bonds. Some of the samurai went into the armed forces, more perhaps into the navy than into the army, but again they had to have germane abilities. The armed forces, particularly the army, early instituted a radical system of promotion on the basis of merit and became a major ladder for social ascent in the new nation. Wryly enough, many of the samurai found positions as policemen, in which roles in the early days at least they could continue to wear their swords. They retained some small measure of authority (under orders, of course) over common people, and their patiently acquired talents could be put to use without too much or too arduous conversion. For many of those nobles the material sacrifices involved were tremendous, but the code of the warriors even in the days of decay had always emphasized the preparation for sacrifice. The new rulers used this habituation. The samurai policemen, however poor, could fulfill the samurai obligations by proper performance in these new roles for their masters.

In the transformation of Japan to a relatively highly industrialized society, particularly given the importance of speed in that conversion, the merchants might have been expected to give the maximum amount of trouble as far as the problem of control was concerned. They formed the group on whom the feudal emphasis of loyalty was least impressed. They were strategic for the conversion because they had some of the skills and attitudes necessary for the changes. They caused little or no trouble, however, for whatever they may have lacked in orientation to higher authorities was made up by the fact that even if they placed their interests as individuals above those of Japan as a unit, they were motivated to seek the same things. They were cut loose by the new regime to do what they were accustomed to doing with relatively slight restrictions. There had to be a place for the heavy industries, and there had to be an orientation to production for export. But there were state subsidies to aid these motivations; there was the fact that the leaders among the merchants were prime movers in the governmental organization itself; and there was the fact that the government measures prevented foreigners from competing with these to their own disadvantage. The new nobility was created, and while there were places in it for many of the more eminent carry-overs from the old nobility, there was a method of continual appointment of new nobles on the basis of achievements useful to the state. The new businessmen and industrialists were prominent among the new nobles. The control was facilitated by another aspect of the situation at the end of the Tokugawa regime. There existed at that time a considerable concentration of wealth and power among the merchants in a few merchant families. This carried over to the new situation particularly when the capital resources of the old feudal nobility were converted out of land and into modern financial forms which gravitated through the banks into the control of the large merchant families who owned the banks. Whatever the social evils may be that are involved in a highly monopolistic situation like that of the zaibatsu, it offers certain advantages in a situation that requires a considerable amount of highly general planning. From the start the control of the key industries was in the hands of a rather restricted group, and the tightness of interstitial relations in a modern economic system means that control of the key industries gives enough leverage if necessary for control of the less strategic industries that are dependent upon the key industries.

But the question of control of determined deviants among the new businessmen and industrialists does not seem to have been seriously raised in the early part of the transition. It is not until the second or third decade of the twentieth century that any element of the society whose interests showed any marked divergence from those of the business and industrial interests came to power in the government. When this did occur, as evidenced in the political struggles for power between the military and the zaibatsu, the struggles were relatively peaceful. There were, it is true, some assassinations of business and industrial figures, but there was no chaotic struggle for power or general resort to arms inside Japan. There was a seesaw political struggle for a time with eventual victory for the military extremists, but despite a difference in their interests the military did not experience any marked difficulty in control of the zaibatsu. Whatever emancipation from the feudal emphasis on loyalty the merchants may have had at the end of the Tokugawa regime, they like everyone else in the society had undergone an intensive and well-conceived program of indoctrination in serving the national interest that dated from the Restoration in 1868. The situation was further complicated in these respects by virtue of the fact that defiance of the military, if successful, would probably have been a Pyrrhic victory for the zaibatsu, but exploration of this matter is beside the point here. In any case there is good reason to believe that the one group that was, perhaps, not well conditioned to stay in line on the basis of an overwhelming concern with loyalty was a group whose members were motivated by other factors to seek exactly the things sought by the rulers of the new Japan among whom the members of this same group were, of course, prominent.

The Resultant Stage

There is not space or need here to describe in detail what was done in the modernization of Japan. The changes were revolutionary as far as the social structure of the society was concerned, and industrialization of a marked degree, far beyond anyone's expectations in the West, was achieved in a very short time. It is perhaps doubtful that any other society ever carried out such marked changes so quickly with so little violence. Land tenure, education, production and consumption systems, political systems — virtually everything — either changed or had its position in the total social structure changed radically. And yet some things were held remarkably constant, though this in itself was a sort of change because those things held constant now existed in a quite different context. The new forces in Japan undercut many of the old patterns just as they had in China, but they did not simultaneously undercut the sole or the major source of control over individuals as they did in China. The Japanese were even able to retard the disintegration of the old type of family system to some extent. By continual emphasis on the "Japanese way" they were able to get individuals to adapt quickly the new ways in spheres in which they were essential and retain the old, at least long enough for a more gradual transition, in other spheres of life. They were not able to prevent a gradual drift toward a more Western and expensive standard of living, but they were able to keep the drift gradual so that the wiping out of their cost differential in certain fields of export was not capricious from the point of view of the economy as a whole. The Japanese paid a price for their tightly controlled change. There is much reason to believe that, in the world context in which they developed, the aggressive international policy that brought about their defeat was intimately related to the very factors that permitted their rapid and smooth transition to an industrialized state. A definite case can be made out for the proposition that in the international environment in which they existed their success at home was bound to get them involved in a failure abroad that would threaten to undo the effects of much of their social engineering. But here we are concerned with the factors that permit of rapid industrialization, and the lesson we may learn from the comparison of the Chinese and Japanese experience consists first of some of the conditions under which modernization may be carried out or facilitated and second of what may be done to offset the difficulties that were attendant on Japanese success in these respects. Japan was able to do the first of these. She was not able to avoid the second.

In the deliberately oversimplified analysis presented here the comparative lesson may be summed up briefly. The new forces in both cases were identical, and it may be added that they will be roughly the same in the case of the modernization of any of the so-called "underdeveloped areas," except for the fact that both the advantages and the disadvantages for latecomers to the process have now been intensified by more than half a century of further development. The basis from which change took place was quite different in the two cases, though both were similar in many respects, especially in their emphasis on highly self-sufficient economic units, relationship requirements different from those accented by modern industry and the importance of the family system as a major focus of attention in the organization of the society. They differed in two respects that were crucial for industrialization if the hypotheses presented here are tenable. In the first place, for all the fact that both societies were a world apart from the structures necessary for a modern industrialized nation, Japan had in the basis from which its change took place patterns that made possible the tight maintenance of control over the vast majority of her individuals even while or after the process of industrialization undercut many of the old structures that figured prominently in control or motivation of deviant activities. China's "traditional" social structure was such that the advent of the new forces undercut virtually the only possibility of such control, and the old system was not, as in Japan, able to maintain its forces until a comparatively sudden end so that the new forces could be prevented from dribbling in uncontrolled. The transition in China was not such that a planned introduction of selected aspects of the new forces could be made even temporarily, as in Japan. In the second place, there existed in Japan a group of people with roles such that the individuals holding them were relatively readily adaptable to some of the roles strategic for the transition. This was true despite the fact that prior to the transition these roles were by no means identical with those that were strategic for the transition. Although China had similar roles in her "traditional" social structure, they differed from those in Japan particularly with regard to the manner in which the holders of those roles were fitted into the total social structure, and the difference was apparently sufficient when combined with other aspects of that situation to preclude the ready adaptation of the persons involved in them to the new roles necessary for a transition like that carried out in Japan.

If the hypotheses presented in this deliberately oversimplified picture of strategic, necessary, but not sufficient factors in the relatively rapid accomplishment of modernization in Japan as contrasted with China's inability to accomplish a similar result have any validity, they indicate the importance for such a problem of what may superficially seem to be small differences in social structure indeed. They would also seem to indicate that for these purposes in these two cases factors such as inanimate resources, climate, population size, the forces introduced from outside, etc., when considered apart from the social structures of the societies concerned, do not contain the necessary but not sufficient conditions to explain the differential result. It is by no means true that all the cases of industrialization or modernization of so-called "backward" areas will present identical or nearly identical problems to those that arose in China and Japan. But there are likely to be some common features. The new forces remain similar in kind, but as time passes they progressively accentuate the problems of conversion from a relatively nonindustrial to a relatively industrial form.[16] The advantages and disadvantages that accrue to the late-comers

---

[16] In the sense of the term used here conversion to a relatively industrial form does not necessarily mean preoccupation of the economic aspects of the system with either light or heavy manufactures. Predominantly agrarian or commercial systems may become highly industrialized, and one of the characteristic problems of this sort of conversion is that relatively nonindustrialized parts of the society are made interdependent with or even completely dependent upon the more industrialized portions of the society long before they are themselves converted in any obvious and direct sense easily appreciated by the persons involved. When this happens, it is very likely both to retard the development of industrialization in some respects and hasten the disintegration of the patterns characteristic of the nonindustrialized portions of the society. But in any case the persons con-

in the process continue to increase, or so it would seem at least. This continues to accent the importance of a technique of control over the actions of individuals in societies making the conversion. The problem is aggravated by the fact that the new patterns are certain to undercut many of the measures of social control characteristic of relatively nonindustrialized societies, particularly those that are dependent on relationships that accent traditional ways of doing things — who a person is rather than what he can do that is germane to his jobs, and vaguely delimited relationships. Furthermore whether the conversion is to be carried out on a predominantly private-enterprise basis or a governmentally controlled basis, administrative talent of a remarkably similar sort is a minimum requirement. In the absence of a group relatively easily converted for these purposes as in the case of Japan, one must be trained. On the balance it is probably doubtful that many of the so-called "backward" areas have a group that is relatively speaking so easily convertible for these purposes as were the merchants in Japan. Finally, another special aspect of control related to both the general need for control cited above and the need for a specialized form of talent must be mentioned. If the conversion is to be successful in the sense of being smooth and rapid, there must be patterns in the society that neutralize at least the possibility of interference from members of those groups that cannot be readily converted for the new purposes. Such patterns have been conspicuously absent in the case of China so far.

There are numerous other problems that must be taken into consideration in the full discussion of these problems of conversion. The "demographic problem" is perhaps the most obvious of these. In general these have not been touched on here because in the particular cases presented here they could be considered both constant for the two cases or not strategic for them. There is no reason to believe that this will be the case with other societies.

Finally, this paper has emphasized the importance of social patterns that facilitate a continuance or institution of tight centralized controls for rapid progress toward industrialization. I believe that to be a sound emphasis in this case, but one must not infer from this more than is stated. It by no means follows that high degrees of industrialization achieved in a manner such as that of Japan are stable in the long run. There is some reason at least to raise the question as to whether any highly industrialized

---

cerned are then involved in industrialization, and so far at least, the change has continued to run in the direction of industrialization and not the reverse. The future may hold a change in these respects, but so far the patterns of highly industrialized societies have shown themselves to be remarkably close to a universal social solvent.

society is not most precariously balanced as a social system. Even apart from this general question, however, those late-comers to industrialization that have carried it far and fast on a highly controlled basis show some signs that may be interpreted as indicative of even greater instability than seems general in those societies that acquired industrialization slowly over an extended period of development. Japan, Germany, and Russia are the only late-comers who have been conspicuously successful at industrialization. No late-comer has yet gotten far with the process by the slow, gradual development route, and indeed the stage of industrialization reached elsewhere may already preclude that route for others. It may well be that the lessons we shall learn from the comparative analysis of the problems of industrialization will have implications for social engineering in an unexpected quarter. They may get us further in the stable maintenance of these societies already having achieved it than in the rapid, easy, and efficient transformation of the societies whose members either appear to "need" it or desire it or both.

18   DENNIS C. MC ELRATH

The Social Areas of Rome:
A Comparative Analysis

Among the most promising aspects of social area analysis is its use as a framework for the comparative study of social differentiation.[1] Indeed, several inter- and intra-city analyses based upon this approach and relying upon census tract measures wholly or in part have appeared since its

From *American Sociological Review*, vol. 27, no. 3 (June 1962), pp. 376-391. Reprinted by permission of the author and the American Sociological Association.
    [1] This approach was introduced in Eshref Shevky and Marilyn Williams, *The Social Areas of Los Angeles*. Berkeley and Los Angeles: University of California Press, 1949; and elaborated in Eshref Shevky and Wendell Bell, *Social Area Analysis: Theory, Illustrative Application and Computational Procedures*, Stanford: Stanford University Press, 1955.

original formulation by Shevky.[2] However, the typology never has been applied for comparative purposes to materials gathered outside the United States. Thus questions concerning the analytical utility of the social areas approach for comparative studies of social differentiation in other societies have been given little attention to date. Can comparable measures be constructed from censuses of urban areas outside the United States? Do such measures meet the requirement of univocality? Does the constructed typology facilitate analysis by permitting interpretation of patterns of social differentiation between societies and within? Limited answers to these questions may be gained by an application of social area analysis to the 1951 Census of Rome, Italy.

The interpretive frame of reference suggested by Shevky proposes that as the social organization of society increases in *scale*, at least three basic forms of social differentiation develop.[3] "Urbanization," "social rank," and "segregation" are considered both as forms of social differentiation

[2] Wendell Bell, "The Social Areas of San Francisco Bay Region," *American Sociological Review*, 18 (February 1953), pp. 39-47; Shevky and Bell, *op. cit.*; Scott Greer, "Urbanism Reconsidered: A Comparative Study of Local Areas in a Metropolis," *American Sociological Review*, 21 (February 1956), pp. 19-25; Scott Greer and Ella Kube, *Urban Worlds*, Laboratory in Urban Culture, Occidental College: mimeographed report, 1955; Wendell Bell and Maryanne T. Force, "Urban Neighborhood Types and Participation in Formal Associations," *American Sociological Review*, 21 (February 1956), pp. 25-34; Wendell Bell and Maryanne T. Force, "Social Structure and Participation in Different Types of Formal Associations," *Social Forces*, 34 (May 1956), pp. 345-350; Wendell Bell and Marion D. Boat, "Urban Neighborhoods and Informal Social Relations," *American Journal of Sociology*, 62 (January 1957), pp. 391-398; Dennis C. McElrath, "Prestige and Esteem in Selected Urban Areas," Proceedings of the Pacific Sociological Society in *Research Studies of the State College of Washington*, 23 (June 1955), pp. 130-137; Aubrey Wendling, "Suicide in the San Francisco Bay Region 1938-1942 and 1948-1952," unpublished Ph.D. dissertation, University of Washington, 1954; John H. Mabry, "The Social Areas of Duluth," unpublished manuscript, 1953; Dean G. Epley, "The Social Areas of Miami, Florida," study in progress; Walter C. Kaufman, "A Factor-Analytic Test of Revisions in the Shevky-Bell Typology for Chicago and San Francisco, 1950," unpublished Ph.D. dissertation, Northwestern University, 1961; Olive Reeks, "The Social Areas of New Orleans," unpublished M.A. Report, University of California, Los Angeles, 1953; Walter C. Kaufman and Scott Greer, "Voting in a Metropolitan Community: An Application of Social Area Analysis," *Social Forces*, 39 (March 1960), pp. 196-204; Maurice D. Van Arsdol, Jr., Santo F. Camilleri, and Calvin F. Schmid, "An Application of the Shevky Social Area Indexes to a Model of Urban Society," *Social Forces*, 37 (October 1958), pp. 26-32; Maurice D. Van Arsdol, Jr., Santo F. Camilleri, and Calvin F. Schmid, "An Investigation of the Utility of Urban Typology," *Pacific Sociological Review*, 4 (Spring 1961), pp. 26-33; Theodore R. Anderson and Janice A. Egeland, "Spatial Aspects of Social Area Analysis," *American Sociological Review*, 26 (June 1961), pp. 392-399.

[3] Shevky and Bell, *op. cit.* and Shevky and Williams, *op. cit.*

characteristic of modern society and as products of increase in scale of social organization experienced by these societies.[4] Urbanization defines differentiation according to "life styles" associated with changes in the structure of productive activity. A precondition for the development of this form of differentiation is the elaboration of distinctive modes of production characteristic of large scale urbanized societies. Social rank, the second dimension of the typology, is viewed as a product of the changing distribution of skills. This change allows for the differentiation of populations in terms of the economic, technical, and social meaning of occupation. Finally, segregation is seen as a form of differentiation based upon changes in the composition of the population attending the rise of industrial societies.[5]

In addition, social area analysis holds that population aggregates within industrial societies may be located within a "social space" or three dimensional typology defined by the three modes of differentiation outlined above. Finally, without directly addressing the theoretical problem of linking a social organization to a spatial organization, forms of differentiation are examined in terms of measures based on population aggregates settled in spatial units (census tracts, blocks, enumeration districts, countries, regions).[6] Using United States census tract statistics, urbanization is determined by measures of the distribution of fertility, women at work, and house type. Social rank, on the other hand, is indexed by measures of the distribution of occupation and education within each tract. The third dimension of the typology, segregation, is indicated by tract measures of the distribution of racial and nationality groups living in relative isolation.[7]

By means of these indexes, then, the approach proposes that observations of sub-area populations ultimately may be interpreted in terms of postulates concerning the increasing scale of social organization experienced by industrial societies.[8] Hence, this frame of reference should be applicable to analyses of other societies experiencing increasing scale.

[4] Shevky and Bell, *op. cit.*, pp. 5 ff.

[5] *Loc. cit.*

[6] An exception to this is the segregation dimension which uses spatial characteristics as part of the definition. Cf., *ibid.*, pp. 17 ff. and Wendell Bell, "A Probability Model for the Measurement of Ecological Segregation," *Social Forces*, 32 (May 1954), pp. 357-364.

[7] The segregation dimension is eliminated from the following analysis since comparable materials are not available. See Shevky and Bell, *op. cit.*, pp. 54-58, for computational procedures.

[8] For evaluation of the approach see reviews of *Social Area Analysis* by Robert W. Buechley, *Journal of the American Statistical Association*, 5 (March 1956), pp. 195-197; David B. Carpenter, *American Sociological Review*, 20 (August 1955), pp. 497-498; and Otis Dudley Duncan, *American Journal of Sociology*, 61 (July 1955), pp. 84-85; as well as the interchange between Bell and Duncan, *American Journal of Sociology*, 61 (November 1955), pp. 260-262.

Italian society may be considered of somewhat smaller scale than the United States. At least, this view is supported by such traditional measures of the relative scale of social organization as the proportion of the labor force engaged in non-agricultural pursuits, the proportion of salaried workers and wage earners, the proportion engaged in primary industries, the degree of urban population concentration, and the degree of metropolitan concentration.[9] On all these crude indicators of scale, Italy falls somewhat below the United States. (See Table 1.) Therefore, several

TABLE 1. SELECTED MEASURES OF RELATIVE SCALE:
UNITED STATES AND ITALY, *CIRCA* 1950

	U.S.	Italy
Percent economically active population[a]		
Engaged in agriculture	12.2%	40.0%
Engaged in primary industries	13.8	62.8
Wage earners and salaried workers	82.1	55.9
Percent total population classified[b]		
Urban	64.0%	40.9%
Metropolitan	55.9	27.3

[a]Computed from International Labor Office, *Year Book of Labour Statistics 1960,* Geneva: I.L.O., 1960, Table 4.

[b]From T. O. Wilkinson, "Urban Structure and Industrialization," *American Sociological Review,* 25 (June, 1960), p. 358.

propositions about the relation of societal scale to patterns of sub-area population differentiation may be examined by comparing findings for United States cities with those of Rome. These propositions may be subjected to analysis along with the previous questions concerning the applicability of the social area approach to areas outside the United States.

Finally, the Roman census materials permit a limited description of several aspects of the spatial distribution of the Roman population. Therefore, one may ask whether or not the spatial patterning of Roman populations "fits" with findings generated from American studies. Are the social areas of Rome distributed in a concentric or sectoral fashion? In what ways do the spatial configurations of differentiated sub-area populations compare and contrast with American patterns? This descriptive material should facilitate linking findings interpreted from a social organization posture with traditional propositions concerning spatial patterns of settlement of locality groups.

It is proposed, then, to use the Roman census findings as a basis for an examination of: (1) the *applicability* of social area analysis to populations outside the United States; (2) the *analytic utility* of this framework; (3)

[9] While these measures are admittedly inadequate, they do convey the general position of Italian and American society.

the *spatial configuration* of population types settled in sub-areas. Such an examination should provide a limited test of the analytic utility and theoretical relevance of this approach.

APPLICATION

Size

One requirement for the application of social area analysis to comparative studies of social differentiation is the delimiting of sub-areas of comparable population magnitude in various societies. In the United States the census tract has been widely adopted as a convenient and relevant unit of study. The analysis of the social areas of the San Francisco Bay Region with a total population of 1,509,678 in 1950, for example, reports findings based on 244 census tracts with a mean tract population of 6,187.[10] In Rome, with almost an identical population in 1951 — 1,530,252 — unpublished data are tabulated for 354 *gruppi di sezione* with a mean *gruppi* population of 4,324 (see Table 2). Thus, while the average sub-area population in Rome is somewhat smaller than in the San Francisco area, the difference is not unreasonable for comparative purposes. Indeed, if sub-areas with extremely small populations were eliminated from consideration in Rome, as was the case in the Bay Region study, the magnitude of difference would be even smaller on the average.[11] A further indication of the

TABLE 2. POPULATION AND AVERAGE SUB-AREA POPULATION OF TWENTY U. S. CITIES, SAN FRANCISCO BAY REGION AND ROME, ITALY[a]

Urban Area	Number of Sub-Areas	Total Population	Mean Sub-Area Population
20 city average	83	382,657	4,807
S.F. bay region[b]	244	1,509,678	6,187
Rome	354	1,530,252	4,342

[a]See text for sources.
[b]Includes only those tracts studied. Cf., Shevky and Bell, *op. cit.,* p. 28.

comparability of *gruppi* and the census tract may be gained from a study of twenty middle-size cities reported by Schmid, C. MacCannell, and Van Arsdol, Jr.[12] This study, based on selected cities with an average population of 382,657 and with an average of 83 tracts per city, indicates

[10] Shevky and Bell, *op. cit.*, pp. 28 ff.
[11] *Ibid.*
[12] Calvin F. Schmid, Earle H. MacCannell, and Maurice D. Van Arsdol, Jr., "The Ecology of the American City: Further Comparison and Validation of Generalizations," *American Sociological Review*, 23 (August 1958), pp. 392-401.

a mean tract population of 4807 for the twenty cities combined (see Table 2). This figure is quite close to the 4324 average found in Rome. This would suggest that tract and *gruppi* are fairly comparable in terms of average population size. Both may be considered as sub-areas for the purpose of comparative analysis with respect to this criterion.

Index Components

Comparative studies are possible only when comparable indexes defining the dimensions of the social area typology are available. Comparability is necessary with respect both to the referent of the index and to the statistical treatment of it.

In their monograph, Shevky and Bell propose that social rank be measured by a single index consisting of two components: (1) occupation ratio, and (2) education ratio.[13] The occupation ratio distinguishes area populations in terms of manual and non-manual skills which, in turn, is linked to the changing distribution of skills in industrializing societies. There is a good deal of support for the use of the manual-nonmanual distinction in studies of social differentiation in a wide range of industrial societies.[14] Therefore, this break in the occupational structure would seem applicable to the sub-area populations in Rome where the distribution of nonmanual workers is tabulated by *gruppi di sezione*.[15]

The second component of the Index of Social Rank is the education ratio. This component reflects the role of a literate and educated population in industrialized and industrializing societies. An accurate indicator of educational achievement, therefore, is considered as necessary for the examination of social differences based on the distribution of skills in large scale societies. Fortunately most governments provide data on the ability to read and write.[16] While data on educational attainment are tabulated for Rome, literacy rates provide an indicator of skill which is readily available for most societies throughout the world. In addition, literacy is

[13] *Occupation ratio:* total number of craftsmen . . . , operatives . . . , and laborers . . . per 1000 employed persons. *Education ratio:* number of persons who have completed no more than grade school per 1000 persons 25 years old and over.

[14] See Seymour M. Lipset and Reinhard Bendix, *Social Mobility in Industrial Society,* London: Heinemann, 1959, Chapter II for summary of research findings and discussion on this point.

[15] *Occupation ratio:* Total number of active population classified as non-cultivating independent farmers or other administrators in agriculture; dependent administrator or clerk in agriculture, hunting or fishing; independent administrator or free professional not in agriculture, hunting or fishing per 1000 active population. *Viz.,* non-manual workers per 1000 workers.

[16] For a discussion of the criteria of literacy used in census enumeration, see UNESCO, *Progress in Literacy in Various Countries,* Monograph on Fundamental Education, No. VI, Paris: UNESCO, 1953, *passim.*

highly related to educational achievement in these societies.[17] Therefore, the second component of the Index of Social Rank used in Rome is the literacy ratio.[18]

The Index of Urbanization proposed by Shevky and Bell has three components: (1) fertility ratio, (2) women in labor force ratio (WLF), and (3) single-family detached dwelling units ratio (SFDU). High urbanization is indicated by low fertility, high WLF ratio and low SFDU. The index is used to measure differentiation based on changes in life style which accompanied the rise of urban industrial societies. Each component touches upon different aspects of this change. Fertility rates reflect the changing role of children in the productive process and the changing age-sex structure.[19] Women in the labor force reflects the movement of women into productive units outside the home.[20] House type indicates the changing role of the household as a unit of economic production as well as the rise of alternative family forms. The referent of fertility and WLF ratios would seem readily translatable to most industrial societies irrespective of the dominant value systems of these societies. The SFDU ratio, on the other hand, may not range across societies as an indicator of family form or household production. This is especially the case where choice of house type is not available either because of cultural traditions, government planning, prevailing topography, or lack of housing opportunities. Under any of these conditions this important component of the urbanization index would not be applicable. Therefore, in Rome, fertility and WLF ratios are used in the construction of the urbanization index.[21] House type, on the other hand, is not applicable since the opportunity for the population to be distributed in terms of detached single family dwellings does not exist to an appreciable degree.

[17] Cf. Hilda Hertz Golden, "Literacy and Social Change in Underdeveloped Countries," *Rural Sociology*, 20 (March, 1955), p. 1.
[18] *Literacy ratio:* resident population six years old and over classified as illiterate per 1000 resident population six years old and over.
[19] *Fertility ratio:* number of children under 5 years per 1000 females age 15 through 44. Cf., Shevky and Bell, *loc. cit.*
[20] *Women in the Labor force ratio:* the number of females in the labor force per 1000 females 14 years old and over. Cf. *ibid.*
[21] *Fertility ratio:* number of resident population less than six per 1000 females in resident population 14 through 44; and *Females in labor force ratio:* number of active females 10 years old and over per 1000 females 10 years old and over. Standard scores for each ratio were computed from the Roman data. Standardization was accomplished by linear transformation so that scores would range from 0 to 100 in Rome. Literacy and occupation standard scores were summed and their average taken as the Index of Social Rank. High social rank areas are characterized by high literacy rates and a high proportion of nonmanual workers. Fertility and WLF scores were also standardized to their ranges in Rome and the average of standardized scores taken as the Index of Urbanization. High urbanization areas are characterized by low fertility rates and a high proportion of women at work.

In the case of both social rank and urbanization, competent ratios are standardized according to their ranges in Rome and combined to form their respective indexes.[22] Sub-areas are grouped by each index in four equal percentile intervals. This provides a classification of sub-areas into sixteen social areas.

The comparability of index components and the resultant classification of social areas would seem to be quite high in terms of referents of the measures and computational procedures. There are three exceptions to this, however: (1) the segregation dimension is eliminated from the typology; (2) the SFDU component of the Index of Urbanization is eliminated, and (3) the standardization procedure consists of standardizing components to their range in Rome.

Elimination of the segregation dimension is required because comparable information is not available from the Roman census. A possibly comparable index could be constructed from the distribution of recent migrants to Rome — and especially from the distribution of immigrants from rural areas. These data, unfortunately, are not available. Neglect of this index is not too serious since segregation is the least independent empirically in studies done in the United States.[23]

The lack of comparable standardization procedures, on the other hand, is a severe limitation on the use of social area typology for inter-societal comparisons. As the typology now stands, the numerical values of the indexes — and consequently the societal area designation — may not be translated from one country's census to another unless identical indexes are computed. And here one faces difficulties with regard to the referent of the measures. One way to solve this difficulty is to develop identical and univocal indicators applicable to a wide range of census classifications. Then, standard dimensions of the social area typology could be described. International standard nomenclature should greatly facilitate this task.

Another possibility is to standardize the ratios to their ranges in the area under study. Inter-societal comparison would then be possible under the assumption that the *range* of ratios in one city was indicative of the same implied reality as the range in another. Thus at least the relative position of a sub-area in relation to others in its city would be standard. This assumption is adopted for the present analysis.

ANALYTIC UTILITY

Contribution of Components

The social area paradigm holds that at least two forms of differentiation of sub-area populations may be found in large scale societies. Further,

[22] Cf. Shevky and Bell, *op. cit.*

[23] Cf. Van Arsdol, Jr., Camilleri and Schmid, *op. cit.*, p. 31; and "The Generality of Urban Social Area Indexes," *American Sociological Review*, 23 (June, 1958), pp. 277-84, by the same authors.

both these forms of differentiation are viewed as necessary to account for sub-area population differentiation.[24] However, inspection of Table 3 which lists the correlation of components reveals that all components are highly related in Rome. Although Van Arsdol, Jr., Camilleri, and Schmid report significant correlations between components in ten U.S. cities combined, as does Bell for San Francisco, only two of these correlations are of the magnitude of those in Rome (see Table 3).[25] Therefore, it

TABLE 3. CORRELATIONS OF FOUR SUB-AREA MEASURES OF URBANIZATION AND SOCIAL RANK COMPONENTS: ROME, TEN U. S. CITIES COMBINED AND THE SAN FRANCISCO BAY REGION[a]

Measure	Area	Literacy or Education	Fertility	Women in Labor Force
Occupation	Rome	.789[b]	.676[b]	.640
	Ten cities	.838	.546	.162
	San Francisco	.760	.291	.021
Literacy or education	Rome	—	.744	.593[b]
	Ten Cities	—	.289	.094
	San Francisco	—	.600	.293
Fertility	Rome	—	—	.685[b]
	Ten cities	—	—	.636
	San Francisco	—	—	.692

[a]The number of sub-areas involved in these comparisons is: Rome = 354; Ten Cities = 767; San Francisco = 244.

[b]Sign has been reversed throughout all tables to be consistent with computation used in other studies.

would seem appropriate to examine whether or not all of these components are, in fact, necessary to account for sub area differentiation. This may be stated in the question: do urbanization variables improve the relationship between social rank variables and the converse? If this is indeed the case, then each component would account for variation unaccounted for by other components. Here correlation analysis seems the appropriate test. If the multiple correlation of components is significantly greater than their zero order correlation, then one would reject the hypothesis that components do not contribute. Table 4 lists the zero order and multiple correlations for Rome, ten cities and San Francisco. In every instance the F test indicates that the coefficient of multiple correlation between components is significantly greater than the zero order coefficients. This indicates that urbanization and social rank components jointly account for greater variation than either set of components. . . .

[24] Cf. Shevky and Bell, *op. cit.*
[25] San Francisco Bay Region data from an unpublished manuscript by Bell, Ten Cities data from Van Arsdol, Jr., Camilleri and Schmid, *op. cit.*

[The] small numerical differences are expected given the high values of the zero order coefficients. Therefore, given these significant, albeit small, differences and given the additional fact that this correlation test holds in the ten cities and in San Francisco where independence of dimensions was established by separate analyses, it clearly must be concluded that urbanization and social rank components cannot be substituted one for another without loss in analytic power.[26]

TABLE 4. ZERO AND MULTIPLE CORRELATIONS BETWEEN COMPONENTS OF INDEXES OF URBANIZATION AND SOCIAL RANK: ROME (1951), TEN U. S. CITIES COMBINED (1950), AND SAN FRANCISCO BAY REGION (1950)

Coefficient[a]	Rome	Ten U.S. Cities	San Francisco Bay Region
r_{12}	.789	.838	.760
$R_{1.23}$	.800[b]	.896[b]	.787[b]
$R_{1.24}$	.817[b]	.872[b]	.789[b]
r_{34}	.685	.636	.692
$R_{8.41}$	.752[b]	.794[b]	.745[b]
$R_{8.42}$	.803[b]	.726[b]	.807[b]
N	354	767	244

[a]Subscripts indicate (1) Occupation ratio; (2) Literacy or education ratio; (3) Fertility ratio; (4) Women in Labor Force ratio.

[b]Significantly greater than zero order coefficient above line. Five percent level of significance adopted.

These data are demonstrative of the analytic utility of the social areas approach. In Rome as in American cities the data fit this aspect of the model proposed by Shevky. Additional examination of the contribution of index components will be presented below in the discussion of population types.

Delimitation of Population Types

Does the social area typology delimit distinctive population types? The answer to this question provides a second test of the analytic utility of the approach. The logic type construction in the context of social areas holds the following: (1) certain characteristics of sub-area populations are highly related to social rank while others are highly related to urbanization; (2) certain characteristics are more closely related to one dimen-

[26] For analyses of independence of components for ten cities and San Francisco see *ibid*. Five per cent level of confidence adopted for the analysis of Tables 4 and 5. For a discussion of multiple correlation test see Robert F. Winch and Douglas M. More, "Does TAT Add Information to Interviews? Statistical Analysis of the Increment," *Journal of Clinical Psychology*, 12 (October 1956), pp. 316-321.

sion than to the other index, its components and characteristics related to it; (3) components and characteristics related to one dimension should be more closely related to each other than are components and characteristics of different dimensions, and (4) both urbanization and social rank *jointly* describe population types more completely with respect to basic sociological factors than either dimension of the typology alone.[27] The typology may be tested in terms of these strictures in Rome.

First, urbanization may be interpreted as delimiting area populations in terms of life style. Substantive findings from several American studies support this view.[28] In contrast with less urbanized areas, highly urbanized sub-areas may be expected to be characterized by (1) a distinctive age structure with the aged composing the bulk of the dependent population, and (2) a small family pattern. Three measures of these characteristics are listed in Table 5. These are: (1) dependent population ratio, (2) proportion of aged, and (3) mean family size.[29] Each of these three measures may be considered as variables related to urbanization.

As the social area framework suggests, correlation with urbanization is significant for each of these three characteristics. In terms of the second stricture, there are twenty-one comparisons between the correlation of these three characteristics with urbanization and the social rank index, its components and characteristics related to it. Using a one-tailed Z' test at .05 confidence, it is evident that these characteristics are significantly more closely related to urbanization than to the other index, its components and characteristics in fifteen out of twenty-one comparisons. The major exception is family size which shows no greater relation to urbanization than to the social rank index, primary industries, crowding and illiteracy ratios. The other two exceptions are the relationship between aged ratio and crowding and the dependent population ratio and crowding.

The third stricture requires a comparison of the average correlation between urban components and characteristics (values included in the lower right triangle in Table 5). The average correlation in the triangle is .64 which is significantly greater than the average correlation of .49 for the rectangle. On the average, characteristics and components of urbaniza-

27 Cf. Paul F. Lazarsfeld and Allen H. Barton, "Qualitative Measurement in the Social Sciences: Classification, Typologies, and Indexes." In Daniel Lerner and Harold D. Lasswell, editors, *The Policy Sciences*, Stanford: Stanford University Press, 1951.
28 See especially works by Greer, Greer and Kube, Bell, Bell and Force, Bell and Boat, and McElrath cited above.
29 *Dependent population:* resident population under six years per 1000 resident population 65 years old and over; *aged:* resident population 65 years old and over per 1000 resident population; *family size:* number of family members divided by number of families.

DENNIS C. MCELRATH

TABLE 5. CORRELATIONS BETWEEN INDEXES, COMPONENTS, AND RELATED CHARACTERISTICS OF 354 SUB-AREAS OF ROME, 1951

Index	Components Characteristics	Multiple R	Zero Order Correlation Coefficients												
			1	2	3	4	5	6	7	8	9	10	11	12	13
Social rank	1		—												
Nonmanual	2		.942	—											
Illiterate	3		−.950	−.789	—										
Crowding	4	(.889)	−.845	−.843	.758	—									
Primary I	5	(.453)	−.442	−.328	.503	.234	—								
Secondary I	6	(.608)	−.574	−.567	.521	.609	.051	—							
Tertiary I	7	(.696)	.690	.637	−.668	−.629	−.427	−.892	—						
Dependent	8	(.736)	−.608	−.520	.626	.659	.250	.457	−.498	—					
Aged	9	(.705)	.532	.456	−.547	−.626	−.167	−.349	.369	−.723	—				
Family size	10	(.646)	−.601	−.474	.656	.587	.538	.266	−.439	.577	−.531	—			
Women in L.F.	11		.651	.641	−.593	−.755	−.147	−.540	.507	−.578	.613	−.475	—		
Fertility	12		−.752	−.676	.744	.783	.344	.515	−.577	.764	−.691	.652	−.685	—	
Urbanization	13		.762	.714	−.728	−.829	−.273	−.567	.586	−.731	.705	−.611	.902	−.903	—

Average Coefficients

.61	.64
.49	

tion are more closely related to one another than are the characteristics and components of different indexes.

In all of the above comparisons, the direction of correlation is as expected. Thus in 15 out of 21 comparisons of individual coefficients and a comparison of average coefficients, the expectation based upon the social area framework is sustained with respect to urbanization sub-area characteristics.

Social rank refers to the level of living characteristic of an area population. The Shevky framework holds that population types are differentiated in terms of living conditions (rather than life style) and work patterns. Four measures of these characteristics are listed in Table 5. High social rank areas would be expected to be characterized by: (1) uncrowded living conditions; and (2) a distinctive industrial composition of the working population with (a) a small proportion engaged in agriculture, (b) a somewhat larger proportion in manufacturing and construction, and (c) a large proportion engaged in such tertiary industries as communications, transportation, commerce, insurance, services, and public administration.[30]

Again, expectations based on the social area framework are largely supported in Rome. First, each of these four characteristics is significantly related to social rank. Secondly, in seventeen out of twenty-four comparisons these characteristics are more closely related to social rank than to the urbanization index, its components and related characteristics. The major exception to this occurs in the case of the secondary industries ratio. This ratio is no more closely associated with social rank than with the urbanization index and its components. Other exceptions occur with: primary industries which show a close relation to average family size and the fertility ratio; tertiary industries and the urbanization index; and crowding and the urbanization index.

The average coefficient for entries in the upper triangle of Table 5 is .61. This is significantly greater than the average coefficient of .49 for the rectangle. If primary and secondary industries ratios are excluded from this comparison on the grounds that all industries ratios add to 1000 for each sub-area, then the corresponding values are .73 for the triangle and .53 for the rectangle. In this case as well, components and characteristics of social rank are significantly more closely related to one another than are components and characteristics of different dimensions.

In every instance the direction of correlation is as expected. Thus

[30] *Crowding:* number of occupants divided by number of occupied rooms; *Primary industries:* Per cent active resident population ten years old and over engaged in agriculture, forestry, and fishing; *Secondary industries:* Per cent active resident population ten years old and over engaged in extractive industries and manufacturing, building and construction, electric energy, gas and water; *Tertiary industries:* Per cent active resident population ten years old and over engaged in transportation and communication, commerce and various services, credit and insurance, and public administration.

seventeen out of twenty-four comparisons of individual coefficients and a comparison of average coefficients based on the strictures implicit in this type construction support the view that social rank defines distinctive sub-area population types.

Finally, social area analysis holds that *both* social rank and urbanization are necessary to describe area types. If this is indeed the case, then these two dimensions of the typology should *jointly* account for greater variation in area population characteristics than either dimension separately. The evidence from Rome is conclusive on this point. The multiple correlation of social rank and urbanization with life style, living conditions, and work pattern characteristics is significantly greater than their correlation with either dimension in 13 out of 14 possible comparisons (see Table 5). Only in the case of the proportion of the aged is there an exception. The multiple correlations for the remaining six characteristics are significantly greater than their correlation with either dimension alone.

The magnitude of these coefficients should not be ignored. In all except two instances, social area accounts for over 40 per cent of the variance in the distribution of external measures of life style living conditions and work patterns. The correlation with crowding (.889) is especially impressive. Here, social area accounts for over 70 per cent of the variance.

These findings demonstrate that the dimensions of social area analysis effectively describe distinctive population types. They also lend support to the view that social area analysis permits interpretation of area types by relating them to an interpretive frame of reference.

The findings presented in Table 5 also support the earlier conclusion about the necessity of various components. Examination of the correlations between related sub-area characteristics and components reveals that, in no instance, does one index component account for significantly more variation in all of the variables related to that index. In the case of social rank components, the illiteracy ratio is more closely related to crowding while the non manual component is more closely related to the primary industries ratio. No significant difference occurs with respect to the relationship of secondary or tertiary industries ratios to either social rank component. The picture is much the same for sub-area characteristics related to urbanization. Here the fertility ratio is more closely related to dependent population and family size but not to the proportion aged. This clearly indicates that each component contributes to the explanation of variation in type characteristics.

Descriptions of Area Populations

Since social rank and urbanization both are necessary and useful in accounting for variation in area characteristics, it would seem profitable to describe sub-area population characteristics in terms of the location of sub-areas in social space.

[Figure 1] presents the distribution of sub-areas by social areas. To simplify presentation and because of the low frequencies of sub-areas in some cells of the table, all except three of the 354 sub-areas of Rome are

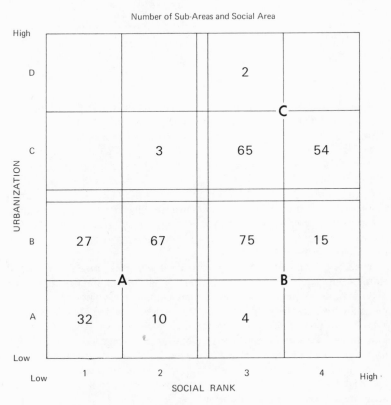

[FIGURE 1]. NUMBER OF SUB-AREAS BY SOCIAL AREA AND
AREA TYPE, ROME, 1951

collapsed into three major social areas: (type A) low social rank and low urbanization, (type B) high social rank and low urbanization, and (type C) high social rank and high urbanization. Each of these areas may be described in terms of available population characteristics. Means for these characteristics are listed in Table [6].[31]

[31] Two measures in addition to those defined above are included for the purpose of this description: *dwelling size:* number of rooms in an area divided by number of dwelling units in that area; *sex ratio:* number of males per hundred females in an area.

TABLE [6]. MEANS OF SELECTED SUB-AREA POPULATION
CHARACTERISTICS, BY SOCIAL AREA TYPE

Characteristic	Low SR Low Urb. (A)	High SR Low Urb. (B)	High SR High Urb. (C)	All Areas Low SR	All Areas High SR	All Areas Low Urb.	All Areas High Urb.	All Areas Total
Dependent pop.	260	141	76	257	104	211	77	164
Aged	5.27	6.89	9.26	5.30	8.22	5.93	9.19	7.07
Family size	4.00	3.63	3.45	3.99	3.53	3.85	3.46	3.71
Crowding	1.94	1.39	1.08	1.93	1.22	1.73	1.09	1.49
Primary industry	5.43	.56	.87	5.35	.74	3.44	.89	2.55
Secondary industry	41.9	26.6	22.8	41.4	24.5	35.7	22.8	31.1
Tertiary industry	52.1	72.7	75.6	52.7	74.3	60.5	75.7	65.8
Dwelling size	2.84	3.58	4.40	2.86	4.04	3.14	4.39	2.90
Sex ratio	105	92	84	104	87	99	84	91
Number of sub-areas	136	94	121	139	215	230	124	354

Type A areas include 38 per cent of all sub-areas and 37 per cent of the total population of Rome. They contain a fairly young population with a low ratio of children to aged. These sub-areas are characterized by large families, and small and crowded dwellings. They contain more men than women. About half their active population is engaged in agriculture and secondary industries. Because these areas contain a high proportion of manual workers and have a fairly high rate of illiteracy, they are termed *low* social rank. Since these areas demonstrate high fertility rates and have a fairly small proportion of women working outside the home, they are termed *low* in urbanization. As noted below, these areas tend to be located near the outskirts of the city.

Type B areas include 26.5 per cent of all sub-areas and 32 per cent of Rome's population. These areas contain about 140 children under 5 per 1000 persons 65 years old or older. They contain fairly large families and moderate size dwellings which tend to be less crowded than in type A areas. Slightly more than one quarter of their active population is engaged in primary and secondary industries. These areas average a sex ratio slightly under 100. Because they are characterized by a fairly high proportion of nonmanual workers and low illiteracy rates, these areas are termed *high* in social rank. With high fertility rates and few women at work, these areas are termed *low* in urbanization.

Type C areas contain 34 per cent of the sub-areas and 30 per cent of the population of Rome. They are characterized by an older population and a fairly low ratio of children to aged. Families tend to be small and dwellings large and uncrowded. Over three-fourths of the active population is engaged in tertiary industries. The sex ratio is appreciably lower than 100. With a high proportion of non-manual workers and a literate population, these areas are classified as *high* social rank. Because of low fertility rates and a fairly high proportion of women working, they are termed high urbanization areas. As will be noted below, these areas tend to be located near the center of the city.

Social Differentiation and Scale

According to the social area formulation it is contended that at least two forms of differentiation (urbanization and social rank) are possible in large scale societies. Further, it is contended that these forms are apparent in the sub-area distributions of populations in large scale societies. Two related questions may be addressed to this view: (1) at what point in scale does either or both of these forms of differentiation develop and become apparent? And (2) is their development sequential or simultaneous?

In order to examine these questions the existence of the following possible situations may be considered.

I. Sub-area populations are not differentiated by either dimension of the typology. Presumably this would occur in societies of minimum scale according to the Shevky formulation.

II. Sub-areas are differentiated by only one dimension of the typology. Presumably this would occur at some point in scale if primacy exists for either dimension.

III. Sub-area populations are differentiated by both dimensions. This would occur in large scale societies either (1) subsequent to situation II if primacy occurs or (2) at some point in scale following the first situation if no primacy occurs.

The first situation would be evidenced by a lack of significant association with either dimension and expected population characteristics. As noted above in Table 5, this situation is certainly not apparent in Rome where all selected characteristics are significantly related to the dimensions of the typology. Of course, studies of the San Francisco Bay Region and of ten U.S. cities indicate that the U.S. cannot be considered as in the first situation of minimal scale with a lack of sub-area differentiation based on urbanization or social rank.[32] As one would expect, one concludes from the available data that both Italy and the United States are beyond the first situation.

The second situation would be evidenced by a strong association between dimensions of the typology and a large relationship between one primary dimension and appropriate population characteristics and a small correlation between the second dimension and such external criteria. Findings from Rome show this situation to be somewhat more the case than is true in available studies of American cities. Data presented in

[32] See Shevky and Bell, *op. cit.* and Van Arsdol Jr., Camilleri, and Schmid, *op. cit.*

Table 3 reveal that Rome exhibits significantly higher correlations between components of the indexes than are found in ten U.S. cities combined or in San Francisco. This is especially the case with the relationship of women in the labor force ratio to the occupation ratio which are components of different indexes. For Rome, the relationship is quite high as indicated by a correlation of $r = .64$. The corresponding coefficient for the ten middlesize cities is .16 and only .02 for San Francisco.

In addition, correlations between the dimensions of the typology are significantly greater in Rome in 1951 ($r = .76$) than in San Francisco, 1940 ($r = .25$) or 1950 ($r = .13$).[33] One interesting interpretation of this finding is that Rome in 1951 is of lesser scale than in the San Francisco Bay Area in 1940 and that the San Francisco area is of lesser scale in 1940 than in 1950. It further indicates that Italian society approximates the second situation described above more closely than American society. These extremely limited longitudinal and cross societal comparisons support the view of a sequential development of the dimensions. For, the lower the scale of a society, the more closely are sub-area populations distributed in the manner expected in the second situation.

However, Table 5 shows that the second condition of a sequential situation — high correlation of test variables with a single dimension of the typology — is not met in Rome. Age structure variables, for example, are significantly more related to urbanization than to social rank. Industrial composition variables, on the other hand, are more closely related to social rank.

Thus, this evidence suggests that both Italian and American society appear to have reached the third situation. In both societies the dimensions jointly account for greater variation in population characteristics than either separately. However, it would seem that Italy is, in some respects, closer to a transition between the second and third situations. While both dimensions of the typology are necessary in accounting for sub-area variation in Italy and in the United States, dealing with only one dimension leaves out more in the U.S. Data from several societies of differing scale should permit further examination of this point.

SPATIAL CONSIDERATIONS

While the social area approach utilized characteristics of sub-area populations to construct a typology of differentiated populations, little has been done rigorously relating this typology to the local area. Theoretical efforts to establish this link have revolved around such concepts as a range

---

[33] Shevky and Bell, *op. cit.*, p. 29. Correlation between social rank and urbanization is higher in Rome than in any *one* of the ten cities studied by Van Arsdol, Jr., Camilleri, and Schmid. The highest coefficient is found for Atlanta ($r = .224$). Cf. "The Generality of Urban Social Area Indexes," *op. cit.*, Table 5.

of residential alternatives and commitments to areas and facilities shared by differentiated sub-populations. Studies oriented to this approach have shed some light on the dynamics of urban patterns of settlement.[34] They have not, however, succeeded in presenting a system of propositions relating sub-area population differentiation to the spatial location of these populations although a spatial unit (the sub-area) defines these populations. Can a relationship between the location of sub-areas and the forms of differentiation characteristic of their populations be established?

Recently an interesting step toward the establishment of an empirical association between social organization and spatial organization by use of the Shevky model has been provided by Anderson and Egeland.[35] Using an analysis of variance technique applied to four typographically regular U.S. cities of 200,000–500,000 population, they effectively demonstrate that Burgess' concentric zone hypothesis is supported with respect to urbanization but not with respect to social rank. Hoyt's sector hypothesis, on the other hand, is supported with respect to social rank but not in the case of urbanization.

These two ecological propositions may be examined by use of social area data from Rome and compared with similar data from American cities. Are social areas arrayed in terms of either of these traditional spatial patterns in Rome? Do the dimensions of social space order sub-areas in a manner similar to that observed in American cities?

In Rome three sectors may be arbitrarily established by including all sub-areas contiguous to three major transportation arteries and their projections. This method provides sector lines which are compatible with Hoyt's hypothesis.[36] Within each sector, sub-areas are classified in terms of three concentric zones circumscribing the central city. The boundaries of these zones are located primarily along traditional administrative lines and demonstrate a roughly circular form.

A two-way classification analysis of variance technique is used to examine sector and zone differences in mean urbanization and mean social rank scores. Table [7] presents an analysis of variance for the 84 sub-areas falling within the selected sectors.

Inspection of Table [7] indicates clearly that both urbanization and social rank are distributed in Rome with respect to both sectors and zones. The null hypothesis of no difference in means between sectors or between zones with respect to urbanization or social rank scores is rejected at the one per cent level of significance.

[34] Cf. Wendell Bell, "Social Areas: Typology of Urban Neighborhoods," in Marvin Sussman, editor, *Community Structure and Analysis*, New York: Crowell and Co., 1959.

[35] *Op. cit.*

[36] Homer Hoyt, *The Structure and Growth of Residential Neighborhoods in American Cities*, Washington, D.C.: United States Government Printing Office, 1939.

TABLE [7]. ANALYSIS OF VARIANCE FOR URBANIZATION
AND SOCIAL RANK BY ZONES AND SECTORS, ROME, 1951

Source	Sum of Squares	df	Variance Estimate	F	Ho[a]
		Urbanization			
Between zones	6,234	2	3,117	39	Reject
Between sectors	4,018	2	2,009	25	Reject
Zones x sectors	852	4	213	2.66	Accept
Remainder	6,002	75	80	....	......
Total	17,106	83	....	....	......
		Social Rank			
Between zones	11,485	2	5,743	29	Reject
Between sectors	11,549	2	5,775	29	Reject
Zones x sectors	2,980	4	745	3.69	Accept
Remainder	15,139	75	202	....	......
Total	41,153	83	....	....	......

[a] .01 level of significance adopted.

On the other hand, interaction between zones and sectors is insignificant in the case of both urbanization and social rank. This indicates that
the null hypotheses, that sectors containing high urbanization or high
social rank areas also contain zones with high urbanization or social rank
areas, cannot be rejected.

To facilitate description of the zonal pattern, all 354 sub-areas of Rome
are classified by zones. Means for these zones and for selected sectors and
zones within sectors are listed in Table [8].

As might be expected, highest urbanization areas are found in the central district of the city with a gradual decline in urbanization toward the
periphery. This finding agrees with the data generated from four U.S.

TABLE [8]. MEANS OF URBANIZATION AND SOCIAL RANK
SCORES BY ZONES, SECTORS AND ZONES WITHIN SECTORS,
ROME, 1951

	Number of Areas	Means[a]		
		(1)	(2)	(3)
Zones (all areas)				
Urbanization	354	52.26	42.94	27.61
Social rank	354	60.48	59.42	22.54
Zones (within sectors)				
Urbanization	84	53.58	46.55	30.35
Social rank	84	64.08	61.03	33.76
Sectors				
Urbanization	84	52.54	49.45	36.41
Social rank	84	72.10	54.55	43.40

[a](1) = Central zone *(Rioni)* or 1st sector (Via Nomentana);
 (2) = Intermediate zone *(Quartieri)* or 2nd sector (Corso—Via Flaminia);
 (3) = Outer zone (mainly *Suburbi*) or 3rd sector (Via Prenestina).

cities described by Anderson and Egeland. Unlike these American cities, however, *social rank is highest in the central district in Rome*. In Rome, social rank is highest in the central zone, then declines slightly in the second zone, and declines sharply in the third or outer zone. Contrary to Roman findings, the study of four U.S. cities did not support the zonal distribution of sub-areas with respect to social rank. In addition, the distribution of areas in terms of social rank in Rome markedly departs from the view of the blighted central city frequently observed in the United States. Rather, the ecology of social rank in Rome apparently is more in accord with traditional patterns observed in older European cities and in Latin America where prestige centers on the central plaza.[37]

The three sectors selected for study in Rome revealed marked differences with respect to both urbanization and social rank. Clearly, areas included in the third sector (Via Prenestina) reveal a lower average urbanization score than either of the other two sectors. This sector also contains the lowest mean social rank score. The first sector (Via Nomentana), on the other hand, contains the highest social rank and highest urbanization areas on the average.

It is interesting to note that sector differences with respect to urbanization were not observed in the four American cities. Of course, this may be due to differences in the way sectors were established in the two studies. In Rome, sectors were located adjacent to three major thoroughfares and their projections. The U.S. study, on the other hand, did not use existing transportation lines to locate sectors. Rather, they arbitrarily constructed thirty degree sectors radiating from the center of the city, then selected four of these for study in each city. The method used in Rome would seem to be more in line with Hoyt's original formulation of the sector hypothesis. However, these findings may represent a real difference between Rome and the four U.S. cities studied.

In sum, Roman data reveal to a significant degree the applicability of both the zonal and sector patterns to the spatial distribution of social areas. Within this city, urbanization and social rank are clearly both concentric and zonal phenomena.

[37] Cf. Asael T. Hansen, "The Ecology of a Latin American City," in E. B. Reuter, editor, *Race and Culture Contacts*, New York: McGraw-Hill Book Co., 1934, pp. 124-142; Norman S. Hayner, "Mexico City: Its Growth and Configuration," *American Journal of Sociology*, 50 (January 1945), pp. 295-304; Harry B. Hawthorn and Audrey E. Hawthorn, "The Shape of a City: Some Observations of Sucre, Bolivia," *Sociology and Social Research*, 3 (November-December 1948), pp. 87-91; Theodore Caplow, "The Social Ecology of Guatamala City," *Social Forces*, 28 (December 1949), pp. 113-135; Dan Stanislawski, "The Anatomy of Eleven Towns in Michoacan," *Latin American Studies* X, Austin: University of Texas Press, 1950, pp. 1-75; and Erdmann D. Beynon, "Budapest: An Ecological Study," *Geographical Review*, 33 (April 1943), pp. 256-275.

288 Dennis C. McElrath

SUMMARY AND CONCLUSIONS

This study has examined the theoretical and analytical power of the interpretive frame of reference proposed by Shevky and Bell. The findings, based on an analysis of 354 sub-areas of Rome, lend strong support to this approach.

1. It is demonstrated that with minor modifications social area analysis may be applied to census districts outside the U.S.
2. All measures of social differentiation which are combined in the present study to form dimensions of the typology are necessary.
3. Characteristics external to the social area typology describing life styles, living conditions and work patterns are significantly related either to social rank or to urbanization in the manner predicted from the theory underlying social area analysis.
4. As expected, both urbanization and social rank jointly describe population types more completely than either separately in terms of life style, living conditions and work patterns.
5. Examination of hypotheses across societies is possible with this approach. The social areas of Rome and of U.S. cities are interrelated in a manner which may be meaningfully interpreted in terms of differences in the scale of Italian and American society.
6. Social rank and urbanization are concentric as well as sectoral phenomena in Rome even when the effects of sector on zone or zone on sector are taken into account.

Generally, all of these findings are supported at relatively high levels of confidence. They constitute a strong case for the utility of this approach for cross-societal analyses.

In addition to permitting a test of the utility of this approach, the social area results from Rome are indeed provocative. The substantive findings include:

1. A high positive relationship between social rank and urbanization (higher than that reported to date in any U.S. study);
2. A zonal occurrence of *low* social rank areas near the periphery of the city;
3. A positive relationship between social rank and crowding and industrial composition of the labor force;
4. A positive relationship of urbanization to such life style characteristics as dependent population, aged population, and family size; and
5. A relationship between social area types and dependent population ratio, proportion of the aged, family size, dwelling size, crowding, and industrial composition of the labor force.

19   MORRIS JANOWITZ AND
      DAVID R. SEGAL

Social Cleavage and Party Affiliation:
Germany, Great Britain, and the United States

Empirical research on the political sociology of the multiparty nations of
western Europe has been pursued with great vigor and a sense of historical
perspective in part because some of the major propositions of the leading
theorists could be explored by means of a growing body of sample-survey
data. One dominant theme has been to marshal evidence describing the
decline of a clear-cut and sharply differentiated social-class basis of party
affiliation, that is, the modulation of "class conflict" politics. With the
emergence of advanced industrialism, the social basis of mass political
behavior becomes more complex and more heterogeneous.[1] In this view,
correspondingly, the content of politics has been transformed from an
ideologically defined and diffuse struggle to a set of demands for concrete
bargaining. Granting this political change in selected industrialized societies, the actual extent and process of the transformation remains to be
determined, especially in terms of cross-national comparisons.

ALTERNATIVE MODELS

Two different models are central for dealing with these issues. The most
widely publicized approach for analyzing the decline of class-conflict
politics in western Europe (and its relative absence in the United States)
is the notion of "middle majority" politics. Fundamentally, this orientation gives priority to changes in social stratification derived from economic
growth and accordingly places lesser importance on the independent and

From the *American Journal of Sociology,* Vol. 72, 1967, pp. 601-618, ©
1967 by The University of Chicago. Reprinted by permission of the authors and
The University of Chicago Press.
[1] See especially the work of the Committee on Political Sociology of the
International Sociological Association. Stein Rokkan, "International Cooperation
in Political Sociology: Current Efforts and Future Possibilities," in Erik Allardt
and Yrjo Littunen (eds.), *Cleavages, Ideologies and Party Systems* (*Transactions
of the Westermarck Society,* Vol. X), pp. 5-18.

autonomous roles of political institutions. Central importance is placed on economic growth and economic affluence, although the complexities of political change are acknowledged.[2] Particularly, changes in economic levels — that is, the rising standard of living — produce greater equality in the social structure, which in turn produces changes in political demands and a broadening of political citizenship. Socioeconomic position, and, more concretely, occupation, is taken as the crucial measure of social stratification. The social structure of a middle-majority society is seen as one in which the number of persons in the upper working class and the lower middle class exceed those in the end groups, the upper middle class and the lower working class. It is a society in which the line between working and middle class is not very distinct, and there is a fusion into the life style of the middle stratum.

In this approach, the social groups who still accept ideological or class-conflict politics are holdouts or residues, and the future decline of their political impact is explicitly asserted as the future growth of class-conflict politics once was. Thus, Lipset writes, "In the long run, however, the remaining bases of ideologically intrinsic politics will continue to decline due to the contradictions between reality and their definition of the situation, and because of the irrelevance of their call to action in terms of a situation which will no longer exist."[3] The politics of the "middle majority" implies, of course, not the end of party divisions, but a narrowing of party differences and a transformation in the political consequences of these divisions.

The alternative model is that of "consensus and cleavage."[4] Politics and political behavior are still seen as derived from the conflicts of social strata, but political affiliations are more than a by-product of social stratification. Political institutions and political leadership are more autonomous elements in the process of change. The social-stratification system is itself molded by political decisions and the action of political parties.

The "consensus and cleavage" approach postulates a more complicated pattern of social stratification, in which political conflict is manifested by new and more differentiated social groupings which reflect economic, professional, and bureaucratic interests. Likewise, religious, ethnic, and linguistic differences can persist or emerge as bases of political cleavage

[2] S. M. Lipset, "The Changing Class Structure and Contemporary European Politics," *Daedalus*, XCIII (Winter 1964), 271-303.

[3] *Ibid.*, pp. 295-96. See also Robert E. Lane, "The Politics of Consensus in an Age of Affluence," *American Political Science Review*, LIX, No. 4 (December 1965), 874-95.

[4] Morris Janowitz, "Political Sociology," in *International Encyclopedia of the Social Sciences* (New York: Macmillan Co., in press); William Kornhauser, *The Politics of Mass Society* (New York: Free Press, 1959).

which include ideological elements. Advanced industrialization produces a changing stratification system which alters older forms of political conflict and provides the basis for newer forms. These new conflicts are more delimited in scope, but they have deep consequences on collective problem-solving, and they may be so aggregated as to produce pervasive strains. Because there are built-in limitations in the trend toward greater social equality, in this view what is crucial is not only the persistence of the social-structural basis of cleavages but also the capacity of the political institutions to adjust and to create the conditions for political consensus.

Moreover, in contrast to the middle-majority model the emphasis on strain places greater importance on the international context and on the impact of foreign affairs. For Western Europe, bargaining politics is an expression not only of changes in internal social structure but of the recent history of adjustment, after intense struggle, with the Soviet Union. The emerging phase of international relations is already producing new bases of internal cleavage in Western Europe, both as nationalistic orientations become more dominant and as neutralist sentiments protrude into domestical political debate. Thus, the "consensus and cleavage" model is not limited to an extrapolation of the elements of the recent past that have produced an increase in political bargaining. Instead it seeks to identify those changes in social structure, in political institutions, and in the international context that have the possibility of introducing new rigidities and new conflicts into the language of politics.

The difference between the middle-majority and the consensus-and-cleavage positions can be briefly summarized along one crucial dimension of political change in an advanced industrial society. The middle-majority outlook assumes that the social sources of rigid ideological orientation or of political extremism are residues or holdouts which, with additional economic expansion, will be incorporated into the political structure. The consensus-and-cleavage approach sees the sources of rigid ideological orientation and political extremism as also being the products of social change and political leadership. It is therefore oriented toward the detection of new sources of resistance to political integration.

These two approaches of political sociology do not exhaust the debate, although they encompass the basic issues investigated by those who make use of sample surveys. Traditional conceptions of social-class conflict, adapted to deal with new issues, still have currency in polemical political writing that makes use of sociological categories.[5] One derivative of these traditional class-conflict notions is applicable to sample-survey data. The argument runs that increased skill and technique in mass manipulation make it possible for the economic elites to pervert and inhibit the political

[5] See George Lichtheim, "Class and Hierarchy: A Critique of Marx?", *European Journal of Sociology*, V, No. 1 (1964), 101-11.

expression of social-class interests. The processes of mass communications, which are particularly overlooked by the middle-majority model, need not be tied to social-class-conflict categories. These issues are still worthy of the most careful investigation, although contemporary survey data do not necessarily assist in the pursuit of this goal.[6] Obviously, our approach included traditional social-class-conflict variables, and it emerged that these variables were as relevant as any particular and delimited source of cleavage, although they hardly supplied the basis for an over-all interpretation of the processes of political change in industrialized societies.

SAMPLE-SURVEY DATA

Sample-survey data supplies a basis for exploring these models. But the investigator who seeks to make use of national sample surveys for the purposes of cross-national comparisons faces a pervasive dilemma. On the one hand he has the option of utilizing for secondary analysis a body of disparate and unco-ordinated surveys which have at least the advantage that they were designed to take into account the historical and institutional setting of each specific country. However, this approach presents extensive problems because of the lack of comparability in the measurement of key variables. More serious limitations operate to the extent that available surveys do not necessarily contain adequate coverage of similar or theoretically related topics so that systematic comparisons are difficult to make. The result is that the existing literature contains many insightful propositions but analysis is often discursive and incomplete.

On the other hand, individual investigators have sought to be both comparable and systematic by organizing a single unified research design and applying it to a number of nations. Such a strategy runs the risk of being criticized as "intellectual imperialism," namely, projecting the political assumptions and definitions of one nation onto another. In this approach there is a danger of searching for uniform variables and failing to develop a survey instrument appropriate for the historical and institutional setting of each country.

This paper is a report of an effort to make national sample-survey materials more relevant for cross-national analysis and to reduce the dilemmas of working in this field. The approach was applied to existing bodies of data, but it could equally be used in planning and developing new research efforts. We were not interested primarily in studying the same variables in each country but in analyzing variables that had comparable meaning and significance in each country. First, this meant it was necessary to state the particular problematic issue of comparative politics under

[6] See Morris Janowitz and Dwaine Marvick, *Competitive Pressure and Democratic Consent: An Interpretation of the 1952 Election* (Chicago: Quadrangle Books, 1965), for an effort to probe these issues.

study in general terms. We were concerned with the consequences of different patterns of social stratification on party affiliation. Second, this meant developing operational measures that reflected the national social structure and its sociopolitical balance but organizing the data in such a fashion as to permit the maximum comparability.

National sample surveys are particularly well suited for cross-national research on the social-stratification bases of party affiliation and political partisanship. Sampling procedures in the United States and in western European countries are based on national parameters and therefore produce data about the nation-state as a whole, at the expense of understanding regional and metropolitan differences. But our comparisons are precisely at the national level.

This type of comparative analysis should include the widest possible range of multi-party states with similar levels of economic development. However, we chose Great Britain, West Germany, and the United States because the stability of their post-war competitive party systems has been similar enough to permit useful paired comparison, and our analysis relies heavily on paired comparisons. The degree of precision in the sample surveys of these countries is great enough to record the relatively small differences that characterize both political change within a nation and numerous types of cross-national differences.

Nevertheless, notions such as middle-majority politics or the politics of consensus and cleavage present complex problems when applied to a specific body of survey data. The variables derived from these frameworks are not readily operationalized and measured. Despite our efforts at explicit definitions, they are overlaid with implicit and subtle political and ideological preferences. Which of the three nations most closely approximates the model of middle-majority politics? Of all the possible measures of social cleavage, which are most politically relevant for each of these three countries? Such questions we shall postpone until we examine the data on the association between social-class position and party affiliation. However, it should be pointed out that our preference was for the "consensus and cleavage" model both on the basis of theoretical considerations and existing data. The results of this empirical investigation served only to strengthen our assumption.

Comparison of these nations involved three paired comparisons. In particular, we believed that Great Britain would reveal a much higher level of partisan polarization on the basis of socioeconomic stratification than the United States.[7] Existing studies indicated this pattern. It seemed rea-

[7] Philip E. Converse defines status polarization as "the strength of the relationship between status and relevant politico-economic variables" (see "The Shifting Role of Class in Political Attitudes and Behavior," in Eleanor Maccoby, Theodore M. Newcomb, and Eugene L. Hartley [eds.], *Readings in Social*

sonable to assume that the Germans would be more polarized than the United States and less polarized than Great Britain. Moreover, in placing Germany between Great Britain and the United States, it would be important to know whether Germany was markedly closer to Great Britain or closer to the pattern in the United States. Yet, as we shall argue, each of these assertions about the relative degree of socioeconomic stratification of party affiliation, if correct, could best be explained and amplified by the consensus-and-cleavage model.

National surveys of political opinion are typically based on rather small probability samples, which produce relevant data on the over-all distribution of voting behavior, party affiliations, and attitudes but are limited for purposes of detailed analysis. This paper is based on the accumulation of similar-type national surveys in each of the three countries. For Germany, the 12,676 cases used were collected by the Institut für angewandte Sozialwissenschaft during a one-year period in 1963-64 and involved seven surveys. For Great Britain, the data were based on 5,628 interviews carried out by Research Services, Ltd., by means of four national surveys during the period before the general election of 1964. In the case of the United States, there were 11,146 cases based on eight national surveys completed during the period of 1961 and 1964, two by the National Opinion Research Center.

The cumulation of cases from a series of national samples is justified on the basis of two assumptions. First, previous research has indicated that political partisanship and its correlates are relatively persistent and stable. Therefore, we assumed that the summation of data collected over a short period of time would not distort the findings encountered.[8] Second, there

---

Psychology [New York: Holt, Rinehart & Winston, 1958], p. 394). Robert R. Alford, in *Party and Society* (Chicago: Rand McNally, 1963), p. 102, assigns Great Britain a mean index of class voting of 40. The magnitude of the same statistic for the United States was 16. For further information on class and partisanship in England see J. Blondel, *Voters, Parties, and Leaders: The Social Fabric of British Politics* (Baltimore, Md.: Penguin Books, 1963), p. 91, and Richard Rose, *Politics in England* (Boston: Little, Brown & Co., 1964), p. 73. See also J. Bonham, *The Middle Class Vote* (London: Faber & Faber, 1954), and Mark Abrams and Richard Rose, *Must Labour Lose?* (Baltimore, Md.: Penguin Books, 1960).

[8] A computer simulation of the 1960 presidential election using poll data collected in the course of an entire decade has claimed, "The benefits of large numbers and broadly based coverage proved to be greater than the benefits of timeliness" (Ithiel de Sola Pool, Robert P. Abelson, and Samuel L. Popkin, *Candidates, Issues, and Strategies* [Cambridge, Mass.: M.I.T. Press, 1964], pp. 65-67). However, the purposes of the analysis and the variables employed must be kept in mind, and there are obvious limits to the time span that can be involved. The Research Services, Ltd., surveys were studies J. 4104, J. 4285, J. 4380, and J. 4475; the National Opinion Research Center studies were S. 110 and S. 640, and those conducted by the Survey Research Center were numbers 706, 714, 720, 734, and 736.

is the question of sampling points, and again it was assumed that, if the probability bases of the samples were similar, it would be possible to cumulate independent national samples without introducing significant distortion for our purposes.

SOCIOECONOMIC STRATIFICATION AND PARTY AFFILIATION

The first step in our analysis was to determine the degree of polarization of party affiliation in the three nations. In order to measure on a comparable basis the relation between socioeconomic position and party affiliation, it was necessary to (*a*) have a general conceptualization of class structure that would be applicable to all three countries and (*b*) to construct operational measures that would accurately reflect each national setting. This task is greatly simplified by the overriding limitation of national probability surveys, which do not collect relevant data on the "upper" or very top social stratum. The actual size of this group is so limited that the procedures of sample surveying do not produce analyzable numbers, and thereby one of the most difficult sociological questions in social stratification is avoided by simple exclusion.

Both the middle-majority model and the consensus-and-cleavage approach emphasize the growing differentiation of the occupational structure. A large and refined number of occupational categories are required to describe the skill structure of an industrialized society. Despite the fact that we have used the largest sized samples to be assembled for comparative political analysis, our categories of analysis remain limited and reflect present practices in national-survey work. These data were classified by the overriding distinction between blue collar (working class) and white collar (middle class). Further differentiation within each of these groupings was both essential and possible. Much comparative research into social mobility has been conducted on the basis of movement from blue- to white-collar positions and vice versa, but the results are indeed oversimplified, and current methodology of the national sample survey at least permits a four-group stratification pattern.

We believed that differentiation within both the working class and the middle class should reflect "style of life," and this could be measured by education level or income or a combination of both. More subtle categorization by content of education, work setting, life cycle, etc., was not possible. However, education and income are highly intercorrelated, and in fact it makes little or no difference which of these criteria are used as the basis for separating the middle-class group into upper-middle and lower-middle strata or for making the equivalent distinction in the working-class group.

The relevant issue is to locate the appropriate cutting points for each specific country which would still produce the most comparable or equivalent patterns of socio-economic stratification. For West Germany, a monthly income of DM. 1,000 or more separated the upper middle class from the lower middle class, while a monthly income of DM. 600 was the dividing line for the upper working class from the lower working class. On an equivalent basis, for the United States an annual income of $10,000 was used to divide the upper middle class from the lower-middle-class group, and for the working class a $5,000 or more annual income was used to differentiate between upper and lower strata. The data in Great Britain were collected on a somewhat different basis, namely, by social-strata grades as judged by the interviewer. These categories were directly translated into the four-strata hierarchy.

The diffuse term "party affiliation" supplied an appropriate measure for cross-national analysis. Differences as to how the electoral systems operate to create a national "regime" cannot, of course, be overlooked. In Germany, the national electoral decision is between parties directly. The national candidates are not on the ballot, and the voter selects a district candidate. In Great Britain the voter makes a similar decision, but the candidate is more of a district representative of the national party leadership. In the United States, the citizen decides between national candidates.

However, party affiliation has a relatively standard meaning in all three nations because the parties are mass parties and are seeking to develop the broadest political allegiance. Party affiliation refers to the diffuse commitment to one or another of the political parties. It is the base from which political parties mobilize electoral support. It is a measure that varies slowly, and it persists between elections when these surveys were conducted.

"Party affiliation" was, in effect, operationalized with slight differences in each country in order to reflect national meanings. For the United States, because national elections are held at regular intervals, respondents were asked, "Generally speaking, do you usually think of yourself as a Republican, a Democrat, an Independent, or what?" Because of the high cultural value in answering "Independent," those who gave this response were probed for their leanings. The category "Independent" was reserved for persons who did not lean to either the Republican or the Democratic party.

For Great Britain, because elections are not periodic, the measure of party affiliation was based first on the question of party voting intention in the event an election were to be held. The relatively large number of undecided were probed as to their party leanings. In Germany, the respondent was aked to express his preference among the various political parties. (See Table 1 for the distribution of reported party affiliation in Germany, Great Britain, and the United States.)

TABLE 1. DISTRIBUTION OF PARTY AFFILIATION
(BASED ON CUMULATED NATIONAL SURVEYS)

	Total Sample	
	N	%
Germany:		
Social Democrat	4,393	34.6
Christian Democrat	5,135	40.5
Other	908	7.2
D.K.; N.A.[a]	2,240	17.7
Total	12,676	100.0
Great Britain:		
Labor	2,030	36.1
Conservative	1,775	31.5
Other	433	7.7
D.K.; N.A.	1,390	24.7
Total	5,628	100.0
United States:		
Democratic	6,080	54.6
Republican	3,416	30.6
Neither[b]	1,650	14.8
Total	11,146	100.0

[a] D.K. = don't know; N.A. = no answer.

[b] The category "Neither" for the United States was composed of approximately equal parts of declared independent and D.K. or N.A. responses.

In developing these measures a research strategy was employed that is at variance with the contemporary data bank and retrieval systems. The current emphasis in the reanalysis of survey data is to store data in electronic data-processing systems and to develop common categories for retrieval. This approach has the advantage of speeding the process of data-handling but removes the analyst further and further from direct contact with and understanding of his data. A general set of categories is developed which is designed to be relevant for all types of analysis. Because of the widely different systems of collection and coding, risks in excessive and rigid standardization are likely.

Instead, these data were handled by a confrontation approach in which procedures for comparison were developed for each research problem. The original data from all of the studies of the three nations were collected at the Institut für angewandte Sozialwissenschaft. In terms of the specific hypothesis to be tested, rubrics that were functionally equivalent but reflected relevant national differences were created. The data were then recoded for each country.

The data presented in Table 2 reveal that party affiliation is the most highly associated with socioeconomic status in Great Britain, less so in West Germany and least in the United States. The measure of association employed was that of Cramér's V, which was calculated in each

TABLE 2. SOCIOECONOMIC STATUS AND PARTY AFFILIATION: UNITED STATES, GERMANY, GREAT BRITAIN (BASED ON CUMULATED NATIONAL SURVEYS)

	Social Status							
	Middle Class				Working Class			
	High Income		Low Income		High Income		Low Income	
Party Affiliation	N	%	N	%	N	%	N	%
United States:								
Democrat	518	47	1,436	51	1,416	61	1,242	61
Republican	446	40	1,003	35	554	24	418	20
Neither	147	13	388	14	346	15	363	18
Total	1,111	100	2,827	100	2,316	100	2,023	100
Germany:								
Social Democrat	340	25	871	28	1,086	50	1,117	49
Christian Democrat	677	49	1,485	47	724	33	720	31
Other	185	14	299	9	85	4	88	4
N.A.[a]	166	12	493	16	277	13	367	16
Total	1,368	100	3,148	100	2,172	100	2,292	100
Great Britain:								
Labor	109	11	229	23	846	45	846	47
Conservative	542	56	388	40	451	24	394	22
Other	76	8	99	10	140	8	118	6
D.K.; N.A.	237	25	259	27	433	23	461	25
Total	964	100	975	100	1,870	100	1,819	100

[a] D.K. = don't know; N.A. = no answer.

country for those persons on whom there was adequate data to locate their positions in this schema of social stratification. The resulting statistics were: for America, $V = .171$; for Germany, $V = .246$; and for England, $V = .372$. As mentioned above, an alternative definition of socioeconomic position (Table 3) based on a more refined eight-strata schema (four categories of occupation, each divided on the basis of income) produced the same relative pattern of polarization of party affiliations (the association was found to be weakest in the United States, $V = .162$; intermediate for West Germany, $V = .284$; highest for Great Britain, $V = .394$). By both schemata of social stratification, these differences are large and noteworthy. Moreover, it appears that Germany falls midway between the United States and Great Britain and is not merely a variant of the pattern in one or the other nation.

These detailed breakdowns reveal in all three countries that the "Left"-oriented party failed to increase in concentration among the lower-working-class group as compared with the upper working class. This is not because of defection to a third party. It is, rather, the result of an ability in all three countries (but particularly in Germany) of the "conservative" party to penetrate this group and reduce its expected losses or the result of the increase in non-partisanship in the lower-working-class group.

TABLE 3. SOCIOECONOMIC STATUS AND PARTY AFFILIATION

A. UNITED STATES

	Party Identification							
	Democrat		Republican		Neither		Total	
Social Status	N	%	N	%	N	%	N	%
Upper middle:								
High income	180	44	172	42	55	14	407	100
Low income	314	46	271	39	105	15	691	100
Lower middle:								
High income	338	48	274	39	92	13	704	100
Low income	1,122	53	731	34	283	13	2,136	100
Upper working:								
High income	1,253	61	493	24	305	15	2,051	100
Low income	905	62	313	21	251	17	1,469	100
Lower working:								
High income	163	62	61	23	41	15	265	100
Low income	337	61	105	19	111	20	553	100

B. GERMANY

	Social Democrat		Christian Democrat — Christian Social Union		Other		N.A.[a]		Total	
	N	%	N	%	N	%	N	%	N	%
Upper middle:										
High income	84	16	282	54	104	20	54	10	524	100
Low income	129	23	272	49	78	14	76	14	555	100
Lower middle:										
High income	256	30	395	47	81	10	112	13	844	100
Low income	742	29	1,213	47	221	8	417	16	2,593	100
Upper working:										
High income	588	49	402	33	52	4	167	14	1,209	100
Low income	523	53	283	28	46	5	144	14	996	100
Lower working:										
High income	498	52	322	34	33	3	110	11	963	100
Low income	594	46	437	34	42	3	223	17	1,296	100

[a]N.A. = no answer.

C. GREAT BRITAIN

	Conservative		Labor		Other		N.A.[a] Ineligible		Total	
	N	%	N	%	N	%	N	%	N	%
Upper middle	542	56	109	11	76	8	237	25	964	100
Lower middle	388	40	229	23	99	10	259	27	975	100
Upper working	451	24	846	45	140	8	433	23	1,870	100
Lower working	394	22	846	47	118	6	461	25	1,819	100

[a]N.A. = no answer.

300   Morris Janowitz and David R. Segal

SOCIAL-SYSTEM CLEAVAGES

The second step in the analysis involves additional dimensions of stratification. The consensus-and-cleavage approach implies that beyond social
class the other major social-system cleavages related to party affiliation
vary from nation to nation. Moreover, the consequences of these cleavages
for political change depend on whether they work to reduce or to heighten
the strains generated by socioeconomic stratification. For the United
States, first, race was taken as a dominant source of party affiliation and
then religious affiliation. For Germany, because of the absense of racial
division, religion supplied a majority dimension, while for Great Britain,
in the absence of racial or religious divisions, sex and age differences were
assumed to operate as potential bases of political cleavage.[9] This is not to
be taken as meaning that racial issues are absent in British politics, as they
are significant. Rather, racial minorities are so small that in general they
do not constitute a significant socioeconomic voting group to which political leaders make appeals. In Table 4 the polarization of party affiliation
by socioeconomic position is presented for each nation holding constant
the above relevant variable of political cleavage.

TABLE 4. SOCIOECONOMIC STATUS, SOCIAL CLEAVAGE,
AND PARTY AFFILIATION: UNITED STATES,
GERMANY, AND ENGLAND

	Total Sample	Social Cleavage	
United States	$V = .162$	White	$V = .149$
		Non-white	$V = .011$
Germany	$V = .284$	Catholic	$V = .297$
		Non-Catholic	$V = .251$
Great Britain	$V = .397$	Males	$V = .412$
		Females	$V = .387$

These data indicate the different consequences of social cleavages for
party affiliation in each of the nations. Is the socioeconomic polarization
higher or lower among these social divisions? For the United States, the
white population reveals a pattern of polarization similar to the total
sample; namely, Democratic affiliation is negatively associated with socioeconomic position at a level just below that for the total sample (Cramér's

[9] Blondel, op. cit., p. 91, and Rose, op. cit., p. 63, point out that in England
women are the politically handicapped group. Robert McKenzie and Allan
Silver attribute disproportionate Tory leanings among English women to a
deferential ideology (see "Conservatism, Industrialism and the Working Class
Tory in England," Transactions of the Fifth World Congress of Sociology, III
[1964], 191-202).

V = .149). By contrast, Negro affiliation is markedly unpolarized because it is unrelated to socioeconomic position. At each level, Negroes hold predominantly Democratic affiliation (Cramér's V = .011). In addition, we explored the relevance of religion as a secondary basis of polarization. The Protestant figure is somewhat greater than for the United States as a whole (Cramér's V = .18). The difference between Protestants (.18) and non-Protestant (.12) is less than the difference between Negroes and whites. Thus, religion in the United States operates as a basis of polarization but not as much as race. For Germany, religion operates to produce some additional polarization among the Catholics (Cramér's V = .297), while among the Protestants socioeconomic polarization of party affiliation is somewhat lower (Cramér's V = .251). In Great Britain, sex operates in the same fashion but with rather slight magnitude. Males are more polarized on the basis of socioeconomic position in their party affiliation, while women are less (Cramér's V = .412 for males and .387 for women). This represents a greater commitment of women to the Conservative party against their socioeconomic position. Alternatively, in Great Britain age serves as another basis of polarization, since the Conservative party has the advantage among old people, both male and, especially, female.

Insofar as party affiliation is an expression of social attachment within the context of economic self-interest, these data reveal with some precision the extent to which specific additional social variables create a base of political cleavage. A simple measure is the difference in the scores measuring polarization of party affiliation within socioeconomic groups; the greater the difference, the more the control variable operates as a basis of political cleavage. Thus the greatest difference is for the United States, where the data demonstrate the obvious reality that Negroes have a political affiliation as a racial group rather than dividing between Democrats and Republicans on the basis of their socioeconomic position. The amount of dissensus introduced by religion in Germany is much less and by sex in Great Britain is even less (differences in scores: for race in United States, .138; for religion in Germany .046; for sex in Great Britain .025). These data underline the obvious reality that the higher consensus on socioeconomic bases in the United States should not overlook the greater degree of polarization on other social bases.

INSTITUTIONAL FACTORS AND POLITICAL INTEGRATION

The third step in the analysis of this body of comparative survey data is to probe further the underlying social-structural variables accounting for party affiliation. It should not be overlooked that even the simple schema of socioeconomic stratification plus *one* selected variable produces social groupings with immensely wide differences in political-party preferences.

302   MORRIS JANOWITZ AND DAVID R. SEGAL

Among the respondents who expressed party preference, the social-structural variation was as follows:

Great Britain:
Upper-middle-class women . . . .   74% Conservative
Lower-working-class men . . . .   25% Conservative
                                               Δ = 49%
Germany:
Upper-middle-class Catholics . . . .   71% Christian Democrat
Lower-working-class Protestants . . . . . .   27% Christian Democrat
                                               Δ = 44%
United States:
Upper-middle-class white . . . .   47% Republican
Lower-working-class Negro . . . .   17% Republican
                                               Δ = 30%

This array seems to give further support to the relevance of the "consensus and cleavage" model. In addition, it seemed relevant to examine on a wide empirical basis whether other variables, especially institutional associations, would also be revealing of the underlying social-structural basis of party affiliation.

In order to maximize the meaningful reduction of unexplained variance in party affiliation, the statistical technique used was based on the non-symmetric splitting of social groups, the so-called tree technique.[10] By this process the ordering of variables and their dichotomizing is based on the results of computer operations.

Our effort was to maintain, as in the other phases of the analysis, an optimal balance of variables which would take into consideration national differences and maintain a basis for comparability among the three countries.

Despite the enormous effort in collecting these studies, standardizing the variables, and analyzing the data by the procedures of the tree analysis, the results indicate that political sociologists do not yet have adequate bodies of data for cross-national analysis, and our goal still must emphasize the collection of adequate empirical materials. Interestingly enough, this is probably due more to the limitations on the available data from the United States and Great Britain than from Germany. It needs to be emphasized that only in the case of Germany are the data sufficiently com-

[10] John A. Sonquist and James N. Morgan, "The Detection of Interaction Effects" (Ann Arbor: Survey Research Center, University of Michigan, 1964). The specific technique applied was that developed by J. H. G. Seegers ("De Contrasgroepen-Methode: Nadere Uitwerking en eel Tweetal Toepassinger," *Sociale Wetenschappen*, No. 3 [1964], pp. 194-225). Because the analysis could be carried out only on those respondents who had expressed a party affiliation, the case base was reduced; United States, 9,431 cases; Great Britain, 3,826; Germany, 9,493.

prehensive to produce meaningful results, but for comparative purpose even the initial branches in the tree analysis are revealing. In the case of Germany, on the basis of previous analysis, a tree of many branches was constructed which explained more of the variance than could be explained by standard methods of analysis (see Table 5). But even these preliminary findings help clarify the patterns of convergence and diversity in social stratification that underlie party affiliation.

For Great Britain, the tree analysis reaffirms that the most important single variable is the split on social-class position. (This variable accounted for 13.2 per cent of the variance.) Only within the working class, the next most important split was the size of household; persons living in large households — those of more than three people — were more prone to be affiliated with the Labor party than those in smaller households. (This variable accounted for only 2.1 per cent additional explanation of the variance.) The high degree of consensus underlying party affiliation can be inferred from the absence of additional bases of cleavage in these data. No other available variable included in surveys to which we had access increased the amount of explained variance by 1 per cent or more.

In the United States, a similar type of simple model emerges with religious affiliation as the most important initial split. Democratic affiliation was linked to "minority religion" (Catholic, Baptist, Jewish, or no pref-

TABLE 5. PARTY AFFILIATION BY SOCIAL-STRATIFICATION GROUPING BASED UPON "TREE ANALYSIS": UNITED STATES, GREAT BRITAIN, AND GERMANY

Group Definition	Size of Group N	%	Affiliation with Major Left Party (%)
United States:			
1. "Minority Religions"/or no preference	2,932	31.0	78
2. "Core Protestants"/working-class occupations	2,139	22.7	67
3. "Core Protestants"/middle-class occupations	4,360	46.3	52
Total	9,431	100.0	
Great Britain:			
1. Working-class strata/large households	1,074	28.1	72
2. Working-class strata/small households	1,485	38.8	64
3. Middle-class strata	1,267	33.1	27
Total	3,826	100.0	
Germany:			
1. Union affiliation/non-practicing Catholics	2,520	26.5	72
2. Working-class strata/no union affiliation/non-Catholics	1,775	18.7	60
3. Working-class/union affiliation/Catholics	531	5.6	41
4. Middle-class strata/no union affiliation/non-Catholics	2,562	27.0	31
5. Practicing Catholics/no union affiliation	2,105	22.2	18
Total	9,493	100.0	

304   MORRIS JANOWITZ AND DAVID R. SEGAL

erence) in contrast to the core Protestants with Republican affiliation.
(This variable reduced the unexplained variance by 6.8 per cent.) The
second step came in dichotomizing the Protestant groups on the basis of
occupation as between a group of working-class occupations and a group
of middle-class occupations (this variable reduced the variance by only
1.6 per cent).[11] In the case of the United States, the tree analysis did not
serve to differentiate the respondents to the same degree as for Great
Britain.

For Germany, the tree analysis resulted in five social groupings which
were built initially on the basis of social-class position (occupation) and
religion. But the increased explanatory power of the model was the result
of the fact that it was able to incorporate institutional variables, such
as trade-union affiliation and church attendance.[12] The extreme groups,
based upon unionism and religion, were on the "Left," union-affiliated
non-practicing Catholics, 72 per cent of whom supported the Social Democratic party, and on the "Right," non-union–affiliated practicing Catholics, of whom only 18 per cent supported the Social Democratic party.

The tree-analysis procedure for Germany highlighted the importance of
the religion variable as a basis of political cleavage, in part because the
measure included actual religious behavior as well as denomination. Further, the effort to explore institutional variables proved rewarding because
trade-union affiliation had a general nation-wide relevance. Thus, for
example, middle-class persons who were not practicing Catholics, but
who had family trade-union affiliations, expressed a 62.1 per cent preference for the Social Democratic party and were subsumed under the
"Left"-oriented group. In contrast, the similar social groupings without
family affiliation to trade unions only reached 49.3 per cent in their Social
Democratic preference.

For Germany trade-union membership is a simple but meaningful
measure of integration into the larger political system. For the United
States, the equivalent integrating structures are so variegated that sample
surveys do not easily permit their precise identification. Finally, for none

[11] These findings were not unexpected. Analyzing data from American Institute
of Public Opinion Survey no. 636K (1960), Alford computed indexes of class
voting that for Protestants were +19 and for Catholics only +6. It should be
pointed out that Roper Survey no. 78 for the same year provides figures of +18
and +10 for the same indexes. The difference in magnitude serves to demonstrate the variability among small samples on such matters. See Alford, op. cit.,
p. 243.
[12] In connection with a study of the 1965 German elections, the analysis of
German data has been expanded to include a greater number of cases and
a set of sociopsychological variables. These data will be presented in a forthcoming paper by Klaus Liepelt and Friederike Golzem.

of the samples was there adequate basis to analyze the mass media as another integrative mechanism to the political system.

POLITICAL CHANGE

What relevance do these data have in helping to understand the processes of political stability and change in advanced industrial societies? How can these findings be integrated with institutional studies of politics?

1. These data reaffirm the conclusion that the degree of social-class polarization of party affiliation varies considerably even among these three nations with relatively comparable social structures. The observation in and of itself that Great Britain is more polarized than the United States or Germany, and, on the basis of other studies, that it has been since 1945, raises important questions about "middle majority theories of political change. It would seem that the persistently higher the degree of party affiliation (and party vote) along socioeconomic lines, the less ideologically based social class-conflict politics decline and the less a nation conforms to a model of bargaining-type politics. But on the basis of this analysis this is not the case in a paired comparison of Great Britain with Germany or with the United States.

Our data dealt with mass political orientations and not with elite perspectives. However, there is no reason to argue that Great Britain has a more ideologically based electorate than Germany or the United States. In fact, we would argue that British mass politics is less ideological and based more on mass consent than Germany.[13] For a comparison of Great Britain with the United States the same holds true, or at least there is no noticeable gap.[14]

For example, we can make use of a series of specific comparisons about mass predisposition as presented by Gabriel Almond and Sidney Verba to indicate that Germany has distinctly less of a "democratic" culture based on consent and political integration, while the differences they report between the United States and Great Britain are at best minor. Popular sentiments toward the national government as measured by positive attitudes on the theme that the national government improves conditions were equal in Great Britain and the United States (76 per cent, 77 per cent), while they were distinctly lower for Germany (61 per cent).[15] The same pattern of attitudes was encountered on expectations of equal treat-

[13] Gabriel Almond and Sidney Verba, *The Civic Culture* (Princeton, N.J.: Princeton University Press, 1963), e.g., pp. 82 ff.

[14] See James B. Christoph, "Consensus and Cleavage in British Political Ideology," *American Political Science Review*, LIX, No. 3 (September 1965), 629-42.

[15] Almond and Verba, *op. cit.*, p. 82.

ment by the public bureaucracy and the police.[16] Even for information on refusal to report voting decision, a crude but revealing measure of consent politics, the results were negligible for Great Britain and the United States but reached 15 per cent of the respondents for Germany.[17]

More important, feelings of civic competence were equal at the national level in the United States (77 per cent) and Great Britain (78 per cent), while for Germany the figure was lower (62 per cent).[18] If the Almond-Verba measures of political competence are combined with expectations of equal treatment by administrative agencies, the United States drops below Britain and Germany. Finally, many of these measures of consent toward the political and electoral system are influenced by educational level, thereby giving the United States a reported over-all advantage. However, when education is held constant, lower-class Americans have lower scores than those for Great Britain. It is frequently argued that the process of social change and the growth of affluence weaken ideological commitment by creating greater equality. However, this process of social change does not guarantee the comparable development of positive commitments to the rules of the "bargaining" game. Here we are dealing with cultural traditions and the impact of political institutions on social structure.

2. In interpretating these findings on socioeconomic position and party affiliation, it is necessary to re-emphasize the limitations in the sample-survey data, especially in relating these data to historical trends. Undoubtedly, there are important elements of convergence in occupational and socioeconomic stratification patterns in the United States, Great Britain, and West Germany, but they have not yet converged, nor is their convergence predetermined.[19] Moreover, the present patterns of convergence are not necessarily the result of similar historical sequences. The emergence of industrialism has not followed the same pattern in Great Britain and Germany as compared with the United States, since the development of occupational systems does not conform to a single "ideal" or "type" pattern. In Great Britain and Germany, industrial processes were introduced into a society that had a relatively well-developed middle stratum of commercial and governmental occupations and a traditional agricultural labor force. In the United States industrialization was grafted

[16] *Ibid.*, p. 108.
[17] *Ibid.*, p. 116.
[18] *Ibid.*, p. 226.
[19] S. M. Lipset and Reinhardt Bendix, *Social Mobility in Industrial Society* (Berkeley: University of California Press, 1959); S. N. Miller, "Comparative Social Mobility: A Trend Report and Bibliography," *Current Sociology*, Vol. IX, No. 1 (1960); see also Morris Janowitz, "Social Stratification and Mobility in West Germany," *American Journal of Sociology*, Vol. XLIV, No. 1 (1958), 6-24.

onto a social structure with a much less well-developed commercial and administrative structure and a very different agricultural base.

These differences in patterns of socio-economic stratification, together with absolute differences in living standards, constitute a central theme in the comparative political sociology of the United States and western Europe. These differences help explain the persistently higher relevance in Great Britain and Germany of socioeconomic position as a basis of political cleavage and the greater polarization of party affiliation as compared with the United States. But, as indicated above, greater socio-economic polarization of party affiliation does not necessarily mean more class conflict or more ideological politics if we are dealing with the comparative analysis of the United States, Great Britain, and West Germany.

3. Our data indicate that a consensus-and-cleavage model that includes both socioeconomic and other structural variables, plus institutional affiliations, supplies a relevant basis of organizing comparative national survey data. The tree analysis, in particular, highlighted the process of social change and the new sources of political cleavages as the older basis of social-class conflict declines.

But survey data supply only a partial basis for examining patterns of social change in order to identify these new sources of political cleavage. On the macro-social-system level, available research, for example, indicates that during the last two decades the built-in trends toward income redistribution associated with the first and earlier developments of the welfare state in Great Britain and the United States have slowed, and may even have reversed themselves.[20] Such trends, unless altered by drastic changes in taxation and wage policies, are likely to contribute new elements of political cleavage.

Likewise, there is every reason to believe that, with the growth of a more complex division of labor and of a more differentiated educational system, the categories of social stratification we used in this analysis become too undifferentiated to capture the realities of social change. Despite the relative success we have had with simple variables in accounting for party affiliation, we agree with Wilensky's formulation of the need for a more refined approach to study mass ideology and mass political references. In fact this is precisely what the tree analysis indicates:

> Our data suggest that we need to slice up social structure in ways that capture both the persistence of older divisions (age, religion, occupation) and the emergence of newer ones (the quality and content of education) and to do it more precisely than usual. To say

[20] See Richard Morris Titmuss, *Income Distribution and Social Change* (Toronto: University of Toronto Press, 1962), and Herman P. Miller, *Rich Man, Poor Man* (New York: Thomas Y. Crowell Co., 1964).

"white collar" or "working class" is to obscure most of what is
central to the experience of the person and the structure of society.
To say "professional, technical, and kindred" captures more of social
life but not much more. "Lawyer" and "engineer" move us closer
to social reality, for these men develop quite different styles of life,
rooted in diverse professional schools, tasks, work schedules, and
organizational contexts. To say "independent practitioner" is to say
even more, and finally, to particularize the matter with "solo lawyer"
vs. "firm lawyer" is to take account of the sharp contrasts in
recruitment base (social origins, religion, quality of professional
training), career pattern and rewards which divide the two.[21]

One important consequence of such social differentiation on political
behavior is observable from the available data. On the basis of the findings of this research and others generally, there is an over-all inverse relationship between higher socioeconomic position and affiliation with the
Labor party, the Social Democratic party, and the Democratic party.
Within the upper-middle stratum, however, persons from non-business
occupations and professions are more likely to hold partisan affiliation
with these political parties than persons in the upper-middle socioeconomic stratum who are business affiliated. This is particularly the case
for the United States and Great Britain.[22] The administrative, professional, and scientific personnel who are employed in educational, governmental, health and welfare institutions, tend to become politically
polarized from their counterparts in industrial and commercial hierarchies.
Clearly, differences in recruitment, educational experience, and, most important, in group interest generated by employment in a different work
setting are all operative factors.[23]

The notion of status crystallization, or more precisely status congruence,
can be used to describe this linkage between social stratification and political partisanship.[24] Status congruence refers to gross characteristics and
can involve large discrepancies in social position such as the case of a
person with "lower class" educational achievement who is earning a very
high income; or it can involve more subtle and smaller but nevertheless
politically important differences. This is what appears to be at work
within the upper-middle-class stratum. The business-connected persons

[21] Harold L. Wilensky, "Mass Society and Mass Culture," in Bernard
Berelson and Morris Janowitz (eds.), *Reader in Public Opinion and Communication* (2d ed.; New York: Free Press, 1966), pp. 317-18.
[22] Angus Campbell, Philip E. Converse, Warren E. Miller, and Donald E.
Stokes, *The American Voter* (New York: John Wiley & Sons, 1960), pp. 482-
83; Mark Abrams, Research Services, Ltd., London, unpublished report, 1966.
[23] The distinction suggested by Daniel R. Miller and Guy E. Swanson, between entrepreneurial and bureaucratic groups, is applicable (see *The Changing
American Parent* [New York: John Wiley & Sons, 1958]).
[24] Gerhard Lenski, "Status Crystallization: A Non-Vertical Dimension of
Social Status," *American Sociological Review*, XIX (August 1954), 405-13.

have less education than their professional and technical counterparts (some college or college, as compared with college and postcollege education), while their income level is on the average higher. This pattern of status incongruence sets the social context within which their political polarization develops.

Survey research can incorporate such more refined variables in order to capture the greater complexity of contemporary work settings. However, there is an inherent limitation in national surveys with limited numbers of cases as currently practiced. If the sequential influence of social origin, education, work experience, and institutional ties is to be probed, even the cumulation of repeated national samples will have to be augmented by subsamples of crucial age and occupational groupings selected on more purposive and theoretical criteria.[25]

4. As stated above, the "consensus and cleavage" model does not assume that the social sources of rigid ideological political orientation or the sources of political extremism are residues or holdouts which additional economic expansion will incorporate into the political structure and therefore eliminate or contain. Instead, it is oriented to identifying new sources of political cleavage and political conflict as well as to transforming old sources. For example, from our data it is clear that in all three societies there is a tendency for persons in the lower working class to have a higher degree of non-party affiliation than in the other strata of society. While the magnitude is not large, it reflects a persistent vulnerability produced by advanced industrialism. The underlying configuration that generates this lack of effective participation is not to be seen in terms of education or income per se but as a series of life experiences which produce persons and families without adequate institutional links to the political system. But we are not dealing only with a lower-class phenomenon, for such disruption can occur at various points in the social structure, for example, among elderly men and women living outside family units or among the downwardly mobile. What is important is that the sources of such disruption persist with the development of an advanced industrial society.

Alternatively, language and ethnic differences have emerged in the last decade in particular regions of Western Europe as important sources of sharp political cleavage. Ethnic and language differences can constitute independent sources of political polarization, but they can be specific manifestations of a more comprehensive process of political conflict under conditions of advanced industrialism, namely, the cleavage between the center and the periphery. In Great Britain, ethnic and regional feelings fuse together to support political cleavages based on reactions to differential rates of economic progress. There is a division between England on the one hand and Scotland and Wales on the other, which have

[25] The design of the German 1965 election study of the Institut für Angewandte Sozialwissenschaft is a step in this direction.

310   MORRIS JANOWITZ AND DAVID R. SEGAL

experienced slower rates of economic development. For each comparable
social grouping the Conservative party has more partisans in England
than in Scotland and Wales.

In Germany, regionalism has been obscured or repressed as a result of
the basic division into East and West Germany. There is still a basis of
polarization between the central urban metropolitan centers and the less
industrialized hinterlands. In the United States, regional differences are
pervasive and complex. Regionalism in the South is based on historical
and racial factors and a lag in economic development; a markedly different type of western regionalism is linked to very rapid and very special
forms of economic development. As a result, ideological and conflict politics has important regional variations, both in the South and in the Far
West.

5. This analysis of the sources of party affiliation has focused on domestic politics. This is what is implied in the transformation of social-class
struggles into bargaining politics. But beyond our findings, consensus and'
cleavage more and more come to involve foreign affairs on a mass basis
as literacy grows and as the nature of warfare becomes completely destructive. In fact, one can make the argument that the decline in ideological
politics since 1945 has been influenced not only by changes in internal
social stratification but also because in all three societies the overriding
concerns with the Cold War made possible the management of the
national economy so as to inhibit political conflict and created a situationally based consensus. We prefer at a minimum to see mass perceptions of
the threat of war and international tensions as a relevant and emerging
basis for political cleavage.

For the recent past, survey data gives conservative-type parties in both
the United States and Great Britain an advantage in that they are seen
as being more effective and skillful in international relations and foreign
policy. In Great Britain this issue helps account for the difficulty of the
Labor party in translating its popular support into electoral success. In the
United States this issue is even more pronounced in that the Democratic
party is viewed as more aggressive in international relations and even
characterized by some as the "war party." In Germany, the differences in
public perceptions about the skill and posture of the two parties in international relations do not vary to any noteworthy extent. As international
relations are transformed away from the patterns of the last twenty years,
foreign policy is likely to supply a basis of political polarization since the
range of alternative policies is certain to become broader and more complex.

In summary, we would conclude that existing quantitative survey data,
with all their limitations, make a contribution to comparative political sociology that goes well beyond common sense and "well-informed" bases

of judgment. For comparative analysis, measures from one nation cannot be mechanically imposed on another even if they have highly similar social structures. The analysis of sample-survey data requires both a concern for national differences and a reliance on equivalent categories. As a result of a series of paired comparisons we found that partisan affiliations were most polarized on the basis of socioeconomic positions in Great Britain, less in Germany, and the least in the United States. In each country, there were different secondary social bases of political cleavage. Our initial assumption was that differences in social stratification per se cannot explain comparative party affiliation or, in turn, differing levels of political consensus. It is obvious that political institutions play an active role in fashioning such mass orientations. The model of consensus and cleavage, which attributes an element of independence to political arrangements, not only helps explain the transformation of social-class conflict but helps avoid overlooking the persistent and emerging sources of political conflict in an advanced industrial society.

20 REINHARD BENDIX

Preconditions of Development:
A Comparison of Japan and Germany

The economic and political development of the modern world was initiated in England and France during the eighteenth century. Influences from abroad had played a role at an earlier time, but with the emergence of modern industry in these countries it became a convenient and useful abstraction to consider changes as indigenous to the societies changing. This model of an "indigenous development" is not very useful for understanding the development of other countries. It is as true of Russia as it is of Japan and Germany that many ideas, technical innovations, and political institutions are either taken over from abroad or developed in

From *Nation-Building and Citizenship* by Reinhard Bendix (New York: John Wiley & Sons, 1964), pp. 177-197. Reprinted with permission of the author and publisher.

conscious reference to changes that have taken place abroad. At times such borrowing and adaptation are part of a concerted political effort to increase the economic and military viability of a country. Military occupation and conquest are another major source of change. The influence of the French Revolution and of French culture on Russia and Germany during the eighteenth and nineteenth centuries; German borrowing of English technology and the prominence of English thought and institutions as a "reference group" of German intellectuals; the effect of the Napoleonic conquest in Germany; England and Prussia as "reference groups" for the modernization of Japan — these examples of cross-cultural influences from the nineteenth century have multiplied greatly in more recent times. As modern technology and various other aspects of modern Western societies have been "transplanted' by one means or another, Germany and Japan along with many other countries have had to cope with the problems arising from the symbiosis of tradition and modernity.

Germany and Japan are today highly industrialized countries. Consequently, the two countries share a large number of characteristics which follow from industrialization itself and are either the direct product of technical and economic change or variable by-products of that change. An incomplete list of the first would include the change from a traditional technology toward one based on the application of scientific knowledge, a change in agriculture from subsistence farming toward commercial production of agricultural goods, a change in industry from the use of human and animal power towards the use of power-driven machines, and a change in work place and residence from the farm and village toward urban centers. An incomplete list of the second would include the effects of a growing market economy upon the division of labor, the substitution of contractual and monetary ties for the earlier familial or quasi-familial relation between employer and worker, the diversification of the occupational structure, increased social mobility, the development of universal elementary education, and others. These and related changes have occurred in all countries that have industrialized successfully, though this is not to deny that quantitative and qualitative distinctions remain even with regard to these comparable products and by-products of industrialization.

Germany and Japan are comparable in a number of other respects. Both countries underwent rapid political changes at roughly the same time, Japan after the Restoration of 1868 and Germany after her political unification following the Franco-Prussian war of 1870-71. This accident of timing is less important than the political comparison. The two countries shared a preference for monarchical institutions and a tradition of bureaucratic government controlled by a ruling oligarchy — a similarity which accounts for the degree to which the Meiji oligarchs took the government of Imperial Germany as their model. In this setting most democratic tendencies were regarded with suspicion; autocratic or dictatorial forms of government were readily preferred to the development of parliamentary institutions. This common tradition of an autocratic and bureaucratic government also imparted a certain similarity to the aristocracies of the two countries, since aristocratic title was often directly associated with high office. Persons from aristocratic families enjoyed a social and political prominence which was a source of envy and resentment in the German and the Japanese "middle class." Economic similarities are not so pronounced, since Germany preceded Japan by several decades both in the development of science and technology and in the rapid industrialization of her economy. Still, both countries were industrial "latecomers" and as such dependent for a time on borrowing technical and economic know-how from abroad.

With reference to each of these similarities it is possible to point to striking differences as well, but the comparison between the Japanese and the German social structure is illuminating just because there is also some common ground between them. The dissimilarities are massive, nevertheless.

Japan is an island empire that was conquered only once in her recorded history — at the end of World War II. The tremendous internal divisions which mark Japanese medieval history had no adverse effect upon the cultural coherence of the country. Because of her insular position, Japan's political divisions and instability never exposed her to the cumulative effect of wars and alliances from the outside. On the other hand, Germany has experienced changes in her territorial composition throughout her history. Her exposure to outside forces at all times greatly intensified her cultural and political heterogeneity. This difference is associated with the dynastic and religious traditions of the two countries. In one case, there is an unbroken tradition of the Emperor as the single source of legitimacy (despite the political impotence of the Emperor for long periods of Japanese history). In the other, there is a succession of reigning houses during the medieval period and a history of conflicts over the principle of legitimacy as well as over questions of succession. Again, Japanese religious history is marked by a high degree of doctrinal syncretism, making for a considerable degree of toleration, whereas Germany reflects the doctrinal orthodoxies of Christianity generally and reveals to this day the legacies of past conflicts based on religious belief.[1]

---

[1] These religious and dynastic differences between Japan and Western Europe have important ramifications for the comparison of feudalism and the preconditions of representative institutions in the two settings. On feudalism, see F. Jonon de Longrais, *L'Est et L'Ouest* (Tokyo: Maison Franco-Japonais, 1958); and now John W. Hall's excellent essay, "Feudalism in Japan: A Reassessment," *Comparative Studies in Society and History*, V (October 1962), pp. 15-51. A

Moreover, the basis from which the two countries began their most rapid industrialization is not the same despite the important similarities noted earlier. By the time of the Meiji Restoration, Japan had had 250 years of exclusion accompanied on the positive side by administrative consolidation, significant developments in agriculture, a population increasingly disciplined both by police supervision and education, and the pent-up preparedness for change on the part of the lower nobility analyzed below. On the negative side, there is the high cost of isolation. The exclusion of ideas from abroad retarded technical advance and contributed to a cultural provincialism which perhaps threatened even the native arts with stagnation. Above all, isolation entailed the danger, visible only in retrospect, that the precipitous industrialization following the opening of the country would subject its social structure to strains of a magnitude difficult to manage politically. By the time Germany became unified in 1870, she had undergone a very different experience. Instead of isolation she had been exposed to the impact of the French Revolution and its Napoleonic aftermath, thus setting the stage for her political bifurcation between revolution and reaction. During the eighteenth and nineteenth centuries, every idea propounded in England or France found a creative response or at least an echo in Germany. Her cultural cosmopolitanism was not matched for decades in the technical and industrial fields but from the late eighteenth century onward there was a steady advance here also, often based on borrowings from England. Her economy was stimulated also (and at an increasing rate) by indigenous developments, at first by bureaucratic initiative and scientific developments at academic institutions and supplemented eventually (roughly from the 1830's on) by entrepreneurial efforts.[2] Germany's liabilities were largely political. Instead of administrative consolidation of more or less equal component territories under the central government as in Japan, Germany was fragmented into very unequal units and hence lacked central authority. Moreover, one of the units (Prussia) was clearly ascendant over all others by

---

comparative study of preconditions of representative institutions is contained in Otto Hintze, "Weltgeschichtliche Bedingungen der Repräsentativverfassung," *Staat und Verfassung* (Göttingen: Vandenhoeck & Ruprecht, 1962), pp. 140-185.

[2] As a result of these early developments, Germany was at a markedly different economic level in the 1870's. In 1871, 36% of the German population was classified as urban whereas as late as 1890 only 10% of the Japanese population was so classified. Germany's railroads measured 37,650 kilometers in 1885, whereas Japanese railroads measured 1024 kilometers in 1887. Japan's distribution of her labor force in 1920 corresponds roughly to the German distribution of the 1880's. Perhaps most striking of all, Prussia had 86% of her children (7-14 years of age) attending school as early as 1820, as contrasted with Japan whose elementary school attendance developed from 28% in 1873 to 94% in 1903!

virtue of military strength and efficient administration. Political unity, ensuing from the Franco-Prussian war, came under the aegis of Prussia, the Prussian army, and the Hohenzollern legacy of monarchical and bureaucratic rule. Economic development after 1870 was not nearly so precipitous in Germany as in Japan, but Germany's oligarchic rule was not nearly so undisputed as that of the Meiji bureaucrats who derived considerable strength from the cumulative legacies of Tokugawa rule, even though these did not include as much economic advance.

Against this background of similarities and differences the following analysis will compare three aspects of Japanese and German modernization. . . . [I]n Western Europe the growth of the nation-state involved the concurrent development of a nation-wide authority, the destruction of inherited privileges, and the gradual universalization of citizenship. In Germany as in other Western European countries this development was ridden with conflicts, since the established ruling groups resisted not only the extension of citizenship but all political reforms jeopardizing their own position. The striking feature of Japan is that her modernization began with the internal, social, and political reconstruction of the ruling groups themselves. Thus, resistance to internal reforms in Prussia as contrasted with the initiation of such reforms by the ruling groups in Japan is the first aspect to be considered. Specifically, why were the Japanese samurai willing to pioneer in this respect and the Prussian *Junkers* not? This first problem is considered in relation to the historical antecedents of the Prussian and Japanese social structure. It will be seen that these different antecedents also help to explain a second and third aspect of Prussian and Japanese modernization. Entering the modern era with an internally reconstituted ruling class, Japan possessed a greater ability of managing the country's political transition in the post-Meiji period than was the case in Germany after her unification under Prussian leadership in 1870-71. This difference in political modernization will be related to a comparison of the "consensus" achieved in Japan and in Germany. In the concluding section of this chapter an attempt is made to relate the comparative evidence examined under these headings to the theoretical problems in studies of social change. . . .

TWO ARISTOCRACIES

All developed countries exemplify a more or less viable symbiosis between their traditional social structures and the consequences of industrialization. The task is, therefore, to distinguish between different types of "partial development." For Germany and Japan this may be attempted by comparisons between the samurai and the *Junkers*, two traditional ruling groups which exemplify how past formations of the social structure can facilitate or hinder the process of modernization.

A word is needed to explain this emphasis on ruling groups. Most

316   REINHARD BENDIX

obviously, ruling groups are best documented in the history of any country. Since political initiative is important in countries that are "industrial
latecomers," it is appropriate to give special attention to the social groups
that were politically prominent in the traditional social structure. Whether
or not such groups take a leading role in the modernization of the
country, it is clear that their social and cultural influence is pervasive. If
we are to understand types of "partial development," then we must give
special attention to the "base line" of tradition with reference to which
these changes are to be gauged. To do this, a knowledge of traditional
ruling groups is indispensable, and a comparative analysis can help us to
define their distinguishing characteristics. Professor Thomas Smith's interpretation of the "aristocratic revolution" in Japan represents and specifically calls for a comparative analysis of the kind attempted here.[3]

Smith points out that ordinarily one expects aristocracies to defend
their established positions, not to take the lead in abolishing their own
privileges and transforming the whole society. Why was Japan different?
In his answer to this question, Smith examines the changes in the position
of the samurai prior to the Restoration, how these changes are related to
Japan's "aristocratic revolution," and what distinctive traits emerge in
Japan because her revolution was aristocratic. On all three points Smith's
treatment is a brilliant summation of research on the social history of
Japan. Several specific points in his analysis invite comparison with the
divergent history of the ruling strata in Prussia and Germany since the
seventeenth century.

Ideological Articulation

Referring first to conditions under the Tokugawa Shogunate, Smith
makes the hypothetical point that the Japanese aristocracy might not
have initiated a wholesale transformation of their own position in society,
if their privileges had ever been challenged by a rising "democratic" movement. They could be revolutionary only because there was no democratic
revolution in Japan. Why did the Japanese townsmen fail to launch such
a challenge? Neither numerical weakness, poverty, illiteracy, political
innocence, nor a lack of resentment can well serve as an explanation.

> There was resentment aplenty and there were many instances of
> private revenge; but for some reason resentment never reached the
> pitch of ideology, never raised private hurts to a great principle of
> struggle between right and wrong.[4]

[3] See Thomas Smith, "Japan's Aristocratic Revolution," *Yale Review* (Spring
1961), pp. 370-383. Two other contributions of the same author, "The Discontented," *Journal of Asian Studies*, XXI (1962), 215-219 and " 'Merit' in
Tokugawa, January 1963), in addition to his earlier works, fit into the framework of this interpretation and will be noted in due course.
[4] Smith, "Japan's Aristocratic Revolution," p. 372.

With this suggestion let us look at Prussia and Germany at the end of the eighteenth century. As in Japan, the aristocracy was *not* challenged in its privileged position. The quietism and pietism of the German burgher are proverbial, coming to consummate expression in Goethe's epic poem, *Hermann und Dorothea*, in which the upheavals of the French Revolution are recorded as from afar, while by contrast the modest well-being and contentment of the average citizen are praised in a quietly glowing panegyric.[5] It is true that liberal tendencies were present, but these were forced "underground" by the police. The Free Masons with their secret assemblies became the forum for mildly liberal, frequently mystical expressions of opinion.[6] However, if liberal views were hardly public enough to account for a strong aristocratic reaction, it was otherwise with their literary expression. The German classical drama of Lessing, Schiller, Goethe, and many lesser writers broadcast the message of the French enlightenment, of liberty and the inviolable claims of the individual personality. In this manner the widest possible audience was reached in a society in which public life, publicity, the expression of political views were virtually nonexistent.[7] Thus, in Germany, "private hurts [were raised] to a great principle of struggle between right and wrong," because the country's opinion leaders were influenced directly by liberal ideas from abroad, even though there was very little internal stimulus in this direction. Conversely, the absence from Japan of a comparable ideological polarization may be attributed, at least proximately, to the effective se-

---

[5] For a documentation of these quietistic tendencies in the middle-class society of the eighteenth century, see W. H. Bruford, *Germany in the 18th Century* (Cambridge: At the University Press, 1939), pp. 206-234. See also Koppel Pinson, *Pietism as a Factor in the Rise of German Nationalism* (New York: Columbia University Press, 1934).

[6] Two studies enable us to follow both trends in detail. For an analysis of the first very mild expressions of opinion and the relation of these expressions to public affairs see Fritz Valjavec, *Die Entstehung der politischen Strömungen in Deutschland, 1770-1815* (Munich: R. Oldenbourg, 1951). The Free Masons as a forum for the formation of "public" or politically relevant opinion are examined in Ernst Manheim, *Die Entstehung der öffentlichen Meinung* (Brünn: R. M. Rohrer, 1933).

[7] From the standpoint of the present we can only look back with nostalgia to a time when it was sufficient for a writer to place his action in the Middle Ages, in Spain, or the far-off Near East in order to disguise the contemporary political relevance of his theme. It should be mentioned, however, that most of the classical German literature originated outside Prussia and, although subject to some police controls, was probably more at liberty to reflect current ideas than would have been the case in Prussia. There are, of course, hundreds of studies of this matter, but one of the most comprehensive and judicious is probably Ernst Cassirer, *Freiheit und Form, Studien zur deutschen Geistesgeschichte* (Berlin: Bruno Cassirer, 1916).

clusion of the country.[8] It is difficult to make a convincing case for the absence of a phenomenon, such as the ideological articulation of middle-class resentments, even where a directly contrasting development can be found as in this instance. But these negative considerations do not stand alone.

Relation to Land and Its Implications

Smith points out that following the Restoration of 1868 the Japanese samurai were in no position to resist the transformation of their position in society, because some three centuries earlier they had been removed from the land. Until the late sixteenth century, warriors had been scattered over the land, where they were overlords of villages, levying taxes, administering justice, and keeping the peace. In the course of the protracted civil wars preceding the Tokugawa Shogunate the great lords restricted the power of these vassals over their fiefs, that is, forbade them to administer justice, eventually took the power of taxation into their own hands, and compensated their warriors directly by stipends in money or in kind. Thus, by 1560 fiefs had been consolidated into large tracts of land and seignorial rights concentrated in the hands of some 200 daimyos, each governing on the average a population of some 100,000 people. These large realms were administered from the newly erected

[8] I am tempted by the intriguing byways which this contrast suggests. To understand the social-psychological correlates of modernization we require some basis for comparison between past and present. In the absence of interviews or questionnaires, we must rely on the indirect evidence of literature, the theater, diaries, and so forth. In this respect a comparison between Japan and Germany would seem to be especially rewarding. Perhaps the most striking contrast in the literature of the two countries is related also to the restrictionism of the Tokugawa regime. In Japan sumptuary laws and police controls sought to regulate the entertainment appropriate for each class and to exclude from the theater any politically suspect themes. As a result, Kabuki seems to have been channeled in the direction of situation comedy, taking its themes from the foibles of stock-characters derived from the social scene of the time. The fact that police controls proved very difficult to enforce and that political themes kept reappearing despite efforts to suppress them, only accentuates the political significance of cultural seclusion. Germany in the eighteenth century also witnessed considerable censorship, but she was the recipient of influences from abroad and her classical literature reflects this in the sense that here themes derived from the suppressed social and political controversies of the time were given a universal meaning. This classic literature then was joined to a romantic idealization of personality, this blend became the dominant "high culture" of Germany during the nineteenth century, and under the influence of a dominant militarism some unsavory syntheses resulted between this humanistic tradition and the power-orientation of *Realpolitik*. A glimpse of the contrast may be had by comparing Donald H. Shively, "Bakufu versus Kabuki," *Harvard Journal of Asiatic Studies*, XVIII (December 1955), 326-356, with Bruford, *op. cit.*, pp. 291 ff.

castle towns in which the expropriated samurai came to reside as retainers and officials of their lords. The chronology of these and related events is instructive. Hall states that most of the first-ranking castle towns were founded between 1580 and 1610 after a large number of lesser castles had been destroyed, a process which culminated in the Shogunal edict of 1615 ordering the destruction of all but one castle in each province.[9] This wholesale removal of warriors from the land was the action most likely to provoke their intense resistance, and there is evidence that it was accomplished by superior force.[10] It is significant in this respect that the first decree promulgating the expulsion of Christian missionaries was issued in 1857, in the midst of the struggles eventuating in the consolidation of daimyo-power. At the national level, the Battle of Sakigahara of 1600 established the supremacy of the Tokugawa family, which consolidated its power by requiring each daimyo family to maintain a residence in Edo. Mandatory attendance at Court by the daimyo or a member of his family (the so-called *sankin-kotai* system) provided the Tokugawa Shogunate with the personal guarantee of the daimyo's continued loyalty. In the 1620's prior to the introduction of this alternate-residence system, the Christian missions were suppressed with great ferocity and the policy of seclusion was introduced. These policies were prompted, in part at least, by the specific fear that continued contact with the West would provoke the warriors to organize a more concerted resistance against the consolidation of daimyo and Tokugawa power.[11] Seclusion insulated the struggles of the Japanese warrior aristocracy sufficiently to enable them to fight it out among themselves, and continued insulation was used by the victors to stabilize the resulting power relationships.

The contrast with Prussia enables us to strengthen this interpretation, though in such complex matters one cannot expect confirmation. Here

[9] See John W. Hall, "The Castle Town and Japan's Modern Urbanization," *Far Eastern Quarterly*, XV (November 1955), 42-44. He cites the case of Bizen which had some 20-30 castles during the fifteenth century, this number was reduced to four by 1615 at which time the edict led to the destruction of three more, leaving the castle town of Okayama.

[10] See the brief description of the principal methods used by Hideyoshi in C. R. Boxer, *The Christian Century in Japan, 1549-1650* (Berkeley: University of California Press, 1951), pp. 173-174.

[11] This is the interpretation of C. R. Boxer. See *ibid.*, especially pp. 338-339. Professor Boxer emphasizes that among Japanese Christian converts who remained true to their faith unto death during the persecution *heimin* (peasants, artisans, and merchants) constituted a much higher proportion than samurai. Out of two to five thousand martyrs who died for their faith in 1614-1643, less than 70 were Europeans (pp. 358, 448). Accordingly, it is probable that the persecution was motivated by the fear that conversion to Christianity would undermine obedience to temporal lords among the population at large as well as by the more specific fear of the disgruntled *ronin* and the possibility of an alliance between these elements and Catholic Spain (pp. 317, 373, and *passim*).

also the struggles among the ruling strata of the country culminated in the
supremacy of one ruling family — the Hohenzollern Dynasty, but political
unification was achieved to the accompaniment of a rapid decline of
towns, the political and economic ascendance of the rural nobility, and an
eventual victory of the ruler over the estates on the basis of military
mobilization and foreign involvements. Toward the end of the sixteenth
century the later state of Prussia consisted of a number of scattered territories in Northeastern Germany and elsewhere, only nominally held together by the Hohenzollern rulers whose center of power lay in the province of Brandenburg.[12] In these territories the towns had been relatively
prosperous and the peasants free under the stimulus of the Hanseatic
towns on the Baltic Sea and the political stability provided by the Teutonic Order. By the sixteenth century, however, the Hanse was declining
and the Order was dissolved in 1525. All resistance to the landed nobility
crumbled. The result was a steady encroachment by the nobility on the
commercial and political prerogatives of the towns and on the customary
rights of the peasants, leading to an almost precipitous decline of the
towns and the establishment of serfdom for the peasants by the middle
of the seventeenth century. Still, the sixteenth century was a period of
peace and prosperity. Feudal knights turned themselves into merchants
and entrepreneurs who, once they had broken the urban monopoly on
trade and industry, proceeded to make the most of the ample opportunities in foreign and domestic trade which were available to them.[13]

At first, the Hohenzollern rulers were entirely powerless against this
landed but commercialized nobility. Although their territories were scattered, during the sixteenth century they succeeded in adding to them by a
series of marriages. These marriages involved them in the power struggles
of Europe — an important vantage point in their later struggles against
the estates. But at the beginning of the seventeenth century the Hohenzollern were at the lowest point in their fortunes. The Thirty-Years' War
(1618-48) engulfed all of their possessions. The Hohenzollern did not
take part in these struggles; while the Elector chose to reside in far-away

[12] The diversity of these territories is suggested by their divergent legal status.
"The Prussian 'kingdom' was confined to the province of East Prussia only. The
'King of Prussia' (since 1701) was at the same time 'Elector' of Brandenburg,
'Duke' of Pomerania, Magdeburg, Cleves, and Silesia (since 1740), 'Prince' of
Halberstandt and Minden, 'Count' of Mark and Ravensberg, etc." See Hans
Rosenberg, *Bureaucracy, Autocracy, and Aristocracy* (Cambridge: Harvard Uni-
versity Press, 1958), p. 28. The territory of "East Prussia" was a Polish fief until
1657 when Poland recognized the sovereignty of Prussia.

[13] For documentation see F. L. Carsten, *The Origins of Prussia* (Oxford: At
the Clarendon Press, 1954), Chap. XII. Note that the towns continued to pay
two thirds of all taxes, even in this period of their decline, while the landed
nobility was tax exempt.

Prussia, his home province of Brandenburg was occupied by Imperial or Swedish troops from 1627 onward. Yet this occupation helped to change the internal balance of power. The foreign army leaders made short shrift of all existing privileges, so that prolonged occupation weakened the political power and economic strength of the landed aristocracy. This weakness played into the hands of the Hohenzollern who strengthened their military preparations especially in connection with the war between Sweden and Poland from 1655 to 1660, in which they took an active part. Frederick William, the Great Elector (1640-88),

> . . . considered it the obvious duty of the Estates not only of Prussia which was directly involved in the war, but equally of Brandenburg and of Cleves, to grant him the money for the conduct of the war. When they failed to do so, he raised it without their consent. At the end of the war he had gained great strength and a standing army, capable of breaking any resistance against the collection of taxes required for its maintenance.[14]

Frederick William and his successors compensated the aristocracy for its submission not only by a continuation of their privileges in all fiscal and local administrative affairs, but also by the transformation of an army of mercenaries into one in which especially the poorer nobility made up the overwhelming majority of the officer corps that was loyal to the Hohenzollern dynasty and indeed opposed to some extent the more parochial interests of the landed nobility.[15]

Japanese and Prussian social history in the sixteenth and seventeenth centuries provide a series of striking contrasts. In Japan, centralization of power occurred in the course of protracted civil wars under conditions of increasing isolation; in Prussia, it occurred as a result of (or in relation to) events outside the country which altered the internal balance of power (e.g., decline of the Hanse, dissolution of the Teutonic Order, Hohenzollern marriage alliances, Thirty-Years' War). The Hohenzollern used foreign involvements and the divisions within the aristocracy to subdue the recalcitrant nobility and weaken its opposition to specific policies. From the standpoint of the internal social structure the importance of

14 *Ibid.*, p. 189. When the Great Elector came to power in 1640, the total revenue of his realm amounted to one million Taler; at the time of his death in 1688 the total came to over three million. During the same period the strength of the standing army increased from approximately 4500 men to some 30,000, although these numbers fluctuated greatly. The financial burden of this effort fell on a population of one million people, who had to pay nearly twice as much per head than their much more prosperous contemporaries in France. See *ibid.*, pp. 266-271.

15 See Rosenberg, *op. cit.*, p. 70. Rosenberg's study contains an excellent comparative analysis of the "Prussian case" in its relation to the general European development. See *ibid.*, pp. 1-45.

external events for this build-up of the Prussian state may be considered "fortuitous." Yet in the present context these "fortuitous" events have significance, because their absence or deliberate exclusion from the course of the Japanese development helps to account for the successful removal of warriors from the land and hence for their greater receptivity to change in comparison with the Prussian landed nobility.

Japan experienced a rapid rise of urbanization, Prussia a rapid decline. In Japan the warrior aristocracy was separated from the land — which was tantamount to its urban concentration, its antirural bias, its relative demilitarization, or, conversely, its increasing bureaucratization. In Prussia the aristocracy strengthened its ties to the land by virtue of the widening economic opportunities that resulted from the destruction of urban monopolies. This development led to a strong antiurban bias and a concerted resistance to the demands of the ruler and his officials; when this resistance was finally overcome in matters of taxation, military affairs, and foreign policy, it continued in all local affairs where the nobility remained paramount.[16]

This difference between an urbanized and a rural aristocracy is related in various ways to the different significance of military affairs for the political unification of the two countries. German unity was achieved through military victory over France. Prussia, the leading German state prior to unification, was itself largely the product of military preparedness and army organization. This accounts for the special position of the Hohenzollern kings and for the special virulence of the constitutional conflict of 1862-66. For the Prussian king was above all the personal leader of the army, the constitution of 1850 specifically noted this position and excluded military affairs from the purview of legislative oversight, so that the Prussian *Landtag's* refusal to endorse the proposed military preparedness struck at the root of the king's prerogative. The subsequent military victory appeared to give a retrospective endorsement to the king's and Bismarck's position and brought about a genuine acceptance of "dynastic militarism" in the ranks of liberal opposition. I note this development of ascendant militarism in Germany in order to emphasize the contrast with Japan. Seen in the large, we may characterize the Tokugawa Shogun-

---

[16] At the same time, we can speak of a "remilitarization" in so far as these Prussian aristocrats who now became army officers were descendants of feudal knights who had cultivated the military arts as a way of life at one time, but had become peaceful landowners and landed merchants during the peace and prosperity of the sixteenth century. However, we should remember that this was East European frontier territory, which had been settled not only by knights, but by "professional promoters of frontier settlements, and numerous noble *condottieri* immigrants." In addition, some of these noble families were descendants of "horse and cattle thieves, dealers in stolen goods, smugglers, usurers, forgers of legal documents, oppressors of the poor and helpless, and appropriators of gifts made over to the Church." See Rosenberg, *op. cit.*, p. 30.

ate as a period of descendant or quiescent militarism. Hideyoshi's sword hunt of 1588, the consolidation of local daimyo rule through the establishment of castle towns (from 1580 to 1610), the consequent removal of samurai from the land, and the formalization of the *sankin-kotai* system for *tozama* daimyo in 1635 (and for *fudai* daimyo in 1642) were major steps in the thorough subjugation and control of the Japanese warrior aristocracy; and this control remained intact until the Meiji Restoration. In terms of their education, bearing, and ideas, the samurai remained attached to their tradition of physical prowess and chivalric honor, as Veblen might say, but this was a militarism without war and above all it was an individualized military stance. Thus, Japan entered the modern world in 1868 under the leadership of a demilitarized aristocracy that was turning its attention to the promotion of education and economic enterprise as a necessary precondition of the country's eventual political and military renaissance, whereas Germany did so under the leadership of the Prussian king, the Prussian army and the Prussian bureaucracy whose *raison d'être* was a military posture and whose success in achieving national unity provided a framework of militancy for the resolution of most internal conflicts.

The foregoing comparative analysis has examined two points. In the absence of a "democratic challenge" the Japanese aristocracy possessed a greater tolerance for change, even in its own privileged position, than would have been the case otherwise. Secondly, the Restoration movement under the leadership of the Meiji oligarchs could accomplish a wholesale transformation in the position of the samurai, because the latter had been removed from the land three centuries earlier and were in no position to resist. Both the lack of ideological articulation and the final failure of the warriors to resist removal from the land may be related to the policy of seclusion, an interpretation which is strengthened by the contrasting development of Prussia during the same period. But it is one thing to show why the Japanese aristocracy did not resist the development of their country; it is another to show why they took the lead in accomplishing this result and in so doing greatly altered the preconditions of their own privileged status. In his answer to this last question, Professor Smith points to a series of conditions which induced the samurai to take an active interest in development under the aegis of the Meiji government, even at the risk of actual or eventual deprivation. Conflicts of interest among the ranks of the aristocracy, the bureaucratization of *han*-government, the development of new aspirations, and changing interpersonal relations between lord and vassal are among these conditions.

Ruling-Class Traditions and Development

The Tokugawa settlement resulted in a genuine class division within the aristocracy. A few thousand families of superior lineage monopolized the important offices of government, while several hundred thousand families of samurai were cut off from all opportunities of appointment. Although some samurai became officials in their respective daimyo domains, most of them were modest retainers. Many samurai families lived in real poverty, resorted to by-employments they considered degrading, and greatly resented the impropriety of merchant wealth. Yet such differences in rank or condition did not affect samurai ideology. The tradition of loyalty to the lord, the cultivation of a militant stance of daring and prowess were not only retained by the samurai but encouraged by the Shogunate and the daimyo. We can suppose that the samurai sensed this discrepancy between their lives and their pretensions. Military men who live as retainers and have little chance to see action may strut about in language and gesture, but the most sensitive among them must have become restless and many more developed strong hostilities against the higher ranks of the aristocracy, especially at the Shogunal Court.

Other considerations support this speculation. The consolidation of daimyo power led to the bureaucratization of *han*-government and hence to increased career opportunities for some of the samurai who had been removed from the land and could now exercise a larger, albeit delegated authority. By the late eighteenth century writers on government were in strong and general agreement on merit as the criterion which should govern selection for office. It is uncertain at what levels and how widely this new principle was applied. But impressive public works were undertaken in some well-administered daimyo domains, and this suggests that merit was recognized occasionally.[17] Where such practices prevailed, upward mobility based on achievement became possible.

> . . . men of lower rank were sometimes promoted to high office; merchants and occasionally even peasants with specialized qualifica-

[17] Both the emphasis on "merit" and the uncertainty of applying this principle under the Tokugawa Shogunate are discussed in Smith, " 'Merit' in Tokugawa Bureaucracy." It would be instructive to know the social position of these writers and in particular whether they have reference primarily to the Tokugawa or the daimyo bureaucracy. The transformation of samurai from vassals into officials and the increasing use of impersonal, administrative considerations is described by John W. Hall, "Foundations of the Modern Japanese Daimyo," *Journal of Asian Studies*, XX (May 1961), 327-328. The same author discusses the construction of waterworks undertaken during and since the seventeenth century in Richard Beardsley, John W. Hall and Robert E. Ward, *Village Japan* (Chicago: University of Chicago Press, 1959), Chap. 3, especially pp. 51-55. However, the two studies cite evidence from the same area (Bizen and environs) and conditions varied among the *han*. One such variation is analyzed in Robert K. Sakai, "Feudal Society and Modern Leadership in Satsuma-han," *Journal of Asian Studies*, XVI (May 1957), 365-376. Note especially the decentralized administration of Satsuma and the quite high proportion of samurai in the population (26% in 1874 against 0.56% of the total population).

tions were ennobled that they might hold office; and promotion in
the bureaucracy became for warriors an important means of improving status.[18]

But however sporadic such instances may have been, the impoverished
samurai families provided a ready audience for writers who made "merit"
their watchword. Since the highest offices usually went to well-placed
families, it was easy to exacerbate the invidious contrast between the in-
competence of high officials and the lowly samurai whose sterling virtues
went unrewarded. Accordingly, an ideology of "merit" was fashioned
which satisfied the pride and aspirations of the samurai, while it also
intensified the invidious contrast between the daimyo-domains and the
corrupt and effete Shogunate in Edo.

Smith argues that the ideal of the warrior was gradually superseded
by ideals of personal conduct more appropriate for a bureaucrat. After the
samurai were removed from the land and the country had become pacified, relations between lord and vassal became more impersonal. The
administration of the consolidated daimyo-domains became bureaucratic
and a new ideology of aspiration developed among the lower samurai.
For two centuries prior to the Restoration, the samurai had been schooled
in envy and emulation by the example of *han* officials of samurai rank,
whose successful careers presumably goaded on the pretensions and self-
confidence of men who had to live on a modest rent or in penury.[19] Accordingly, the very rapid expansion of opportunities after 1868 was
tailor-made for men who suffered from the acute discrepancy between
their high social rank and their lowly economic position, who were free of
bias against change since they had long since been severed from the land,
whose educational preferment under the Tokugawa regime provided them
with an immediate advantage over all competitors, and whose traditional
cult of action, habits of frugality, aristocratic aversion to money making,
and ideology of aspiration had prepared them psychologically for a
bureaucratic career.[20] In a society which heavily underscored status dis-

[18] Smith, "Japan's Aristocratic Revolution," p. 375.

[19] In this context, Smith refers in a review article to "able and rising men
destined to form a new ruling class who felt unjustly cut off from positions of
power and respect." See his "The Discontented," 218. Although this charac-
terization applied to men from all social ranks, it applied with special force to
the lower samurai. The curious combination of radicalism and conservatism
among these petty and frustrated aristocrats may be explained by the fact that
some of their number were successful; there was hope in principle, a condition
highly conducive to revolution as Tocqueville already suggested; but no one in
high office questioned that men of samurai rank had first claim, certainly a
reassuring note even in a dismal economic situation.

[20] Smith, "Japan's Aristocratic Revolution," pp. 378-379. Ronald Dore,
"Mobility, Equality and Individuation in Modern Japan," *Second Conference
on Modern Japan* (Bermuda, January 1963) states (p. 2) that the samurai

326 REINHARD BENDIX

tinctions, the samurai could now hope to rise to the highest positions. This hope, combined as it was with the collectivist ideal of national advance, outweighed the real deprivations to which they were at first exposed and this occurred the more easily because the Restoration leaders left no doubt that the new government's obligations toward the ex-samurai were taken seriously.[21]

Once again, comparisons and contrasts with Prussia and Germany may be made. The consolidation of Tokugawa and Hohenzollern power was similar in one respect: the daimyos and the *Junkers* were left with considerable local powers in contrast to a country like France, where dynastic absolutism greatly disorganized or actually destroyed the old aristocracy. Yet, daimyos and *Junkers* or the samurai and the lower landed nobility of Prussia were not aristocrats of the same type, either in their relation to local government, in their military role, or in their manners and general culture.

In Prussia, the Hohenzollern rulers subjected a once-free peasantry to serfdom and thus vastly increased the local power of the landed aristocracy (even of its lesser ranks) in return for political submission. The Prussian nobles remained on the land and lorded it over a servile peasantry as landowners, administrators, judges, prosecutors, and police officers, thus combining personal dominance with governmental authority. In Japan, the samurai were removed from the land in the sixteenth century, while the social structure of the village community remained intact. The daimyos along with their samurai retainers became town residents and as such did not intervene in village affairs as long as they received their stipends and contributions from the villagers. This setting greatly encouraged local autonomy, albeit one combined with a strongly collectivist orientation. Under the Tokugawa Shogunate governmental controls were

---

class made up 6% of all families, and that two samples of samurai participation in the Meiji elite yield the proportions of 45 and 53% respectively. That the response of the samurai was instantaneous and disproportionately high is suggested by the fact that in the years 1863-1871 Fukuzawa's Western-oriented Keio school was attended by 40 commoners and 1289 samurai. See Johannes Hirschmeier, S.V.D., *Entrepreneurship in Meiji Japan* (Ph.D. Dissertation, Harvard University), p. 69.

[21] In 1867 payments in rice to the samurai amounted to 34.6 million yen, while in 1876 the value of yearly interest paid on a commutation basis had fallen to 11.5 million. But this decline should be compared with the fact that in 1871 the government spent 15.3 million yen or some 36% of its total budget on stipends for *han*-samurai who had become prefectural samurai. See Hirschmeier, *op. cit.*, p. 62. Note also Ito Hirobumi's telling comments that "most of the men of spirit and argument have come from among the former samurai," that these men have been deprived of their former high position in society and are, consequently, the source of unrest. Quoted in George Beckmann, *The Making of the Meiji Constitution* (Lawrence: University of Kansas Press, 1957), p. 131.

highly centralized, and responsibilities were imposed on the community as a whole. As a result the exercise of local authority by government officials tended to be relatively impersonal, in contrast to the Prussian estates with their highly personal exercise of authority. It is probable, therefore, that these two countries possess strikingly different traditions of interpersonal relations, despite their common and long-standing emphasis on status distinctions and hierarchy. For *in the sphere of local government* high social rank and governmental authority went hand in hand in Prussia, whereas in Tokugawa Japan the vast majority of samurai possessed rank but not authority.

In the military sphere the contrast is sharp also. The Tokugawa Shogunate pacified the country as a whole and sought to control their aristocratic vassals by elaborate police controls. At the same time the Shoguns protected the exclusive right of daimyos and samurai to carry a sword; this right was an index of high social rank. At first, Meiji military reforms retained this right in the new army, but eventually the right was abolished and a system of national conscription introduced a significant measure of equality through the army. In Prussia, the Hohenzollern kings also suppressed all independent military action on the part of the nobility while protecting its high social rank. But in this case supremacy was achieved by the organization of a standing army directly subordinate to the monarch. Both the high rank and the loyalty of the nobility were ensured by giving the sons of noble families exclusive access to the officer corps. High military rank in the standing army and high social rank were closely related. In the army, relations between officers and men were very harsh and tended to replicate and reinforce the harsh civilian relations between landlords and peasants, since the composition of the two groups largely overlapped. Accordingly, interpersonal relations between military ranks were a major buttress of inequality and invidious status distinctions in Germany. The individual militancy of the samurai in Tokugawa Japan contrasts sharply with this organized militarism of the Prussian nobility.

There are parallel distinctions in the field of culture and manners. The Tokugawa Shoguns required that all daimyos maintain a residence in Edo in which the daimyo or his relations by their presence at court vouchsafed for the loyalty of the absent. This *sankin-kotai* system imposed very heavy expenditures, increased still further by the conspicuous consumption through which the daimyo and his relations sought to hold their own in the competition for preferment at the Shogunal Court.[22] It would be of interest to compare the resulting refinement in etiquette with the

---

[22] Incidentally, this put a premium on a more efficient organization of the *han*, which in many instances passed into the hands of samurai officials. May this not be an instance in which "wasteful expenditures" proved to be on occasion at least a positive incentive for a more efficient administration of the *han*-domains, Veblen to the contrary nothwithstanding?

328 REINHARD BENDIX

development of polite manners at the French Court in Versailles, since both may be considered a by-product of absolutism following the decline of feudalism.[23] By contrast, the Prussian nobility was not subjected to comparable controls. The individual lord (*Gutsherr*) was complete master in his own domains, especially east of the Elbe River. As such he combined the arbitrary benevolence or punitiveness of the personal master with the authoritarianism of the government official and military commander. In the East these landlords became "experts in local tyranny" (Rosenberg) for several reasons. As colonizing territory East Germany attracted its complement of adventurers and outlaws. The serfdom of the peasantry brutalized masters and servants alike. And the masters, who stayed on the land and entertained themselves with the crude pleasures of provincial squires, lacked the polished manners and cultural refinements which in the seventeenth and eighteenth centuries were typical by-products of court life.[24] In the Prussian "garrison state" there was little room for the cultivation of manners, with the result that civilian life was "militarized" exacerbating the class and status distinctions of German society until well into the twentieth century.[25]

As a consequence of these and related differences the two aristocracies played quite different roles in the development of their countries. In Japan, the samurai took the initiative and at the beginning furnished the majority of the key figures in the economic as well as the political fields.[26] Among the samurai there was a strong antirural bias and much indignant envy of wealthy merchants, but the prejudice against materialism and money-making disappeared quickly after 1868 when development of the country became a national cause. Among the *Junkers* an antiurban bias prevailed, which was combined with a strong prejudice against merchants and commercialism. These attitudes were buttressed by the real conflicts of interest between the agrarian East and the industrial West of Germany, and by the anticommercial sentiments typical among military officers. All this did not preclude an intense interest in money-making. Max Weber observes that these landlords from East of the Elbe had become rural capitalists with aristocratic pretensions, who use their privileged social position to exact economic concessions from the government and resist

[23] Such an interpretation of the evidence from France is contained in Norbert Elias, *Über den Prozess der Zivilisation* (Basel: Haus zum Falken, 1942), two volumes.
[24] Until well into the eighteenth century many of these *Junkers* definitely preferred a military as against a bureaucratic career, because they lacked the educational background for the latter. See Rosenberg, *op. cit.*, p. 59.
[25] See Otto Büsch, *Militärsystem und Sozialleben im Alten Preussen, 1713-1807* (Vol. 7 of Veröffentlichungen der Berliner Historischen Kommission; Berlin: W. de Gruyter, 1962).
[26] See Dore, "Mobility, Equality and Individuation in Modern Japan," *passim*.

all attempts at constitutional reforms. Thus, in Germany initiative for reform came, not from the landed aristocracy but from the officials of an absolutist regime. These reforms met with determined opposition with the result that German nineteenth century history is marked by a basic cleavage between defenders of tradition and advocates of reform.

No comparable cleavage seems to have developed in Japan. As in other societies undergoing rapid change, there was considerable tension between tradition and modernity in Japan as well. But Professor Smith points out that in the absence of an aristocratic defense of the old regime there was no "radical cleavage of the two by ideology." When all parties are more or less reformist and more or less traditional, the past does not appear as a barrier to progress, but rather as an obstacle in some respects and an aid in others.[27] On the other hand, tradition and modernity appeared mutually exclusive where, as in Germany, the ideals of the French Revolution were brought into direct confrontation with "stiffly martial concepts of authority and of military virtues . . . as models for civil life in general."[28] Again, in Japan the absence of a revolutionary struggle against inequality meant that class consciousness remains relatively weak, even though status consciousness is strong. Professor Smith sees no contradiction in this, since the Japanese concern with status is relatively free of class feeling as long as higher-ups are looked on "as superior extensions of the self."[29] We have seen that this view is a typical feature of societies which take the existence of inequality for granted. Professor Smith's assessment implies, therefore, that in Japanese society inequality remains unchallenged until well into the modern era and, perhaps, is rather widely accepted still. In Germany, on the other hand, inequality becomes controversial early in the nineteenth century, with the result that status differences are challenged and class consciousness increases. To this day, interpersonal relations tend to be marked by strong feelings of class in Germany, whereas in Japan such relations seem to be characterized by an acceptance of status differences, softened by kinship simulations and an elaborate ritual of collaboration among status equals, which have no analogue in Germany as far as I am aware.

[27] Smith, "Japan's Aristocratic Revolution," p. 382.
[28] Rosenberg, *op. cit.*, p. 41.
[29] Smith, "Japan's Aristocratic Revolution," p. 382.

21   RICHARD D. SCHWARTZ AND
       JAMES C. MILLER

       Legal Evolution and
       Societal Complexity

The study of legal evolution has traditionally commended itself to
scholars in a variety of fields. To mention only a few, it has been a concern in sociology of Weber[1] and Durkheim;[2] in jurisprudence of Dicey,[3]
Holmes,[4] Pound,[5] and Llewellyn;[6] in anthropology of Maine[7] and Hoebel;[8] in legal history of Savigny[9] and Vinogradoff.[10]

"Legal Evolution and Societal Complexity," by Richard D. Schwartz and
James C. Miller, from the *American Journal of Sociology*, Vol. LXX, 1964, pp.
159-169, © 1964 by The University of Chicago; "Dynamic Inferences from
Static Data," by Stanley Udy, and "Reply," by Richard D. Schwartz, from the
American Journal of Sociology, Vol. LXX, 1965, pp. 625-628, © by The Uni-
versity of Chicago. All reprinted by permission of the authors and The University
of Chicago Press.
    [1] Max Weber, *Law in Economy and Society*, ed. Max Rheinstein (Cambridge,
Mass.: Harvard University Press, 1954). For a discussion and development of
Weber's thinking on legal evolution, see Talcott Parsons, "Evolutionary Uni-
versals in Society," *American Sociological Review*, XXIX (June 1964), 350-53.
    [2] Émile Durkheim, *The Division of Labor in Society*, trans. George Simpson
(Glencoe, Ill.: Free Press, 1947).
    [3] A. V. Dicey, *Lectures on the Relation between Law and Public Opinion in
England during the Nineteenth Century* (London: Macmillan Co., 1905).
    [4] Oliver Wendell Holmes, Jr., *The Common Law* (Boston: Little, Brown &
Co., 1881). Holmes's discussion of the place and limitations of historical analysis
provides an appropriate background for the present study. "The law embodies
the story of a nation's development through many centuries, and it cannot be
dealt with as if it contained only the axioms and corollaries of a book of
mathematics. In order to know what it is, we must know what it has been,
and what it tends to become. But the most difficult labor will be to understand
the combination of the two into new products at every stage. The substance of
the law at any given time pretty nearly corresponds, so far as it goes, with what
is then understood to be convenient; but its form and machinery, and the degree to which it is able to work out desired results depend very much on its
past" (pp. 1-2). In stressing history as providing an explanation for procedure
rather than substance, Holmes points to those aspects of legal development that
—in the present study at least—appear to follow highly uniform sequences of
change.

There are theoretical and practical reasons for this interest. Legal evolution[11] provides an opportunity to investigate the relations between law and other major aspects and institutions of society. Thus Maine explained the rise of contract in terms of the declining role of kinship as an exclusive basis of social organization, Durkheim saw restitutive sanctions replacing repressive ones as a result of the growth of the division of labor and the corresponding shift from mechanical to organic solidarity. Dicey traced the growth of statutory law-making in terms of the increasing articulateness and power of public opinion. Weber viewed the development of formal legal rationality as an expression of, and precondition for, the growth of modern capitalism.

For the most part, these writers were interested in the development of legal norms and not in the evolution of legal organization. The latter subject warrants attention for several reasons. As the mechanism through which substantive law is formulated, invoked, and administered, legal organization is of primary importance for understanding the process by which legal norms are evolved and implemented. Moreover, legal organization seems to develop with a degree of regularity that in itself invites attention and explanation. The present study suggests that elements of legal organization emerge in a sequence, such that each constitutes a necessary condition for the next. A second type of regularity appears in the relationship between changes in legal organization and other aspects of social organization, notably the division of labor.

By exploring such regularities intensively, it may be possible to learn more about the dynamics of institutional differentiation. Legal organization is a particularly promising subject from this point of view. It tends toward a unified, easily identifiable structure in any given society. Its form

5 Roscoe Pound, "Limits of Effective Legal Action," *International Journal of Ethics*, XXVII (1917), 150-65; and *Outlines of Lectures on Jurisprudence* (5th ed.; Cambridge, Mass.: Harvard University Press, 1943). See also his *Interpretations of Legal History* (London: Macmillan Co., 1930).

6 Karl N. Llewellyn, *The Common Law Tradition: Deciding Appeals* (Boston: Little, Brown & Co., 1960).

7 Sir Henry Maine, *Ancient Law* (London: J. M. Dent, 1917).

8 E. Adamson Hoebel, *The Law of Primitive Man* (Cambridge, Mass.: Harvard University Press, 1954).

9 Frederick von Savigny, *Of the Vocation of Our Age for Legislation and Jurisprudence*, trans. Abraham Hayward (London: Littlewood & Co., 1831).

10 Paul Vinogradoff, *Outlines of Historical Jurisprudence*, Vols. I and II (London: Oxford University Press, 1920-22).

11 The term "evolution" is used here in the minimal sense of a regular sequence of changes over time in a given type of unit, in this case, societies. This usage neither implies nor precludes causal links among the items in the sequence. For a discussion of diverse uses of, and reactions to, the term "evolution," see Sol Tax (ed.), *Issues in Evolution* (Chicago: University of Chicago Press, 1960).

RICHARD D. SCHWARTZ AND JAMES C. MILLER

and procedures are likely to be explicitly stated. Its central function, legitimation, promotes crossculturally recurrent instances of conflict with, and adaptation to, other institutional systems such as religion, polity, economy, and family. Before these relationships can be adequately explored, however, certain gross regularities of development should be noted and it is with these that the present paper is primarily concerned.

This article reports preliminary findings from cross-cultural research that show a rather startling consistency in the pattern of legal evolution. In a sample of fifty-one societies, compensatory damages and mediation of disputes were found in every society having specialized legal counsel. In addition, a large majority (85 per cent) of societies that develop specialized police also employ damages and mediation. These findings suggest a variety of explanations. It may be necessary, for instance, for a society to accept the principles of mediation and compensation before formalized agencies of adjudication and control can be evolved. Alternatively or concurrently, non-legal changes may explain the results. A formalized means of exchange, some degree of specialization, and writing appear almost universally to follow certain of these legal developments and to precede others. If such sequences are inevitable, they suggest theoretically interesting causative relationships and provide a possible basis for assigning priorities in stimulating the evolution of complex legal institutions in the contemporary world.

METHOD

This research employed a method used by Freeman and Winch in their analysis of societal complexity.[12] Studying a sample of forty-eight societies, they noted a Guttman-scale relationship among six items associated with the folk-urban continuum. The following items were found to fall in a single dimension ranging, the authors suggest, from simple to complex: a symbolic medium of exchange; punishment of crimes through government action; religious, educational, and government specialization; and writing.[13]

[12] Linton C. Freeman and Robert F. Winch, "Societal Complexity: An Empirical Test of a Typology of Societies," *American Journal of Sociology*, LXII (March 1957), 461-66.

[13] This ordering has not been reproduced in other studies that followed similar procedures. Freeman repeated the study on another sample and included four of the six items used in the first study. They scaled in a markedly different order, from simple to complex: government specialization, religious specialization, symbolic medium of exchange, writing. The marked change in position of the first and third items appears attributable to changes in definition for these terms (Linton C. Freeman, "An Empirical Test of Folk-Urbanism," [unpublished Ph.D. dissertation, Northwestern University, 1957], pp. 45, 49-50, 80-83). Young and Young studied all six items in a cross-cultural sample of communities, changing only the definition of punishment. Their ordering is somewhat closer

To permit the location of legal characteristics on the Freeman-Winch scale, substantially the same sample was used in this study. Three societies were dropped because of uncertainty as to date and source of description[14] or because of inadequate material on legal characteristics.[15] Six societies were added, three to cover the legally developed societies more adequately[16] and three to permit the inclusion of certáin well-described control systems.[17]

Several characteristics of a fully developed legal system were isolated for purposes of study. These included counsel, mediation, and police. These

---

to, but not identical with, that found by Freeman and Winch (*op. cit.*). From simple to complex, the items were ordered as follows: punishment, symbolic medium of exchange, governmental specialization, religious specialization, writing, educational specialization (Frank W. and Ruth C. Young, "The Sequence and Direction of Community Growth: A Cross-Cultural Generalization," *Rural Sociology*, XXVII [December 1962], 374-86, esp. 378-79).

In the present study, we will rely on the Freeman-Winch ratings and orderings, since the samples overlap so heavily. The reader should bear in mind, however, that the order is tentative and contingent upon the specific definitions used in that study.

[14] Southeastern American Negroes and ancient Hebrews.

[15] Sanpoil.

[16] Three societies—Cambodian, Indonesian, and Syrian—were selected from the Human Relations Area Files to increase the number of societies with counsel. The procedure for selection consisted of a random ordering of the societies in the Human Relations Area Files until three with counsel were located in geographically separate regions. These were then examined to determine the presence or absence of other legal characteristics. The random search eliminated the possibility of a bias in favor of societies conforming to the scale type.

The three societies were quota sampled by region to represent a randomly determined three of the following six regions: Asia, Africa, the Middle East, North America, South America, and Oceania. Purposely omitted from the sample were Europe and Russia because they were already represented in the "counsel" type in the Freeman-Winch sample. Selection from different regions was designed to avoid the problem, first noted by Francis Galton, that cross-cultural regularities might be due to diffusion rather than to functional interrelationships. For a discussion of the problem and evidence of the importance of geographical separateness in sampling, see Raoul Naroll, "Two Solutions to Galton's Problem," *Philosophy of Science*, XXVIII (1961), 15-39; Raoul Naroll and Roy G. D'Andrade, "Two Further Solutions to Galton's Problem," *American Anthropologist*, LXV (October 1963), 1053-67; and Raoul Naroll, "A Fifth Solution to Galton's Problem," *American Anthropologist*, Vol. LXVI (forthcoming).

[17] These three — Cheyenne, Comanche, and Trobrianders — were selected by James C. Miller before the hypothesis was known to him. Selection of both the Comanche and Cheyenne is subject to some criticism on the grounds that they were prone to diffusion, but this hardly seems a serious difficulty in view of the difference in their scale positions. At all events, the coefficients of reproducibility and scalability would not be seriously lowered by eliminating one of the two.

three characteristics, which will constitute the focus of the present paper,[18] are defined as follows:

counsel: regular use of specialized non-kin advocates in the settlement of disputes

mediation: regular use of non-kin third party intervention in dispute settlement

police: specialized armed force used partially or wholly for norm enforcement.

These three items, all referring to specialized roles relevant to dispute resolution, were found to fall in a near-perfect Guttman scale. Before the central findings are described and discussed, several methodological limitations should be noted.

First, despite efforts by Murdock[19] and others, no wholly satisfactory method has been devised for obtaining a representative sample of the world's societies. Since the universe of separate societies has not been adequately defined, much less enumerated, the representativeness of the sample cannot be ascertained. Nevertheless, an effort has been made to include societies drawn from the major culture areas and from diverse stages of technological development.

Second, societies have been selected in terms of the availability of adequate ethnographic reports. As a result, a bias may have entered the sample through the selection of societies that were particularly accessible — and hospitable — to anthropological observers. Such societies may differ in their patterns of development from societies that have been less well studied.

Third, despite the selection of relatively well-studied societies, the quality of reports varies widely. Like the preceding limitations, this problem is common to all cross-cultural comparisons. The difficulty is mitigated, however, by the fact that the results of this study are positive. The effect of poor reporting should generally be to randomize the apparent occurrence of the variables studied. Where systematic patterns of relationship emerge, as they do in the present research, it would seem to indicate considerable accuracy in the original reports.[20]

[18] The original study also included damages, imprisonment, and execution. These were dropped from the present analysis, even though this unfortunately limited the scale to three items, to permit focus on statuses rather than sanction. Data on damages will be introduced, however, where relevant to the discussion of restitution.

[19] George Peter Murdock, "World Ethnographic Sample," *American Anthropologist*, LIX (August 1957), 664-87.

[20] On this point see Donald T. Campbell, "The Mutual Methodological Relevance of Anthropology and Psychology," in Francis L. K. Hsu (ed.), *Psychological Anthropology* (Homewood, Ill.: Dorsey Press, 1961), p. 347. This

Fourth, this study deals with characteristics whose presence or absence can be determined with relative accuracy. In so doing, it may neglect elements of fundamental importance to the basic inquiry. Thus no effort is made to observe the presence of such important phenomena as respect for law, the use of generalized norms, and the pervasiveness of deviance-induced disturbance. Although all of these should be included in a comprehensive theory of legal evolution, they are omitted here in the interest of observational reliability.[21]

Fifth, the Guttman scale is here pressed into service beyond that for which it was developed. Originally conceived as a technique for the isolation of uni-dimensional attitudes, it has also been used as a means of

---

inference should be treated with caution, however, in light of Raoul Naroll's observation that systematic observer bias can lead to spurious correlations (*Data Quality Control: A New Research Technique* [New York: Free Press of Glencoe, 1962]).

[21] Determination of the presence of a characteristic was made after a detailed search by Miller of the materials on each society in the Human Relations Area Files. His search began with a thorough reading for all societies of the material filed under category 18, "total culture." (All categories used are described in detail in George P. Murdock *et al., Outline of Cultural Materials* [4th rev. ed.; New Haven, Conn.: Human Relations Area Files, 1961].) This was followed by a search of the annotated bibliography (category 111) to locate any works specifically dealing with legal or dispute settling processes. When found, works of this kind were examined in detail. In addition, materials filed under the following categories were read: community structure (621), headmen (622), councils (623), police (625), informal in-group justice (627), inter-community relations (628), territorial hierarchy (631), legal norms (671), liability (672), offenses and sanctions (68), litigation (691), judicial authority (692), legal and judicial personnel (693), initiation of judicial proceedings (694), trial procedure (695), execution of justice (696), prisons and jails (697), and special courts (698). If this search did not reveal the presence of the practice or status under investigation, it was assumed absent. The principal sources relied on for these determinations are given in a mimeographed bibliography which will be supplied by the authors on request.

A reliability check on Miller's judgments was provided by Robert C. Scholl, to whom the writers are indebted. Working independently and without knowledge of the hypotheses, Scholl examined a randomly selected third of the total sample. His judgments agreed with those of Miller 88 per cent, disagreed 4 per cent, and he was unable to reach conclusions on 8 per cent of the items. If the inconclusive judgments are excluded, the reliability reaches the remarkable level of 96 per cent.

The use of a single person to check reliability falls short of the desired standard. In a more detailed and extensive projected study of the relationships reported here, we plan to use a set of three independent naïve judges. For discussion of the problems involved in judging cross-cultural materials see John W. M. Whiting and Irvin L. Child, *Child Training and Personality* (New Haven, Conn.: Yale University Press, 1953), pp. 39-62; and Guy E. Swanson, *The Birth of the Gods* (Ann Arbor: Michigan University Press, 1960), pp. 32-54.

studying the interrelationship of behavior patterns. It should be particularly valuable, however, in testing hypotheses concerning developmental
sequences, whether in individuals or in societies.[22] Thus, if we hypothesize
that A must precede B, supporting data should show three scale types:
neither A nor B, A but not B, and A and B. All instances of B occurring
without A represent errors which lower the reproducibility of the scale
and, by the same token, throw doubt in measurable degree on the developmental hypothesis.[23] Although the occurrence of developmental sequences
ultimately requires verification by the observation of historic changes in
given units, substantiating evidence can be derived from the comparative
study of units at varying stages of development. The Guttman scale seems
an appropriate quantitative instrument for this purpose.

FINDINGS

In the fifty-one societies studied, as indicated in Table 1, four scale types
emerged. Eleven societies showed none of the three characteristics; eighteen had only mediation and police; and seven had mediation, police, and

[22] The use of the Guttman scale is extensively treated by Robert L. Carneiro
in "Scale Analysis as an Instrument for the Study of Cultural Evolution,"
Southwestern Journal of Anthropology, XVIII (1962), 149-69. In a sophisticated
critique of the Carneiro paper, Ward L. Goodenough suggests that quasi-scales
may be needed for charting general evolutionary trends and for treating the
traits that develop and then fail to persist because they are superseded by functional equivalents ("Some Applications of Guttman Scale Analysis to Ethnography and Culture Theory," *Southwestern Journal of Anthropology*, XIX
[Autumn 1963], 235-50). While the quasi-scale is a desirable instrument for
analyzing supersedence, Goodenough appears unduly pessimistic about the
possible occurrence of approximately perfect scales, see p. 246. Studies that obtained such scales, in addition to the one reported here, include Freeman and
Winch, *op. cit.*; Stanley H. Udy, "'Bureaucratic' Elements in Organizations:
Some Research Findings," *American Sociological Review*, XXII (1958), 415-
18; Frank W. and Ruth C. Young, "Social Integration and Change in Twenty-
four Mexican Villages," *Economic Development and Cultural Change*, VIII
(July 1960), 366-77; and Robert L. Carneiro and Stephen L. Tobias, "The
Application of Scale Analysis to the Study of Cultural Evolution," *Transactions
of the New York Academy of Sciences*, Series II, XXVI (1963), 196-207.
    The suggestion that Guttman scales could be used for discovering and test-
ing temporal sequences was made earlier by Norman G. Hawkins and Joan
K. Jackson in "Scale Analysis and the Prediction of Life Processes," *American
Sociological Review*, XXII (1957), 579-81. Their proposal referred, however, to
individuals rather than societies.
[23] The developmental inference does not preclude the possibility of reversal
of the usual sequence. It merely indicates which item will be added if any
is acquired. Cf. S. N. Eisenstadt, "Social Change, Differentiation and Evolution," *American Sociological Review*, XXIX (June 1964), 378-81. The finding
of a scale also does not rule out the possibility that two items may sometimes
occur simultaneously, although the existence of all possible scale types indicates
that no two items invariably occur simultaneously and that when they occur
separately one regularly precedes the other.

specialized counsel. Two societies departed from these patterns: the Crow and the Thonga had police, but showed no evidence of mediation. While these deviant cases merit detailed study, they reduce the reproducibility of the scale by less than 2 per cent, leaving the coefficient at the extraordinarily high level of better than .98.[24] Each characteristic of legal organization may now be discussed in terms of the sociolegal conditions in which it is found.

MEDIATION

Societies that lack mediation, constituting less than a third of the entire sample, appear to be the simplest societies. None of them has writing or any substantial degree of specialization.[25] Only three of the thirteen (Yurok, Kababish, and Thonga) use money, whereas almost three-fourths of the societies with mediation have a symbolic means of exchange. We can only speculate at present on the reasons why mediation is absent in these societies. Data on size, using Naroll's definition of the social unit,[26] indicate that the maximum community size of societies without mediation is substantially smaller than that of societies with mediation.[27] Because of their small size, mediationless societies may have fewer disputes and thus have less opportunity to evolve regularized patterns of dispute settlement. Moreover, smaller societies may be better able to develop

---

[24] This coefficient of reproducibility far exceeds the .90 level suggested by Guttman as an "efficient approximation . . . of perfect scales" (Samuel Stouffer [ed.], *Measurement and Prediction* [Princeton, N.J.: Princeton University Press, 1950]). The coefficient of scalability, designed by Menzel to take account of extremeness in the distribution of items and individuals, far exceeds the .65 level that he generated from a scalability analysis of Guttman's American Soldier data. Herbert A. Menzel, "A New Coefficient for Scalogram Analysis," *Public Opinion Quarterly*, XVII (Summer 1953), 268-80, esp. 276. The problem of determining goodness of fit for the Guttman scale has still not been satisfactorily resolved (see W. S. Torgerson, *Theory and Methods of Scaling* [New York: John Wiley & Sons, 1958], esp. p. 324). A method utilizing χ^2 to test the hypothesis that observed scale frequencies deviate from a rectangular distribution no more than would be expected by chance is suggested by Karl F. Schuessler, "A Note on Statistical Significance of Scalogram," *Sociometry*, XXIV (September 1961), 312-18. Applied to these data, Schuessler's Test II permits the rejection of the chance hypothesis at the .001 level. $\chi^2 = 60.985 \ (7df)$.

[25] Statements of this type are based on the ratings in the Freeman-Winch study, as noted in n. 13 above. For societies that did not appear in their sample, we have made our own ratings on the basis of their definitions.

[26] Raoul Naroll, "A Preliminary Index of Social Development," *American Anthropologist*, LVIII (August 1956), 687-720.

[27] Data were obtained for thirty-nine of the fifty-one societies in the sample on the size of their largest settlement. Societies with mediation have a median largest settlement size of 1,000, while those without mediation have a median of 346. Even eliminating the societies with developed cities, the median largest settlement size remains above 500 for societies with mediation.

RICHARD D. SCHWARTZ AND JAMES C. MILLER

TABLE 1. SCALE OF LEGAL CHARACTERISTICS

Society	Counsel	Police	Mediation	Errors	Legal Scale Type	Freeman-Winch Scale Type
Cambodians	x	x	x	. . .	3	*
Czechs	x	x	x	. . .	3	6
Elizabethan English	x	x	x	. . .	3	6
Imperial Romans	x	x	x	. . .	3	6
Indonesians	x	x	x	. . .	3	*
Syrians	x	x	x	. . .	3	*
Ukrainians	x	x	x	. . .	3	6
Ashanti	. . .	x	x	. . .	2	5
Cheyenne	. . .	x	x	. . .	2	*
Creek	. . .	x	x	. . .	2	5
Cuna	. . .	x	x	. . .	2	4
Crow	. . .	x	. . .	1	2	0
Hopi	. . .	x	x	. . .	2	5
Iranians	. . .	x	x	. . .	2	6
Koreans	. . .	x	x	. . .	2	6
Lapps	. . .	x	x	. . .	2	6
Maori	. . .	x	x	. . .	2	4
Riffians	. . .	x	x	. . .	2	6
Thonga	. . .	x	. . .	1	2	2
Vietnamese	. . .	x	x	. . .	2	6
Andamanese	. . .	. . .	x	. . .	1	0
Azande	. . .	. . .	x	. . .	1	0
Balinese	. . .	. . .	x	. . .	1	4
Cayapa	. . .	. . .	x	. . .	1	2
Chagga	. . .	. . .	x	. . .	1	4
Formosan aborigines	. . .	. . .	x	. . .	1	0
Hottentot	. . .	. . .	x	. . .	1	0
Ifugao	. . .	. . .	x	. . .	1	0
Lakher	. . .	. . .	x	. . .	1	2
Lepcha	. . .	. . .	x	. . .	1	3
Menomini	. . .	. . .	x	. . .	1	0
Mbundu	. . .	. . .	x	. . .	1	3
Navaho	. . .	. . .	x	. . .	1	5
Ossett	. . .	. . .	x	. . .	1	1
Siwans	. . .	. . .	x	. . .	1	1
Trobrianders	. . .	. . .	x	. . .	1	*
Tupinamba	. . .	. . .	x	. . .	1	0
Venda	. . .	. . .	x	. . .	1	5
Woleaians	. . .	. . .	x	. . .	1	0
Yakut	. . .	. . .	x	. . .	1	1
Aranda	. . .	. . .	. . .	. . .	0	0
Buka	. . .	. . .	. . .	. . .	0	0
Chukchee	. . .	. . .	. . .	. . .	0	0
Comanche	. . .	. . .	. . .	. . .	0	*
Copper Eskimo	. . .	. . .	. . .	. . .	0	0
Jivaro	. . .	. . .	. . .	. . .	0	0
Kababish	. . .	. . .	. . .	. . .	0	1
Kazak	. . .	. . .	. . .	. . .	0	0
Siriono	. . .	. . .	. . .	. . .	0	0
Yaruro	. . .	. . .	. . .	. . .	0	0
Yurok	. . .	. . .	. . .	. . .	0	1

* Not included in Freeman-Winch sample.
Coefficient of reproducibility = $1 - 2/153$ = .987; coefficient of scalability = $1 - 2/153-120$ = .94; Kendall's tau = +.68.

mores and informal controls which tend to prevent the occurrence of disputes. Also, the usually desperate struggle for existence of such societies may strengthen the common goal of survival and thus produce a lessening of intragroup hostility.

The lack of money and substantial property may also help to explain the absence of mediation in these societies. There is much evidence to support the hypothesis that property provides something to quarrel about. In addition, it seems to provide something to mediate with as well. Where private property is extremely limited, one would be less likely to find a concept of damages, that is, property payments in lieu of other sanctions. The development of a concept of damages should greatly increase the range of alternative settlements. This in turn might be expected to create a place for the mediator as a person charged with locating a settlement point satisfactory to the parties and the society.

This hypothesis derives support from the data in Table 2. The concept of damages occurs in all but four of the thirty-eight societies that have mediation and thus appears to be virtually a precondition for mediation. It should be noted, however, that damages are also found in several (seven of thirteen) of the societies that lack mediation. The relationship that emerges is one of damages as a necessary but not sufficient condition for mediation. At present it is impossible to ascertain whether the absence of mediation in societies having the damage concept results from a simple time lag or whether some other factor, not considered in this study, distinguishes these societies from those that have developed mediation.

TABLE 2. DAMAGES IN RELATION TO LEGAL FUNCTIONARIES

	No Mediation	Mediation Only	Mediation and Police	Mediation, Police, and Counsel	Total
Damages	7	17	10	7	41
No damages	6[a]	3	1	0	10
Total	13	20	11	7	51

[a] Includes Thonga, who have neither mediation nor damages, but have police.

POLICE

Twenty societies in the sample had police — that is, a specialized armed force available for norm enforcement. As noted, all of these but the Crow and Thonga had the concept of damages and some kind of mediation as well. Nevertheless, the occurrence of twenty societies with mediation but without police makes it clear that mediation is not inevitably accompanied by the systematic enforcement of decisions. The separability of these two characteristics is graphically illustrated in ethnographic reports. A striking

340   RICHARD D. SCHWARTZ AND JAMES C. MILLER

instance is found among the Albanian tribesmen whose elaborately developed code for settling disputes, Lek's Kanun, was used for centuries as a basis for mediation. But in the absence of mutual agreements by the disputants, feuds often began immediately after adjudication and continued unhampered by any constituted police.[28]

From the data it is possible to determine some of the characteristics of societies that develop police. Eighteen of the twenty in our sample are economically advanced enough to use money. They also have a substantial degree of specialization, with full-time priests and teachers found in all but three (Cheyenne, Thonga, and Crow), and full-time governmental officials, not mere relatives of the chief, present in all but four (Cuna, Maori, Thonga, and Crow).

Superficially at least, these findings seem directly contradictory to Durkheim's major thesis in *The Division of Labor in Society*. He hypothesized that penal law — the effort of the organized society to punish offenses against itself — occurs in societies with the simplest division of labor. As indicated, however, our data show that police are found only in association with a substantial degree of division of labor. Even the practice of governmental punishment for wrongs against the society (as noted by Freeman and Winch) does not appear in simpler societies. By contrast, restitutive sanctions — damages and mediation — which Durkheim believed to be associated with an increasing division of labor, are found in many societies that lack even rudimentary specialization. Thus Durkheim's hypothesis seems the reverse of the empirical situation in the range of societies studied here.[29]

[28] Margaret Hasluck, *The Unwritten Law in Albania* (Cambridge: Cambridge University Press, 1954).

[29] A basic difficulty in testing Durkheim's thesis arises from his manner of formulating it. His principal interest, as we understand it, was to show the relationship between division of labor and type of sanction (using type of solidarity as the intervening variable). However, in distinguishing systems of law, he added the criterion of organization. The difficulty is that he was very broad in his criterion of organization required for penal law, but quite narrow in describing the kind of organization needed for non-penal law. For the former, the "assembly of the whole people" sufficed (*op. cit.*, p. 76); for the latter, on the other hand, he suggested the following criteria: "restitutive law creates organs which are more and more specialized: consular tribunals, councils of arbitration, administrative tribunals of every sort. Even in its most general part, that which pertains to civil law, it is exercised only through particular functionaries: magistrates, lawyers, etc., who have become apt in this role because of very special training" (p. 113). In thus suggesting that restitutive law exists only with highly complex organizational forms, Durkheim virtually insured that his thesis would be proven — that restitutive law would be found only in complex societies.

Such a "proof," however, would miss the major point of his argument. In testing the main hypothesis it would seem preferable, therefore, to specify a common and minimal organizational criterion, such as public support. Then

COUNSEL

Seven societies in the sample employ specialized advocates in the settlement of disputes. As noted, all of these societies also use mediation. There
are, however, another thirty-one societies that have mediation but do not
employ specialized counsel. It is a striking feature of the data that damages
and mediation are characteristic of the simplest (as well as the most complex) societies, while legal counsel are found only in the most complex.
The societies with counsel also have, without exception, not only damages, mediation, and police but, in addition, all of the complexity characteristics identified by Freeman and Winch.

It is not surprising that mediation is not universally associated with
counsel. In many mediation systems the parties are expected to speak
for themselves. The mediator tends to perform a variety of functions,
questioning disputants as well as deciding on the facts and interpreting
the law. Such a system is found even in complex societies, such as Imperial China. There the prefect acted as counsel, judge, and jury, using a
whip to wring the truth from the parties who were assumed a priori to be
lying.[30] To serve as counsel in that setting would have been painful as
well as superfluous. Even where specialized counsel emerge, their role
tends to be ambiguous. In ancient Greece, for instance, counsel acted principally as advisors on strategy. Upon appearance in court they sought to
conceal the fact that they were specialists in legal matters, presenting
themselves merely as friends of the parties or even on occasion assuming
the identity of the parties themselves.[31]

At all events, lawyers are here found only in quite urbanized societies,
all of which are based upon fully developed agricultural economies. The
data suggest at least two possible combinations. First, all of the sample
societies with counsel have a substantial division of labor, including
priests, teachers, police, and government officials. This implies an economic base strong enough to support a variety of secondary and tertiary
occupations as well as an understanding of the advantages of specializa-

---

the key question might be phrased: Is there a tendency toward restitutive rather
than repressive sanctions which develops as an increasing function of the
division of labor? Although our present data are not conclusive, the finding
of damages and mediation in societies with minimal division of labor implies
a negative answer. This suggests that the restitutive principle is not contingent
on social heterogeneity or that heterogeneity is not contingent on the division
of labor.

[30] Sybille van der Sprenkel, *Legal Institutions in Manchu China* (London:
Athlone Press, 1962). See also Ch'ü T'ung-tsu, *Law and Society in Traditional
China* (Vancouver, B.C.: Institute of Pacific Relations, 1961).

[31] A. H. Chroust, "The Legal Profession in Ancient Athens," *Notre Dame
Law Review*, XXIX (Spring 1954), 339-89.

tion. Eleven societies in the sample, however, have all of these specialized statuses but lack specialized counsel. What distinguishes the societies that develop counsel? Literacy would seem to be an important factor. Only five of the twelve literate societies in the sample do not have counsel. Writing, of course, makes possible the formulation of a legal code with its advantages of forewarning the violator and promoting uniformity in judicial administration. The need to interpret a legal code provides a niche for specialized counsel, especially where a substantial segment of the population is illiterate.[32]

CONCLUSIONS

These data, taken as a whole, lend support to the belief that an evolutionary sequence occurs in the development of legal institutions. Alternative interpretations are, to be sure, not precluded. The scale analysis might fail to discern short-lived occurrences of items. For instance, counsel might regularly develop as a variation in simple societies even before police, only to drop out rapidly enough so that the sample picks up no such instances. Even though this is a possibility in principle, no cases of this kind have come to the authors' attention.

Another and more realistic possibility is that the sequence noted in this sample does not occur in societies in a state of rapid transition. Developing

[32] Throughout the discussion, two sets of explanatory factors have been utilized. The observed pattern could be due to an internal process inherent in legal control systems, or it could be dependent upon the emergence of urban characteristics. It does seem clear, however, that the legal developments coincide to a considerable extent with increased "urbanism" as measured by Freeman and Winch. Evidence for this assertion is to be found in the correlation between the Freeman-Winch data and the legal scale types discerned. For the forty-five societies appearing in both samples, the rank correlation coefficient (Kendall's tau) between positions on the legal and urbanism scales is + .68. While this coefficient suggests a close relationship between the two processes, it does not justify the assertion that legal evolution is wholly determined by increasing urbanism. A scatter diagram of the interrelationship reveals that legal characteristics tend to straddle the regression line for five of the seven folk-urban scale positions, omitting only scale types 2 (punishment) and 3 (religious specialization). This suggests that some other factor might emerge upon further analysis that would explain why roughly half of the societies at each stage of urbanism appear to have gone on to the next stage of legal evolution while the others lag behind. A promising candidate for such a factor is the one located by Gouldner and Peterson in their cross-cultural factor analysis of Simmons' data and described by them as "Apollonianism" or "Norm-sending" (Alvin W. Gouldner and Richard A. Peterson, *Technology and the Moral Order* [Indianapolis: Bobbs-Merrill Co., 1962], pp. 30-53).

To test whether the legal sequence has a "dynamic of its own," it would seem necessary to examine the growth of legal systems independent of folk-urban changes, as in subsystems or in societies where the process of urbanization has already occurred. The data covered here do not permit such a test.

societies undergoing intensive cultural contact might provide an economic and social basis for specialized lawyers, even in the absence of police or dispute mediation. Until such societies are included in the sample, these findings must be limited to relatively isolated, slowly changing societies.

The study also raises but does not answer the questions concerning the evolution of an international legal order. It would be foolhardy to generalize from the primitive world directly to the international scene and to assume that the same-sequences must occur here as there. There is no certainty that subtribal units can be analogized to nations, because the latter tend to be so much more powerful, independent, and relatively deficient in common culture and interests. In other ways, the individual nations are farther along the path of legal development than subtribal units because all of them have their own domestic systems of mediation, police, and counsel. This state of affairs might well provide a basis for short-circuiting an evolutionary tendency operative in primitive societies. Then too, the emergent world order appears to lack the incentive of common interest against a hostile environment that gave primitive societies a motive for legal control. Even though the survival value of a legal system may be fully as great for today's world as for primitive societies, the existence of multiple units in the latter case permitted selection for survival of those societies that had developed the adaptive characteristic. The same principle cannot be expected to operate where the existence of "one world" permits no opportunity for variation and consequent selection.

Nonetheless, it is worth speculating that some of the same forces may operate in both situations.[33] We have seen that damages and mediation almost always precede police in the primitive world. This sequence could result from the need to build certain cultural foundations in the community before a central regime of control, as reflected in a police force, can develop. Hypothetically, this cultural foundation might include a determination to avoid disputes, an appreciation of the value of third-party intervention, and the development of a set of norms both for preventive purposes and as a basis for allocating blame and punishment when disputes arise. Compensation by damages and the use of mediators might well contribute to the development of such a cultural foundation, as well as reflecting its growth. If so, their occurrence prior to specialized police would be understandable. This raises the question as to whether the same kind of cultural foundation is not a necessary condition for the establishment of an effective world police force and whether, in the in-

[33] For an interesting attempt to develop a general theory of legal control, applicable both to discrete societies and to the international order, see Kenneth S. Carlston, *Law and Organization in World Society* (Urbana: University of Illinois Press, 1962).

terest of that objective, it might not be appropriate to stress the principles of compensatory damages and mediation as preconditions for the growth of a world rule of law.

STANLEY UDY

Dynamic Inferences from Static Data

The paper "Legal Evolution and Societal Complexity" by Richard D. Schwartz and James C. Miller employs a method which has become increasingly commonplace in cross-cultural analysis, and raises what I think is an interesting question; namely: What conclusions, if any, can one draw regarding evolution or development through time by inspecting a Guttman scale constructed from cross-sectional static data? Schwartz and Miller evidently assume, as I did in an article cited by them[1] . . . that the sequence of appearance of the items in the scale can validly be interpreted as denoting a developmental or evolutionary sequence. To be sure, Schwartz and Miller occasionally enter some demurrers in this regard, even to the point of briefly proposing and rejecting an alternative interpretation at one juncture. Furthermore, it is only fair to point out that in their footnotes, they allude to some of the problems commented upon here. Nevertheless, their basic position is quite clear; they do not really seriously consider that the method they use is basically affected by these problems, and it is evident that their occasional apparent ambivalence on this score was not allowed to have any effect on their conclusions. For example, on page 114 they state: "We have seen that damages and mediation almost always *precede* police in the primitive world" (italics added).

I find myself in the rather awkward position of now objecting to this method, despite the fact that I used it myself some years back in the article cited above, and did so without exhibiting any disquietude or ambivalence whatsoever. But it would appear that this procedure is, at best, of highly dubious merit. The essential difficulty lies in the inference of dynamic conclusions from static data. It does not seem inconceivable that under certain rather highly restrictive conditions this could be done

[1] Stanley H Udy, " 'Bureaucratic' Elements in Organizations: Some Research Findings," *American Sociological Review*, XXII (1958), 415-18. A later article, "Administrative Rationality, Social Setting, and Organizational Development," *American Journal of Sociology*, LXVIII (1962), 299-308, sought to correct the earlier error and substitute a more appropriate interpretation.

from a Guttman scale, but the problem is much more complex than has often been assumed. So far as I am aware the logic of such a process has never been systematically explored and developed *in abstracto*; the sources cited by Schwartz and Miller either simply employ the method uncritically in an empirical investigation or are concerned with problems of its immediate application other than those deriving from its basic logical properties. Nevertheless, despite the absence of such an exploration, one can at least hazard some suggestions as to the conditions under which the order of appearance of items in a Guttman scale would reflect a developmental or evolutionary sequence. Even the most casual efforts in this direction are sufficient to cast serious doubts on the validity of this method under most ordinary research circumstances. For example, one crucial condition would seem to be the absence of simultaneous or nearly simultaneous development of the characteristics in question. For if such characteristics do develop simultaneously — or so nearly simultaneously that a cross-sectional sample would be unlikely to yield any cases in the process of development — the researcher cannot exclude the possibilities that (1) the scale types represent qualitatively different types of units which in fact develop independently of one another; (2) more complex types develop first and subsequently drop some characteristics; or (3) some combination of the above occurs, together and/or singly, or together with some development congruent with the scale pattern.

Therefore, unless one can realistically assume this condition of "non-simultaneity," one is faced with a situation wherein any developmental sequence whatsoever is consistent with any scale pattern at all.[2] Although, as indicated earlier, Schwartz and Miller are not entirely unaware of this problem, they certainly do not seem to take it very seriously. At no point do they present any data or theoretical argument in support of the implied contention that their material meets any conditions essential to the argument they make from it. Perhaps it does, but in view of the rather highly restrictive nature of at least one necessary assumption, the burden of proof would seem appropriately to fall on them. "Alternative interpretations" involving simultaneous or nearly simultaneous development of traits with subsequent dropping of some of the traits are . . . possibilities which cannot be dismissed a priori as merely farfetched. For example, I had er-

---

[2] Perhaps not quite. It is conceivable that a method might be devised whereby developmental sequences could, under certain conditions admitting of at least some simultaneous development, be inferred not by inspecting the order of items in the scale but by analyzing the pattern of errors. However, the exact procedure which would have to be followed, and the necessary assumptions, are by no means obvious in the absence of more extensive exploration of the formal properties of the situation. It remains clear, however, that in the absence of the condition of non-simultaneity, the method followed by Schwartz and Miller is not appropriate.

roneously assumed[3] in the article previously cited that a scale expressing different degrees of bureaucratic complexity indicated a developmental sequence. The scale had been developed from cross-sectional, static data. However, dynamic historical data from voluntary associations suggested subsequently that the actual developmental sequence might well be virtually the reverse of the scale pattern: a more or less effective way of infusing a voluntary association with some modicum of rational bureaucratic administration is to start with more bureaucratic complexity than is really technically necessary to its task with the prospect that certain of the most complex characteristics will subsequently drop out.[4]

I do not mean to insist that a parallel situation necessarily obtains with the Schwartz-Miller data, but merely to point out that there is no reason to believe that it does not. On the contrary, it seems quite reasonable to presume that, at least under conditions of centralized authority, several characteristics of a legal system would be quite likely to be promulgated at once. To be sure, Miller and Schwartz indicate that no cases involving sequences different from the one they presume have come to their attention. But since they present no dynamic historical data, it would appear that in a very real sense no cases involving the sequence they do presume have come to their attention either. We are left with the fact that, in the absence of at least an assumption of non-simultaneity, which assumption seems highly questionable in the present context, no inferences concerning developmental sequences can be made without recourse to dynamic historical data. Moreover, a thorough exploration of the matter might reveal that further assumptions are necessary as well.

Are we to conclude that construction of scales such as that of Schwartz and Miller is a useless exercise? I think not. It would seem quite appropriate to employ such scales in the analysis of requisite, as opposed to prerequisite, structures. Thus if one assumes that all of the societies studied are basically alike, and that no structural substitutions are possible, one can, for example, infer from the Schwartz-Miller data that societies possessing police but not mediation are unstable, as would be societies with counsel but not police and/or mediation, and so forth. From this point of view one can then develop hypotheses regarding differential problems involved in various specified developmental sequences. But data of an altogether different order are necessary to discover which sequences actually occur.

---

[3] See my " 'Bureaucratic' Elements . . . ," op. cit.

[4] F. S. Chapin and J. Tsouderos, "Formalization Observed in Ten Voluntary Associations," Social Forces, XXXIII (1955), 306-9; and their "The Formalization Process in Voluntary Associations," Social Forces, XXXIV (1956), 342-44; A. Meister, "Démocratie et participation dans les associations volontaires," Sociologie du Travail, III (1961), 236-52.

It has not been my purpose here particularly to castigate Schwartz and Miller, who have written an article which I found to be very interesting and stimulating, and which contains an error that I too was guilty of committing. Neither has it been my purpose to present a definitive solution to the problem, other than to suggest that if one is found, it may be extremely difficult to apply in practice. Rather, my intent has been to call general attention to a difficulty which I think is an important one and which came forcibly to my attention since I was caught in it myself.

RICHARD D. SCHWARTZ

Reply

I am grateful to Stanley Udy for his comments on the Schwartz-Miller paper. He is quite right in calling for a systematic exploration of the method. Nevertheless, I think that the method will stand up under close scrutiny. As a first step toward such an examination, let me spell out some of the assumptions which underlay the work.

Our scale analysis of cross-cultural data was aimed at discovering the sequence in which legal roles would be added if they were acquired one at a time. In principle, the scale might serve equally well to predict which item or items would be dropped if change were in the opposite direction, toward a less complex legal system. While we recognized this as a possibility (p. 111, n. 23), we assumed that the usual sequence of change would move in the direction of greater rather than lesser complexity. The findings of archeology and culture history lend plausibility to this assumption.[1]

In facing the problem of simultaneity, we took a conservative view. Admitting the possibility that two (it should have been two or more) items "might sometimes occur simultaneously," we noted that the finding of all possible scale types indicated that no two items invariably did so. From this fact, we inferred only that "when they occur separately, one

[1] An outstanding authority for this statement is Ralph E. Turner, *The Great Cultural Traditions* (2 vols.; New York: McGraw-Hill Book Co., 1941). A similar picture emerges from the separated reports and summary chapter in Robert J. Braidwood and Malcolm M. Willey (eds.), *Courses toward Urban Life* (Chicago: Aldine Publishing Co., 1962). Cf. also V. Gordon Childe, *Man Makes Himself* (New York: New American Library, 1951), and *What Happened in History* (rev. ed.; New York: Penguin Books, 1954), as well as Julian H. Steward, *Theory of Culture Change* (Urbana: University of Illinois Press, 1955).

regularly precedes the other." The process of reasoning may be schema-
tized in the following way. For each of the societies with items A and B
we asked which of these items did *that* society have, at an earlier point
in time, when and if it did not have both. In the absence of historical
data, we had to infer the answer from those known societies which had A
or B. Admitting that the A and B society might earlier have had neither,
we asserted that, if it had one or the other, the item it had was in all
probability A. This seemed likely, since all of the cases which we found
with A or B had A and not B. What reason was there to suppose that such
societies, currently having characteristics A and B, had earlier been different from current societies with one of the two items? If there were societies which had B but not A, they escaped our attention. This might
have occurred because of the limitations of our sample, but that is surely
not a problem unique to this method. It might have occurred because
societies with B but not A are in an unstable state, maintaining that combination for a limited time before dropping B or acquiring A. The short
duration of B without A might explain our failure to note any such instances. It would also suggest, however, that A, if not a temporal predecessor of B, is at least a requisite needed for the maintenance of B, but this
would hardly alter the basic evolutionary picture presented.

I agree with Udy that it would help confirm our developmental inference, and help test the "requisite" rival hypothesis, if we had historical
data showing the diachronic development of these roles in given societies.
The absence of such data for the types of societies studied here has long
been lamented by anthropologists. The history we have amounts, in Scott
Greer's phrase, to "a few scattered postage stamps in a big empty
album." I would welcome a test of our hypothesis against such data,
but I wonder whether, considering the paucity and bias of available historical materials, inferences drawn from them would be nearly as trust-
worthy as ours. If such information convincingly disconfirms our hypothesis, fine. Should not the burden of proof lie on those who believe that it
might?

VII

Methods

22   GABRIEL ALMOND and SIDNEY VERBA

Some Methodological Problems in
Cross-National Research

The cross-national survey faces all the problems of the national survey —
problems of conceptualization, sampling, interview design, interviewer
training, and so forth. There is, however, one major difference. In the
cross-national survey all these problems, with the possible exception of
devising the questionnaire, are multiplied by the number of nations
studied: in this case five samples were drawn, the no-response problem had
to be faced five times, five interviewing staffs had to be trained, and so

From *The Civic Culture: Political Attitudes and Democracy in Five Nations*,
by Gabriel Almond and Sidney Verba (Princeton: Princeton University Press,
1963); pp. 56-72. Reprinted with permission of the authors and Princeton University Press.

on. In effect, then, we are presenting the results of five simultaneous surveys.*

But this in itself would introduce no new problems over ordinary single-nation survey research if the five surveys were treated and analyzed independently. The new and intriguing problems begin when one attempts to treat the five surveys as comparable, and to concentrate, not on individual nations, but on comparisons across nations. In most cases, however, even these problems are not different in *kind* from those encountered in systematic research in a single nation: they are the same difficulties, only much more so. For example, one problem in cross-national research is the possible lack of standardization in the interview situation. Attitudes toward interviewing may vary from one nation to another: in some nations it may be better known than in others, or the relationship between the interviewer and the respondent may not be uniform in all nations. And these differences may act to lower the comparability of the interviews. This is a serious problem, but is no different in kind from the problem of standardization within individual nations. Just as the "Italian" interview situation may differ from the "British," so may interviews with upper-class respondents differ from those with respondents of lower status within the same nation; likewise, interviews may differ between regions of the same nation. Even the most striking problem in cross-national research, that of the use of more than one language, resembles in kind the problem of regional dialect or of differences in the uses of words among the strata of one society.

But though the problems differ more often in degree than in kind, the difference in degree is so great as to make it worthwhile to look more closely at some of these problems. In fact, one possible methodological advantage of the cross-national survey is that many of the problems that can be ignored when one is dealing with a single nation must now be faced explicitly. If the meaning of questions varies among the geographical regions or the social strata of a nation, this may receive little consideration; but if one must write an equivalent interview schedule in English, Italian, German, and Spanish, such problems must be carefully considered.

THE PROBLEM OF EQUIVALENCE

The two broad problems in comparative research are the standardization of the interview situation and the interpretation of the data gathered through the interviews.

The interview carried on with each of the five thousand respondents is

* [*The Civic Culture* is a study of the political culture of democracy based on more than 5,000 interviews conducted in Germany, Italy, Mexico, Great Britain, and the United States in 1959 and 1960. This excerpt from the book deals mainly with the methodological approach to cross-national research used by the authors to conduct their study. — Eds.]

essentially a stimulus that produces responses. The responses are the data we analyze. But for these responses to be comparable, the stimulus situation itself must be comparable. The differences that are found in response patterns from nation to nation or group to group within nations have little meaning if they are artifacts of the interview situation: that is, if the situation changes from nation to nation or group to group. The first task, then, in cross-national survey research is to develop a research instrument that will represent an equivalent stimulus in each nation.

In achieving such equivalence, the most obvious problem faced by the practitioner of cross-national research is that of language. Can one translate an interview from one language to another so that it represents an equivalent instrument in both languages? The answer is probably "no." Obviously one wants not a literal translation but an equivalent translation. What exactly is equivalence? In the first place, the words used must refer to equivalent objects in the several languages. But this is not enough. Even if words with equivalent meaning can be found, they may not be equivalent stimuli in the interview situation. They may, for instance, differ in the frequency with which they are used in the respective languages, and hence in the extent to which they are familiar to respondents. Or, though the words refer to equivalent objects, they may in one language have a wider range of meanings than in another; and the other meanings of the word may affect responses. Furthermore, the desire to obtain words of equal familiarity may conflict with the desire to obtain words that are both equally precise in referring to an object and "uncontaminated" by other meanings. For example: one set of questions in our survey has to do with attitudes toward the local government under which the respondent lives. Interviewers were instructed in the selection of the governmental units about which questions were to be asked. In most cases the names of the local units were well known and caused little problem. But in the common parlance of Mexico City the local government (essentially the government of the Federal District) is identified with the name of the extremely popular governor of the district, Ernesto Uruchurtu. Our pretest suggested that if we asked about the government of the Federal District we would find many residents in Mexico City who had never heard of it or confused it with the federal government itself. Everyone, however, knew of "*el gobierno de Uruchurtu*," and it was in this form that the question was asked. But though in the familiarity of the terms we achieved rough equivalence with other nations (and other locales in Mexico), we obviously introduced new problems of nonequivalence through the use of the name of a specific man.

Other examples of this sort could be mustered from our experience with translation — and there are probably many others of which we do not know, since information on the relative familiarity of words is not readily available. In fact, the most serious problem in attempting to attain equivalence is that there is no way of recognizing it when one has attained it. When one uses linguistic stimuli such as questions, there are no rules that specify when one has equivalent stimuli.[1]

The problem of language illustrates the difficulty of achieving equivalent stimuli from nation to nation. Yet the researcher has control (though not complete control) over a number of other factors that make equivalence possible. These include the level of skills of the interviewers, the training they receive, the "tightness" of control over their actions, and so forth. One attempt to achieve equivalence — by controlling the interviewer's behavior somewhat more tightly than would be necessary in a single-nation survey — was described above in the discussion of the modification of our research instrument in response to the results of our pretest. When it became apparent that interviewers in different countries used different practices in following up the answer to an open-ended question, it was possible for the research directors to specify more precisely the exact nature of the follow-up questions to be used. Other differences in the interview situation are not under as close control of the researcher. One such factor is the familiarity of populations in various nations with political surveys. It is not so much that populations differ in the frequency of the experience itself; it is unlikely that more than a handful of respondents in any of the nations studied had ever been interviewed before in a social survey. But the nations do differ in the extent to which social surveys are well known; in our case, in the United States, Britain, and perhaps Germany, pre-election surveys are quite familiar. In the other two nations they are not. Differences in reactions to the interview situation, or perhaps general differences in willingness to talk to strangers, can affect the results of a cross-national survey and are hard to eliminate.

One other possible source of nonequivalence is the time at which the survey is carried on. This too is difficult to standardize from nation to nation. Even if all five surveys are carried on simultaneously, there may be events taking place in one nation that temporarily affect political attitudes in ways that are relevant to the concerns of the researcher. The height of an election campaign and the aftermath of a major crisis are clearly noncomparable situations in which to survey the extent of interest in politics. And again, it is impossible for the researcher to standardize the situation in the several nations.[2]

[1] For other problems involved in obtaining equivalent meanings, see Susan Ervin and Robert T. Bower, "Translation Problems in International Surveys," *Public Opinion Quarterly*, XIV (1952-1953), pp. 595-604; and Eugene Jacobson, Hideya Kumata, and Jeanne E. Gullahorn, "Cross-Cultural Contributions to Attitude Research," *Public Opinion Quarterly*, XXIV (1960), pp. 205-23.

[2] In four of the nations our interviews were carried out simultaneously in June-July, 1959; in the United States they were carried out in April 1960. In Mexico

What then can one do? Equivalent questionnaires — that one is *sure* are equivalent — appear impossible to obtain. Two possible approaches suggest themselves. First, one can let the availability of methods dictate one's approach; one can aim at developing stimuli that are as cross-national as possible. This can be accomplished, perhaps, by dropping the use of ordinary questions or by using non-verbal techniques. It may be that one significant future task of political science is to develop such techniques. But the techniques of this sort that are currently available are not applicable to many substantive problems. To use them would increase cross-national comparability, but would limit the range of one's substantive interests.[3]

The second possible approach — and the one we have used in our study — is to follow one's substantive interests wherever they lead, in full realization that even the best available techniques are far from perfect. And though one cannot achieve perfect comparability, there are a number of ways in which one can hope to come somewhat closer to it. By careful translation, for instance, one can attempt to minimize linguistic problems.[4] Furthermore, there is some evidence that the difficulty of achieving

the interviewing took place during a crisis over fishing rights with Guatemala (and the Mexican press carried rumors of a possible war). Obviously an event of this sort, if it had any effect at all, would affect political interest — and only in Mexico and Guatemala. Similarly, the interviewing in Britain and the United States took place several months before a general election, though in both cases well before the beginning of the campaign; while in Mexico the interviewing occurred in the year following a general election. Though it is impossible to dismiss the possible contaminating effects of these events, there is little evidence that these events had any effect on the interviews.

[3] Some possible nonverbal techniques that have been used cross-culturally include the thematic apperception test and the Rorschach test. See J. Henry and M. E. Spiro, "Psychological Techniques: Projective Tests in Field Work," in A. L. Krocher (ed.), *Anthropology Today*, Chicago, 1953, pp. 417-29. As yet they are of limited usefulness in the analysis of political attitudes. In fact, there is some evidence that even these nonverbal techniques do not have equivalent meaning cross-nationally.

A very promising approach to cross-national equivalence is the semantic differential. Osgood and his associates, using pairs of opposite adjectives that appear to be cross-cultural, have found common judgment dimensions. See Charles E. Osgood, "The Cross-Cultural Generality of Visual-Verbal Synethestic Tendencies," *Behavioral Science*, V (1960), pp. 146-61, and Howard Maclay and Edward E. Ware, "Cross-Cultural Use of the Semantic Differential," *Behavioral Science*, VI (1961), pp. 185-90.

[4] The interviews used in this study were translated from English into the foreign language by bilinguals. They were then "blindly" translated back to English by other bilinguals who were not familiar with the original English version. This process was repeated several times. Furthermore, the several pretest waves of interviews were also translated, and the responses to these interviews highlighted some translation problems.

equivalent meanings diminishes as one moves from abstract words to concrete ones. If the questions can be kept simple and relatively straightforward, it is easier to attain some degree of equivalence.[5] The desire to avoid ambiguity in the results often means that subtle distinctions in the data must be ignored. Intensity questions — where respondents are asked if they agree with a statement "strongly," "somewhat," and so forth — can be dichotomized into positive and negative answers. This may eliminate any differences among nations in their propensity to use extreme language (as in slang, where even the "mildly good" becomes the "greatest"). The use of open-ended questions, where the respondent has the opportunity to respond freely, may also improve comparability. The questions may still be nonequivalent, but the free responses allow one to catch at least gross deviation from equivalence. And lastly, there are ways of analyzing the resulting data that reduce the extent to which one is dependent on complete equivalence; this we shall discuss in the following section.

So much for the mechanical difficulties in designing an equivalent stimulus situation when one is using an interview cross-nationally. The reader should consider himself forewarned as to the limitations of our data. We shall present many tables with cold and solid figures as to the numbers who said such-and-such in a nation. The figures may not be as solid as they appear. On the other hand, this warning ought not to lead the reader to despair. Though the material presented in here is far from perfect, it does have the advantage that its weaknesses can be at least made explicit. In fact, one can certainly argue that no cross-national study can avoid the problems listed above — problems of translation from one language to another, temporary differences in the situation at the time the material is gathered, and so forth. No matter what sort of study is contemplated, one must contend with these difficulties.

THE INTERPRETATION OF RESULTS

The search for equivalent questions and an equivalent interview situation is but the first step toward meaningful comparisons of the political behavior of citizens in various nations. One must still select equivalent dimensions of political behavior, as well as indicators for those dimensions. Assume, for example, that a question on some aspect of political behavior

[5] Buchanan and Cantril found that words such as "peace" and "democracy" were likely to cause the most trouble in attempts to find equivalent meanings (see Buchanan and Cantril, How Nations See Each Other, pp. 106-7). Yet in one of the first international surveys it was discovered that as concrete a word as "washing machine" meant different things in different countries. In some it was an expensive electrical appliance; in others it referred to any hand-turned device, however simple. See D. Wallace et al., "Experience in the Time International Survey," Public Opinion Quarterly, XII (1947), pp. 8-21.

(say, on the frequency of political discussion) is translated accurately; that the German respondent who says he discussed politics means by this what the Mexican respondent does (perhaps any informal discussion in which politics or public affairs is mentioned); assume that there are no differences in ease of interviewing, in the respondent's honesty, and so forth. Nevertheless, the problem of inference from the response is still difficult, because the dimensions and indicators of political behavior are being applied to differing political systems.

The more general a dimension, the more likely it is to have cross-national validity. One can, for instance, place American voters on a dimension that ranges from "strong Republican" to "strong Democrat," with various levels of partisan affiliation in between. Such a scale is useful in the United States, but obviously makes no sense elsewhere; either other nations will have no two parties with those names, or, even if there are parties with similar names (as in Turkey), these parties may be of so different a nature from those in America that it would make no sense to compare the dimensions. Or one might array voters on a left-right continuum, but even this more general dimension might not apply to all nations. On a more general level one might use, as we have done, the dimensions of activity-passivity, awareness-unawareness, or alienation-nonalienation. It is likely that individuals in all political systems can be arrayed along these.

But if the use of general dimensions solves some of the problems of cross-national comparability, these problems re-emerge when one attempts to find precise indicators for the dimension. Consider the dimension of "political activity." As in all social research one does not observe "political activity" directly, but tries to develop *indicators* of political activity. Does a man report he discusses politics? This might indicate that he is active politically. Does he vote? This might be another indicator. Yet the problem always arises as to the relationship of a particular indicator to the underlying dimension. Is the respondent who discusses politics more "active" than the man who does not? That we are dealing with five different political systems complicates this relationship even further.

Though one can easily think of indicators of political activity, it is a subtler problem to find indicators of equivalent meaning cross-nationally. Assume that a particular type of behavior — let us call it "behavior A" — is of political significance. We want to compare the rates of performance of "behavior A" in a variety of countries. The important point is that, if the comparison is to be meaningful, the behavior must be the same in each country. We obviously will learn little if we compare the rate of "behavior A" in one country with that of "behavior B" in another — it makes little sense to compare the rate of voting turnout in Germany with the rate of party membership in Italy. This is clear and obvious, but we stress the point here because, not only may voting be different from party membership, but voting in one country may differ from voting in another country, just as party membership in one country may differ from party membership in another. In other words, what we label "behavior A" in one country may appear the same as, yet differ sharply from, that to which we commonly give the same label in another.[6]

It may differ in two ways: in its meaning for the individual who is acting, or in its meaning for the political system in which the act is performed. Consider voting as an example. As far as the individual is concerned, the vote may represent a conscious attempt to bring into power a party or candidate who stands for policies the individual desires; or it may involve ritualistic conformity to traditional party affiliations. Similarly, the vote may involve a great effort for some individuals or a minimum effort for others. Surely the Southern Negro in America who registers and votes at great personal risk is participating in a much more intense way than is the voter who lives in a situation where voting is relatively easy and expected. These variations in the meaning of the vote or of other political acts occur within nations, but they also occur, often more sharply, between nations. It would make little sense to compare the rate of voting in Australia, where voting is compulsory by law, with the rate of voting in a nation that has no such legal provision — especially if one wants to use the frequency of voting participation as an indicator of political interest and activity.[7]

In its impact upon the political system in which it takes place, voting has another kind of differential meaning. Under an authoritarian government the vote is essentially a symbol of solidarity; in a multiparty democracy, however, it has an effect on who runs the country. Certainly the vote cannot be considered the same act in those two circumstances. (It must be noted that the countries dealt with in this book [The Civic Culture], though they might be considered democracies, all differ in this respect. There are, for instance, large one-party areas in the United States. And Mexico is essentially a one-party system.)

What has been said about voting applies with more or less validity to other forms of political behavior: party membership, organizational mem-

[6] On this general subject, see Angus Campbell and Stein Rokkan, "Norway and the United States," International Social Science Journal.

[7] This problem is an old one for those anthropologists who have wanted to make cross-national comparisons. As Whiting points out, physiologically a belch is a belch in any society, but in one society it may be a compliment and in another an insult. But this, he goes on to say, does not eliminate the possibility of cross-national comparisons. A belch may not always be a belch, but an insult is always an insult. One can compare insults, if one can find some adequate index. See John W. M. Whiting, "The Cross-Cultural Method," in Gardner Lindzey (ed.), The Handbook of Social Psychology, I, Cambridge, Mass., 1954, p. 528.

bership, even media exposure and knowledge of politics. Party membership, for instance, represents one act for the individual who is in a mass party with structures of indirect membership, and another act for someone who is in a party with no structure of mass membership. From the point of view of the political system, these two kinds of membership mean something else. Lastly, it should be pointed out that the individual and systemic meanings of an act, though usually related, may vary independently. Thus the vote may mean different things to two different individuals but have identical effects on the political system: to one individual it may be a highly affect-laden protest against the current government, to another it may be traditional conformity to family voting patterns. But both may vote for the same party. Or the vote may mean the same to two individuals and different things to the system: two civic-minded citizens may vote on the basis of careful calculation, but one may live in a community where, unknown to him, his vote is not counted.[8]

That an act may mean one thing in regard to the political system and another in regard to the individual suggests that differences in the frequencies of particular behavior from nation to nation may reflect differences in the political systems as much as in the perspectives and attitudes of individuals. For example, we asked about watching news broadcasts on television and learned that a much higher proportion of Americans than Mexicans watch such programs. There is little doubt that our data are correct on this point (there are no particular translation problems, for example); but how does one interpret such a result? One could not conclude from this that Americans are more interested in politics and involved in governmental affairs. The bulk of the difference in watching broadcasts is probably due to the greater ease of access to television sets in the United States. This does not mean that one can infer nothing from the difference. If one is interested in the amount of time spent exposed to communications about politics, the difference will be important. On the other hand, one cannot very well use these data to infer differences in the level of motivation to obtain information about politics in these two countries.

The same problem applies to the interpretation of differences in fre-

---

[8] A related problem, which does not raise such serious methodological difficulties, is that the relationship between a particular behavior and a set of attitudes (or among attitudes) may differ from nation to nation. Rates of voting and attitudes toward voting, for instance, may vary independently. A high frequency of voting may not be matched by a high frequency of interest in the vote or of belief in the efficacy of the vote. It may well be that in some nations or among some groups, frequent voting is associated with lack of interest in the vote (one votes for other reasons).

However, this problem can be handled by comparing attitudes and behavior within nations, to see what attitudes are associated with what behavior, or with what other attitudes. A further discussion of the advantages of this approach will appear below. . . .

358   GABRIEL ALMOND AND SIDNEY VERBA

quency of political attitudes. Here the major difficulty is that the *object of orientation* for the attitude differs from nation to nation — that is, Italians were asked about Italian government and Britons were asked about British government. Again if we solve the mechanical problems of creating a similar stimulus situation, we are still faced with the problems of interpretation. If the citizens in one country report more frequently than those in another that their government operates in their interest or that it can be trusted, this is a real difference in attitude with real consequences. But because the object of orientation differs (we are not, for instance, comparing, as one does in a single-nation survey, the attitudes of men and women toward the same government), it is more difficult to explain these differences in attitude toward government. To some extent the explanation may lie among the factors usually adduced in surveys to explain attitudes — social group, personality, other attitudes, and so forth. On the other hand, it may simply be that one government is in fact more beneficial in its operation or more to be trusted than another. Or it may be both — the two types of explanation do not necessarily contradict each other. Again the differences are real, but what they mean is harder to say.[9]

Finally, there is the difficulty in attaining comparable social categories for matching respondents across national lines. In all survey research analysis one attempts to compare matched subgroups of a sample in order to isolate nonspurious relationships among variables. If one wants to estimate the impact of income on political participation, one compares various income groups within matched educational groups to eliminate the possibility that what appears to be a relationship between income and political participation is, instead, largely due to the fact that those with higher income are likely also to have more education. In cross-national research in political behavior the isolation of such matching groups is useful. If one can compare matching groups cross-nationally — Americans with Italians of similar educational attainment; British working-class men with German working-class men — one can begin to estimate the extent to which differences between the average responses in a cross-section sample can be explained by the uneven distribution of some important social attribute in the cross-section samples. For instance, a much larger

[9] Here, the problems in cross-national survey research seem to differ in kind from those in single-nation research. Yet single-nation surveys have this in common with cross-national surveys: in the first place, from the subjective points of view of the respondents, the objects of orientation may differ. One Mexican, when asked about his government, might have one view of it; another might have a different view. Furthermore, one often asks about objects that differ from respondent to respondent. This is true when one asks the respondent about himself or his family. And as will be discussed below, this raises similar problems in single-nation and cross-national surveys.

proportion of respondents in the United States than in Italy reported exposure to political communications. One reason for this might be that a much higher proportion of Italians than of Americans reported no formal education or only primary education (both samples seem fairly accurately to reflect the distribution of educational attainment in the two nations). If one can show that a larger proportion of American respondents are exposed to political communications, whereas among American and Italian respondents of equivalent educational attainment there is little or no difference in rate of exposure, then one has gone a long way toward explaining why the two nations differ in this aspect of political behavior. The difference in exposure would appear to be due to differences in educational levels from one nation to another rather than to some aspect of Italian politics or Italian "national character." In fact, if, when one controls for a demographic characteristic or some other attribute, one can remove the differences among the response patterns in the various nations, one has a powerful tool for explaining the differences among various nations. (The difference in, say, exposure to political communications remains, however, a "real" difference between the nations; as real as the difference in the educational systems.)

Though achieving matched subgroups cross-nationally would be desirable, it is very difficult. This is not because the measures are inaccurate, but because again the interpretation is difficult. One cannot, of course, "translate literally" demographic measures from nation to nation. Such a translation would involve, for instance, matching income groups by their equivalence in each other's currency at the going rate of exchange. This would lead to such obvious distortion as matching respondents whose positions in the income hierarchy within each nation were quite different. A better way would be to match respondents by their position on the income ladder in each country — compare those in the top twenty per cent of earners in each nation, and so forth. But even this does not produce equivalent groups. Real incomes will differ, as will perhaps such important characteristics as the difference in income from that of people lower on the scale.

This problem can best be illustrated by considering how to obtain matched educational groups cross-nationally.[10] One approach would be to match groups in terms of number of school years completed. Yet obviously the quality and content of education differ from nation to nation. (Again this is a problem found within nations as well.) More important, perhaps, the social implications of equivalent levels of education, in terms of num-

---

[10] This is a useful example, for educational attainment seems to be the most significant demographic variable in our study, and the one most able to explain differences among nations. It is also the demographic control we use most frequently.

ber of years, may differ as well. In a nation where secondary education is almost universal and college education widespread, higher educational attainment is not as clear an indicator of higher social status as it would be in nations where there is a generally lower level of education.[11] The problem of matching groups cross-nationally, like the problem of equivalent indicators, is probably insoluble *if one is looking for complete equivalence.* (As we shall suggest below, one can get by with much less.)

The above discussion should make it clear that cross-national systematic comparisons are difficult indeed. The problem in finding equivalent indicators from nation to nation is, however, not specific to this type of research (although, as suggested earlier, it may be most explicit in this sort of research endeavor). In all comparative research we have to isolate comparable variables: one cannot simply compare "totalities." Yet in the social sciences this isolation of variables is difficult. As yet we cannot adequately separate those aspects of politics that we want to compare from other aspects; we cannot hold constant or ignore the large number of aspects of a phenomenon that the natural scientists can leave out of his calculations. Most of the variables we attempt to isolate are completely meaningful only when considered in their contexts, but to compare complete contexts is not really possible. Is there any way out of this dilemma — the general social science dilemma or the specific one of cross-national research in political behavior? The answer is "no" if we are looking for a perfect solution, but "yes" if we are looking for a reasonable solution: a solution through which we pursue problems of substantive interest with as much rigor as possible, but do not let the concern for rigor dominate our willingness to tackle problems of significance.

MAXIMIZING COMPARABILITY

There are a number of ways to maximize comparability in survey research. One way, as was suggested above, is to take general dimensions of political behavior. As will be seen, many of the variables we use — such as the activity-passivity dimension — are of this sort. Second, if we want data on individual political orientations and not on the political structures of the system (the latter might better be studied by some means other than a systematic survey), it is well to concentrate on the behavior or attitudes that are least determined by the structure of the situation. Of course, all

---

[11] We are dealing here with "composition" effects: that is, the impact on an individual, not of his own position on a variable (e.g., his level of educational attainment), but of the distribution of that variable in the group to which he belongs (e.g., the proportion of university educated within the group). Composition effects have obvious relevance to cross-national research. See Peter M. Blau, "Structural Effects," *American Sociological Review,* XXV (1960), pp. 178-93, and James A. Davies, *Great Books and Small Groups,* New York, 1961, Chap. 1.

the attitudes we deal with are in part situationally determined. If one is interested in political orientation and not in basic dimensions of personality, one must expect to study attitudes and behavior that are affected by structural characteristics. Nevertheless, one can search for that type of attitude or behavior that is relatively independent of structural constraints.

That frequency of exposure to news broadcasts on television was found inappropriate as a measure of political interest suggests what sort of behavior one ought to concentrate on. If television sets are more widely distributed in one nation than another, there is clear structural constraint on the relative ability of individuals to watch television. Assume that individuals in the United States and Mexico have the same desire to watch news broadcasts on television (if that could be measured independently of actual watching); it would take much more effort by the average Mexican than by the average American to overcome structural resistance to his desire to watch. Similarly, given the same level of intensity of desire to vote, the force required to vote is greater for a Southern Negro than for a Northern Negro. Thus one cannot infer differences in intensity of political affiliation from lower voting rates among Southern Negroes. If, then, one wants to compare the rates of political acts cross-nationally in order to infer the nature of political orientation in various countries, one ought to compare acts to which the social structural obstacles to performance are minimal or roughly the same from nation to nation. Rather than concentrating on voting behavior or party membership or exposure to formal media of communications, one might concentrate on more informal political acts. Political discussion might be this kind of act. Or one might concentrate on expressed political attitudes, such as political interest. Behavior and attitudes of this sort are not independent of various social pressures and structural constraints: they do not spring solely from some internal individual mechanism. It is more difficult to discuss politics even if one so desires if there are few others interested in such discussion. Yet the constraints on such informal activities and attitudes are not as clear and insuperable as are structural obstacles in other fields.[12]

12 However, comparison of the rates of formal activity, such as voting behavior, party membership, or exposure to formal media of communications, is still important if one recognizes the uses to which it can be put. That these data cannot be used to infer national differences in political attitudes or perspectives does not mean that the formal differences, in exposure to a particular type of communications, for example, do not have real effects on the nature of political communication and on the way a political system operates. Furthermore, the fact that more Americans than Mexicans watch the news on television, or that more British workers than American workers are members of a political party, or that more Northern than Southern Negroes vote (all of these differences could be traced mostly to structural inhibitions that operate regardless of individual propensities) does have significant implications for the political behavior of individuals. For even if a particular behavior varies from group to

Differences in political structure can also be minimized, at least in part, by concentrating on the individual as object of orientation. One asks questions, not about the government nor even about the individual's perception of the government, but about the individual's perception of *himself* in relation to the government. Does the individual believe the government benefits *him?* Does he think *he* can influence it? With questions of this sort one focuses attention on the individual's subjective view of the political system and compares these subjective views cross-nationally. While this does not eliminate the fact that one is dealing with differing political systems, it does make the measures used somewhat more comparable.

Though the judicious choice of indicators helps eliminate some of the problems of nonequivalence in cross-national research, perhaps the most important way in which such problems must be handled is in the analysis of the data. The fact that a particular indicator has to be interpreted to some extent in terms of its context has led those interested in cross-national comparisons to stress, not direct comparisons of variables cross-nationally, but cross-national comparisons of the *pattern* of relations among variables.[13] For instance, one does not compare the rate of performance of a particular act or of expression of a particular attitude from nation to nation; instead, one compares cross-nationally the differences among groups within each nation. The question is not whether Germans more frequently vote or more frequently report interest in politics than do Italians, or even if German and Italian males differ in these respects. Rather, one asks if males vote more frequently than females in both countries, or if those with high income are more interested in politics in both countries. By phrasing the comparison *between* nations in terms of the similarities and differences in the *patterns* of relations *among* variables *within* each country, one controls somewhat for the difference in meaning that these variables may have from one nation to another.

Even if an activity (say, voting) has a somewhat different meaning from nation to nation, this does not invalidate cross-national comparisons

---

group because of structural differences, the chain of causality does not end there. The behavior, no matter why it is performed, affects the individual who performs it. Thus the Northern Negro who votes may not have started out any more involved in politics than his Southern counterpart. But the act of voting makes him a different political person. If greater involvement did not lead him to vote, voting may lead to greater involvement. Whatever their origin, differences in rates of behavior have different effects upon the political system and upon the individuals within that system.

[13] See Stein Rokkan, "The Comparative Study of Political Participation," in Austin Ranney (ed.), *Recent Developments in the Behavioral Study of Politics*, Urbana, Ill., 1962; and Campbell and Rokkan, "Norway and the United States," *International Social Science Journal*.

of the internal distribution of voting behavior in a nation. The differences in voting rates that one compares are differences among various groups within each nation, and one can assume the meaning of the variable has greater stability within than across nations. Furthermore, the variables presented to explain the political activity or attitude (the independent variables) can be made more comparable when patterns of relationships are compared. The difficulty of obtaining matched groups on such characteristics as education or income is eased. Even though one does not know what constitutes an equivalent level of income or education cross-nationally, one can without much difficulty locate individuals within each nation on an income or educational hierarchy. Though university education is not the same in the United States as in Italy, it is in both countries a higher level of education than primary or secondary education. And this is the only assumption one needs to make for this type of comparison. The same applies to the use of variables of political behavior or attitude as independent variables to explain other political behavior or attitudes. Just as it is easier to rank individuals in a single society in terms of educational attainment or income than to compare income or educational levels across societies, so it is easier to rank individuals on dimensions of political behavior than to compare levels of political behavior cross-nationally. It is more difficult to say what are equivalent levels of political interest, or political information, or exposure to political communications from nation to nation than it is to rank individuals within each nation in terms of their interest, or information, or exposure. Ranking individuals within each nation, one can then raise such questions as: "How do those who are more highly exposed to political communications differ in their political attitudes from those less exposed?" And one can compare cross-nationally the differences in political attitudes between those well exposed to political communications and those not so well exposed. This approach partially eases the problem that the meaning of each variable depends somewhat upon the political system in which it is embedded. By comparing patterns of relationships, one has to some extent placed the relevant variables into their context before drawing comparisons.

Many of the comparisons made in this book [*The Civic Culture*] will be of the pattern of relationship among variables. We shall compare demographic distribution of attitudes and behavior, as well as the ways in which several attitudes and behaviors are related. In this way we hope to increase the cross-national validity of our comparisons.[14]

[14] Though cross-national comparison of the pattern of relations among variables eases some of the problems mentioned above, it does not completely eliminate them. For instance, if such patterned comparison allows one to consider particular variables within their own context, it does not eliminate the fact that the

Having argued for the greater validity of cross-national comparisons of patterns, we must warn the reader that we shall also present a large number of direct comparisons of rates of adherence to a particular attitude or performance of a particular act — direct comparisons either among entire samples or among particular subgroups. These comparisons can answer a number of descriptive questions about differences among nations that could not be answered through the patterned comparisons described above. The direct comparisons must, however, be viewed with caution. In particular, it is important to look, not merely for differences among nations on a particular measure, but for a consistent set of differences among nations on a number of measures. If a particular measure of political activity tends to inflate the level of participation in one nation over another — due perhaps to some translation problem, or some characteristic of the political system — there is no reason to expect a distortion in the same direction on another measure of activity. Therefore, if we can locate consistent differences in political orientation among nations on a variety of measures, we can have somewhat more confidence that our observation is a real difference among the nations and not merely an artifact of the interview situation. . . .

---

variables must be comparable to begin with. If the meaning of an indicator is not related to some underlying dimension — if the vote, for instance, cannot even be considered a measure of activity in *one* of the nations — then any cross-national comparison will be meaningless.

Second, there is the danger that national differences in a political act or attitude will mean differences, not only in the absolute *frequency* of performance of the act or of adherence to the attitude, but also in the *distribution* of that act or attitude. For instance, we argued earlier that comparative rates of party membership in Britain and the United States could not be used as an index of political activity, since membership in Britain meant something quite different from membership in the United States. This difference in meaning (the particular example given was the existence in Britain of a large amount of non-individual affiliation through trade unions) describes the national differences in absolute level of membership. But it also describes national differences in the class distribution of membership. The inflation of British membership figures through the existence of nonindividual membership has a differential effect on members of the various classes. Cross-national comparisons of class patterns of activity on this measure would therefore be distorted.

23   ERWIN K. SCHEUCH

Cross-National Comparisons
Using Aggregate Data

PROBLEM FORMULATION IN DISCUSSING
THE USES OF AGGREGATE DATA FOR
CROSS-CULTURAL COMPARISONS

Until very recently, in most social science disciplines except cultural anthropology, cross-national comparisons involving numbers meant using aggregate data. Since World War II, and especially during the last several years, we have observed a number of important examples of comparing large territories such as nation-states by using survey research.[1] The use of aggregate data (specifically of statistical information about nation-states) and cross-societal comparisons via survey research have proceeded simultaneously and separately without so far causing a major methodological debate.

Within the past two years we have witnessed the publication of books on the two most ambitious and voluminous cross-cultural comparisons ever on the basis of national aggregates: The Yale Political Data Program (the YPDP) initiated by Karl Deutsch and Harold Lasswell, and the Cross-Polity Survey (CPS) by Arthur Banks and Robert Textor.[2] These

---

From *Comparing Nations*, edited by Richard L. Merritt and Stein Rokkan, pp. 135-156 and 158-164. Copyright © 1966 by Yale University. Reprinted by permission of the author and the publisher.

[1] Alex Inkeles, "Industrial Man: The Relations of Status to Experience, Perception, and Value," *Society and Self*, ed. Bartlett Hicks Stoodley (Glencoe: Free Press, 1962); Seymour Martin Lipset, "Democracy and Working-Class Authoritarianism," *American Sociological Review*, 24 (1959), 482-501; Gabriel A. Almond and Sidney Verba, *The Civic Culture: Political Attitudes and Democracy in Five Nations* (Princeton: Princeton University Press, 1963).

[2] Arthur S. Banks and Robert B. Textor, *A Cross-Polity Survey* (Cambridge: M.I.T. Press, 1963). Both the YPDP and the CPS so far have concentrated on aggregates. However, the CPS largely works with nominal and ordinal variables derived from judgmental coding, while the YPDP preferred quantitative variables that may be treated as interval measurements. Thus, the following discussion refers to problems that are specifically relevant for the YPDP.

The YPDP and the CPS are both conceived as being applicable to individual measurements and specifically to survey data, and such application is envisaged

first true world surveys of polities attempt to provide the empirical basis
for generalizing propositions about polities as concrete units determined
by general factors, instead of emphasizing the unique features.

In trying to implement similar programs, the two surveys follow quite
different strategies in the processing of data. The differences in strategy,
the scope of the comparisons, and especially the abstract way of dealing
with politics are aspects of the YPDP and the CPS which call for major
attention and should trigger a lively methodological debate. Hopefully,
in this debate there will be some carry-over from previous methodological
discussions about the use of aggregates in other social science fields which
usually referred to much smaller units for aggregation than whole nation-
states.

One very important example is the controversy in the early 1950s which
centered around a problem referred to as the "ecological fallacy."[3] This
debate cleared some important points and led to some unfortunate problem definitions, but appears to have had only a limited long-run impact.

The discussion of the "ecological fallacy" was in part just a repetition
of an earlier and more generally posed controversy over the use of grouped
data. And this debate again proceeded as if the character of aggregate
data, the advantages of working with them, had to be discussed as a new
topic.[4] Thus, the earlier heated controversy over an attempt of the "Lau-
sanne School of Marginal Utility" in economics to construct, e.g., aggregate demand curves from the estimation of individual preferences was
ignored. In general, there has been very little carry-over between disciplines or fields of interest whenever the problem of aggregate versus individual data caught the attention of a particular group of scholars; and,
characteristically, such methodological discussions proceed from a prob-

---

by the authors of both data programs. The Yale Political Science Research
Library has collected survey material, and this will be processed for the purposes
of the YPDP in the same way as the aggregate statistics used so far. A central
element of the CPS is the Pattern Search and Table Translation Technique,
and this technique has already been applied to some survey data; plans call for
its application to survey data gathered from more than one country.

The YPDP and the CPS differ fundamentally in their approaches to data; in
this context it is, however, important to note one agreement: the YPDP and
the CPS are not only prepared to handle individual measurement, but want to
combine aggregate and individual descriptors.

[3] William S. Robinson, "Ecological Correlations and the Behavior of Individuals," *American Sociological Review*, 15 (1950), 351-57; Herbert Menzel,
"Comment on Robinson's 'Ecological Correlations and the Behaviour of Individuals,'" *American Sociological Review*, 15 (1950), 674.

[4] For some earlier discussions see, e.g., G. Udney Yule and M. G. Kendall, *An
Introduction to the Theory of Statistics* (14th ed. New York: Hafner,
1950), pp. 310-15; and Roy G. Francis, "On the Relations of Data to Theory,"
Rural Sociology, 22 (1957), 258-66.

lem formulation that is peculiar to the particular situation of a discipline at a given time.

Survey research is not available throughout the world, and statistical services — not only the regular census, but also sampling by official statistical offices — have expanded in many Western countries. It will be an obvious research strategy to make use of both kinds of data, and indeed the YPDP and the CPS programs envisage just that. However, even a great number of impressive international data still means that the results are subject to the errors that triggered the methodological debates on aggregates, with the one qualification that the problems are *ceteris paribus* much greater when one deals with such large territorial units as nations. Combining aggregate and individual measurements creates additional problems, and some methodologists argue that it should not be done at all.

The following aspects most often cause uneasiness to those reviewing the use of aggregate data in social research, and they need to be considered when combining aggregates with individual measurements (specifically with survey research data):

1. *The accuracy of aggregate data.* There is a suspicion that on the level of aggregates the information may be more faulty than in using smaller units.

2. *The comparability of measurements for aggregates.* This question arises especially when territorial units are compared that provide information essentially by a process of self-enumeration.

3. *The representativeness of aggregate data for properties of the collective* — a problem akin to the use of summary statistics, such as averages in general (what do we know about a collective when we know its average?).

4. *Types of inference* which are permissible when using aggregate data.

In addition, we shall suggest a particular use of aggregates that, if it were more consciously employed, should contribute to the development of empirically substantiated macrotheories. This, then, is the major aim of this paper: to make suggestions for a more conscious use of aggregate data, and to attempt some clarification — rather than to continue a mistaken argument for or against using aggregates.

ON THE ACCURACY OF AGGREGATE DATA

Researchers who have dealt mostly with observations of individual units often feel uncomfortable about the accuracy of numbers reported for large aggregates — just as many researchers working with aggregates feel uneasy about the stability and generalizability of sample survey results. Aggregation obviously means being further removed from the original observations, and the greater number of cases to which a number refers (e.g. occupational distribution on the basis of a national census as against a sample survey) may indeed be purchased by sacrificing exactitude, or control over the recordings for each case. Using aggregate data for polities usually means working with complete enumerations, and it has been empirically demonstrated that these may be less accurate than samples. One of the effects of sample surveys has been to make census bureaus more conscious of the errors connected with complete enumerations, and consequently official statistical agencies now will use sampling to check on the adequacy of individual measurements prior to their aggregation.[5] These attempts to improve the quality of complete enumerations have been carried out mostly in advanced societies (with the notable exception of India) whose statistical services were already unusually developed. Thus, we know more about the problems of national statistics for those countries whose statistical services are already exceptionally well developed — at least in comparison to the majority of countries represented in the YPDP and CPS.

Some types of aggregate data that even in developed societies with strong central bureaus for statistics are subject to systematic errors and need to be interpreted with caution are (1) unemployment figures; (2) statistics for certain crimes, especially crimes against persons such as murder, assault, sex offenses, and juvenile delinquency in general; (3) statistics of traffic accidents; and (4) statistics for residential and occupational mobility. It is by no means possible in all instances to arrive at intelligent guesses (e.g. for crime statistics), and especially disturbing for time series analyses are changes in definition or policy. Thus, ethnicity in the U.S. Census has sometimes been defined as "foreign-born" and sometimes as "foreign stock." To give two examples for Germany: Rates of juvenile delinquency — especially for delinquency of well-off children — suddenly increased in Nazi Germany as a result of an order from the central government to treat as offenses acts of minors from families which, in the opinion of the prosecution, were better able to correct the child than the court would be. Traffic deaths also increased considerably in the late fifties partly as a consequence of now classifying the traffic fatalities those deaths of injured persons who died after a period of hospitalization. Even the number of households — a seemingly simple measure — is partly a function of the particular and changing definition employed, and not

[5] Cf. William E. Deming, *Some Theory of Sampling* (New York: John Wiley, 1950), e.g. p. 358. Samples as a means of quality control for a complete enumeration led to the discarding of a French economic statistic after World War II. The German census of 1946 was found to be highly deficient, as an example, for the attribute "occupation." Sampling also uncovered the amount of error caused by field workers for the Indian statistical office.

just an expression of preferences in family living; thus, statements about the strength of the movement to the nuclear family have to be somewhat tempered by the recognition that "household" has become more strictly defined.

We thought it necessary to caution against a tendency, especially (though by no means exclusively) among demographers and ecologists, to consider data from complete enumerations for that very reason safe material to work with. This is clearly an unwarranted assumption — whether explicitly made or implied in one's proceedings. However, aggregate data may also be superior for the same reason that the grouping of data often results in the improvement of estimates (e.g. by reducing spuriously high degrees of dispersion).[6] This effect is most noticeable when the individual measurements are unstable, and it is questionable when the individual observations are biased. Also, different analytical operations are of varying sensitivity,[7] and too little attention is often paid to the degree to which a summary measure responds to the faultiness of data.

From these considerations follows a general caveat in treating aggregate data, but in our opinion also a simple rule of thumb: the intervals for grouped data (or when grouping them) and the threshold of sensitivity for a measure should be just greater than the possible errors in the data. *Ceteris paribus*, for distributions some further grouping of data would be advisable. If there is any reason to suspect error, one should sacrifice some information and settle for a rougher measure.

THE COMPARABILITY OF AGGREGATE MEASUREMENTS

The quality of aggregate data needs to be even more carefully examined when the data are compared, and the dangers become greatest when the aggregates are polities. A relatively safe form is comparing aggregate measures over a period of time, that is, performing time-series analysis. Obviously, even faulty measurements may permit statements about change, provided the "faultiness" remains constant; this, however, is somewhat unlikely for longer time periods.

[6] This is also often the reason for measuring a factor through some index rather than relying on one direct measurement. See in this connection the argument of Stouffer for the use of "contrived" items (combining several primary observations) rather than individual indicators. Cf. Samuel A. Stouffer, "Measurement in Sociology," *American Sociological Review*, 18 (1953), 591-97. Of course, here several observations of one case are combined rather than a single observation for many cases. Although the logical problems are similar, only the latter operation is the theme of this contribution.

[7] Cf. Oskar Anderson, *Probleme der statistischen Methodenlehre in den Sozialwissenschaften* (2d ed. Würzburg, Physica-Verlag, 1954), pp. 106-09 et passim. Basic to this much neglected aspect of statistics are the writings of Arthur L. Bowley.

The same principle operates when making comparisons between collectives that commit the same kind of error — e.g. underenumerating rural areas — provided that one intends to make statements about determinants of variability between collectives. Thus, even though data on individual income in various European societies systematically underestimate the actual income (e.g. through the difficulties in accounting for nonmonetary income and for public services), this may not be too serious for a comparison between these countries; indeed, comparative measures are likely to be better than incomes for *one* society. However, if one compares income figures for Europe and the United States, the likelihood of error increases significantly through the higher monetization of the U.S. society and the relative paucity of public services. To account for the types of inaccuracy and yet prevent the bypassing of comparable information, we suggest stratifying the universe of polities into groups with presumably the same sources of error.

In spite of the efforts of the U.N. Statistical Office, statistical data for underdeveloped countries are by and large quite inaccurate. Many of the countries included in the Yale Political Data Program do not know even the size of their population. However, that by no means renders their statistical material in general valueless for the purposes of the YPDP. Apart from the possibility of comparing societies with comparable degrees of inaccuracy, this inaccuracy differs for the type of datum. While one may not know the size of one's population, the volume of newspaper circulation or of letter-writing is nearly as accurate for these countries as for developed countries.

In comparing aggregate data, the most troublesome problems arise when each of the units determines its own data collection, thus producing data essentially by a process of self-enumeration. From studies on response errors in official census work we know about the danger of this process even if a common questionnaire is supplied. Most of the data supplied by nation-states, and most of the variables represented in the YPDP, are based on self-enumeration. In the case of polities, this often means employing different definitions of the categories in counting. Efforts to standardize categories have been partly successful — as in the case of import-export statistics and postal statistics — but partly quite unsuccessful as in the case of many demographic variables.

This is partly a consequence of the real difficulties inherent in the subject matter; thus, defining a household remains a topic of controversy within the most developed countries (e.g. unit of consumption, unit in preparing meals, unit around one main provider, shared use of incomes, etc.), and differences in definition result in differences in findings which are by no means trivial. The difficulties of defining income in societies with different economic and social systems have already been referred to, and it is safe to say that differences in income between industrialized and nonindustrialized societies are probably exaggerated — if the income figures are meant to signify differences in the standard of living.

Comparisons based on monetary units are obviously affected by the meaning of exchange rates between currencies. Such exchange rates are more often than not "political prices" for a currency. This is obvious for countries which have not liberalized the exchange of currencies and sometimes have several exchange rates (as is true for some of the Communist countries with different rates of exchange for tourists, commercial transactions, and their own citizens desiring foreign currencies). Determining the meaning of monetary units, however, is also problematical for freely convertible currencies. It is luckily not our task to make statements about the determinants of the exchange rate of a currency but we can safely state that such rates are — even for freely convertible currencies — the result of many factors: a currency may be an international medium of exchange (e.g. the U.S. dollar) and may, as such, have a (partly monetarily determined) price; a currency may be undervalued as a means of export-dumping (as in efforts to export one's unemployment to other countries) or it may be overvalued to benefit capital owners investing abroad (as in the case of the U.S.).[8] The notion that exchange rates for freely convertible currencies can be easily interpreted as parities in any other sense (and as buying power) is patently ridiculous, although by implication widely accepted by the predominantly economically naïve sociologists and political scientists.[9]

Even if the definition of categories is fairly simple and standard, their meanings may differ considerably. A prime example of this is educational statistics. Secondary education in Europe has a different meaning in terms of curriculum (i.e. content) and social significance (e.g. social prestige) than in the United States; in the U.S. the term "university" embraces institutions of world fame which are functionally equivalent to any European university as well as institutions for secondary education in the European sense. On the other hand, there are in the United States no

[8] As an example we might refer to the many measures adopted by European countries to support the present exchange rate of the U.S. dollar. Thus, the German Federal Republic buys U.S. military equipment in part solely to support the U.S. dollar — even though some of it is considered not first rate. Even France refrains from exchanging the greater part of its holdings in U.S. paper money into U.S.-held gold. Other examples are the rescue operations in 1964 for the Italian lire and the English pound.

[9] These problems associated with using variables expressed in monetary terms have been fully realized by the researchers of the YPDP. Cf. the admirable discussion in Bruce M. Russett with Hayward R. Alker, Jr., Karl W. Deutsch, and Harold D. Lasswell, *World Handbook of Political and Social Indicators* (New Haven: Yale University Press, 1964), pp. 149-51 et passim.

real equivalents for certain forms of secondary education in Europe, such as the German *Berufsschule*. These difficulties in comparing educational statistics and in the way these statistics are used as indicators reflect real structural differences — e.g. general education versus elitist systems.[10]

Many distortions result from a tendency to look at statistical reports as neither socially nor politically neutral. Prime examples are reports on literacy rates. Given the value structure of elites in the developing nations, literacy figures for their countries must show rapid increase as a yardstick of success in modernization efforts. In general, figures relating to standard of living (wage level, distribution of tax burden, food prices) have political and often legal implications. Thus, some Communist countries look at income figures or such a datum as rooms-per-person as information relevant to the cold war. In the France of the Fourth Republic the consumer price index for years was manipulated, deliberately and with public knowledge, in order to prevent escalator clauses in wage contracts from becoming effective. (One means of manipulation, for example, was to substitute a new item for a changing component of the index.) During the 1960 presidential election in the United States, a major political topic was the growth rate of the American economy and its insufficiency relative to the growth rates of other industrial nations. Items for defense spending are often ingeniously buried among other budget categories, and not merely for security reasons. Thus one should conclude that whenever a polity defines a statistic as relevant to its domestic or international politics, data need to be interpreted with some caution.

It is not just the categories that may present problems of comparability when using aggregate data; in terms of the usages made, the very units themselves for which properties are being aggregated may not be comparable. This is even true when the unit is a "polity." It may be acceptable to include in a data program — and assign a place in a total rank ordering of cases — such diverse units as Mauritania, Luxembourg, the USSR, Singapore, Gabon, Malta and Gozo, Japan, Sarawak, the U.S.A., and Kuwait, if the variable is population. It is a bit difficult to imagine what such a rank ordering should be correlated with, if the variables are "percentage of population of working age" (first three ranks: Luxembourg, Gabon, West Germany); "percentage of population in cities over 20,000" (first five ranks: Hong Kong, Trinidad and Tobago, Surinam, New Zealand, Great Britain); "votes for socialist parties as a percentage of total vote" (first five ranks: Singapore, Burma, Australia, Jamaica, Nor-

---

[10] Taking a "hard-headed" position, i.e. maintaining that the higher number of high school graduates in the U.S. as compared to Great Britain would mean after all a better educated general population, does not avoid the problem. Compare the results of a knowledge test in England and the U.S. as reported in the *Public Opinion Quarterly*, 27 (1963), 133-41.

way); "cinema attendance per capita" (first five ranks: Hong Kong, Lebanon, Australia, Israel, USSR); or "GNP per capita" (first three ranks: Kuwait, U.S.A., Canada).[11]

No amount of checking will reduce erroneous conclusions in a cross-national comparison that result from treating as polities in a substantive sense those units which are polities only in a purely formalistic sense, and which by no stretch of the imagination refer to units that are usually meant when discussing polities. The fact that in the United Nations something is defined as a polity and has a vote in that organization does not make it necessary to treat the units as comparable in contexts other than membership or votes in the U.N. This error is, of course, not peculiar to cross-national comparison; it is, however, logically equivalent to defining as a worker anyone subject to a special form of social security, and then discussing "worker" as being a status in a social science sense.[12]

THE REPRESENTATIVENESS OF AGGREGATE DATA

The greater the number of units that are aggregated and summarily reported for aggregates, the more likely it is *ceteris paribus* that the number does not meaningfully represent the property of the aggregate one intends to represent. The *ceteris paribus* is the degree of internal variation for the property in question. Especially affected are summary statistics such as measures of central tendency, presumably the best representation of a selected aspect of a collectivity. For example, everyone learns (or should learn) in introductory statistics the danger of using an arithmetic mean for a highly skewed distribution; computing the average income for a town with 98 farmers with an income of $6,000 each and 2 millionaires results

---

11 The examples are taken from Russett *et al.*, *World Handbook*. The authors of the *Handbook* are aware of this problem, and, compared to earlier versions, have already eliminated a number of units that are polities in name only.

12 "Worker" in the official German statistic is someone in a special old age insurance system, the "Invalidenversicherung." In principle, the occupational categories of the German census are conceived in terms of type of income and thus, for example, include a category for all those with derived income (the "selbstständigen Berufslosen"), lumping together students, retired workers, prison inmates, and persons living on capital income only. In several investigations these categories are then treated as referring to persons with comparable occupational status. We do not want to imply that this system of categorization renders occupational statistics by the census bureau valueless. Theodor Geiger, *Die Klassenschichtung des deutschen Volkes* (Stuttgart, Enke, 1932), is based entirely on census material, and can be considered as a demonstration of what can be done with a critically conscious use of such figures (in this case a breaking down of larger aggregates and recombination under different criteria than those used by the census). However, the prevailing use of such terms as "nation" or "worker" in research based on aggregate data amounts to a *quaternia terminorum*.

in an average of $25,880 which represents neither the farmers nor the millionaires in any meaningful (i.e. interpretable) way.[13] While we do not doubt the work of desk calculators (or computers) leading to the report of a higher per capita income in Kuwait than in the U.S.A., we doubt that many uses can be specified where this difference would have an interpretable meaning.[14] Correlations based on averages are obviously sensitive to the internal variability of an aggregate, and for most of the measures of central tendency they are in general sensitive to the form of the distribution. The problem presents itself, however, also for the aggregation of qualitative factors. Thus, the education continuum in the U.S. is cut into "qualitative" steps in such a way that the variability of the setting tagged as "college education" is extremely great — so great as to obscure partly the effect of the factor one intends to measure.

Especially important for a study of polities is the rapid change in the societies. In comparing polities this may just be the phenomenon one wants to track, but it need not be so at all. In an example from the YPDP, cinema attendance is reported for South Africa in 1950, for Italy in 1959, and for the U.S.A. in 1961; movie attendance, however, is one of the most rapidly changing behaviors. If cinema attendance were to be included in an index of communication density or an index of mobilization, the differences in time would quite materially affect the results.

And even if the time referents are identical — as in the YPDP for number of TV sets or for the Gross National Product — the problem of representativeness of a number is by no means solved except in a purely formalistic sense. Countries may differ in terms of the property represented only by a few years (as for density of TV and Gross National Product) largely due to a slightly different beginning for a growth process — but these polities may not at all represent different "stages" or different types. Thus, in 1957, the rank order in terms of GNP was United Kingdom rank #3, West Germany #4, and France #6; in 1963 the rank order was West Germany before England, and France practically identical with the United Kingdom. If, for example, rank order of GNP, based on a single observation, were correlated with turnout in national elections, the relationship one intends to measure would be obscured by many accidental factors. The following analogy may be dangerous and easily misunderstood, and is meant to illustrate just this point: One would hardly base a study of the

[13] A highly ingenious strategy in dealing with this problem can be found in the *World Handbook* where a new measure for expressing inequality is proposed. Cf. Hayward R. Alker, Jr., and Bruce M. Russett, "Indices for Comparing Inequality," in [Richard L. Merritt and Stein Rokkan, *Comparing Nations* (New Haven: Yale University Press, 1963).]

[14] To avoid misunderstandings, we do indeed consider the reporting of "average number of children = 2.5" useful, even though decimal children are not known to exist.

relationship between the athletic skill of 100 schoolchildren of all different age levels with the socioeconomic status of their parents on a single observation in time for each case. Abstractly, one can formulate this as a warning against resting satisfied with single observations of units in a state of rapid fluctuation.

In general, and especially for such varied, unstable, and heterogeneous units as polities, we would recommend as a strategy: (1) reliance on several descriptions in addition to averages (at least a measure of dispersion); (2) in many cases averaging between repeated observations over a short period of time; (3) grouping cases into comparable classes; and (4) discarding units that are not units in terms of the inferences drawn.

THE TYPES OF INFERENCE PERMISSIBLE WHEN USING AGGREGATES

The Controversy over the Ecological Fallacy

The main controversies over the use of aggregate data center around the types of inference that appear permissible or dangerous. However, especially in sociology it is not in these terms that the issues are discussed; here the problem has been more specifically defined as the "ecological fallacy." Most influential has been an article by W. S. Robinson in 1950 which triggered one of the liveliest methodological debates in the postwar period.[15]

Robinson advised a distinction between "individual correlations" and "ecological correlations." The former he defined as a correlation in which the statistical object or thing described is indivisible, while in the latter correlation the statistical object is defined as a group of persons.[16] After surveying a number of studies, especially in the fields of delinquency and political behavior, Robinson warned against treating ecological correlations as if they were individual correlations. Using data obtained for territorial units as if they were measurements of individual units was called "ecological fallacy."

The danger of this widespread practice was empirically documented when the findings of several studies were recalculated. Thus, the ecological correlation between percentage of colored population and illiteracy (based on 1930 U.S. census data) results in a Pearsonian $r = .946$ when using the large-scale area subdivision of the U.S. census for the whole country; the same correlation coefficient drops to $r = .773$ when the correlations are

---

[15] Robinson, "Ecological Correlations and the Behavior of Individuals"; cf. also note 3. The only other recent methodological debate of comparable intensity was the discussion of the use of tests of significance, beginning with Hanan C. Selvin's "A Critique of Tests of Significance," *American Sociological Review*, 22 (1957), 519-27.

[16] Robinson, p. 351.

computed on the basis of results for 48 states. Both correlations were shown to be spuriously high, if they were intended to demonstrate a direct relationship between color and illiteracy. Using "individual data," Robinson arrived at a correlation of .203. While "ecological correlations" on the basis of large territorial units yielded a coefficient of determination of 89 per cent, "individual correlations" resulted in an $r^2 = 4$ per cent. From this Robinson concluded that ecological correlations should only be used for ecological purposes, i.e. if statements about territorial units are intended.

The great differences between correlations computed on the basis of aggregates and those computed on the basis of individual measurements are essentially a function of the increase in homogeneity between larger-scale units, resulting in a reduction of variability in the data. To use the language of Robinson, individual correlation depends on the internal frequencies of within-areas individual correlations, while ecological correlation depends upon the marginal frequencies of the within-areas correlations. Obviously it is an empirical question as to what degree marginal frequencies determine cell frequencies, but even for a fourfold table a large number of internal frequencies will fit exactly the same marginal distributions.

Working with averages or other summary statistics when relating two distributions, instead of with the individual observations that enter into the computation, quite obviously reduces variability. In the technique of computing correlation coefficients (and not least in the Pearsonian r), variability among units entering into the computation reduces the correlation coefficient. Consequently, the larger the contexts for which units are aggregated, the higher (*ceteris paribus*) the resulting correlation coefficient. Accordingly, in Robinson's example, we find that the larger the territories on which the data are based, the higher the correlation.[17]

The subsequent discussion was somewhat diverted from important issues by an unnecessary contention of Robinson's: "In each study which uses ecological correlations, the obvious purpose is to discover something about the behavior of individuals. Ecological correlations are used simply because correlations between the properties of individuals are not available."[18] Herbert Menzel quite correctly challenged this notion that the only reason for working with aggregated data — and specifically with census figures for territorial units — was technical, that is, substituting

[17] Leo A. Goodman, "Ecological Regressions and the Behavior of Individuals," *American Sociological Review*, 18 (1953), 663-64; see also Paul F. Lazarsfeld and Allen H. Barton, "Quantitative Measurement in the Social Sciences," *The Policy Sciences*, eds. Daniel Lerner and Harold D. Lasswell (Stanford: Stanford University Press, 1951), pp. 182-92.
[18] Robinson, p. 352.

territorial data for individual observations, since individual measurements were not available.[19]

It is factually true that in political science and political sociology the data reported for territorial units are often used for inferences about the behavior of individuals, sometimes even for statements about their motivations. However, a factually correct statement is obviously something different from a logical necessity, such as Robinson has contended. Thus, territorial units are obviously a part of reality, and as such may be a variable in an explanation process. In Robinson's main example, identical historical circumstances and aspects of economic development probably caused certain states both (a) to import and retain large Negro populations and (b) to neglect their school systems.[20] Using territorial units to observe the correlation between the literacy rate and the percentage of Negro population is obviously justified, if one uses the territory as a contextual property in accounting for the variations in the other variables. Another example would be indicators of social disorganization computed on the basis of census tracts, where one would assume that the areas as such influence the values of the variables for social disorganization. Also, territories or other units arrived at by a process of aggregation may be elements in a social process in their own right. (I shall refer further to this at the end of the chapter.)

A number of classical investigations are guilty of committing the ecological fallacy, and their results may have to be largely discarded. This is a disturbing realization, and adding to this the vested interest in certain fields of learning in aggregate data (which for reasons that are by now obvious give one a better chance to "find" high correlations), it was to be expected that there would be strong objections and attempts to refuse the argument. Especially political scientists of the more traditional bent rejected altogether the notion that to identify the determinants of voting one should rely on individual measurements. Electoral statistics are, of course, one of the prime bodies of aggregate data in political science and will remain so. This factual condition is, however, sometimes given the status of a principle, and the following quotation is representative of the thinking of a considerable number of political scientists (even though they may be a bit more careful in their writing):[21] "It is impossible and *undesirable* [italics mine] to know how each individual votes, but it is

[19] The following is based on Menzel's "Comment on Robinson's 'Ecological Correlation and the Behavior of Individuals.' "
[20] Robinson, p. 352.
[21] E. B. Olds and D. W. Salmon, *St. Louis Voting Behavior Study* (St. Louis, 1948). Cf. also David Butler, "Voting Behavior and Its Study in Britain," *British Journal of Sociology*, 6 (1955), 97 et passim; Jean Stoetzel, "Voting Behavior in France," *British Journal of Sociology*, 6 (1955), 110 et passim; Ranney, "The Utility and Limitations of Aggregate Data," p. 96 et passim.

possible to learn how voters in each precinct vote as a party; and since
these citizens in these small election units have many characteristics in
common, it is possible to generalize with accuracy regarding the relationship between a certain way of voting and a certain kind of people."
Methodologically, this type of argument of course need not be taken too
seriously; it is quoted here only to show how resistant part of the audience
is when important vested interests are at stake.

Determinants of the Ecological Fallacy

One cannot argue on principle against the statement that individual correlation and ecological correlation will usually not coincide — but neither
can one rest with such an observation. While it may be satisfactory for
discussions of the logic of inquiry to stop here, for actual empirical research it is of course more important to give an answer to the questions:
What factors determine the difference between the two correlations? How
important will this difference be in a concrete case? A satisfactory answer
to these two questions, and preferably an answer formulated in algebraic
terms, would retain the usefulness of aggregated data for research even if
aggregated data are used to arrive at statements about individual behavior.

While some methodologists thought the conditions quite unusual under which ecological correlations and individual correlations would approximate each other,[22] a number of other researchers — and especially
demographers — suggested general and differentiated answers. It will be
recalled that the difference between individual and ecological correlations
is dependent on the degree to which cell frequencies can be predicted
from marginals; it will also be recalled that *ceteris paribus* the larger the
unit, the more likely a strong difference between individual and ecological
correlations. From these observations, Duncan and Davis developed an
estimate of the size of error when using aggregate data in predicting
individual units.[23] In principle, they employ successive sub-divisions of a
superordinate territorial unit; the differences in the ecological correlations
that are obtained for units of varying size are used as a best estimate for
the size of the ecological fallacy. "Although different systems of territorial
subdivision give different results, as is the case with ecological correlation,
the criterion for the choice among these results is clear. The individual
correlation is approximated most closely by the least maximum and the
greatest minimum amongst the results for several systems of territorial
subdivision."[24]

This is in my opinion a too mechanistic formulation, since the sizes of

[22] Cf. Goodman, p. 663.
[23] Otis D. Duncan and Beverly Davis, "An Alternative to Ecological Correlation," *American Sociological Review*, 18 (1953), 665-66.
[24] *Ibid.*, p. 666.

ecological correlations obtained in a succession of subdivisions of a superordinate unit are not just a function of the size of that unit but also a function of the type of subdivision. Thus, computing correlations first for the towns of a state and then for the enumeration districts of a census may give some indication of the size of the ecological fallacy; however, if the enumeration districts of the census coincide largely with the effect of a latent third factor, influencing both the variables being correlated, the subdivision of the unit city into the smaller districts will give a quite imperfect estimate. After all, the reductions in ecological correlations which usually result from successive subdivisions of larger territorial units are a function of the increasing control over the variability of individual units. Whether this control will be effectively increased by subdividing is a question of fact, although when working with territorial units this will often be the case. In principle, some kind of weighted average for the different (not just successive) subdivisions of larger aggregates appears as the safest possible measure, and the difference between the various correlations may be undertaken as a rough indicator of whether such averaging should be undertaken at all.

Difficulties in Arriving at Inferences
When Using Aggregate Data

The contention that ecological units are always used as a mere substitute for individual measurements, the contrary assertion that in some fields individual measurements are inherently inferior to aggregate data, and the technical discussion of best estimates (given the attempt to use ecological correlations as a substitute for observations of individual units) — these debates have tended to distract us from a more general problem formulation. Although the ecological fallacy is indeed especially relevant for work with such large units as polities, it is unfortunate that the issues were only discussed in terms of territorial units. Actually, the debate that I have reviewed has had little lasting impact. The ecological fallacy is still widespread, and we still come across hardly any examples where consequent use is made of Duncan's and Davis' suggestions.

What has been discussed as the ecological fallacy is, of course, only a special case of the difficulties in making inferences when working with grouped data. One of the earlier behavioral scientists to demonstrate the problems associated with the use of grouped data was E. L. Thorndike, in the course of his studies on determinants of intelligence.[25] Correlating intelligence quotients and crowded living conditions, Thorndike observed a correlation coefficient of .90 when using grouped data; the correlation

[25] E. L. Thorndike, "On the Fallacy of Imputing the Correlations Found for Groups to the Individuals or Smaller Groups Composing Them," *American Journal of Psychology*, 3 (1939), 122-24.

between the same variables was reduced to .45 when using individual data.

In the logic of inquiry it does not make any difference whether the basis for grouping individual units is a territory or some other criterion; what is essential is the effect that this criterion has on the control over the internal variability of units. Thus, the general issue underlying the discussion of the ecological fallacy is really *the relation of the criterion, according to which units are grouped, to the types of inference intended when using the results of aggregated units.*

This more general problem formulation makes it easier to specify the conditions under which territorial units — and specifically polities — can be used with tolerable accuracy or even employed to greater advantage. A general problem formulation also makes it easier to recognize that the effect discussed under the term "ecological fallacy" occurs in various guises. In the definition of what constitutes an ecological fallacy, let us substitute for the term "territorial" the term "grouped," and it becomes immediately apparent that the whole discussion so far applies to many fields and topics.

To give a few examples of the variety of circumstances under which the group fallacy becomes relevant:[26]

1. Let us assume that the higher the proportion of farm boys in a university, the higher the median score of that university's students on a Graduate Record Examination; and let us assume further that within any university farm boys consistently average lower on Graduate Record Examinations than other students. This seemingly contradictory information can easily be explained in terms of differential recruitment, a phenomenon which affects a wide variety of groups that one might compare by means of group data. However, when comparing polities, this will be less often a factor that one will have to consider, except in the rarer cases of highly selective and very substantial migration.

2. In a voluntary political organization, the records of every member show that he has become less active since joining. Grouping the members by length of membership, we also observe that those who have been in the organization for ten years are more active than those who have belonged for nine years; and those with nine years' membership are more active than those with fewer years. Again, there is an easy explanation for this seeming contradiction: membership turnover. While this factor is likely to affect the comparability between polities, it does have to be taken into account when comparing smaller territorial units. The fact that a territorial unit is a constant obviously does not mean that it is a constant in the substantive sense that one uses it in the process of explanation.

[26] I am indebted to Charles H. Tilly for these examples, although he is not responsible for the use I make of them.

3. Let us assume we are comparing the census figures for a polity from the year 1920 with those from 1960. We may observe that the proportion of men whose sons were in the same occupation as they themselves was higher in 1960 than in 1920. Before concluding that occupational mobility has decreased, however, we might also note that the proportion of men in the same occupation as their fathers was lower in 1960 than in 1920. Only by taking into account both sets of results do we identify massive demographic changes in possible determinants.

4. Suppose that we want to compare the proportion of foremen to workers in industry between a capitalist and a socialist country, using this proportion as an index of direct control over the workers. Since in general the factories are larger in the socialist countries, we hold constant the size of industrial establishments. We then observe that the proportion of supervisors to workers is higher in each size class of industrial enterprises in the capitalist country than in the socialist country. Do we conclude that capitalist economies have to rely more on direct supervision? Obviously, as least one further control we would have to employ is a grouping of factories by types of products, and even then we would not be sure of accounting for structural differences as underlying factors.

This list is by no means a complete inventory of instances in which quite often the group fallacy is committed. It should also not be taken as an argument in principle against working with aggregate data. However, the list should be understood as a warning to treat grouped data just as individual observations. These cases were intended to demonstrate that — due to the more indirect relation between datum and inference — in working with grouped data the number of controls and checks against which to test an explanation has to be *ceteris paribus* greater than in the case of individual data.

.   .   .

THE INDIVIDUALISTIC FALLACY[27]

Today there is a strong and probably increasing tendency in the social sciences to commit what I would suggest be termed the "individualistic fallacy," and the preference for using ecological correlations merely as a substitute for inferences about the individual is closely connected with this orientation. Thus, the fallacious use of ecological correlations or of other correlations on the basis of grouped data can — ironically — be understood partly as a result of the individualistic fallacy.

[27] Related to this notion of an *individualistic fallacy* is the concept of "universalistic fallacy" as proposed by Hayward R. Alker, Jr. Compare for this discussion here Alker's treatment of "Regionalism versus Universalism in Comparing Nations," in Russett *et al.*, *World Handbook*. See also, Hayward R. Alker, Jr. and Bruce M. Russett, "Correlations between Political and Social Indices," in Russett *et al.*

The individualistic fallacy is the negation (explicitly or in one's research procedure) of the usefulness of an explanation that treats the collectivity as a collectivity, of working on a system level, and the phrasing of explanations for properties of the collectivity entirely in terms of the individual units, whose aggregated values should be the "true" value for the collectivity. Of course, this aggregation may no longer be thought of as necessarily a simple addition of individual observations but may also be based on values for the individual observations that are modified prior to their summation.

While traditionally political science may have been guilty of frequently committing the ecological fallacy, there appears to be a tendency among the newer behavioral political scientists to rely on individual measurement and in so doing to commit what we termed the individualistic fallacy. In its most naïve version, this fallacy takes the following form: In a cross-national comparative survey, samples of populations are asked whether they believe that a gifted and diligent person has a good chance of upward social mobility; the different percentages in various countries of persons agreeing that indeed there is such a chance are taken as an index of the degree to which a particular society is still basically ascriptive. Another example is to count the percentage of authoritarian persons, or to ascertain the proportion of individuals who come close to a particular notion of a "democratic, civic culture" in their opinions, and take this as an index of the degree to which a society is democratic. In such studies as the international citizenship survey,[28] what is ignored is that one may have a democratic system with few "democratic" personalities, and various types of authoritarian systems with high percentages of democratic personalities. Democracy is the term for a political system, and a political system is obviously not just the aggregate of the individuals comprising it.

Peculiarly, small-group researchers — though maintaining that they are discussing groups — have often committed the individualistic fallacy too. As James S. Coleman points out, small-group research primarily works with individual measurements which are then summed up or averaged as a group measure.[29] This type of aggregation often does not lead to difficulties if one holds constant the groups to be dealt with. Obviously, when keeping the groups constant, or for the same type of group (in the sense of comparable structures), such a simple aggregation of individual measurements partly by-passes the effects of group structure. If one makes comparisons across families, friendship groups, office groups, and voluntary associations by simply adding the scores for the number of interactions as

[28] Almond and Verba, *The Civic Culture.*
[29] James S. Coleman, "The Mathematical Study of Small Groups," *Mathematical Thinking in the Measurement of Behavior,* ed. Herbert Solomon (Glencoe: Free Press, 1960), pp. 5-149.

an expression of friendliness or antagonism, defining group cohesion would immediately result in problems.

If logical arguments should not be sufficiently convincing, let us turn to one of the (to our knowledge) extremely few empirical studies on the relation between aggregate and individual values.[30] Subjects of the study were committees of the oil industry; the method was the personal interview with questions both about the respondent's own attitudes and behavior and about his report of the attitudes and behavior of other committee members. In the analysis, the individual responses were treated as predictors of other responses by the same individual; the responses for a given group were then averaged and used as predictors for responses of the individual group members. Altogether there were 430 possible comparisons of the predictive power of aggregate versus individual values. As one would expect, the individual responses were the best predictor of variables describing the behavior of individuals — but the aggregated values predicted behavior referring to group process better than the individual responses. It could further be demonstrated that the predictive power of aggregate values was a function of group cohesion, and especially of the strength of sanctions exercised in a group against deviating behavior.

A reference to economics might again help to define more clearly the problems of a common fallacy in social research. Presently, economics emphasizes the use of aggregates, and the group fallacy now constitutes a more acute problem; but there is also the continuing tradition of dealing with an economy by reference to individual observations only. This tendency was quite strong toward the end of the nineteenth century when, for instance, Bentham and Edgeworth advocated the addition of individual utilities to arrive at social welfare functions. The schools of marginal utility were based on this premise, as has already been mentioned. Post-Keynesian welfare economists (such as Bergson, O. Lange, A. P. Lerner, Samuelson, and Hicks) are continuing the discussion as to whether the summation of individual preferences is legitimate when specifying the greatest welfare of the collective — and whether in turn aggregate utility curves can be used as the basic empirical material of welfare economics.[31]

This particular discussion makes quite clear the fact that reductionism,

[30] Robert L. Kahn, "Consequences of the Joint Consideration of Individual and Aggregate Data in Correlational Social Research" (unpublished doctoral dissertation, University of Michigan, 1958).

[31] For details of this discussion see, e.g., Leo Goodman, "On Methods of Amalgamation," and Clyde H. Coombs, "Social Choice and Individual Preference," both in *Decision Processes*, eds. R. M. Thrall, C. H. Coombs, and R. L. Davies (New York: John Wiley, 1954), pp. 39-49; Leo Goodman and Harry Markowitz, "Social Welfare Functions Based on Individual Rankings," *American Journal of Sociology*, 63 (1952), 257-62; Kenneth Arrow, *Social Choice and Individual Values* (New York, John Wiley, 1951).

the individual fallacy, and the group fallacy are all quite closely related. All consider the collective as a direct aggregate of individual units, and all (explicitly or implicitly) negate the relevance of the higher order units as such.

The use of indifference curves or utility functions to which I referred above should not be simply equated with the newer consumer economics. This rapidly developing branch of an empirical economics relies mainly on the prevailing field methods for data collection in social research, and is in effect just one more field of behavioral science (in the same sense as the "new" political science). For example, interviewing regularly a cross-section of the U.S. population, the Survey Research Center provided basic intelligence for the monetary policy of the Federal Reserve Board. To characterize the changes, and specifically the stages of growth of consumer markets in Western European nations, cross-national comparative surveys are increasingly used.[32] In Germany, the IFO-Institute regularly conducts a poll of executives in industry and business, and forecasts, on the basis of this information, changes in aggregate economic activity; in this prediction the technique of polling is in constant competition with both the historically descriptive and the econometric techniques of forecasting fluctuations on the level of aggregates by using aggregate data — and the poll of executives is proving worthwhile enough to have been continued for over a decade.

This kind of empirical consumer economics is uncontroversial for micro-economic purposes. It is the more successful in accounting for changes on the level of aggregate activity, the more the individual units (be they "executives" or "consumers") can be treated as comparable with regard to economic outcome, or where structural factors are relatively simple and well known (as, for example, in the case of the IFO-forecasts). Accordingly, one may now argue that the economics postulating the aggregation of individual values — such as Pareto's — was not fallacious in principle, but merely too simpleminded, always treating the various units of an economy as essentially interchangeable. Predicting in general the processes of such a complicated institution as a national economy obviously requires a high degree of information about structure.

When the use of aggregates versus individual values is discussed in economics, two issues are debated more or less simultaneously: (1) whether it is technically feasible to go from individual values to aggregates (or the reverse) in order to obtain a technically more advantageous unit to operate with; and (2) whether the collective (or economy) should be treated as a higher order unit that should not be reduced to its compo-

---

[32] The newest, and in my opinion especially impressive, example of such cross-national comparisons is the project "Products and People," Reader's Digest Association, London, 1963.

nents.[33] I want to postpone the second question to point out how difficult it is even in a discipline that deals with a relatively restricted range of activities, with a specialized institutional sphere, and that relies on rather "hard" information, to meet the conditions for aggregating individual values in a way that fully accounts for variations in the higher order units. These problems are by no means peculiar to economics, and if anything are easier to deal with in this specialized discipline; it is also easier in economics to specify the problems, and this accounts for the usefulness of the debate there.

The first problem-area for those refusing to accept different levels of argumentation or contexts of explanation is the structure of collectives, which gives differing relevance to the individual units and provides the outlets for effective choices. However, even if there were no structural arrangements among the units of a system, the preferences of the individual would only coincide with the choices made if the product choices were divisible into as many units as there are individual preferences. Instructive is an earlier discussion in economics about the consequences of the lack of a direct match between the number of preferences and the number of product choices possible; this debate was conducted under the somewhat misleading title, "The Paradox of Voting."[34]

The clearest example is perhaps political voting itself. In a multiparty system (such as that of the Fourth French Republic) individual preferences can express themselves in a considerable number of choices; but even here, the same act may result from a different combination of motives. In a two party system, where the individuals have learned that the defeated vote carries no influence, a small number of outlets (essentially three choices: vote for A, vote for B, abstain) becomes combined with strategic considerations of making the most of one's vote within the given system. As Kenneth Arrow points out: "The methods of voting and the market . . . are methods of amalgamating the tastes of many individuals in the making of a social choice."[35] Thus, for social behavior in general, there should be little argument that the same preference may result in different action, and that different actions may be based on the same preferences.

Contrary to some present tendencies in political science and sociology,

[33] This argumentation may be somewhat reminiscent of the rather fruitless controversy over whether the whole is more than the sum of its parts — but it is not identical at all. By way of contrast, we would accuse those refusing to deal with higher order units as units in their own right of committing the same error as the "wholists": assigning a "higher" reality to one kind of unit in an explanation process than to another.

[34] E. J. Nanson, "Methods of Election," *Transactions and Proceedings of the Royal Society of Victoria*, 19 (1882), 197-240.

[35] Kenneth Arrow, *Social Choice and Individual Values*, p. 2.

polities and societies are not generally directly affected by the motives, attitudes, and opinions of their constituent parts. The referendum is an unusual provision for relating the individual preference to the system — and even here the relation may be more indirect than is implied by the writing of, for instance, Talcott Parsons.[36]

Economics can be taken as a model case for justifying working at different levels instead of claiming the superiority of one over the other. There is no general, simple way of passing from one context of explanation to another — whether by reducing a larger context to smaller components or by aggregating smaller contexts into a larger one.

Let us state again, but this time more abstractly, the logical structure of the group fallacy: *The group fallacy (and, as a special case, the ecological fallacy) results from the difference between units of observation and units of inference. The danger of committing this fallacy is always present when the unit to which the inference refers is smaller than the unit either of observation or of counting.* This abstract statement should help us to see that this fallacy is, in its formal structure, analogous to the more rarely discussed individualistic fallacy. *The danger of the individualistic fallacy is then present when the units of observation or counting are smaller than the units to which inferences are made.*

---

[36] For a discussion of the logical problems of constructing a procedure for passing from a set of known (!) individual tasks to a pattern of social decision-making, see Arrow. Talcott Parsons in his more recent theorizing about generalized media of exchange may be close to a form of the individualistic fallacy in conceiving of a generalized medium as a means of directly relating processes at the system level and choices of the constituent units. Of course, it would not be correct to single out Talcott Parsons in this context; he is only cited as a borderline example of how widespread the danger of the individualistic fallacy presently is. A more representative case is George Homans, who makes what we have termed the individualistic fallacy his scientific program; cf. George C. Homans, *Social Behavior in Its Elementary Forms* (New York: Harcourt, Brace & World, 1961).

*Problems of Translation and
Meaning in Field Work*

. . . At the outset, three points must be emphasized. First, many of the issues discussed here were encountered while the author was conducting a culture-personality study in a Thai (Siamese) village. Because this particular type of research depended almost entirely on verbal instruments and reports, language became the lifeblood of the project, and it was essential to devote a great deal of time and attention to the translation process. One can imagine research projects — a study of material culture, for example — where such careful attention to word meanings might not be necessary. At the same time, however, the kinds of problems described here are present in principle in all research where the language of the people under study is different from one's own or that of the write-up. The basic issue is to recognize that there are translation problems, sometimes brutal ones, and then to decide how much time and effort will be devoted to solving them.

Second, accuracy of translation depends upon a number of factors, some of which may be beyond the field worker's control: The amount of time he has in the field and the size of his budget; the need, availability, and competence of interpreters; and his own knowledge of the native language. These practical considerations are mentioned because, despite the field worker's best intentions, he may have neither time, money, nor personnel to commit himself too rigorously to the translation task.

In most field work, translation accuracy is usually not an end in itself. Ultimately, the researcher's commitment must depend on the nature of his project. For many purposes, it may make little analytic difference, for example, whether the two Thai phrases, *khon mâj dii* and *khon leew* are both translated "a bad person," or whether their meanings are more carefully specified so that the former reads, "a person who is not good" and

From *Human Organization*, 17 (1960), pp. 184–192. Reprinted with permission of the author and the Society for Applied Anthropology.

the latter, "a contemptible person."[1] In either case, the reader would get the point: "a person with negative qualities." Yet, as will be seen below, there are numerous instances where such distinctions may be crucial to one's analyses and interpretations. For example, most Thai-English bilinguals and the two best Thai-English dictionaries translate the words *chïw* and *moo-hŏo* identically — "to be angry." Careful analysis, however, indicates that *chïw* means "to feel anger in one's heart toward another person, but to conceal its expression," while *moo-hŏo* means "to be angry at the situation in which one finds oneself, rather than toward another person." For the student interested in how an informant handles his aggression, these two translations lead to major differences in interpretation which would never be detected from the single phrase, "to be angry."

Finally, the field worker should be frank to admit that no matter how much care he devotes to the translation process, it is in absolute terms an unsolvable problem, and the best that he can hope for are good *approximations* between the meanings of the two languages. Complete semantic equivalence is a statistical fiction. The reasons for this are clear: Almost any utterance in any language carries with it a set of assumptions, feelings, and values which the speaker may or may not be aware of, but which the field worker, as an outsider, usually is not. This accompanying semantic baggage — what Bloomfield[2] and Osgood[3] have called "connotative meaning"[4] — exists in even very simple statements. For instance, "he

---

[1] Although for illustrative purposes these two translations are more accurate than "a bad person," they are, as the reader might suspect, incomplete. The original terms differ not only in intensity, but in specificity and in the extent to which they are linked with overt behavior: *khon mâj dii* is the more abstract term, usually referring to a generalized quality of "badness," the cause of which may be unclear; *khon leew*'s badness is relatively specific (although unmentioned) and is due to some particular act the person has committed. However, interesting as these additional specifications might be, they may have little analytic significance.

[2] Leonard Bloomfield, *Language*, Henry Holt & Company, New York, 1933.

[3] Charles E. Osgood, George J. Suci, and Percy H. Tannenbaum, *The Measurement of Meaning*, University of Illinois Press, Urbana, Ill., 1957.

[4] For discussions of the theory of meaning and the relation of connotative meaning to other semantic concepts, see also, C. K. Ogden and I. A. Richards, *The Meaning of Meaning*, Harcourt Brace & Company, New York, 1923; Charles W. Morris, "Foundations of the Theory of Signs," in *International Encyclopedia of Unified Science*, I, No. 2, University of Chicago Press, 1938, and *Signs, Language, and Behavior*, Prentice Hall, Inc., New York, 1946; Paul Kecskemeti, *Meaning, Communication, and Value*, University of Chicago Press, Chicago, Ill., 1952; Charles E. Osgood, "The Nature and Measurement of Meaning, *Psychological Bulletin*, XLIX, No. 3 (1952), 197-237; and Charles E. Osgood and Thomas A. Sebeok (eds.), *Psycholinguistics: A Survey of Theory and Research Problems*, Indiana University Publications in Anthropology and Linguistics, Memoir 10, Bloomington, Indiana, 1954. (Also published as a supplement to *Journal of Abnormal and Social Psychology*, XLIX, 1954.)

has tables and chairs" is a rough, but reasonably accurate translation for
the Thai statement, *khǎw mii tó lé kâwii*. In an interlinear, or word-by-
word, translation, only one of the five words in the original Thai has a
perfect equivalent in English — the conjunction *lé*, meaning "and"; *khǎw*
can be translated "he, she, or they"; *mii* can mean "has, is, or are"; and *tó*
and *kâwii* can be either singular or plural. But the real semantic difficulty
is at a more abstract level. In most settings, "he has tables and chairs" is a
relatively flat, uninteresting piece of information. However, in a Thai village, the statement can easily mean that the person referred to has higher
status than the speaker, or is foolish for wasting his money on non-utili-
tarian objects. None of this implied meaning can be traced to the words
themselves, but is suggested by the cultural context in which the words
occur. There is also a structural factor involved here: because Thai has a
wide variety of pronouns, all of which are associated semantically with an
attribute of social status, the particular pronoun used in a statement is
frequently a clue as to the speaker's emotional intent. In the above statement, *khǎw* is a pronoun of equality, used between peers. But, had the
speaker used another, equally available pronoun — *than*, the pronoun
for a superior — the statement would have suggested respect or admira-
tion; had he used *man*, it would have indicated anger against, or jealousy
of, the table owner. The very fact that he chooses *khǎw*, and excludes the
other pronominal forms, may be the speaker's way of denying these feelings. None of these connotative possibilities come through the English
pronoun, "he."

As was suggested above, the fundamental problem for the field worker
is the fact that he must not only translate language, but inevitably must
translate culture. This was recognized a number of years ago by Malinowski,[5] but received its most cogent expression in a recent statement by
Casagrande:

> . . . To achieve absolute equivalence in this process of transcod-
> ing presupposes an identity of cultural or socially shared experience
> between the two speech communities. Unless one subscribes to the
> view that two groups can have identical cultures yet speak different
> languages, this state of affairs is a virtual contradiction in terms. It
> seems to the writer that many of the more subtle problems of trans-
> lation are obscured or glossed over by the fact that most translations
> with which we are familiar are from FL ["From Language"] Indo-
> European to TL ["Target Language"] Indo-European, whose speak-
> ers share in large measure a common cultural heritage.
>
> The attitudes and values, the experience and tradition of a
> people, inevitably become involved in the freight of meaning carried

[5] Bronislaw Malinowski, "The Problem of Meaning in Primitive Languages,"
Supplement I in Ogden and Richards, *op. cit.*, pp. 296-336.

by a language. In effect, one does not translate LANGUAGES, one translates CULTURES. Ethnography may, in fact, be thought of as a form of translation. That it is possible to translate one language into another at all attests to the universalities in culture, to common vicissitudes of human life, and to the like capabilities of men throughout the earth, as well as to the inherent nature of language and the character of the communication process itself; and, a cynic might add, to the arrogance of the translator. . . .[6]

Following Casagrande, it is clear that for the anthropologist much of the translation process involves the explication of material and experiences which are not culturally or socially shared. This explication is not so much a matter of "translation," in the usual sense, as it is of explanation, analysis, and interpretation: the field worker must *talk about* language rather than render it. Many of the "translations" noted here are not translations at all, but commentaries on the meanings of terms.

It should be noted that this approach contrasts with that usually favored in the translation of literary works. Eugene A. Nida, director of the vast translating project of the American Bible Society, has said: ". . . a good translation should not reveal its non-native source,"[7] i.e., should not betray the fact that it is a translation. Although this principle undoubtedly makes for smooth reading and easy comprehension, it is antithetical to the goals of anthropological field work. The very aim of ethnographic translation is to disclose as much as possible of the assumptions and values underlying the nonnative language.[8] Attaining this end may result in disconnected texts, clumsy constructions, and perhaps a volume which is burdened with explanatory notes, but, as Malinowski has shown

[6] Joseph B. Casagrande, "The Ends of Translation," *International Journal of American Linguistics*, XX, No. 4 (1954), 335-340.

[7] Eugene A. Nida, "Principles of Translation as Exemplified by Bible Translating," in Reuben A. Brower (ed.), *On Translation*, Harvard University Press, Cambridge, Mass., 1959, pp. 11-31.

[8] Ethnographic translation is, of course, only one type of translation. In his excellent essay, Casagrande distinguishes and discusses four types: *pragmatic* translation which focuses on the content of a message and the transfer of information as such (recipes, scientific treatises, etc.); *aesthetic-poetic* translation where emphasis is on the expressive and affective elements of a message; *linguistic* translation where primary attention is given to structural or grammatical form; and *ethnographic* translation. One might posit a fifth type, *psychological* translation, which focuses on the unconscious motives which prompt a message (articulated dreams and fantasies, Rorschach protocols, etc.). This type of translation, of course, presupposes and is in some respects akin to ethnographic translation. Almost all the recent attempts at machine translation are pragmatic translations. See William N. Locke and A. Donald Booth (eds.), *Machine Translation of Languages*, published jointly by The Technology Press of the Massachusetts Institute of Technology and John Wiley & Sons, Inc., Cambridge, Mass. and New York, 1955.

with his Trobriand materials,[9] this is not only a justifiable price for accuracy, but has led to a more profound understanding of primitive culture.

THE TRANSLATION PROCESS

Despite the fact that cultural anthropology is the one discipline whose practitioners must almost all translate, comparatively little attention has been given to analyzing the translation process as such. This, of course, does not apply to the linguistic section of the anthropological fraternity, but, except for the work of Nida[10] and some recent work in psycholinguistics,[11] linguists have traditionally confined themselves to the translation of morphemes and an emphasis on grammatical form, with little concern for the ethnographic relevance of the material they are translating.[12] Linguists, of course, have given much attention to the whole question of the relationship between thought, language, and culture — of which the "translation problem" is undoubtedly a case in point. Work in this area has been broadly theoretical[13] or confined to small, empirical universes such as color categories, kinship terminology, or particular kinds of verb stems.[14] However, for those ethnographers who do not work on linguistic

[9] Malinowski, *op. cit.* See also *Argonauts of the Western Pacific*, George Routledge & Sons, Ltd., London, 1922 and *Coral Gardens and Their Magic, Volume II: The Language of Magic and Gardening*, George Allen & Unwin, Ltd., London, 1935. For a re-evaluation of Malinowski's data and an example of the kind of contrastive analysis which careful translation procedures permit, see D. Demetracopoulou Lee, "A Primitive System of Values," *Philosophy of Science*, VII, No. 3 (1940), 355-378.

[10] Nida, *op. cit.*, and "Linguistics and Ethnology in Translation Problems," *Word*, I, No. 2 (1945), 194-208.

[11] Susan M. Ervin, "Translation Procedures," in John B. Carroll and Susan M. Ervin (eds.), *Field Manual: Southwest Project in Comparative Psycholinguistics*, unpublished Mss., Harvard University, 1956.

[12] An important exception is C. F. Voegelin and Z. S. Harris, "Linguistics in Ethnology," *Southwestern Journal of Anthropology*, I, No. 4 (1945), 455-465.

[13] See David G. Mandelbaum (ed.), *Selected Writings of Edward Sapir*, University of California Press, Berkeley, Cal., 1951; John B. Carroll (ed.), *Language, Thought, and Reality: Selected Writings of Benjamin Lee Whorf*, published jointly by the Technology Press of the Massachusetts Institute of Technology and John Wiley and Sons, Inc., Cambridge, Mass. and New York, 1956; and Harry Hoijer (ed.), *Language in Culture: Proceedings of a Conference on the Interrelations of Language and Other Aspects of Culture*, University of Chicago Press, Chicago, Ill., 1954. (Also issued as Memoir 79 of the American Anthropological Association.)

[14] Some representative studies are: Harold C. Conklin, "Hanunóo Color Categories," *Southwestern Journal of Anthropology*, XI, No. 4 (1955), 339-344; Roger W. Brown, "Language and Categories," in Jerome S. Bruner, Jacqueline J. Goodnow, and George A. Austin, *A Study of Thinking*, John Wiley & Sons, Inc., New York, 1956, pp. 247-312; Eric H. Lenneberg and

problems, and they are the majority, the question of translation procedures has often seemed wrapped in a conspiracy of silence. The extent of ethnographic interest in (or avoidance of) the translation issue is, perhaps, attested to by the fact that, in a recent interdisciplinary study of the problem,[15] not one of the seventeen contributors is a professional anthropologist.

To this writer's knowledge, only Malinowski,[16] Henry,[17] Kluckhohn,[18] and Paul[19] have discussed translation procedures in any detail. Boas and his students translated numerous texts of North American Indian languages, but one looks in vain in the volumes of the *Handbook of American Indian Languages*[20] for guiding principles, other than grammatical ones. Similarly, the spirited debate between Mead and Lowie on the use of native languages in field work,[21] repeated, in part, a generation later

---

John M. Roberts, *The Language of Experience*, Memoir XXII, No. 13, *International Journal of American Linguistics*; Roger W. Brown and Eric H. Lenneberg, "Studies in Linguistic Relativity," in Eleanor E. Maccoby, Theodore M. Newcomb, and Eugene L. Hartley (eds.), *Readings in Social Psychology*, 3rd ed., Henry Holt & Co., New York, 1958, pp. 9-18; Floyd G. Lounsbury, "A Semantic Analysis of the Pawnee Kinship Usage," *Language*, XXXII, No. 1 (1956), 158-194; Ward H. Goodenough, "Componential Analysis and the Study of Meaning," *Language*, XXXII, No. 1 (1956), 195-216; John B. Carroll and Joseph B. Casagrande, "The Functions of Language Classifications in Behavior," in Maccoby, Newcomb, and Hartley, *op. cit.*, pp. 18-31; Howard Maclay, "An Experimental Study of Language and Non-Linguistic Behavior," *Southwestern Journal of Anthropology*, XIV, No. 2 (1958), 220-229.

[15] Reuben A. Brower (ed.), *On Translation*, Harvard University Press, Cambridge, Mass., 1959.

[16] Malinowski, *op. cit.*

[17] Jules Henry, "A Method for Learning to Talk Primitive Languages," *American Anthropologist*, XLII, No. 4 (1940), 635-641; and "Rorschach Technique in Primitive Cultures," *American Journal of Orthopsychiatry*, XI, No. 2 (1941), 230-234.

[18] Clyde Kluckhohn, "The Personal Document in Anthropological Science," in Louis Gottschalk, Clyde Kluckhohn, and Robert Angell, *The Use of Personal Documents in History, Anthropology, and Sociology*, Social Research Council Bulletin 53, New York, 1945, pp. 79-173.

[19] Benjamin D. Paul, "Interview Techniques and Field Relationships," in A. L. Kroeber (ed.), *Anthropology Today*, University of Chicago Press, Chicago, Ill., 1953, pp. 430-451.

[20] See particularly Franz Boas, "Introduction," in *Handbook of American Indian Languages*, Part I, Government Printing Office, Washington, D.C., 1911, pp. 1-83.

[21] Margaret Mead, "Native Languages as Field Work Tools," *American Anthropologist*, XLI, No. 2 (1939), 189-205; Robert H. Lowie, "Native Languages as Ethnographic Tools," *op. cit.*, XLII, No. 1 (1940), 81-89. See also A. P. Elkin, "Native Languages and the Field Worker in Australia," *op. cit.*, XLIII, No. 1 (1941), 89-94.

by Beals, Bohannan, and Taylor,[22] says little about translation procedures as such. All of these writers, however, do stress the importance of analyzing and understanding the cultural context of native statements.

Malinowski's theory of translation is concerned with both grammar and semantics. Most linguists now reject his grammatic notions as inadequate,[23] but his concept of "meaning" is still persuasive. The crux of the concept is that language should be regarded "as a mode of action, rather than as a countersign of thought."[24] Malinowski completely rejects the notion that words have "cores of meaning," and argues instead that they must be defined and translated by ethnographic analysis:

> The correct translation of each native term . . . is achieved by reference to ethnographic descriptions and by placing the word in its context of culture, in the context of cognate words and opposites and in the context of appropriate utterances.[25]

His technique of translation involves four steps:[26] 1) an interlinear, or word-by-word, translation; 2) a "free" translation in which clarifying terms, conjuctions, etc. are added and words reinterpreted; 3) an analysis and collation of the two translations, leading to: 4) a contextual specification of meaning.

To what extent other anthropologists can use these specific procedures in their field work is problematic. Malinowski was ultimately interested in a theory of language, particularly in the psychosocial function of the language of magic; most of his presentation is an explication, from a number of contexts, of the magical significance of Trobriand speech. However, it may be presumed that a large part of even the Kiriwinian language is of pragmatic, i.e., non-magical significance, and that Malinowski did not put *all* of his ethnographic data to the above translation test. Also, for some ethnographic purposes, steps (1) and (3) may be more confusing — and

---

[22] Ralph L. Beals, "Native Terms and Anthropological Methods," *American Anthropologist*, LIX, No. 4 (1957), 716-717; Paul Bohannan, "On Anthropologists' Use of Language," *op. cit.*, LX, No. 1 (1958), 161-162; Douglas Taylor, "On Anthropologists' Use of Linguistics," *op. cit.*, LX, No. 5 (1958), 940-941; Paul Bohannan, "Rejoinder to Taylor," *op. cit.*, LX, No. 5 (1958), 941-942.

[23] For a comprehensive critique of Malinowski's theory of translation, see J. R. Firth, "Ethnographic Analysis and Language with Reference to Malinowski's Views," in Raymond Firth (ed.), *Man and Culture: An Evaluation of the Work of Bronislaw Malinowski*, Routledge & Kegan Paul, Ltd., London, 1957.

[24] Malinowski, Supplement in Ogden and Richards, *op. cit.*, p. 326.

[25] Malinowski, *Coral Gardens, op. cit.*, p. 21.

[26] Firth, *op. cit.*

even dangerous — than useful. For example, Radin,[27] in analyzing non-Western thought processes, has warned that to argue from an interlinear translation of the Winnebago word for "sacrifice" — which translates to-cut-off-a-fingerjoint — that the Winnebago have a low capacity for abstract thinking or generalized thought would be as ridiculous as to draw inferences from the etymology of words like *understand* and *hypothesis* concerning the inability of Europeans to think abstractedly. Casagrande has suggested[28] that some of the assertions about the habitual modes of thought and world view of a people which have been made by such writers as Whorf[29] and Lee[30] may be due to "pseudo" or "half-translations" which result from too heavy a reliance on interlinear techniques.

Drawing on his experience among the Kaingang and Pilaga, Henry makes three important points. First, although he uses essentially the same translating steps as Malinowski, he follows an entirely different sequence:

> In textual analysis I have found the following procedures useful: (1) I first obtain a free translation of the whole text; (2) I obtain a sentence by sentence translation; (3) I obtain a word by word translation. . . .[31]

This procedure would seem to be psychologically more sensible than Malinowski's since it aims first at broad understanding of an idea cluster, and offers less opportunity for the analyst to become fixated on a particular word or construction. Second, Henry notes a problem which, although not intrinsic to the translation process, undoubtedly affects both it and the validity of one's data, *viz.*, the tendency for informants (and interpreters, for that matter) to simplify their own language in order to make their work easier:

> . . . they easily fall into stereotyped syntactical forms that oversimplify the language and act as an obstacle to understanding.[32]

Finally, Henry recommends that the field worker exercise particular care in translating when recording psychological data.

Kluckhohn and Paul are concerned mostly with the social and communicative aspects of the translation situation. Accepting Lowie's realistic appraisal — "we use interpreters, not because we like to, but because we

[27] Paul Radin, *Primitive Man as Philosopher*, D. Appleton & Co., New York, 1927.
[28] Casagrande, *op. cit.*
[29] Carroll, *Selected Writings of Whorf*, *op. cit.*
[30] Lee, *op. cit.*
[31] Henry, "Learning to Talk Primitive Languages," 637.
[32] *Ibid.*

have no other choice"[33] — they discuss the role of the interpreter and his effect on data. Kluckhohn expresses it almost poignantly:

> . . . At worst, an interview carried on through an interpreter resembles, as someone has said, "an exchange of telegrams." At best, an awkward third set of variables have been introduced into an already complex problem. What the subject says and fails to say will be influenced by his fear of, admiration for, social relation to, the interpreter as well as by the manner in which the interpreter puts questions, his general bearing, his aside comments, etc. What the investigator hears will be entirely filtered through a selective screening which is hard to allow for with any precision. The interpreter will suppress and distort both consciously and unconsciously. He will omit what seems to him unimportant or irrelevant or whatever is embarrassing to him. These omissions can largely be checked if the field worker has a measure of control over the native language. But the subtle distortions of translation cannot be prevented unless the anthropologist knows the language so well as hardly to need an interpreter or unless the whole interview is first recorded in native text and then worked out with, preferably, a battery of interpreters. . . .[34]

THE USE OF INTERPRETERS

Kluckhohn's comment recommends the three basic problems which arise from the use of interpreters: 1) the interpreter's effect on the informant; 2) the interpreter's effect on the communicative process; and 3) the interpreter's effect on the translation.

Without discussing the qualifications of a good interpreter, it is clear that the interpreter's effect on the informant — on what the informant may or may not say — is theoretically no different from the anthropologist's effect on the informant. What a native informant will discuss or withhold depends on factors which are present in *every* interviewing situation — rapport, motivation, relative status, personal trust, etc. — and these factors apply to both interpreter and anthropologist, independently or together. Frequently, an interpreter, because he is a member of the culture under study, can obtain information which is closed to the foreign anthropologist. In the early stages of his research, when the author, despite his six months language training prior to leaving for the field, knew next to nothing about what was going on in the Thai half of an interview, informants would often say to his assistant:

> I'll tell you this because you are a Thai, but I'm ashamed to tell Professor Herb, so don't tell him. . . .

[33] Lowie, *op. cit.*
[34] Kluckhohn, *op. cit.*

Of course, this is a double, and perhaps triple-edged sword; the author is sure that there were many times when the assistant, because of his own interests, did not tell him; and later on in the field work, when the writer became reasonably competent in the language, an informant would occasionally whisper to him:

> I did not tell Kham Sing [the assistant] because he is a Thai, and is an expert at gossiping, but . . .

The interpreter's effect on the communicative process is considerably more complex. Ideally, the interpreter should be nothing more than an agent for transferring messages between the informant and the field worker — a kind of passive instrument for the anthropologist. Empirically, however, this is not only difficult, but perhaps impossible.

From the point of view of small group interaction, there seems to be a natural tendency in three-person groups for a psychosocial coalition to be formed between two of the participants, the third member becoming an isolate to a greater or lesser extent. Georg Simmel called attention to this process a number of years ago,[35] and, more recently, Mills tested it with regard to power relations in problem-solving groups.[36] In the informant-interpreter-anthropologist relationship, this pairing-isolating tendency takes a unique form. Although many interviews begin as "an exchange of telegrams," the participants tire quickly from the strain of this unnatural mode of communication, and the locus of interaction settles on the informant-interpreter relationship. The informant, the most important person in the triad, looks at, responds to, and deals with the person *who understands him*, and who thus is psychologically (and often, spatially) closest to him — the interpreter, not the anthropologist. The ultimate source of questions and respository of answers is, of course, the anthropologist, but the immediate contact is with the interpreter. Also, since the interpreter can frequently anticipate the anthropologist's questions more easily than he can the informant's answers — because of a prearranged interview schedule, or because of his familiarity with the repetitive research task, or simply because he has been in more sustained contact with the researcher, a single person, than with a *number* of different informants — he tends to be more interested in what the informant, rather than the anthropologist, has to say. The informant's statements are more novel and interesting. Finally, the interpreter's bilingualism is a crucial factor here. Since the interpreter almost always shares his primary language with the informant, his secondary language with the anthropologist, and since

[35] Kurt H. Wolff (translator and ed.), *The Sociology of Georg Simmel*, The Free Press, Glencoe, Ill., 1950.

[36] Theodore M. Mills, "Power Relations in Three Person Groups," *American Sociological Review*, XVIII, No. 4 (1953), 351-357.

interaction in one's primary language is always easier and more natural,[37] the interpreter will unconsciously, but inevitably, orient himself toward the informant. Although nobody has even undertaken a time study of who talks most with whom in the field interviewing situation, the highest frequency would undoubtedly fall to the informant and interpreter rather than to the anthropologist and interpreter.

These tendencies can be partially counteracted if the anthropologist always looks at, addresses questions to, and is in close physical proximity to the informant, not the interpreter. (A triangular seating arrangement is usually best. A linear arrangement — the anthropologist seated between the informant and interpreter — may well facilitate the anthropologist-informant contact, but in no time at all the informant and interpreter will be talking around or above the anthropologist, an impossible means of communication.) However, these techniques are effective only in brief or initial interviews. In lengthy or sustained sessions they will not prevent the informant, and eventually the anthropologist, from lapsing into the more natural process of communicating with the person who understands his language.

Three considerations underlie the interpreter's effect on the translation: the time factor, the interpreter's primary and secondary language competence, and, because of these, the inescapable tendency for him to introduce distortions into the data.[38]

In the actual interviewing situation, no interpreter, not even a perfect bilingual, has the time to think through a completely accurate translation of the informant's words and, at the same time, maintain a natural, free-flowing interview. The anthropologist can, of course, get many translations which are as correct at that particular moment as they will ever be. But, because of time pressures, he will also receive translations which are completely askew, but which were offered him because the interpreter had to say *something*, correct or not. Translating difficult passages requires analysis and reflection, all of which presupposes time. Should the anthropologist and interpreter take time during the interview — thus ignoring the informant — it would all but destroy the data-collecting process. If the interpreter is honest with himself and the anthropologist, he will offer translations which in the majority of cases are followed by the comment, ". . . or it is something like that." It is with a sense of frustration, but

---

[37] See Einar Haugen, *Bilingualism in the Americas: A Bibliography and Research Guide*, Publication No. 26 of the American Dialect Society, University of Alabama Press, Alabama, 1956.

[38] For excellent surveys of the various types of translation distortions, see Nida, "Bible Translating," *op. cit.* and Susan Ervin and Robert T. Bower, "Translation Problems in International Surveys," *Public Opinion Quarterly*, XVI, No. 4 (1952-53), 595-604.

thanks, that the author recalls "or it is something like that" as one of the most frequently occurring phrases he heard in Thailand.

There are two ways of reducing the error resulting from time pressures. In one case, the interview is conducted and recorded entirely in the native language, and all translation is done later. In effect, this means training the assistant to be able to carry the burden of the interview. During the early stages of his field work, this was the procedure the author followed. But, after repeated translating sessions, he gained enough control over the native language so that he could actively participate in interviewing — all interviews still conducted completely in Thai. The second method is more efficient, but also more expensive: it requires two assistants, one to serve as an interpreter, and one to record the informant's data, in the native language, for later translation. Two people are required because it is almost impossible for a single person both to translate and record simultaneously; it would mean juggling not only two languages, but two operations. Here, the interpreter does not aim for translation perfection but simply the best approximation, insofar as time and good interviewing technique allow. The anthropologist can also be recording the interpreter's English language version for later comparison.

These procedures do not eliminate translation error. What they do offer is time and freedom to examine and discuss the informant's statements, and thus reduce the error. The amount of time they consume, however, is not insignificant: for every hour of interviewing, the writer later spent from six to ten hours translating, depending on the type of data and method of translation.

With regard to primary and secondary language competence, most linguists would probably agree that, no matter how well one knows a second language, it is always easier to translate from the second language into the first than vice versa. For example, no matter how well a Thai interpreter knows English, he will always translate English into Thai with greater facility than he will Thai into English. The reason for this is that he is fully aware of the semantic alternatives in his own language, but has only an incomplete grasp of the alternatives in the other language. This factor is, perhaps, the primary reason for translation distortion. An example will make this clear.

Card number four on the TAT[39] portrays a woman grasping the shoulders of a man whose face and body are averted as if he were pulling away from or about to move toward her. The man's face could be interpreted as indicating anger, frustration, preoccupation, etc.; the woman's, re-

[39] The TAT used in this study was comprised of eleven of the original Murray-Morgan cards with facial features, clothes, flora, fauna, furniture, etc., redrawn to fit Thai conditions. The social situations and aesthetic effects, however, were the same as in the originals.

straint, succourance, supplication, and the like. The key sentence in a villager's story to this picture was (pointing at the man): *"khon níi chǐw mâag."* Without a moment's hesitation, the interpreter translated the statement as, "This person is very angry." However, as was noted earlier, "angry" is only partial, and, on analysis, misleading, equivalent for the word *chǐw;* the term specifically means "anger that is felt toward another person, but not expressed." This latter translation assumes particular importance when contrasted with other "angrys" in the Thai lexicon. Excluding terms which are simply variations on the intensity of "angry" ("irritated" vs. "enraged"), the informant could have said, "This person is very . . ."

kroòd — generally equivalent to our angry
moo-hǒo — angry at the situation in which he is entangled, rather than toward another person
chǔn — angry at the action of another person, but not the person himself, with a suggestion of helplessness (the blast of a radio as one is falling asleep, or in this TAT story, perhaps while making love)
moo-hǒo-chǔn-chiǎw — angry all the time — at anything — because he has a character trait to be angry
khùn-khaéaen — angry, with the desire to hurt, because the other person has done something harmful to him; akin to our "revengeful."

To feel *chǐw* is a very different psychological experience from feeling *moo-hǒo-chǔn-chiǎw.* The interpreter knows this in Thai. But, had the informant used *moo-hǒo-chǔn-chiǎw* or any other terms listed above, the interpreter would have translated them all as "angry." (He has.) He does not have a grasp of the range and variation of English terms, or circumlocutions, which will describe these feelings. Thus, he selects an English word which has the ring of familiarity and is abstract enough to comprehend the meaning of all the terms, but which is clearly a deceptive description of the speaker's intent.

Related to the above is the tenacious problem of "official" translations, that is, translations which the interpreter learned in school and which often are supported by the authority of a dictionary, but which, in actual usage, are often misleading. The problem is particularly irritating because in a number of contexts the interpreter's translation may be correct, reinforcing him in the use of the term and convincing him that it has the same semantic range in both languages. Yet, there are always those few contexts where the official translation is deceptive. For example, almost all English-speaking Thai learn that the "correct" translation for the word *plaèaeg* is "strange." in English, a semantic mapping of "strange" immediately demonstrates the word's affinity to adjectives such as "unusual, queer, odd, and wierd." This is also the case in Thai with *plaèaeg.* But, in

Thai, the map for *plaèaeg* is more extensive, embracing terms like "marvelous, wonderful, and breath-taking." Thus, in English, calling a beautiful, scenic vista "strange" would indeed be that; but, in Thai, calling it *plaèaeg* would be an appreciation of its beauty. During an election campaign in the village, farmers often discussed the magical significance of the name of the then Prime Minister, who was one of the candidates. His name, ironically, was "*plaèaeg*." Since the term had always been dutifully translating to me as "strange," I assumed the villagers were indulging in the happy game of mocking the Premier. But it soon became clear that, to many of them, the Prime Minister was anything but "strange." The fact that he had escaped three assassination attempts and was "our commander during wars and revolutions" proved how *plaèaeg* he really was — a man of extraordinary and even miraculous talents.

Perhaps the ultimate misrepresentation of these terms, a confusion compounded, was expressed by the author's interpreter when he said, in English, of an eccentric and somewhat disordered acquaintance (for whom he clearly had no love): "Mr. Smith is such a wonderful person."

TRANSLATION METHODS

The research reported here involved translation from both English into Thai and Thai into English. The former was the smaller part of the task — fortunately, since the field worker exercises considerably less control when translating into his non-native language.

At first glance, the English-into-Thai assignment seemed relatively simple. It required translating 203 Sentence Completion Test items (which, after pre-testing, were reduced to two batteries of 72 items each). The items, covering various areas of psychological concern, were half sentences which informants were asked to complete "in any way you wish, so long as the completion fits the first part of the sentence and makes sense." The SCT is, of course, a projective technique based on the rationale that, when informants are presented with a semi-structured stimulus, they will structure the rest of it by projecting into the stimulus their own needs and experiences. There was nothing seemingly complex about these SCT items. They described very basic human experiences, and the author very carefully tried to select items which would be appropriate in *any* culture: "When people annoy me, I . . . ," "He wishes he were . . . ," "When luck turned against him, he. . . ."

It soon became apparent, however, that even "very basic human experiences" resist translation. Using two translators, the author first tried the usual technique of "back-translating": one person translated the items from English into Thai, his Thai version was then translated back into English by the other person, and the two versions were compared. The results of this procedure, however, were so dismal that it was abandoned after a dozen items. That the majority of the translations were not coming through accurately was obvious, but the source of error could be discovered only after prolonged discussion. Items, which originally read "He often daydreams of . . ." or "Sometimes a good quarrel is necessary because . . . ," appeared in the retranslated versions as "When he sleeps during the day he dreams of . . ." or "Sometimes a quarrel brings good results because. . . ." (This last item later proved to be utterly untranslatable. After much discussion, the translators decided that, although it was conceivable that an American might enjoy a quarrel for its cathartic effects, the notion would be incomprehensible to a Thai.)

In order to save discussion time and to profit from the accuracy of a consensus, the following procedure was substituted. Both translators, working independently, translated the remaining items into Thai. All items which were identical in *every* respect, 28 percent of the remaining total, were set aside. The assistants then discussed among themselves the balance of the items: what their English intent and meanings were and how these could be best communicated in *simple* Thai. If after fifteen minutes they could not reach agreement on a particular item, they were to put it aside for later discussion with the author. The percentage of agreement on these items was 53. All the "complete agreement" items were then read to the writer who, by combining his limited Thai with what he hoped were proper probes and the translators' explanations of why they originally disagreed and now agreed, decided on the acceptability of the items; in effect, this step substituted for the English retranslations of "back-translating." Of the 53 "identical" items, only eight were changed in the checking process, but, of the 73 "disagree-agree" items, 21 were changed. In the latter group, two items were also rejected as untranslatable. The whole procedure took approximately a week and a half.

The 65 remaining items, however, were considerably more difficult. For one thing, they required more than three weeks discussion. The differences between the translators were always small, but crucial. For example, in the item, "His most attractive quality is . . . ," there is no Thai equivalent for "quality." There are terms for "inborn personality traits," "characteristic personality traits," "behavior," "manners (politeness, etc.)," and "physical characteristics." One translator was sure I meant "behavior," the other, "manners," and, during their disagreement, the other alternatives did not even occur to them. It took a half hour to tease them out. Sometimes the translators could not come to any decision: there is no way to say in Thai, at least in a half sentence, "He feels frustrated when. . . ." This item, along with three others, was eventually rejected.

Before the items were finalized, they were all reviewed by an American linguist thoroughly conversant in Thai. Despite all our previous efforts, he suggested lexical changes in approximately 30 items and pointed out a basic, but easily remedied, grammatical flaw (with semantic implications) which ran through almost the entire test.

Assuming that the anthropologist has enough control over the native language to participate even to a limited extent in the translation process, this technique has two advantages over "back-translating." First, despite appearances, it saves time. By utilizing the knowledge of two persons, rather than one, it increases the number of accurate items, and speeds up the procedure. Had all the items been back-translated, it probably would have taken twice as long. The economy comes from having the translators first discuss their disagreements between themselves; a monolingual discussion is always faster than a bilingual one. When the translations are presented to an anthropologist, they are either in a relatively finished state or their possible meanings have been sorted out and crystallized, and the anthropologist does not start from scratch. In back-translating, the translators cannot begin discussing until the anthropologist has first seen the retranslated version and pointed out the error in English; then the translators have to decide whether the cause of the difficulty is on the English side or the Thai side; and having decided this, they can then begin to try to agree on the best Thai version. All of this takes time. Second, by participating directly in the translation process, the anthropologist not only gains greater control over the results but also learns a considerable amount about the culture. To learn, for example, that it is impossible to say, in Thai, "They hurt his feelings by . . .," without also implying that "he " feels resentment, tells us something noteworthy about social and psychological relations in Thailand.

In translating from Thai into English, two procedures were followed, one for the SCT and one for the TAT and life histories.

For the 122 SCT protocols, the writer managed to obtain the services of two urban Thai translators, both graduates of British universities. The only contact these translators had with informants was through the SCT responses. The theory and method of the test was explained to them, as was a list of twenty instructions which were to be used as translation guides. Some of the more important of these are listed below. After each test was translated (the translator working independently of his colleague and the author), it was checked by the anthropologist for ambiguities, multiple meanings, and statements which simply did not make sense. These questionable items, which averaged approximately one-third of each test, were then analyzed and discussed by the author and a third person and, when necessary, changed or qualified. Thus, responses which were originally translated as, "Most high government officials are . . . *kind people. They speak nicely, but some of them don't,*" or, "People have to help each other because . . . *of humanity's sake,*" became, after analysis, "*kind people. They speak nicely (use nice sounding words), but some of them don't,"* and, *"of humanity's sake (because it is in the nature of hu-man beings, because they are human, to help each other),"* respectively. Each test took an average of seven hours: three hours for the translation, one hour to check, and three hours to clarify questionable points. After about 80 of these tests had been completed, the translations started to become very sloppy and their clarifications more difficult, so that toward the end it took a minimum of ten hours per test.

In addition, ten per cent of the tests underwent translation reliability checks. Twelve of the tests, selected at random, were translated by both translators, and were then checked and clarified by the writer (with at least a month separating each version, so that reliability would not be falsely increased by the writer's bias). The measure of reliability is the extent to which two translations of the same completion fall into the same coding category. Construction of coding categories for the analysis of the SCT is only in its preliminary stages, but the author can report, tentatively, a translation error of 16 per cent. Thus, in the item, "When his subordinates refused to do what they were told, he . . . ," the following translations of the completion are too divergent to be considered part of the same psychological constellation and thus fall in two different coding categories: a) *"felt annoyed a little bit,"* and b) *"felt indignant."* But in the item, "People who criticize others in public are . . . ," the following translations do belong to the same category: a) *"bad. It is not their business. They should not blame other people,"* and b) *"not good. It is none of their business. They should not damage other people."* Because of the small N used in this study, the above figure of 16 per cent will probably be reduced. But some of the responses which must be merged because of statistical necessity are, for many analytic purposes, clearly different.

The TAT's and life histories were translated by the author working with the assistant, who had recorded the material verbatim in his own shorthand during the interviewing session. The assistant would read a message to the author in Thai, and the author, speaking aloud and using the translation guides listed below, would attempt to translate it. When the author committed an error, or, far more frequently, when he could not translate a passage, the assistant would take over. About half the time, the assistant's versions would be acceptable, and we would continue. But the other half of the time, we would analyze and haggle over the translation until it was satisfactory. On the average, six hours of translation were spent for every hour of interview.

Listed below are some of the translation instructions which were used in this research, restated in places to have general applicability. Although they are phrased with Thai examples, the reader will have little difficulty in substituting more familiar illustrations. Thus, instruction number ten, which deals with "areas unusually rich in subtle distinctions not found in English," will be readily understandable to a researcher working in Russian, who has tried to translate terms describing human suffering and psychological depression. Similarly, instruction number eight may prove particularly useful to researchers working in Malayo-Polynesian- or Sinitic-speaking areas.

1. The translator should be sensitive to the intensity of words. For example, in the sentence, "When he hit him, he ran away," and "When he hit him, he turned away," the difference between *ran* and *turned* is important.

2. Be careful of the difference between "he *does* such and such," "he *should do* such and such," and "he *wants to do* such and such." There are great psychological gaps between doing, wanting to do, and being obliged to do because of some kind of compulsion.

3. Indirect objects have a way of sneaking into statements without being noticed. Therefore, try to be particularly attentive to their presence or absence. For example, one informant supposedly said, "The thing they most like about him is that he gives good advice." A check of the original statement, however, indicated that the informant actually said, "The thing they most like about him is that he gives *me* good advice."

4. Be careful of primary and secondary verb constructions, i.e., "he must think of doing it himself" vs. "he must do it himself." Select the translation which is most accurate from the point of view of the native language, not English. A good guide here is the following: if the phrase cannot be said in the native language without using both the primary and secondary verbs, then it is not necessary to note both verbs in the English translation; if the phrase can be said in the native language without using the secondary verb, then note the secondary verb in the translation.

5. Statements which have implied within them something more than the literal translation must have these implications spelled out. Take as much space as necessary, but write the implications out as *parenthetical comments*, specifying whether the implications are *probable* or *possible* and to what extent.

6. If the informant's statement includes words or phrases which seem redundant — Thai words which, if translated into English, seem like extra baggage in the English — include these redundancies in the translation. They can always be removed later. However, if they impede understanding, do not include them.

7. Please keep in mind that our informants are peasants, not educated city people. Therefore, try to keep your translations as simple as possible. It is not necessary to use "proper" or "big" English words. For example,

it is almost always better to translate the word *lôob* as "greed," rather than "covetousness." In this connection, if you encounter any unusual peasant idioms, do not attempt to translate them. Instead, write them out in phonetic Thai, and they will be translated later in discussion.

8. Since the Thai language is unusually rich in puns and *double entendres*, and since our tests offer ideal opportunities to play word games, please be attentive to statements with a humorous cast. This also applies to poetic-sounding phrases, or to any statement which *sounds nice* or *rhythmic* in spoken form. Note these possibilities as parenthetical comments.

9. Avoid using a Thai-English dictionary. This is mandatory for words which you know have more than two or three meanings. (The definitions provided in most bilingual dictionaries tend to be unusually abstract and, for our purposes, are just as likely to be wrong as right.) There are two exceptions to this rule: those occasions when you really do "know" the English term, but cannot remember it; and when you are dealing with words which clearly have only one definition. In Thai, for example, *tônsaj* means "banyan tree" and nothing else.

10. There are a number of areas of the Thai lexicon which are unusually rich in subtle distinctions not found in English. The terms which fall in these areas are translatable, but they require careful qualification. The very fact that these areas contain a wide variety of specific terms indicates their importance to Thai culture. We will undoubtedly encounter many more as we continue translating, but, as of now, be aware of the following areas and do *not* translate terms which in any way are related to them: words of social status; moral and ethical terms; words describing aggression, honesty, loyalty, trust, and truth; and terms describing any aspect of human character or personality. All these words should be written out in phonetic Thai and will be translated later in discussion.

11. There are probably many other Thai words for which it is difficult to find precise English translations. Therefore, please follow this general rule, the most important of all: do *not* work too hard in trying to find the correct English equivalent for a Thai word or phrase; in many cases, it may be non-existent; in other cases, it may exist, but in ambiguous form and will require amplification. If you feel *any* doubt or uncertainty about the English equivalent, do not attempt to translate. Write the word out in phonetic Thai for translation later.

CONCLUSION

Having described the above procedures, there remains the question: what of their value? Do they contribute anything which cannot be obtained through the more customary, casual (and often, undivulged) methods of translating anthropological, and particularly culture-personality, materials?

The answer is threefold. First, in the very act of placing data through such procedures, the field worker learns a great deal about the native culture and native thought processes. Second, by conducting a translation reliability check, the researcher has some idea of the amount of error introduced into his data; although this check is ultimately arbitrary, it is at least an objective account of the quality of the data, with direct reference to the way data are used and analyzed. Finally, and most important, by introducing such translation procedures, the field worker has gotten a grasp on a previously unknown quantity. This grasp is, perhaps, inchoate and vulnerable. But how much less vulnerable it is than those cases where field workers simply ignore translation problems (at least insofar as they represent themselves to their readers). If, after translating with a set of detailed instructions and checking and clarifying the translations, the research described here still resulted in an error of 16 per cent, how much error exists in those cases where translation is left to the hasty, unchecked decisions of an interpreter involved in the complexities of the interviewing situation?

Translation can be expensive, time-consuming, and aggravating. Its central importance to anthropology, however, is obvious when one considers that almost all the data the anthropologist brings home from the field must pass through the translation process at one time or another. If this paper stimulates other field workers to be more explicit in describing their translation procedures, or better, to develop more systematic and precise methods of translation, it will have achieved its end.

Techniques for Determining Cultural
Biases in Comparative Research

IDENTIFYING "THE SAME" TRAIT
IN DIFFERENT CULTURES

A recurrent problem in the comparative study of culture is that of identifying corresponding cultural items in two societies.[1] Analysis of this problem shows that it again requires the anchoring of the specific by a context. And concomitantly a limitation is placed upon its successful achievement. As Professor Northrop has repeatedly made explicit, our thinking on such matters may be biased by the carry-over of the atomistic radical empiricism of British associationism. In this instance it leads us to the anticipation that culture-elements are more certainly identifiable than culture complexes. The reverse is in fact the case.

An analogy may help. Consider the task of identifying corresponding dots of black of which two copies of a newspaper photograph are built. The task is impossible if the dots are taken singly, but becomes more possible the larger the area of the photographs available. Insofar as particular elements can be matched it is only because of the prior matching of the wholes. Similarly for matching elements between languages. A given word cannot usually be translated by a single word when it is in isolation, but can be when it is a part of a sentence or a speech. A paragraph is more accurately translated than a word. To the extent that the translation of a word is anchored, it is because the paragraph of which it is a part has been successfully translated.

From pp. 330-333 of "Distinguishing Differences of Perception from Failures in Communication in Cross-Cultural Studies," by Donald T. Campbell, in *Cross-Cultural Understanding: Epistemology in Anthropology*, edited by F. S. C. Northrop and Helen H. Livingston. Copyright © 1964 by Wenner-Gren Foundation for Anthropological Research, Inc. Reprinted by permission of the author and Harper & Row Publishers.

[1] Sears, R. R., "Transcultural Variables and Conceptual Equivalence," in B. Kaplan (ed.), *Studying Personality Cross-Culturally*, Harper & Row, New York: 1961, pp. 445-456; Norbeck, E., D. E. Walker, and M. Cohen, "The Interpretation of Data: Puberty Rites," *American Anthropologist*, vol. 64, 1962, pp. 463-483.

In a similar way, it takes acquaintance with the larger cultural context to identify the appropriate parallel or classificatory assignment of any particular cultural item. This context dependence correspondingly removes the possibility of certainty and makes ever present the possibility of erroneously alleging cultural differences as a result of mismatching.

TRIANGULATION THROUGH THE OWN-CULTURE BIAS OF OBSERVERS

The achievement of useful hypothetically realistic constructs in a science requires multiple methods focused on the diagnosis of the same construct from independent points of observation, through a kind of triangulation.[2] This is required because the sense data or meter readings are now understood as the result of a transaction in which both the observer (or meter) and the object of investigation contribute to the form of the data. With a single observation at hand, it is impossible to separate the subjective and the objective component. When, however, observations through separate instruments and separate vantage points can be matched as reflecting "the same" objects, then it is possible to separate out the components in the data due to observer (instrument) and observed. It turns out that this disentangling process requires both multiple observers (methods) and multiple, dissimilar, objects of study.[3]

Applied to the study of the philosophy of a culture, this implies that our typical one-observer one-culture study is inherently ambiguous. For any given feature of the report it is equivocal whether or not it is a trait of the observer or a trait of the object observed. To correct this the ideal paradigm might be as shown in Figure [1] (a). In the most general model, two anthropologists from different cultures would each study a third and fourth culture. Of the four ethnographies resulting, the common attributes in ethnographies 1 and 3 not shared with 2 and 4 could be attributed to ethnographer A, the common attributes in 2 and 4 not elsewhere present to ethnographer B. Looking at row consistencies in the figure, the common attributes in ethnographies 1 and 2 not present in 3 and 4 could be attributed to culture C as "objectively" known. Attributes common to all four ethnographies are inherently ambiguous, interpretable as either shared biases on the part of the ethnographers or shared culture on the part of the societies studied. Note the desirability in this regard of comparing ethnologists with as widely differing cultural backgrounds as possible. Insofar as the ethnologists come from the same culture, the

[2] Campbell, Donald T., and Donald W. Fiske, "Convergent and Discriminant Validation by the Multitrait-Multimethod Matrix," *Psychological Bulletin,* vol. 56, 1959, pp. 81-105; "Methodological Suggestions from a Comparative Psychology of Knowledge Processes," *Inquiry,* vol. 2, 1959, pp. 152-182.

[3] Campbell, Donald T., and Donald W. Fiske, "Convergent and Discriminant Validation by the Multitrait-Multimethod Matrix," *op. cit.*

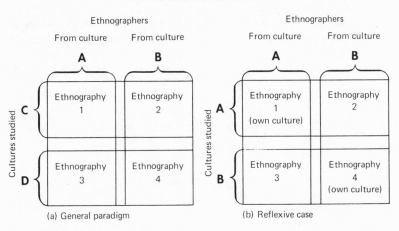

FIGURE [1]. Multiple-Ethnography Schedules to Extricate the Ethnographer-contributed Content from the Culture-studied Content:

(a) General paradigm   (b) Reflexive case

replication of results becomes more a matter of reliability than validity, as these terms are used in discussions of psychological tests. Were such a study carried out by using four ethnographers, two from each ethnographer cultures A and B, studying separate villages of cultures C and D to avoid interference and collusion, then the attributes unique to any one of the ethnographies would be attributable to an equivocal pool of village specificities within its culture, to personality specifics of the ethnographer, and interaction of specific ethnographer culture and studied culture. (If only one ethnologist were used from each culture, and if each of the two studied in turn the same village in the target cultures, then the features unique to any one of the four ethnographies would be equivocally due to ethnographer-culture interactions, time-order effects in which the ethnographer reacted differently to his second culture, time-order effects in which the society reacted differently to the second student of it, historical trends, and interactions among these.) The presence of these indeterminacies should neither be suppressed nor be allowed to overshadow the great gains in understanding which such multiple ethnographer studies would introduce.

While multiplicity of both ethnographer cultures and cultures studied is ideal, it would also be a great gain to achieve only the upper half of Figure [1] (a), i.e., two ethnographer cultures focused on the study of a single target culture. In all such triangulations, we again face the paradox of inability to use differences when these so dominate as to make it impossible to match the corresponding aspects of the reports being compared. The necessity of this common denominator provides one justification for Hockett's advocacy . . . of including material and behavioral cultural details even in ethnographies focused on the determination of the philosophy of the cultures.

Another version of the multiethnographer, multiple-target design is that in which two cultures study each other, as diagrammed in Figure [1] (b). Usually the focus is on ethnographies 2 and 3, A's report on B and B's report on A. Implicitly, however, A's description of A and B's description of B are contained as bases of reference. There is probably some scientific value to be gained from such reports, even at the level of mutual stereotype sets or of reputational consensus from neighboring peoples.[4] Once the evaluative component (each tribe viewing itself as best) is removed, such mutual stereotype sets show remarkable agreement in confirming the direction of group differences.

[4] Campbell, Donald T., and Robert A. LeVine, "A Proposal for Cooperative Cross-Cultural Research on Ethnocentrism," *Journal of Conflict Resolution*, vol. 5, 1961, pp. 86, 91.